Every Psalm for Easy Singing

Expanded Study Edition

Every Psalm
for
Easy Singing

Expanded Study Edition

A translation for singing
arranged in daily portions
with
Textual and Exegetical Notes on the Translation

Prepared and translated by
C.W.H. Griffiths, M.A.

Pearl publications

pearlpublications.co.uk

Contact: info@pearlpublications.co.uk

Every Psalm for Easy Singing: A translation for singing arranged in daily portions. Expanded Study Edition

Paperback: ISBN 978-1-901397-09-3
Hardback: ISBN 978-1-901397-10-9
E Book: ISBN 978-1-901397-11-6

First published 2023.

The moral rights of the author are asserted.

British Library CIP Data available.

BISAC: REL006120; REL006770; REL055020

We acknowledge with thanks permission from Christian Focus Publications to quote Alec Motyer, *Psalms by the Day* and also Alec Motyer, Journey. *Psalms for Pilgrim People*.

The help of David Legg, Hendrik van der Poel, Margaret Maclean, Angharad Griffiths and Margaret Watkinson in the completion of this book is gratefully acknowledged.

Dedicated to the memory of

my beloved daughter,

Naomi

who now sings a new song

CONTENTS

Preface 1

Core principles 3

Introduction to the Expanded Edition 4

Psalms Book 1 (1-41) 11

Psalms Book 2 (42-72) 84

Psalms Book 3 (73-89) 141

Psalms Book 4 (90-106) 186

Psalms Book 5 (108 -150) 229

Appendices.. 322

   1. Transliteration 323

   2. Notes on some Hebrew words 325

   3. Psalm titles, Selah and Higgaion 347

   4. Resources used by this Psalter 349

   5. How to sing this book 355

Advertisement 381

PREFACE

Personal and family praise and worship has been neglected by Christians and Churches for generations. For most Christians the 'voice of praise' at home comes from our favourite singers and groups at the press of a button. If we sing God's praise at all at home, it is a sort of sing-along karaoke to our CD player or iPad.

When Governments introduced restrictions in response to the Covid 19 pandemic Churches closed their doors. When restrictions were eased, they re-opened, but with congregations gagged by face coverings, and forbidden to sing. Churches turned for solutions, not to the old paths of family and personal worship under the supervision of the local Church, but to untried and untested innovation. For many people, the local 'body of Christ' was replaced by virtual association with Churches in distant places, and perhaps even distant lands.

This reinforced the idea that praise is something that we listen to, rather than 'the fruit of our lips' - what is pleasing to the ear, rather than 'teaching and admonishing one another in psalms and hymns and spiritual songs, singing, with grace in your hearts, to the Lord'.

We hope that this Psalm book in daily portions for singing; together with its companion *A Help for Using the Psalms in Personal and Family Worship*, will encourage the old habit and discipline of personal and family worship that includes singing praise to God. If it does, that will help to build a stronger defence against future State restrictions, or even persecution of the Church.

1

Although I am ill-equipped to attempt the task of translating the Psalms into a form faithful to the original and suitable for singing, I have felt compelled to make an attempt. There is a need for something on different lines to what is currently available in print or online. The reader will have to judge how far I have succeeded.

Chris Griffiths

February 2023

CORE PRINCIPLES

This book grew from the following convictions.

1. That the Psalms, as inspired writings, are fundamentally different from hymns, choruses and worship songs (2 Sam 23:2).

2. That Scripture requires God's people in the New Testament (1 Corinthians 14.26) as well as in the Old Testament (Psalm 105:2) to sing the Psalms.

3. That it is 'profitable' to sing all the Psalms (2 Timothy 3:16).

4. That by singing the Psalms the believer glorifies God, is instructed in the will and purposes of God (Psalm 101:1, Colossians 3:16), and expresses his or her own spiritual aspirations - mourning and joy - in the words of Scripture (Psalm 22:1, James 5:13).

5. That praise to God is essentially 'the fruit of our lips' (Hebrews 13:15). All the Psalms should be singable without needing knowledge of dozens of metres and hundreds of tunes, and without needing musical accompaniment.

6. That any translation of the Scriptures, whether for reading or for singing, should keep as close to the inspired words as possible (Jeremiah 36, Revelation 22:19).

7. That any translation should be transparent regarding the translation decisions made (Acts 17:11). We have been guided in our translation primarily by the translators of the Reformation period.

8. That a translation of the Scriptures should avoid novelty or originality (2 Peter 1:20). We have constantly consulted well-respected expositors of a previous age (see Appendix 4).

3

INTRODUCTION
TO THE EXPANDED EDITION

This Expanded Edition is intended for serious Bible study, and to assist anyone who leads group, or family, worship with this version of the Psalms.

It includes extensive footnotes, appendices, and explanation of the approach adopted and materials used. A manual edition without the footnotes and appendices is also available.

Every Psalm for Easy Singing enables the singing of the entire Book of Psalms in a year. It is divided into 365 portions

It can be used with *A Help for using the Psalms in Personal and Family Worship,* (also published by Pearl Publications), which gives devotional and expository comment on the same 365 portions.

The object of Psalm-singing is to sing words given by the Holy Spirit for use in worship. What we sing should therefore be as close as possible to the original, in a form that anyone can sing. That is the aim of this translation.

To sing words given by God necessarily involves concentration of the mind. It should, indeed, at times be joyful, but the Psalms are not simple choruses, or repetitive 'worship songs'. The Psalms must therefore be sung thoughtfully at a measured speed, looking to the Lord to bless and instruct us. It is a different worship-form from that used in almost all modern Churches. Appendix 5 gives guidance on singing through this book, with suggested tunes. There are more resources, including audio resources, on the Pearl Publications website.

The older Bible versions are literal translations. However, they use archaic language which makes them difficult to understand in a day when English is a world language. Many English readers and speakers have no knowledge of past, or earlier forms of the English language. On the other hand modern Bible versions favour dynamic translation that smoothes over difficulties in the Hebrew text, often based on scholarly guesswork. Psalm translations for singing are no different: older versions are more literal, but archaic; newer versions are contemporary but interpretive. Since the days of Isaac Watts there has also been a strong tendency to try to make the Psalms 'speak the language of the New Testament'.

Our translation for singing is not a word for word translation of the Hebrew. This is not possible, even with a prose translation. We have sought to avoid being so literal and mechanical that the meaning is obscured. On the other hand we have sought to avoid dynamic translation that interprets difficult lines with little regard to the original words.

In Hebrew poetry the writer often changes from the first to the third person and vice versa without explanation. A Psalm changes from speaking about God (The LORD is my Shepherd) to speaking to him (I will fear no evil for you are with me) to addressing others (Surely goodness and mercy shall follow me). Sometimes it uses a plural verb with a single noun (e.g. Ps. 66:4). Such features can make the sense difficult to follow without careful thought. What may appear as confusing is generally faithfully represented in the Authorised Version, but is 'corrected' in many modern versions. We have left such difficulties (and others, as in Psalm 68) in the translation, rather than amending, or attempting to give a commentary as well as a book for worship!

A rhyming metre increases the difficulty of accurate translation. Rhyme severely limits the choice of words available to convey the meaning. The shortness of the lines in the metres used in traditional English language psalters can increase the difficulty. It frequently results in the meaning being broken up over two or more lines, with a new sentence beginning half way through a line.

The use of 'blank verse' in Psalm books has been sadly neglected. Blank verse is the use of unrhymed, five stress lines (iambic

5

pentameter). 'It has become the most widely used of English verse forms, and is the one closest to the rhythms of everyday English speech'[a]. Milton's *Paradise Lost* is written in blank verse, as are many of Shakespeare's plays.

Unrhymed metre removes the need to restrict to a small vocabulary of rhyming words, the need to elide, or to 'butcher', words to make them rhyme. At the same time, using a longer metre can accommodate more words in each line, and often results in less fragmentation of the sense. Blank verse is not without its difficulties in translating Scripture. Some of the difficulties mentioned will occur whatever the metre.

Hebrew poetry is very different from English poetry. The second line often represents a restating, or opposite, of the first. Sometimes three lines are linked together. The lengths of the lines may vary within the Psalm.

We have not tried to imitate the literary form: rather, we have attempted to convey the meaning of the words accurately, and in clear modern English. It is better that the poetry be imperfect than the original language be distorted. Singing the Psalms should be 'with understanding'.

Where the New Testament quotes a verse, the meaning given in the New Testament has been noted and often used, sometimes in addition to the apparent meaning of the Hebrew as it stands. The New Testament sometimes simply represents a different vowel pointing (*niqud*) from the Hebrew Masoretic text. We have on occasion noted the Septuagint reading where this represents a different vowel pointing, and also the corrections of the text as proposed by the Jewish soferim (*qerê*). The Hebrew Masoretic text has been very faithfully preserved, but it represents the text as set by normative Judaism after the rejection and crucifixion of Christ. It should not be departed from without very good reason, but we do not consider the vowel points to be inspired.

---

[a] J.A. Cuddon, *Penguin Dictionary of Literary Terms and Literary Theory*.

It has been our constant prayer that we should not add to, diminish, or introduce interpretations of the written word of God in attempting this translation. All versions are imperfect, and the knowledge, even of the best Hebraists, is limited: we do not claim that accolade. We have therefore added many footnotes to this edition to enable those that are better skilled to make judgement of what has been done. We hope the notes will enable others to understand the principles on which we have worked, and the limitations that are inevitable in expressing Scripture in another language, and within the constraints of metre.

Key Features

1. The division into 365 portions has been made giving careful consideration to their subject matter and sub-divisions suggested by commentators. The portions therefore vary in length, and our versification has had to fit the portions, rather than vice versa.

2. Because of the limitation imposed by the portion lengths, on occasion a line has been repeated to complete the final stanza. Usually, the last line has been repeated, unless emphasis is appropriate elsewhere in the portion.

3. The translation does not attempt to convey the strict parallelism (lines repeat, contrast etc) of the Hebrew. The four-line stanzas do not therefore always correspond to the verses of the Psalms.

4. Whenever we have had difficulty accommodating the words to the metre, we have always turned to the root meaning of the Hebrew word and to its alternative meanings. We believe that any variation or expansion of meaning we have made can be justified from the Hebrew.

5. Sometimes the translation has been 'amplified' to convey the greater or more varied meaning of the Hebrew, using two or more words to translate one. Hebrew is a very compact language, and this is sometimes desirable.

6. The use of 'makeweight' redundant words, introduced simply to make the metre work, have been avoided.

7. Where it has been necessary to extend a line for the sake of the metre, we have avoided expressions (however theologically sound) that introduce ideas not in the text, or which interpret the words of the original.

8. We have occasionally given an explanatory translation to express an unfamiliar word or expression, for example 'winnow' (1:4), 'giving the neck' (18:40) 'edge of the sword' (89:43).

9. English idioms similar to the Hebrew have occasionally been used – e.g. 'hound and harry' to translate Ps. 56:1; 'the great and the good' Ps. 118:9. This has been done carefully and sparingly.

10. It is difficult to achieve consistency of translation within the constraints of versification. Attention has been drawn in the footnotes of this expanded edition to some Hebrew words that have a range of meanings.

11. Appendix 2 gives notes on particular words, and the translation standard that we have adopted. For example, we have translated the Hebrew verb *zamar* by 'sing Psalms'.

12. The different Hebrew names of God have been identified throughout. See Appendix 2.

13. The different Hebrew words for 'man' are identified, and translated appropriately where possible. See Appendix 2.

14. The word 'Selah' has been marked throughout the Psalms by the symbol ✝. See Appendix 3.

15. We have sought to avoid poetic and archaic forms of speech. There are some exceptions; 'unto' is often a very useful word to achieve the metre!

16. Words have not been shortened to make them fit (o'er, Isr'el etc), and words have not been stretched over more than their

8

usual syllables to make them fill out the metre. However, use has been made of familiar contractions from everyday speech (I've, they're, I'll, etc).

17. The *Oxford Spelling Dictionary* has been used in dividing syllables, and on rare occasions we have made the syllable division clear by the use of hyphens.

18. We have followed normal English word order wherever possible. However, we have neither sought nor achieved perfect English grammar or syntax. We have tried as much as possible to retain the force of the Hebrew original, regardless of the requirements of 'good English'.

19. Pronouns have not been capitalised to indicate that they refer to God. This is a comparatively modern convention, and sometimes imposes an interpretation on the text, giving an opinion that the pronoun refers to God, whereas it may not. Likewise, at times where perhaps 'the wicked one' refers to Antichrist or Satan, the words have not been capitalised. On rare occasions this rule has been broken where the sense might otherwise be confused in translation.

Book 1

Psalms 1 - 41

Day 1   Psalm 1

[1] *Blessings and happiness*[a] are on that man[b]
who does not walk as wicked ones advise,
who does not linger in the sinners' path[c],
who does not sit down in the scorners' seat.

[2] But in the LORD's Law he has his delight:
That Law, his constant thought[d] both day and night.
[3] He's like a tree by streams[e] of water set,
Which fruits in season, and its leaves don't fade.

Whatever work he does shall prosper well;
[4] Not so the wicked – they are like the chaff,
Which wind blows from the harvest threshing floors.[f]
[5] Therefore, in judgment, wicked ones won't stand.

Sinners will not rise up. They will not stand[g]
within the company of righteous ones.
[6] The LORD well knows[h] the path the righteous take;
The path the wicked take will pass away.[i]

---

[a] Blessings and happiness] The Hebrew word (*'ašrê* - אַשְׁרֵי) is plural. We could
translate 'O the happinesses of that man!' But it also indicates 'that man' lives
under the blessing of God, 'when God blesses, happiness results'. See
Appendix 2 - Blessing.

[b] Man] Hebrew *'îš* - אִישׁ - Man as an individual. Here singular in contrast to the
wicked (plural). Compare Jer. 17:7,8, where the word for 'man' is *gebher* - גֶּבֶר.
See Appendix 2 - Man.

[c] Path] The same word as v6.

[d] Thought] Meditate. The same word as 'make plans' 2:1.

[e] Streams] Literally, 'rivulets', or 'irrigation channels'.

[f] Which the wind blows from harvest threshing floors] Hebrew 'as the chaff that
the wind blows away'. The reference is to winnowing. We have expanded the
meaning as this is now a little-known practice. Winnowing was used to
separate the grain from the chaff after harvest. See Matt. 3:12. Compare Dan.
2:35.

[g] Not rise up ... stand] We have repeated the verb from the previous line. This
verb may be translated 'rise up' (as in resurrection, Septuagint *anastesontai* -
ἀναστήσονται) or 'stand'. 'Stand' here does not contradict Rev. 20:11,12. The
wicked will not be able to withstand the LORD when he acts in judgment (Rev.
6:17). De Burgh comments that the wicked shall have no part in the first
resurrection. We have given both translations, but see Newton (2).

[h] Well knows] This is a participle - the LORD is 'the knowing one'. He is omniscient.

[i] Will pass away] Hebrew *'abhadh* - אָבַד. Compare Ps. 9:6,7 and 41:5.

Day 2   Psalm 2:1-6

¹ Why do the nations^a gather in their rage^b?
Why do the peoples make such foolish plans^c?
² Earth's kings have set themselves in readiness^d;
Together^e rulers meet to plot and plan^f -

Against the LORD and his Anointed One!^g
³ Saying, 'Let's break their chains and ties from us'.
⁴ But he who sits^h in heaven will just laugh;
My Lordⁱ will mock them, and treat them with scorn.

⁵ Then in his anger he will speak to them
And in his fury will strike them with fear.
⁶ 'I have anointed and set^j my own King
On Zion^k, mountain of my holiness'.^l

---

^a Nations] Hebrew *gôyîm* - גּוֹיִם, always used of the Gentile, or non-Jewish, nations. Not 'heathen'.

^b Gather in their rage] AV margin 'tumultuously assemble'. 'Conspire'.

^c Make ... plans] The word translated 'meditate' in 1:2. Literally, 'meditate vain things'. The apostles applied this to their experience Acts 4:25,26.

^d Set themselves in readiness] Literally, 'set in array' or 'stand in a hostile position', as against an enemy. See Deut. 7:24 and 9:2. As Goliath, 1 Sam. 17:16 (AV 'presented himself').

^e Together] The Hebrew word means 'in union', 'unitedly'. The words show 'strength and compactness'.

^f Plot and plan] The meaning is 'gathering to take and establish counsel for a course of action'.

^g Anointed One] Hebrew 'Messiah'.

^h Sits] i.e. enthroned. In the context, the kingship of the LORD is evident (see Isa. 6:1; Rev. 4:10; 20:11; Ezek. 43:7).

ⁱ My Lord] Hebrew *'Adhonay* - אֲדֹנָי. See Appendix 2 - Names of God - *'Adhonay*.

^j Anointed and set] One word in Hebrew. The root meaning of the verb is 'to pour out', and hence 'to melt' as in casting metal (Isa. 40:19) and 'to set' (Prov. 8:23). Note v2. 'Inaugurated' Newton (4).

^k Zion] The mount of David in Jerusalem. See Ezek. 43:7; Ps. 132:13.

^l My holiness] This is the literal Hebrew, as AV margin - i.e. - 'my holy hill'. The 'I' in the verse is emphatic.

Day 3   Psalm 2:7-12

⁷ I will declare the LORD's decree to me,
'I have begotten^a you, my Son, this day;
⁸ Ask me, I'll give you an inheritance -
The nations! You'll possess earth's farthest lands'^b. →

⁹ 'You shall, as with a rod of iron, break
And you will smash them like a potter's jar'.
¹⁰ So, kings be wise. Earth's judges[c] all be warned.
¹¹ Rejoice, with trembling. Serve the LORD with fear.[d]

¹² O kiss the Son, lest he should be enraged
And you will then be cut off from the way[e],
For soon and quickly[f] does his anger burn.
Blest[g] are all those who take refuge in him[h].

---

[a] Begotten] 'Became a father to'. Christ was begotten 'before all worlds', eternally equal with his Father. This Psalm relates to his manifestation as Son of God and his installation in his office as Messiah (see Heb. 1:5,6; Acts 13:32,33).

[b] Farthest lands] Literally, 'the ends of the earth'. Cf. Ps. 22:27; 72:8.

[c] Judges] Hebrew *šopheṭîm* - שֹׁפְטִים - not restricted to the judicial functions. The judges (Samson, Gideon, etc) ruled. Motyer (1) suggests 'the world's decision makers', but more than mere 'decisions' are intended. See Appendix 2 - Law - Judgment.

[d] Rejoice with trembling. Serve the LORD with fear] We have reversed these two commands to achieve the metre.

[e] From the way] Either 'from the right way' (Septuagint) or from your own way (compare Ps. 1:6). The outcome is destruction.

[f] Soon and quickly] Either meaning has been suggested for the words which the AV translates by 'but a little'.

[g] Blest] As Ps. 1:1. Hebrew *'ašrê* - אַשְׁרֵי. See Appendix 2 - Blessing.

[h] Who take refuge in him] AV 'put their trust in'. The Hebrew verb is *ḥasâ* - חָסָה 'to flee to a refuge and a place of safety'. See Appendix 2 - Refuge.

Day 4   Psalm 3

¹ O LORD how many are my enemies!
Many are those who rise up against me!
² So many people say about my soul[a]
'There's no deliverance[b] for him in God'. ‖

³ But yet, O LORD, you are a shield for me
My glory and the lifter of my head.
⁴ My voice has cried aloud unto the LORD;
From his own holy hill[c] he answered me. ‖

⁵ I lay down and I slept; and then I woke,
Because the LORD upholds me. ⁶ I'll not fear
10,000 set against me[d] round about.
⁷ Arise, O LORD, and save me, O my God.   →

14

For all my foes you have hit on the cheek;
Broken in pieces are the wicked's teeth.
⁸ Deliverance belongs unto the LORD.
Upon your people will your blessing rest! ‖

---

^a My soul] Used throughout the psalms meaning 'me' or perhaps here 'my very
  person'.
^b Deliverance] AV 'help'. The same word translated 'salvation' (AV) v.8.
^c His own holy hill] as in Ps. 2:6 - Mount Zion. Literally, 'the hill of his holiness'.
^d 10,000 set against me] Literally, 'ten-thousands of the people who have set
  themselves against me'. The Hebrew word may mean 'a very large number'
  (Numb. 10:36). 'Set themselves' is a military expression, as Isa. 22:7.

Day 5   Psalm 4

¹ Answer me when I call, my righteous God^a.
You gave relief when I was in distress
When I was hemmed in, you then gave me room^b
Be gracious to me. Listen to my prayer!

² O you great men^c, just how long will it be?
For how long will my glory be disgraced?
How long will you love what is vanity?
How long will you seek what are only lies? ‖

³ Know this: the LORD selects^d the one he loves^e
The LORD will hear me when I call to him
⁴ Tremble in awe^f and see that you don't sin.
Speak to your heart upon your bed. Be still. ‖

⁵ Give offerings of righteous sacrifice^g.
And place your confidence upon the LORD.
⁶ Many are saying, 'Who will show us good?'
O Lift the light of your face on us, LORD!

⁷ You have bestowed more gladness to my heart,
More than the time their corn and wine increased.
⁸ In quiet peace I will lie down and sleep;
For you alone LORD, make me dwell secure^h.

---

^a My righteous God] Literally, 'God of my righteousness', i.e. 'the God who

15

vindicates me'.

[b] You gave relief ... gave me room] We have given the literal translation in the second line.

[c] Great men] Hebrew sons of man, *benê 'îš* - בְנֵי־אִישׁ. Cf. Ps. 49:2. There is irony in the word used for 'man' here. See Appendix 2 - Man.

[d] Selects] The word means 'sets apart', 'distinguishes', 'singles out'. The Hebrew adds 'for himself'.

[e] The one he loves] Hebrew *ḥaṣîdh* - חָסִיד singular. The AV translates 'him that is godly'. See Appendix 2 - Loving-kindness - *ḥaṣîdh*.

[f] Tremble in awe] The word can mean agitation in both fear and anger, hence the Septuagint translation 'be angry', which is used in Eph. 4:26.

[g] Give ... sacrifice] Literally, 'sacrifice sacrifices of righteousness' (as Deut. 33:19 and Ps. 51:19). The word 'sacrifice' here is used of blood sacrifice (Hebrew *zebaḥ* - זֶבַח).

[h] This line may be translated, 'You LORD make me dwell alone in safety' (compare 'alone' Jer. 49:31). The word *betaḥ* - בֶּטַח may be taken as either 'secure'', 'safe', or 'trusting' (as v5).

Day 6   Psalm 5:1-6

¹ Incline your ear unto my words[a] O LORD.
My inmost thoughts O do consider now!
² O heed my cry, my King, my God, I pray.
³ LORD, in the morning, you will hear my voice.

I will prepare[b] at morning, and keep watch,
⁴ You're not a GOD, who takes delight in sin.
You will not harbour[c] any wickedness
⁵ The boastful shall not stand before your eyes.

You hate all those who work iniquity.
⁶ You will destroy all those who speak a lie.
The LORD abhors the man who would shed blood.
The LORD abhors the man who would deceive[d].

[a] My words] Hebrew *'emer* - אֵמֶר (from *'amar* - אָמַר : to say). See Appendix 2 - Word.

[b] Prepare] 'Set out in order'. The word is used in connection with the priestly preparation of sacrifice (cf. Lev. 1:7,8; 6:12). There is no word for 'prayer' here.

[c] Harbour] The word means 'to lodge', 'to sojourn', rather than 'to dwell'.

[d] The Lord detests ... deceive] We have broken this one line into two.

Day 7 Psalm 5:7-12

[7] But, as for me, through your great steadfast love [a],
I'll come into your house. And in your fear
I will bow down toward your holy place:
Even the Temple of your holiness [b].

[8] O lead and guide [c] me in your righteousness,
Because my foes do lie in wait [d], O LORD.
Before me make your pathway smooth and straight. [e]
[9] For nothing in their mouth is fixed or sure. [f]

Inside they are so full of wickedness; [g]
Their mouth is like a yawning open grave;
Their tongue they use to flatter and deceive. [h]
[10] Charge guilt upon them - punish them [i], O God.

By their own wicked counsels [j] make them fall.
For all their trespasses thrust them away
Because it is against you they rebelled.
[11] But let all those who trust [k] in you rejoice.

Let them for ever sing [l]: you'll shelter them.
Let them that love your name rejoice in you.
[12] Because you'll bless the righteous one, O LORD.
Surround him with your favour as a shield. [m]

---

[a] Steadfast love] Hebrew ḥeṣedh - חֶסֶד. See Appendix 2 - Loving- kindness - ḥeṣedh.

[b] Temple of your holiness] The Hebrew is literally, 'the Palace (Hebrew hêkhal - הֵיכַל) of your holiness'. We have added 'your holy place' in apposition to 'Temple of your holiness', as, being a psalm of David, the 'Temple' was not yet built. Therefore, as in 1 Sam. 1:9 and 3:3 the term here applies to Shiloh and the tented Tabernacle of David's time.

[c] Lead and Guide] One word in Hebrew. Literally, 'shepherd me'.

[d] Foes do lie in wait] 'Those who watch me spitefully'. See de Burgh. The word (Hebrew šarar - שָׁרָר) is only used in Scripture in this Psalm and at 27:11; 54:5; 56:2; 59:10.

[e] Make your pathway smooth and straight] i.e. Make it level and straightforward to travel. Cf. 27:11 and 143:10

[f] Is fixed or sure] One word; literally, 'is fixed', or 'is steady - i.e. 'You cannot rely on anything they say'. Different verbs are used in Hebrew, but the Welsh Bible links the thought with the last phrase of verse 8 - 'Make straight (uniona) my path before me, because there is no straightness (uniondeb - rectitude) in their

17

mouth'.

g So full of wickedness] AV 'very wickedness', margin 'wickednesses'. The plural indicates excessive wickedness.

h To flatter and deceive] Literally, 'to make smooth their tongue'. 'smooth talk runs off their tongue' NEB.

i Charge guilt upon them - punish them] The same word means both guilt and punishment (see Jer. 2:3, etc). AV mg. 'make them guilty'.

j Wicked counsels] 'counsels', but as Ps. 1:1. Compare Haman.

k Trust] Hebrew ḥaṣâ - חסה. See Appendix 2 - Refuge.

l Sing] This word in Hebrew is strongly associated with expression of joy and is usually translated 'shout for joy' or 'sing for joy'.

m Shield] The larger, great, shield Hebrew tsinnâ - צנה. See Appendix 2 - Shields.

Day 8   Psalm 6:1-5

¹ Do not rebuke me in your anger, LORD,
Nor in your hot displeasure chasten me.
² Be merciful, O LORD, for I am weak.
My very bones are aching. Heal me LORD!

³ My soul is greatly troubled and dismayed.ᵃ
How long? How long? O LORD, I cry to you!
⁴ Return again, O LORD, rescue my soul,
And for your mercy'sᵇ sake, O LORD save me.

⁵ For your remembrance is not there in deathᶜ
And there is no memorial to youᵈ.
In Sheol who is there that gives you thanks?
In Sheol who will offer thanks to you?ᵉ

a Troubled and dismayed] The same word translated 'aching' in the previous line.

b Mercy] Hebrew ḥeṣedh - חסד. See Appendix 2 - Loving-kindness - ḥeṣedh.

c In death] Literally, 'in the death'. The parallel of the following line (Sheol - šeʾôl - שאול) indicates that the reference is to the place of the dead. See Appendix 2 - Sheol.

d Remembrance is not there ... no memorial] This verse does not teach 'soul sleep'. The absence of a memorial of the LORD, and not a loss of memory of him, is intended (see de Burgh).

e We have expanded each of the two lines of this verse.

Day 9   Psalm 6:6-10

⁶ I am worn out with all my sighs and groans.
I cry and weep through each and every night.
I make my bed to swim with all my tears.
My couch I water as my tears do fall.

⁷ Because of grief my eyesight wastes away.
Through all of my oppressors it grows old.
⁸ Depart from me, all who do wickedness.
The LORD has listened to my tearful cry.

⁹ The LORD has heard my earnest cry for grace^a.
So, therefore, will the LORD accept my prayer.
¹⁰ All those who hate me shall be shamed and vexed^b.
They shall turn back; at once be put to shame.

---

^a Cry for grace] The word is linked with the verb meaning 'to be gracious', 'to pity'.
^b Vexed] Hebrew 'greatly vexed' or 'suddenly made very fearful'.

Day 10   Psalm 7:1-8

¹ O LORD, my God, in you I put my trust^a.
Save me from all who hunt me and pursue.
Deliver me. ² Lest he should rend my soul,
Lest lion-like he tears with none to help.

³ O LORD my God, if I have done this thing;
And if injustice^b be upon my hands;
⁴ If I rewarded evil to my friend;
(I rescued him who wrongly was my foe).

⁵ Then let the enemy pursue my soul,
And overtake it, and tread down my life.
Let him tread down my life into the ground
And lay my honour down unto the dust. ⧺

⁶ O LORD, rise up and show your anger^c now.
Stand up against the fury of my foes.
Wake as from sleep - arouse yourself for me,
For you command that judgment^d should be done.

⁷ Around you will the peoples congregate
And for their sake return to the high place^e
⁸ Judge peoples, LORD and justly treat me^f, LORD.
After^g my righteousness and uprightness.

---

^a Put my trust] Hebrew ḥaṣâ - חָסָה. See Appendix 2 - Refuge.

^b Injustice] AV 'iniquity'. Hebrew ʿawel - עָוֶל. 'To decline, turn aside, especially from what is just', Gesenius *Lexicon*.

^c Show your anger] The Hebrew word comes for the word for nostrils. Compare Acts 9:1. It means not just anger, but the expression of it.

^d Judgment] The meaning here is nearer that of justice. Hebrew *mišpaṭ* - מִשְׁפָּט. See Appendix 2 - Law - Judgment.

^e For their sake return to your high place] This is the literal translation, as given by the Welsh Bible, reading the Hebrew *lammarôm* (לַמָּרוֹם) as 'on', or 'to', 'the High-place'. The exegesis is therefore an appeal for the Lord to return to 'his holy hill', to the 'height of Zion'. Compare Jer. 31:12; Ezek. 20:40; Psalms 2:6; 4:4; and even Zech. 14:4, and Ezek. 11:23; 43:2. See de Burgh, Newton (1), and Tregelles (3).

^f Judge ... justly treat] The first word is *dîn* - דִּין a judicial word. 'justly treat' is *šaphaṭ* - שָׁפַט, which relates more to God's government. See Appendix 2 - Law – Judgment.

^g After] According to.

Day 11   Psalm 7:9-17

⁹ Oh, make the evil of the wicked cease^a.
Confirm the righteous^b. You search mind and heart^c
O righteous God, ¹⁰ My shield is upon God^d.
He saves the men of honest, upright hearts^e.

¹¹ God - righteous Judge^f! GOD - outraged every day!^g
¹² If one will not turn back^h, he'll whet his sword.
He's surely bent his bowⁱ, ready to shoot
¹³ With deadly weapons and with bolts of fire.

¹⁴ Behold!^j one travails to bear wickedness
Conceiving mischief, gives birth to a lie.
¹⁵ He made a pit, and when he'd dug it out
He fell into the ditch that he'd prepared.

¹⁶ His mischief shall return on his own head,
And on his skull^k will violence descend.
¹⁷ My thanks will answer^l the LORD's righteousness.
Sing psalms unto his name - the LORD Most High^m.

a Oh make ... cease] The Hebrew word of entreaty *(na' - נָא)* here emphasises the verb. See note on Ps. 118:2.

b The righteous] Singular - 'The righteous one'. Hebrew *tsadîq* – צַדִיק.

c Mind and heart] Literally, 'heart and reins [kidneys]'. This Hebrew expression (26:2; Jer. 11:20; 17:10; 20:12) represents the mind and emotions of a person by referring to their internal organs. See also note on 16:2.

d My shield is upon God] i.e. 'God who holds my shield as my shield bearer'. Compare 1 Chr. 18:7. The 'shield' in this verse is *maghen* - מָגֵן. See Appendix 2 - Shields.

e Men of honest, upright hearts] Literally, 'Ones of straight heart'.

f Judge] Hebrew *šôphet* - שׁוֹפֵט. See Appendix 2 - Law - Judgment.

g God - outraged every day] The AV supplies the object of God's outrage 'God is angry *with the wicked* every day'.

h Turn back] i.e. repent.

i Bent his bow] Hebrew 'trodden his bow'. The bow string was not attached until just before the battle, in order not to strain the bow unduly. The foot was used to bend the bow to string it. See Yadin, *The Art of Warfare in Biblical Lands*, p62ff.

j Behold!] Hebrew *hinneh* - הִנֵּה an urgent interjection to draw attention to something important. There a change of subject here as he describes the rebel against God. See Appendix 2 - Behold!

k Skull] The Hebrew word means 'the crown of the head'.

l Will answer] 'Will answer to', 'will be in accord with'. Hebrew 'I will give thanks according to his righteousness'.

m LORD Most High] Hebrew LORD *'Elyôn* - יהוה עֶלְיוֹן. See Appendix 2 - Names of God.

Day 12   Psalm 8

¹ O LORD, our Lord[a], how splendid is your name –
How splendid is your name in all the earth!
Over the heavens you your glory set.
Display your glory over them above![b]

² Out of the mouth of infants and of babes
You have established strength, perfected praise[c].
Because of those who are your hurtful foes[d],
To still the enemy and vengeful one[e].

³ Seeing your heavens that your fingers made,
The moon and stars that you have put in place
⁴ What is frail man[f] that you remember him?
The son of man that you would visit him? [g]

21

⁵ You've made him little less than^h the angelsⁱ are.
Honour and glory gave him, as a crown
⁶ Over your handiwork you gave him rule.
You have set all things underneath his feet.

⁷ All sheep and cattle; wild beasts^j; ⁸ birds that fly^k;
Fish and all creatures that swim in the sea.
⁹ O LORD, our Lord, how splendid is your name –
How splendid is your name in all the earth!

---

^a Our Lord] This Hebrew word 'Lord' is *Adhôn* - אָדוֹן. It is not the word uniquely
used of God (*'Adhonay* – אֲדֹנָי). 'LORD, our Lord' suggests the investiture of the
Lord Jesus (Dan. 7:14). The Prayer Book Version translates 'Governor'.

^b Over the heavens ... over them above] We have given two translations of this
line in our two lines. It is generally assumed to be, and is commonly translated
as, a past event - the Creation. The verb ('to set', 'to give', 'to display') is used
in Gen. 1:17. However, the Hebrew verb here is in the imperative. As de Burgh
demonstrates, this is primarily a prophetic statement regarding a future event
(Heb. 2:5), hence the translation of the second line.

^c Perfected praise] We have added this alternative Septuagint translation of the
words translated 'ordained strength' by the AV, which is adopted in Matt. 21:7.
The Hebrew word '*oz* - עֹז (AV strength) has a range of meanings and is
translated by 23 different words in the Septuagint (Muraoka).

^d 'Hurtful foes'] One word in Hebrew = 'adversaries'. A different word from
'enemy' in the next line. See the *Dutch Annotations* on 'because of'.

^e The vengeful one] The word is only elsewhere used in Ps. 44:16.

^f Frail man] Hebrew *'enôš* - אֱנוֹשׁ - frail, mortal man, with stress on weakness and
so applied to Christ in his humanity Heb.2:6. 'Man' in the following line is
Hebrew *'adham* - אָדָם, man as a child of Adam. See Appendix 2 - Man.

^g Visit him, etc] Compare v2,3 with Jer. 15:15.

^h You've made him little less than] The emphasis of verses 5 and 6 is that God has
done all this. It speaks of Christ in his humiliation and glorification (Heb. 2:5-
8).

ⁱ The angels] Hebrew *'elohîm* - אֱלֹהִים. The Septuagint, and the Jewish Targum,
translate 'angels', although the word usually refers to God. We, as the AV,
translate 'angels', following the New Testament use of the passage (Heb. 2:6-
8).

^j Wild beasts] Hebrew 'beasts of the field'. In contrast to the domesticated 'sheep
and cattle'.

^k Birds that fly] Hebrew 'birds of the heavens'.

Day 13   Psalm 9:1-10

¹ I will praise you, O LORD, with all my heart.
I will declare the wonders you have done.
² I will be glad and will rejoice in you.
Sing psalms unto your name. You are Most High^a!   →

³ Because my enemies are driven back
They shall be cast down^b, cut off from your sight.
⁴ You have upheld my judgment^c and my cause^d.
You are enthroned and judge^e in righteousness.
⁵ You censured nations: crushed the wicked one.
You blotted out their name for evermore^f.
⁶ Ruined for ever is the enemy.
Forgotten^g are the cities you plucked up^h.

⁷ The LORD will take his seatⁱ for evermore.
He has set up his throne, his judgment^j seat.
⁸ He'll judge and rule the world^k with righteousness.
In uprightness the peoples he will judge^l.

⁹ The LORD's a refuge for all those oppressed:
A place of refuge in distressing times^m.
¹⁰ And those who know your name will trust in you.
You've not abandoned those who seek you, LORD.

---

^a Most High] Hebrew *'Elyôn* - עֶלְיוֹן. See Appendix 2 - Names of God - *'Elyôn*.
^b Shall be cast down] Literally, 'be weakened', hence translations relating to
   stumbling, falling headlong etc.
^c Upheld my judgment] AV 'maintained my right'. Hebrew *mišpaṭ* - מִשְׁפָּט. See
   Appendix 2 - Law - Judgment.
^d My cause] 'My legal claim'. Hebrew *dîn* - דִּין. See Appendix 2 - Law - Judgment.
^e You ... judge] Hebrew *šôpheṭ* - שׁוֹפֵט from Hebrew *šaphaṭ* - שָׁפַט. This line may
   be translated, 'You are enthroned, a judge in righteousness [or righteous
   judge]'. See Appendix 2 - Law - Judgment.
^f For evermore] Hebrew 'for ever and ever'
^g Forgotten] Hebrew 'their memorial is destroyed'.
^h The second half of this verse is capable of a range of meanings. The AV margin,
   Horsley, and Calvin have been followed. They read this as speaking to God
   ('you' singular), rather than taking it a parenthesis speaking to the enemy. The
   root meaning of the word translated 'plucked up' is 'to uproot' or 'to tear up'.
ⁱ Will take his seat] 'Will sit'. This is the literal meaning of the verb. It links to 'his
   throne' in the next line'.
^j Judgment] Hebrew *mišpaṭ* - מִשְׁפָּט. The same word as in v4 and v16.
^k The world] The inhabited earth. Hebrew *tebhel* - תֵּבֵל. See Appendix 2 - Earth.
^l Judge and rule ... judge] AV 'judge ... minister judgment'. 'Judge and rule' is
   šaphaṭ - שָׁפַט, which relates to God's government in the broadest sense. The
   second word *dîn* - דִּין is a judicial word. See v4,5 and Appendix 2 - Law -
   Judgment and (2).
^m Distressing times] See note on 10:1.

23

Day 14   Psalm 9:11-20

¹¹ Sing praises, sing with psalms[a], unto the LORD,
Unto the LORD, he who in Zion dwells!
Among the peoples make known what he's done.
¹² He who avenges blood remembers them!

The LORD does not forget the anguished cry[b],
When the afflicted ones call out for help.
¹³ See my affliction LORD, and pity me[c],
For it was from my hateful enemies

You raise me from the very gates of death:
¹⁴ In Zion's daughter's gates[d], I will praise you.
In your deliverance I will rejoice.
¹⁵ The nations are sunk in the pit they made.

Their foot's caught in the net that they had hid.
¹⁶ The LORD is now made known. Judgment[e] is done!
The wicked one[f] is trapped in his own schemes.
Higgaion. Selah. Think upon these things![g] ⧺

¹⁷ The wicked ones to Sheol shall descend[h],
All nations who do not remember[i] God.
¹⁸ The needy[j] shall not always be forgot,
The hope of the afflicted shall not cease.

¹⁹ Arise, O LORD, and let not man[k] prevail!
Bring judgment to the nations in your sight.
²⁰ Cause them to know your terror and your fear[l],
So shall the nations know they are but men[m]. ⧺

---

[a] Sing praises, sing with psalms] One word in Hebrew, *zamar* - זָמַר. See Appendix 2 - Sing Psalms.

[b] Anguished cry] The word is used of the cry of the woman in danger of rape (Deut. 22:27), and of the cries of Israel in Egypt.

[c] See my affliction, LORD and pity me] Hebrew, 'Have pity (mercy) on me and see my suffering (affliction)'.

[d] In Zion's daughter's gates] i.e. in the place where the inhabitants of Zion gather.

[e] Judgment] Hebrew *mišpaṭ* - מִשְׁפָּט. See Appendix 2 - Law - Judgment.

[f] The wicked one] Singular as v5. See de Burgh and Newton (1). Plural in v17.

[g] Higgaion. Selah. Think upon these things!] The Hebrew words mean 'to

24

meditate' and 'to pause'. See Appendix 3.
^h To Sheol shall descend] The place of the dead. Sheol *(še'ôl* - שְׁאוֹל) is always
spoken of as 'down'. The verb literally means, 'shall return', but going back to
the same place is clearly not intended. Compare Job 1:21. See Appendix 2 -
Sheol.
ⁱ Do not remember] Hebrew - forget.
^j Needy] singular. 'The afflicted' of the following line is plural.
^k Man] Hebrew *'enôš* - אֱנוֹשׁ - Frail, mortal man. See Appendix 2 - Man. Also in
v20.
^l Cause them to know your terror and your fear] Hebrew literally, 'set terror for
them'.
^m That they are but men] Singular in Hebrew. Hebrew *'enôš* - אֱנוֹשׁ, as in v19.

Day 15   Psalm 10:1-11

¹ Why do you stand so far away, O LORD?
Why hide yourself in times of great distress^a?
² The wicked in his pride hunts down the poor,
And they are caught in schemes that they devised^b.

³ The wicked one boasts of his soul's desire^c,
Blesses the greedy and reviles the LORD^d.
⁴ In angry pride^e the wicked does not seek –
In all his thoughts there is no room for God.

⁵ And yet his ways at all times do succeed
(Your judgments are on high, out of his sight).
He scorns^f all foes, ⁶ and says within his heart
'Nothing will shake me. Always trouble-free!'

⁷ His mouth is full of curses, lies, and threats^g,
Under his tongue vexatious vanity^h.
⁸ In villages in ambush he awaits.
The innocent he murders secretly.

His eyes watch slyly for the helpless oneⁱ.
⁹ He lies in wait as in a lion's den.
He lies in wait that he may catch the poor;
Seizes the poor and draws him in his net.

¹⁰ He crouches, and he gets himself down low^j.
Thus do the helpless fall down by his power.
¹¹ 'GOD has forgot' he says unto his heart,
'He's hid his face, and he will never see'.

25

[a] Times of great distress] As in 9:9. Times of great tribulation. Septuagint _thlipsis_ - θλιψις cf. Matt. 24:29.

[b] And they are taken ... devised] AV 'let them [i.e. 'the wicked'] be taken ...' It is better to take this as a statement that the innocent suffer and the wicked triumph. De Burgh notes there are no petitions in this Psalm until we reach v12. The Hebrew changes from singular (both 'wicked' and 'poor') to plural ('they') in the second line.

[c] Soul's desire] So the Hebrew. See de Burgh.

[d] Blesses ... the LORD] See Perowne's note discussing this line, which is capable of several different translations. The usual meaning of the Hebrew word for 'bless' has been retained rather than 'curses'. Tregelles (1) questions the use of 'curses' here.

[e] Angry pride] Hebrew 'in pride of face'.

[f] Scorns] Hebrew 'puffs at'. See Mal. 1:13.

[g] Curses, lies, and threats] Rom. 3:14 'his mouth is full of cursing and bitterness'. Septuagint 'cursing, bitterness, and trouble'. The Greek word for 'bitterness' here also means 'animosity'.

[h] Vexatious vanity] The word 'vexatious' means 'putting burdensome trouble upon'. The word here rendered 'vanity' or 'emptiness', may also be translated 'iniquity'.

[i] The helpless one] This word only occurs in this Psalm (v8,10,14). The meaning is apparently 'one who is unfortunate / hapless'.

[j] Crouches and gets himself down low] i.e. as a lion about to pounce. However, this line may refer to those whom the wicked one pursues, in which case the translation would be '[The helpless ones] are crushed and they sink low".

Day 16   Psalm 10:12-18)

[12] Arise, O LORD! Lift up your hand, O GOD!
Do not forget the ones who are oppressed.
[13] Why does the wicked one disparage God?
And, in his heart, say 'You will not enquire!'

[14] But you have seen, and you yourself regard
Trouble and grief, to pay back by your hand[a].
The helpless one commits himself to you.
You are the helper of the fatherless.

[15] Break the arm of the wicked evil one.
Seek out his wickedness till you find none.
[16] The LORD is king for ever, evermore:
The nations have been cut off from his land.   →

26

¹⁷ O LORD you heard the longing of the poor.
Strengthen their heart. Incline your ear to them
¹⁸ To vindicate the orphan and oppressed
To end the terror of the man of earth^b.

---

^a To pay back by your hand] Literally, 'to give by (or 'into') your hand'.
^b Man of earth] Or 'Man of the land' (Hebrew *'enôš min ha 'arets* - אֱנוֹשׁ מִן־הָאָרֶץ)
see the AV. We take this to be a title of a specific man - the Antichrist - as
contrasted with the Lord from heaven (cf. 1 Cor. 15:47. Note the Hebrew New
Testament translation). 'Man' here is Hebrew *'enôš* - אֱנוֹשׁ - Frail, mortal man.
So he is, when met by the power of God. See Appendix 2 - Man and Earth.

Day 17   Psalm 11

¹ I trust^a the LORD, so why say to my soul
'Flee to your mountain as a bird takes flight'?
² For, surely, look^b - the wicked bend their bow^c.
See! - how they set their arrow on the string.

They darkly shoot at men of upright heart^d.
³ Whatever should a righteous person do
If the foundations are to be destroyed?
⁴ The LORD is in his holy temple^e still.

It's in the heavens the LORD has his throne.
His eyes behold. He tries^f the sons of men.
⁵ The righteous^g the LORD tries: but his soul hates
He who is wicked and loves cruelty.

⁶ He will make snares fall on^h the wicked ones –
Fire, brimstone, tempest! This shall be their lotⁱ.
⁷ The LORD is righteous and loves righteousness;
He who is upright shall behold his face.

---

^a Trust] Hebrew *ḥaṣâ* - חָסָה to flee to a refuge and a place of safety. See Appendix
2 - Refuge.
^b Surely, look!'] Drawing attention to what is a remarkably brazen and evil action.
We have repeated with 'See!' on the second line as it clearly covers both
actions. Hebrew *hinneh* - הִנֵּה. See Appendix 2 - Behold!
^c Bend their bow] Literally, 'tread their bow'. As 7:12
^d They darkly shoot at men of upright heart] Hebrew 'they shoot in darkness at
the upright in heart'.
^e His holy temple] Literally, 'the Palace (Hebrew *hêkhal* - הֵיכָל) of his holiness'. It is
applied to the Temple, but also, perhaps, to the heavens.

^{f} He tries] Literally, 'his eyelids try'. Delitzsch 'when we observe a thing closely or ponder over it, we draw the eyelids together, in order that our vision may be more concentrated and direct'.

^{g} The righteous] Singular, as 'he who is wicked' in the next line.

^{h} He will make snares fall on] Hebrew literally, 'rain down traps', a mixed metaphor.

^{i} Their lot] Hebrew literally, 'the portion of their cup'.

Day 18   Psalm 12

^{1} Save^a LORD! The gracious man^b is at an end,
The faithful from the sons of men are gone.
^{2} Each one unto his neighbour speaks vain things^c.
They speak so smoothly^d with a double heart^e.

^{3} O may the LORD cut off all smooth lips now.
May he cut off the tongue that speaks great things.
^{4} Those who have said, 'We'll triumph by our tongues,
These are *our* lips, so who will master us?' ^{f}

^{5} 'Because the poor are plundered and laid waste^g;
Because the needy do lament and sigh', ^{h}
'I will rise up' is what the LORD now says.
'From him who shows contempt^i I'll make them safe'.

^{6} (The LORD's words are words^j that are pure and clean^k,
As silver melted when it's purified,
As passing through a furnace seven times,
As in a melting pot^l they are refined.)

^{7} You will protect and you will keep^m them, LORD.
You will preserve him^n now and evermore^o.
^{8} On every side the wicked strut about
When vileness is exalted among men^p.

^{a} Save!] The Hebrew is emphatic insofar as no object is expressed (see Perowne). It is a simple and earnest cry for help.

^{b} Gracious man] AV 'godly man'. Hebrew ḥaṣîdh - חָסִיד. See Appendix 2 - Loving-kindness - ḥaṣîdh.

^{c} Vain things] Vanity, emptiness, lying.

^{d} So smoothly] Hebrew 'with a lip of smoothnesses' and so in v3. Smooth, slippery, as with flattery.

^{e} Double heart] Hebrew 'with a heart and a heart' i.e. with deception, two-faced.

Compare 1 Chr. 12:33,38.
^f Who will master us?] Literally, 'Who is Lord over us?' 'Lord' / 'master' here is
'adhôn - אָדוֹן. It is not the word uniquely used of God 'Adhonay - אֲדֹנָי).
^g Plundered and laid waste] One word in Hebrew.
^h Lament and sigh] One word in Hebrew.
ⁱ Those who show contempt] AV 'from him that puffeth at him'. See 10:5. See de
Burgh and modern translations, which favour translating 'for which he pants
(or longs)', i.e. referring the phrase to the afflicted poor desiring safety.
^j Words ... words] Hebrew 'imrâ - אִמְרָה - the spoken word. This is with special
reference to what the LORD has said in v5, and in contrast to v2-4. See
Appendix 2 - Word.
^k Pure and clean] One word in Hebrew.
^l Melting pot] An earthen crucible (see Calvin).
^m Protect ... keep] One word in Hebrew.
ⁿ Him] In the Masoretic text there is a change in this verse from 'them' (i.e. the
poor and needy of v5) to 'him' (i.e. each one of whom the LORD preserves of
that oppressed company). This is the translation of Geneva, Calvin, and NASB.
The Septuagint and Vulgate, and some Hebrew Mss, read 'them' throughout
this verse and are followed by Statenvertaling, AV, NIV, NEB.
^o Now and evermore] Literally, 'from this generation for ever'.
^p Men] Hebrew 'the sons of man' benê 'adham -בְּנֵי אָדָם .. 'Men' as children of
Adam. See Appendix 2 - Man.

Day 19   Psalm 13

¹ How long? Will you forget me always, LORD?
How long will you conceal your face from me?
² How long shall I keep scheming in my soul?
How long will daily sorrow grieve my heart?

And how long will my enemy rise up^a?
³ Look on me, answer me, O LORD, my God.
Lighten my eyes^b, lest I should sleep in death.
⁴ My enemy will say, 'I have prevailed!'

When I should fall, my foes would then rejoice,
⁵ But in your mercy^c I have put my trust.
In your salvation my heart will rejoice.
⁶ I'll sing unto the LORD. He's good to me!^d

---

^a Rise up] 'Rise up against me', Hebrew.
^b Lighten my eyes] i.e. give fresh vision and vitality. Compare 1 Sam. 14:27.
^c Mercy] Hebrew ḥeṣedh - חֶסֶד. See Appendix 2 - Loving-kindness.
^d He's good to me] i.e. for what he's done for me. AV 'He hath dealt bountifully
with me'. Motyer (1) translates 'he is sure to deal fully with me'. See the note

Day 20   Psalm 14

¹ 'There is no God'. The fool says in his heart.
They are corrupt and what they do is vile.
No one does good, no not a single one.ᵃ
² The LORD from heaven sees the sons of men.ᵇ

He looks to see if any understand,
If there are any who seek after God.
³ They've turned away. They're all together foul.
No one does good, no not a single one.

⁴ Do those who work such wickedness not know?
Who eat my people just as they eat bread –
These are the ones who don't call on the LORD.
⁵ But there they were, afraid with trembling fear.

For God is with the righteous companyᶜ.
⁶ Though you deride the counsel of the poor,
Yet, nonetheless, his refuge is the LORD.
⁷ O give salvation unto Israel!

Salvation out of Zion may he giveᵈ,
The LORD will bring his people back again.
When he shall turn them from captivityᵉ.
Jacob will joy and Israel be glad.

ᵃ No one does good, no not a single one] Rom. 3:10-12 develops this, under the
   inspiration of the Holy Spirit, as 'there is none righteous'. We have added 'not
   a single one', from the translation of the Septuagint and Rom. 3:10-12.
   Compare v3
ᵇ Sons of men] Hebrew *benê 'adham* -בְּנֵי אָדָם . 'Men' as children of Adam. See
   Appendix 2 - Man.
ᶜThe righteous company] Literally, 'the generation of the righteous', meaning the
   whole company of those who are righteous, those who are of the same spirit
   with the righteous. cf. Scottish Metrical Psalter 'the whole race of the just'.
ᵈ O give salvation ... may he give] We have split this sentence between the two
   stanzas. It appears to read 'Who will give from Zion the salvation of Israel?'
   However, Gesenius *Grammar*, states that here the Hebrew particle *(mî -*מִי*)*,
   usually indicating a question, is used here as an expression of the optative - 'Oh

that ...': as Deut. 28:67 (literally, 'who will give evening?'). Ewald *Syntax* likewise states 'it is a wish, whose fulfilment is expected from others'.
[e] When he shall turn them from captivity] AV 'When the LORD bringeth back the captivity of his people'.

Day 21   Psalm 15

[1] LORD, who will be a guest[a] within your tent?[b]
Who will abide upon your holy hill?[c]
[2] It is the one whose walk is blemish-free,
For he does right and truth speaks in his heart.

[3] He does not utter slander with his tongue.
Harms not his friend, nor slurs one near to him,
[4] But in his eyes the vile one[d] is despised.
He honours those who truly fear the LORD.

He keeps his word, though it should cost him dear.
[5] He does not lend his money at a price.[e]
Nor takes reward to hurt the innocent.
He never shall be moved who does such things.

[a] Guest ... abide] The first word means 'sojourn', 'temporary residence' of a client or guest, the word in the second line means 'continuing to dwell'.
[b] Tent] The word is used of the holy tent at Shiloh where Eli and Samuel dwelt.
[c] Holy hill] This always means Mount Zion.
[d] The vile one] Literally, 'the reprobate one', 'the rejected or refused one' (see Jer. 6:30).
[e] Lend his money at a price] Literally, 'give out his money for (extortionate) interest' (or 'usury').

Day 22   Psalm 16:1-6

[1] O GOD preserve me, please do keep me safe[a].
You are my refuge and in you I trust[b].
[2] 'You are My Lord'[c] I say unto the LORD,
The good I do brings nothing unto you[d].

[3] Saints of the earth[e] are truly excellent,
All my delight is in those holy ones;[f]
[4] But sorrows will be multiplied to those
Who hastily run after[g] other gods.   →

Their offerings of blood[h] I will not make,
Nor will I take their names upon my lips
5 The LORD's my portion and he is my cup.
He takes good care of what he's given me.

6 In pleasant places the lines have been cast[i].
They measured out a pleasant place for me.
Yet more than that is my inheritance
It is a bright and pleasing thing for me[j].

---

[a] Preserve ... keep me safe] One word here in Hebrew. We have expanded the meaning.

[b] You are my refuge and in you I trust] We have expanded the translation. Here the Hebrew verb is ḥaṣâ - חָסָה 'to flee to a refuge and a place of safety', AV 'trust'. See Appendix 2 - Refuge.

[c] My Lord] A unique name of God. The one who exercises lordship over me. Hebrew 'Adhonay - אֲדֹנָי. See Appendix 2 - Names of God - 'Adhonay.

[d] The good I do ... nothing to you] Various translations are offered of this sentence. We have followed the sense of the Dutch Annotations. David's 'goodness' can contribute nothing to God. Likewise, taking this psalm as Messianic, Christ's 'good' adds nothing to God - it was for imputation to us (see Canons of the Synod of Dort, Part 2, Rejection of Errors 2). Compare the next verse; there is yet an excellence in earthly saints.

[e] The earth] Or 'the land'. The Hebrew word can mean either. In the latter case the psalm would be prophetic (compare Zech. 14:20,21).

[f] Saints ... holy ones] We have given two translations of the same word. The word means 'separated to', and 'in relationship with', God. See Girdlestone.

[g] Hastily run after] So AV and de Burgh. Perowne and Delitzsch contest this use of the verb. They, and most modern translations, favour the meaning of exchanging [the true God] for another. See Exod. 22:16 - AV 'pay a dowry'; Hence Horsley translates 'betroth themselves to another'.

[h] Offerings of blood] Literally, 'drink offerings of blood'.

[i] In pleasant places ... cast] The reference is to casting a measuring line over a field to be divided up. We have continued the translation and expanded the meaning in the following line.

[j] Yet more than that ... a pleasing thing for me] We have expanded the sense of the previous line. This statement is preceded by the Hebrew word aph - אַף. It emphasises something added - 'more than that!' Delitzsch comments on this verse 'with אַף he rises from the fact [his lines have fallen, etc] to the perfect contentment that it secures for him'. The adjective ('beautiful', 'bright', AV 'goodly') has the root meaning 'brightness' or 'clarity' (cf. the sound of the shofar).

Day 23   Psalm 16:7-11

[7] I'll bless the LORD, the one who counsels me.
Indeed[a], my heart[b] instructs me in the night!
[8] I keep the LORD before me all the time.
I'll not be moved with him at my right hand.
[9] My heart is glad. My glory full of joy[c].
For yet[d] my flesh shall dwell secure in hope.
[10] To Sheol you will not forsake my soul[e],
Nor give the One you love[f] to see the Pit[g].

[11] You will reveal – you will make known to me[h]
The path that leads to everlasting life. [i]
Abundant joy[j] is there before your face.
At your right hand are pleasures evermore.[k]

---

[a] Indeed] The word *aph* - אַף again. See v6 and v 9.
[b] My heart] AV 'reins' (as the adjective 'renal'). Literally, 'kidneys'. The seat of the feelings and affections. See note on 7:9.
[c] My glory full of joy] Literally, 'my glory rejoices'. Acts 2:26 confirms the Septuagint translation. The Septuagint translates and interprets 'my glory' as 'my tongue'. Most commentators follow Rabbi Kimchi, and interpret 'my glory' as 'my soul'. However, 'my tongue' fits perfectly well here and elsewhere in the Psalms (30:12; 57:8; and 108:1). In the only other use of the expression (Gen. 49:6), the usual meaning of the word is satisfactory (the AV translates 'my honour').
[d] For yet] The word *aph* - אַף again. See v6 and v 7.
[e] To Sheol ... my soul] Hebrew *še'ôl* - שְׁאוֹל. The place of the spirits of the dead. Acts 2:27, 'in Hades' - ᾅδης. Bishop Pearson *(On the Creed)*, commenting on Acts 2:31, observes that Christ's spirit and body, though temporarily separated at death, did not remain long either in Sheol or the grave. See Appendix 2 - Sheol.
[f] The one you love] Compare Matt. 3:17; 17:5. AV 'your holy one'. Hebrew *ḥaṣîdh* - חָסִיד. See Appendix 2 - Loving-kindness.
[g] Nor give the one you love to see the Pit] Hebrew. This is the literal rendering of the Hebrew. Acts 2:27 and Acts 2:31 'neither will you give your Holy One [Greek *hosios* - ὅσιος] to see corruption', following the Septuagint. Acts 2:31 makes the meaning clear. It was *'his flesh'* that was preserved from 'corruption'.
[h] You will reveal ... make known] We have expanded the meaning.
[i] Everlasting life] Hebrew simply 'life', but the two following expressions 'in your presence' and 'at your right hand' make plain that this is not a reference to our present life. This follows *The Dutch Annotations*.
[j] Abundant joy] Hebrew 'fulness of joys'.
[k] Acts 2:28 follows the Septuagint paraphrase of v11.

33

Day 24   Psalm 17:1-7

[1] Hear a just cause. Attend, LORD, to my cry[a].
Please hear my prayer from lips free of deceit.
[2] Send judgment out for me before your face -
Your eyes behold things that are true and right[b].

[3] You tried my heart, examined me by night.
You tested and found nothing that was wrong.
I purposed that my mouth should not transgress.
[4] The word you spoke[c] kept me from things men do[d].

Thus, I avoided the Destroyer's ways.
[5] Sustain me as I follow in your paths[e].
O keep my footsteps, so they may not slip.
[6] To you I call. You'll answer me, O GOD.

Incline your ear to what I have to say[f].
[7] Display the wonder of your steadfast love[g].
O Saviour of those seeking for refuge[h],
Save from those rising against your right hand[i].

---

[a] Cry] The word is normally associated with joy, but can mean 'entreaty' or 'supplication', as here.

[b] True and right] One word in Hebrew. It means rectitude or straightness.

[c] The word you spoke] Hebrew 'the word of your lips'.

[d] From things men do] Literally, 'as regards deeds of man (Hebrew *'adham* - אָדָם)' - the erring ways of man as a child of Adam; human; *'adham* is used collectively for mankind. See Appendix 2 - Man.

[e] Paths] Properly, 'tracks' left by someone, or something, that has gone before. The same word used in Ps. 23:3.

[f] What I have to say] Hebrew *'imrâ* - אִמְרָה - the spoken word. See Appendix 2 - Word.

[g] Steadfast love] Plural, emphasising the greatness of his love. Hebrew *ḥeṣedh* - חֶסֶד. See Appendix 2 - Loving-kindness.

[h] Those seeking for refuge] The Hebrew verb is *ḥaṣâ* - חָסָה 'to flee to a refuge and a place of safety'. See Appendix 2 - Refuge.

[i] Save from those who rise against your right hand] This verse is just 6 words in Hebrew, and various suggestions have been made (see AV mg etc). We have followed Calvin here. The Psalmist's assailants are setting themselves against the very hand of God

Day 25   Psalm 17:8-15

[8] O keep me as the apple of your eye.
Hide me beneath the shadow of your wings,
[9] From wicked ones who hurt me and oppress,
From deadly foes who circle me around.

[10] Closed to all feeling, shut up in their fat[a],
They speak: their mouth is lifted up with pride.
[11] We are beset by them at every step.
Their eyes are set to cast us to the ground.

[12] He, like a lion, longs to rip and tear:[b]
Like a young lion crouching in its hides.
[13] Arise, O LORD, confront him, bring him down.
Save my soul from the wicked[c] by your sword.

[14] From mortal men[d], LORD, rescue with your hand,
From earthly men, whose portion is this life.
For with your treasure you fill up their womb[e].
With children[f] in abundance they're supplied.

They leave their goods unto their little ones.
[15] But I will see your face in righteousness.
I shall be satisfied when I awake,
For, in your likeness, I shall then appear[g].

---

[a] Closed ... fat] Literally, 'their fat they have shut up'. Gesenius judges this to mean 'torpid, unfeeling' as the heart in Isa. 6:10 and its quotation in the New Testament (Greek pachunō - παχυνω). Most commentators link this 'fat' to pride and prosperity. Cf. Job 15:27; Ps. 73:7. However, the meaning may both literal and figurative
[b] Rip and tear] One word in Hebrew.
[c] Wicked] Singular, as in the rest of this verse - 'the wicked one'.
[d] From mortal men ... earthly men] The word used for 'men' both times in this verse is Hebrew methîm - מְתִים. The second line is 'earthly' men or men 'of the world'. The word used for 'earth' or 'world' here (Hebrew heledh - חֶלֶד) is a word relating to time. It emphasises its transitory nature, and therefore the mortality of such men. See on these words in Appendix 2 - Man; and Earth.
[e] Womb] Hebrew beten - בֶּטֶן. AV and most versions translate 'belly', but the Hebrew word is translated an equal number of times in the AV by 'womb' and this fits the context better.
[f] Children] Hebrew 'sons'.
[g] For I shall be satisfied ... appear] AV 'I shall be satisfied ... with thy likeness', either the manifestation of God's glory when we 'see his face', or satisfied with

his glory to be imparted to us at the resurrection (1 John 3:2).

Day 26   Psalm 18:1-6

¹ I love you fervently^a, O LORD, my strength.
² The LORD's my rock, a fortress unto me.
He's my deliverer. He is my GOD.
He's my strong rock. I take my refuge there^b.

He is my shield – my buckler^c for the fight:
Horn of salvation^d and my high stronghold.
³ I'll call upon the LORD, for praise is due,
I will be saved from all my enemies.

⁴ Twined round about me were the cords of Death.
Belial's^e torrents made me so afraid.
⁵ Sheol had cords around about me bound.
I was confronted by the snares of death.

⁶ In my distress I cried unto the LORD.
I cried aloud for help unto my God.
Within his Temple he then heard my voice.
My cry before his face^f came to his ears.

---

^a Love you fervently] This is a strong verb, linked with emotion and compassion. It is its only time it is used in a simple active sense of the believer's love of God - Motyer (1).

^b I take my refuge] The Hebrew verb is ḥaṣâ - חָסָה 'to flee to a refuge and a place of safety'. See Appendix 2 - Refuge.

^c My shield - my buckler] One word in Hebrew - maghen - מָגֵן, a buckler, a small, round shield. See Appendix 2 - Shields.

^d Horn of salvation] 'Horn' is here either a symbol of power (see 1 Kgs. 22:11; Ps. 75:10, as a bull etc), or a metaphor based on the horns of the altar as the place of atonement (Exod. 29:12; 30:10).

^e Belial's] So the Hebrew (see AV mg), A thing of worthlessness and uselessness. Hebrew Belial (beliya'al - בְּלִיַּעַל), literally, 'without-profit. It is used more strongly as 'wickedness' and 'vileness' in Scripture. In later use, and in the New Testament, it became a proper name for Satan. De Burgh argues it should be rendered here as 'the Wicked One', or just 'Belial', making the parallel with Death in the previous line. The word is also used in Ps. 41:8 and 101:3. Cf. 2 Cor. 6:15.

^f Before his face] The literal Hebrew. Usually translated 'before'.

36

Day 27   Psalm 18:7-15

⁷ His anger burned. The earth then shook and quaked.
To their foundations, hills were moved and shook.
⁸ Smoke from his nostrils, and fire from his mouth!
By it were burning coals of fire consumed.

⁹ He bowedᵃ the heavens, and he then came down:
Darkness - thick darkness - underneath his feet!
¹⁰ Mounted upon a cherubᵇ he flew down.
Yes, he flew swiftlyᶜ on the wings of wind.

¹¹ Darkness his secret place, his boothᵈ around
Darkness of watersᵉ, thick clouds of the skies
¹² Out of his brightnessᶠ, his thick clouds went forth.
They went with hailstones and with coals of fire

¹³ The LORD in heavenᵍ sent forth thunder's sound.
The Highestʰ gave his voice: hail, coals of fire!
¹⁴ He sent his arrows, and he scattered them:
Abundant lightnings, and he panicked themⁱ.

¹⁵ The channels of the waters were then seen.
Foundations of the earthʲ were then revealed.
All this occurred at your rebuke, O LORD.
It was accomplished by your nostrils' breath.

ᵃ Bowed] Or 'rent'. The imagery is perhaps of descending storm clouds, or as Rev.
   1:7 'Behold he comes with clouds'.
ᵇ Cherub] First mentioned in Gen. 3:24 as the executive power of God. In Rev.
   4:6-8 (compare Ezek. 1:10) and 5:8,9 the cherubim are associated with the
   throne of God.
ᶜ Flew swiftly] A different word from the previous line. 2 Sam. 22:11 (the parallel
   passage) reads 'appeared', which we may sing here. The word used there has
   the same Hebrew consonants, but different vowels.
ᵈ Booth] AV 'pavilion'. The word is used of the booths made at the Feast of
   Tabernacles (Succoth).
ᵉ Darkness of waters] 'The darkness of the rain-charged storm cloud is the tent in
   which JEHOVAH shrouds his majesty' Kirkpatrick.
ᶠ His brightness] Hebrew 'the brightness in front of him'
ᵍ Heaven] Hebrew 'The heavens'. It can mean both the visible heavens and the
   dwelling place of God.
ʰ The Highest] Hebrew 'Elyôn - עֶלְיוֹן. See Appendix 2 - Names of God - 'Elyôn.
ⁱ He panicked them] Hebrew hamam - הָמַם. Koehler Lexicon 'to bring into
   motion and confusion'.

37

Day 28   Psalm 18:16-19

¹⁶ He sent down from on high - took hold of me;
And from great waters he then drew me out.
¹⁷ Delivered me from my strong enemy:
Stronger than I, were those who hated me.

¹⁸ They had opposed in my day of distress,
But still the LORD was a support to me.
¹⁹ He brought me out into a spacious place.
He rescued me, for I was his delight.

Day 29   Psalm 18:20-26

²⁰ Therefore the LORD gave his reward to me:
According to my righteousness he gave.
Just as my hands were clean, as they were pure,
His recompense he rendered unto me.

²¹ For I have kept the pathways of the LORD.
And did not wickedly go from my God.
²² All of his judgments are before me set.
And his decrees^a I have not turned away.

²³ I was without a blemish before him.
I kept myself from my iniquity.
²⁴ Therefore the LORD rewarded righteousness:
Just as my hands were clean before his eyes

²⁵ You will show mercy to the merciful^b,
Act without blame unto the blameless man^c.
²⁶ He who is pure will know your purity.
The stubborn one will find you hostile too.

---

^a Decrees] Here the feminine form of *ḥoq* - חֹק. See Appendix 2 - Law - Decree.
^b Merciful] Hebrew *ḥasîdh* - חָסִיד - one who is the object of God's loving-kindness and covenant love. See Appendix 2 - Loving-kindness.
^c Man] Hebrew *gebher* - גֶּבֶר - a strong man. See Appendix 2 - Man.

Day 30   Psalm 18:27-36

²⁷ You – you yourself[a] – the humble people save.
But haughty and conceited looks bring down.
²⁸ You are the one who lights my lamp, O LORD.
Into my darkness, my God will shine light!

²⁹ For by you, LORD, I run against a troop,
And by my God can even jump a wall.
³⁰ GOD's way is perfect[b]; the LORD's word[c] is tried.
He is a shield[d] to all who trust[e] in him.

³¹ For who is <u>God</u>[f] except the LORD alone?
Who is a rock of refuge, but our God?
³² He is the GOD who clothes me round with strength.
He gives to me a perfect, blameless way.

³³ He makes my feet just like the feet of deer.
On my high places[g] he makes me to stand.
³⁴ He trains my hands for battle and for war[h].
So, with my arms, I can press down the bow[i].

³⁵ To me you've given your salvation's shield.
It is your right hand that has held me up.
Your lowly gentleness has made me great.
³⁶ You gave a wide place, lest my feet should slip[j].

---

[a] You – you yourself] 'You' is emphasised in the Hebrew. Salvation is the work of God.

[b] GOD's way is perfect] Literally, 'GOD is blameless as to his way'. The same word 'perfect' or 'blameless' is used in v32. GOD is here, and in v32 and v47 of this Psalm, called *the 'El* - אֵל, emphasising both his uniqueness and his power. See Appendix 2 - Names of God - *'El*.

[c] Word] The spoken word. Hebrew *'imrâ* - אִמְרָה. This psalm is also recorded in 2 Sam. 22, and is followed by the last words of David, where he says in 2 Sam. 23:2,3 that the LORD spoke by him and to him. See Appendix 2 - Word.

[d] Shield] Hebrew *maghen* - מָגֵן, a 'buckler', a small, round shield. Verses 29,30 describe attack, not defence. See Appendix 2 - Shields.

[e] Trust] The Hebrew verb is *ḥaṣâ* - חָסָה 'to flee to a refuge and a place of safety'. See Appendix 2 - Refuge.

[f] God] Hebrew *'Elôah* - אֱלוֹהַ. See Appendix 2 - Names of God - *'Elôah*.

[g] The 'high places' in David's case were the strongholds of the hills and mountains where he found refuge in the days of Saul.

[h] Battle ... war] One word in Hebrew.

[i] So ... bow] The bow was re-strung before battle, usually by pressing or 'treading'

39

it (see note on 7:12). The Hebrew calls the bow here 'a bow of bronze' (AV 'bow of steel' is an anachronism). The expression is also used in the parallel 2 Sam. 22:35, and in Job 20:24. Archaeology has not brought any such bows to light. Bows needed to be lightweight and pliable, and bronze or brass would be unsuitable. Convex bows were widely in use in David's time (see Yadin, *The Art of Warfare in Biblical Lands*, See 2 Kgs. 9:24 for the power of the bow), and Aron Pinker *(Journal of Hebrew Scriptures* 5:12*)* has plausibly suggested the word here is a technical term for such a (serpentine shaped) bow. The cognate word then would not then be related to bronze *(nehosheth* - נְחֹשֶׁת*)* but to its snakelike, or serpentine, shape *(nahash* - נָחָשׁ*)*. Cf. Numb. 21:9.

^j Wide place] Hebrew perhaps means 'You have made a wide place under my feet (or 'my steps') so that my ankles should not give way' (see Calvin etc).

Day 31   Psalm 18:37-45

³⁷ I chased my foes - have overtaken them;
Did not turn back until they were destroyed.
³⁸ I cut them through so that they could not rise,
And they were cast down underneath my feet.

³⁹ For you have bound me round with strength for war.
Those who rose up against me you subdued.
⁴⁰ You made my foes to turn their backs in flight^a,
So those that hate me I might then destroy.

⁴¹ They cried for help - there was no-one to save -
- cried to the LORD - but he no answer gave.
⁴² I beat them fine as dust, blown by the wind;
I cast them out, like dirt of muddy streets.

⁴³ You've saved me from the strifes the people make.
Over the nations you have made me head.
Even a people that I have not known -
That people will give service unto me.

⁴⁴ They will obey when they shall hear of me,
And strangers^b will submit themselves to me.
⁴⁵ The strangers will lose heart and fade away,
And come with trembling from where they have hid.

---

^a You made ... flight] Hebrew 'you have given me the neck of my enemies'. We may translate this literally and relate this to Josh. 10:34, but a different word for 'neck' is used there, and it is generally agreed that the meaning is as we

[b] Strangers] Hebrew 'sons of the stranger', here and in the following verse. The word refers to non-Israelites.

Day 32   Psalm 18:46-50

[46] The LORD most surely lives![a] Blest be my Rock!
Lift up the God of my salvation high.
[47] He is the GOD who thus avenges me,
Who makes the peoples subject under me.

[48] He sets me free from all my enemies.
Above my foes you have exalted me,
And from the cruel man[b] you rescued me.
[49] Among the nations I will thank you, LORD!

I will, with psalms, sing praises[c] to your name.
[50] Great victories the LORD gives to his king.
To his Anointed he shows steadfast love[d];
To David and his offspring evermore.

---

[a] The LORD most surely lives] 'The LORD lives!' (חַי־יהוה) occurs 43 times in the Old Testament, but in the Psalms only here. It is the strongest form of averment, or affirmation, of truth.

[b] Man] Hebrew *'îš* - אִישׁ - Man as an individual. See Appendix 2 - Man.

[c] I will, with psalms, sing praises] Hebrew *zamar* - זָמַֿר. Septuagint and the Rom. 15:9 translation give *psallo* (ψαλλω). See Appendix 2 - Sing Psalms.

[d] Steadfast love] Hebrew *ḥeṣedh* - חֶֿסֶֿד. See Appendix 2 - Loving-kindness.

Day 33   Psalm 19:1-6

[1] The heavens do declare - GOD's glory tell;
The sky above shows what his hand has done.
[2] From day to day continually they speak;[a]
Fresh knowledge night to night they do declare.

[3] Though they are without speech[b] and without words,
and (even though their voice cannot be heard)
[4] Their line's[c] extended throughout all the earth -
Their words unto the limit of the world.[d]   →

He set in them a dwelling^e for the sun.
⁵ It is just like a bridegroom coming forth.
The sun comes forth out of his canopy^f -
Glad, like a strong man, now to run his course.

⁶ He rises from the heavens' farthest end;
Completes the circuit to its end again.
And there is nothing hidden from its warmth,
No-one is hidden from its scorching heat.^g

---

^a They speak] Hebrew 'they utter speech'. 'Speech' here is Hebrew *'omer* - אֹמֶר
  (from *'amar* - אָמַר, to say). See Appendix 2 - Word.
^b Speech] as the note on v2.
^c Line] The Hebrew word means a 'rope' or a 'measuring cord', in which sense it
  describes the extent the voice of the heavens reaches. Gesenius *Lexicon*
  suggests it may mean the string (of a harp). From this last meaning, 'a (musical
  -1 Cor. 14:7) sound', the Septuagint renders it with a word meaning a sound,
  tone, or voice. So it is quoted in Rom. 10:18, which compares the glory of the
  heavens with the preaching of the Gospel - See Alford *in loco*.
^d World] The inhabited earth. *tebhel* - תֵּבֵל. See Appendix 2 - Earth.
^e Dwelling] Hebrew 'tent'. Cf. Hab. 3:11
^f Canopy] Hebrew *ḥuppâ* - חֻפָּה. At Jewish weddings the marriage ceremony is
  conducted under a *ḥuppâ*.
^g We have repeated this line with different wording, noting that the words can be
  understood as 'nothing' or as 'no-one', and the sun's warmth can be
  understood in a positive sense, or as scorching heat. See Calvin.

Day 34   Psalm 19:7-14

⁷ The LORD's, full, perfect^a Law restores^b the soul.
Sure is his Testimony. It makes wise.^c
⁸ Right precepts of the LORD rejoice the heart.
The LORD's command is pure - lights up the eyes.

⁹ Fear of the LORD is clean and it endures.
The judgments of the LORD are true and right.
¹⁰ Desirable much more than gold – pure gold.
Sweeter than honey and the honeycomb.

¹¹ Moreover by them is your servant warned.
The keeping of them gives a great reward.
¹² As for his errors - who can understand?
From hidden faults declare me innocent!^d   →

42

¹³ Keep back your servant from presumptuous sins.^e
Let them not have dominion over me.
Then I will be both blameless and complete.^f
From great transgression I shall be kept free.

¹⁴ O may the words I utter with my mouth,
The meditation^g of my heart in me,
Make it accepted - pleasing in your sight.
Be my strong Rock, Kinsman–Redeemer^h, LORD.

---

^a Full, perfect] One word in Hebrew *(tamîm - תָּמִים)*. The word conveys, fullness, perfection, completeness.
^b Restores] literally, 'brings back'.
^c His Testimony ... wise] Hebrew 'the Testimony of the LORD is sure, making wise the simple [literally, 'those who are open']'
^d Declare me innocent] The same word can mean 'cleanse'. The word is translated 'innocent', by the AV in v13.
^e Presumptuous sins] The word 'sins' is not in the Hebrew. Perhaps, 'presumptuous people'.
^f Blameless and complete] The same Hebrew word as in verse 7. AV 'perfect'.
^g Meditation] The word here is *higgaion* - הִגָּיוֹן. See Appendix 3.
^h Kinsman-Redeemer] Hebrew *gô 'el* - גוֹאֵל the one who gives restitution, as in Lev. 25:25,26; and in the story of Boaz and Ruth (Ruth 2:20ff).

Day 35   Psalm 20

¹ The LORD reply^a to you when trouble comes^b
And by the name of Jacob's God keep safe^c.
² Send you your help out of the Holy Place.
And out of Zion may he give you strength.

³ Remember all the offerings you made,
And your burnt sacrifice may he accept. ⊬
⁴ Give you according to your heart's desire;
Bring to completion all you plan to do.

⁵ We'll shout for joy^d in your deliverance!
And set our banners up in our God's name!
All your petitions may the LORD fulfil.
⁶ I know the LORD saves his Anointed One!   →

He, from his holy heaven, answers him,
With all the saving strength of his right hand.
⁷ Some put their trust in chariot, or horse; ^e
The LORD's name we'll recall. He is our God.

⁸ Though they're brought down unto their knees and fall;
We have arisen and we stand upright.
⁹ O LORD, give your deliverance, and save. ^f
The king will answer in the day we call.

---

^a Reply] The verb means more than just 'hear'. It means hearing and giving an answer. So too verse 9 and Ps. 22:2. See Appendix 2 Hear and Answer. It obviously implies a cry for help has been made.
^b When trouble comes] Hebrew 'in the day of trouble', or 'affliction'. The expression is used 8 times in the Old Testament (e.g. Ps. 50:15, Jer. 16:19; Nahum 1:7).
^c Keep safe] AV 'defend'. The word means 'to lift up', as to a safe defensible place. See *Statenvertaling* and the *Dutch Annotations*.
^d Shout for joy] AV 'rejoice', but the verb is usually 'shout for joy' or 'sing for joy'.
^e Some [put their trust] in chariot or horse] In the Hebrew there is no verb in this line. 'Trust' is also supplied by AV.
^f Give your deliverance and save] One word Hebrew.

Day 36   Psalm 21:1-7

¹ The king rejoices in your strength, O LORD.
In your salvation he'll be full of joy.
² You've given to him what his heart desired,
What he requested^a you did not withhold. ╫

³ You meet him with the blessings of what's good.
You put a crown of pure gold on his head.
⁴ He asked for life and you gave it to him -
Days that will last for ever, evermore

⁵ Great is his glory through your saving work.
Majestic splendour you bestow on him.
⁶ You have made him most blest for evermore.^b
You gladden him with joy before your face.

⁷ Because the king is trusting in the LORD -
Because he rests in his unfailing love
(The loving-kindness^c of the Most High God^d) -
So, he shall not be shaken or removed.

44

a What he requested] Hebrew, 'what his lips requested'.
b You have made him most blessed] Hebrew 'You make him blessings'.
c Unfailing love ... loving-kindness] Hebrew ḥeṣedh - חֶסֶד. See Appendix 2 -
   Loving-kindness.
d The Most High God] Hebrew 'Elyôn - עֶלְיוֹן. See Appendix 2 - Names of God -
   'Elyôn.

Day 37   Psalm 21:8-13

⁸ Your hand will find out all your enemies.
Yes, those who hate you, your right hand will find.
⁹ And you will make them as a blazing fire,
When it is time for you to show your face[a].

The LORD will then engulf them in his wrath;
And with a fire he will devour them up.
¹⁰ Their offspring[b] he'll destroy out of the earth;
Their issue[c] from among the sons of men.

¹¹ For they intended evil against you.
They made a plot that they could not perform.
¹² For you will make them back away from you,[d]
When in their sight you shall prepare your bow.[e]

¹³ O be exalted; LORD, be lifted high!
O be exalted in your strength and might!
So, we will sing, and surely we will praise,
And, singing psalms, will celebrate your power[f].→

---

a Time for you to show your face] Hebrew 'at the season of your face' (or
   presence). This no doubt refers to the Lord Jesus's *Parousia* (παρουσια) or
   presence (AV 'coming'), as in Matt. 24:3,27,37; 2 Thess. 2:8. AV translates 'at
   the time of your anger'.
b Their offspring] Hebrew 'their fruit'.
c Their issue] Hebrew 'their seed'.
d Back away from you] Hebrew 'turn their shoulder [in flight]'.
e You shall prepare your bow] Hebrew 'in your strings you will fix [arrows]'.
   Geneva Bible 'the strings of thy bow shalt thou make ready before their faces'.
f We have extended the last phrases of the Psalm, amplifying the meaning.

Day 38   Psalm 22:1-5

¹ My GOD, my GOD, why have you left me so?
Far off from helping: from my groaning words!
² My God, I cry by day. You answer not.
There is no quiet for me in the night.

³ But you are holy: throned[a] in Israel's praise.
⁴ Our fathers trusted: You delivered them.
⁵ They cried to you: and then they were set free
In you they trusted: They were not ashamed.

---

[a] Throned] The verb has a range of meanings, from the root 'to sit' - hence to be
enthroned, to abide or inhabit, cf. Ps. 80:1.

Day 39   Psalm 22:6-13

⁶ I am a worm, and I'm not like a man[a]:
Reproach of men, and by the people scorned.
⁷ All those who see me laugh at me and mock:
Make mouths at me, and joking shake their head

⁸ 'He cast himself, and trusted[b], on the LORD.
Let him deliver, since he pleases him!'
⁹ But you are he who took me from the womb,
And made me hope upon my mother's breasts.

¹⁰ I was cast forth upon you from my birth: [c]
And from my mother's womb you've been my GOD.
¹¹ O be not distant or remote from me!
Trouble is near, and there's no-one to help.

¹² There are so many bulls surrounding me.
Strong bulls of Bashan circle me around.
¹³ And they have gaped upon me with their mouth,
Just as a lion goes to tear and roar.

---

[a] Not like a man] Hebrew 'îš - אִישׁ -Man as an individual. This is not a denial of his
humanity, but a statement of his felt weakness. Cf. 1 Kgs. 2:2. See Appendix 2
- Man. The word in the following line, 'men' 'adham - אָדָם, is mankind in the
general sense
[b] He cast himself and trusted] One word in Hebrew. Literally, 'he rolled himself
upon'. Compare Ps. 37:5 (AV 'commit').

^c From my birth] Literally, 'from the womb', but a different word is used here from that which we have translated 'womb' in v9 and v10. The word here is more closely linked to the uterus, hence from the context ('cast forth') we have translated 'from my birth'. The other word may be translated 'belly' or 'lower abdomen' of man or woman, or the inmost part of something, as Jonah 2:2 in reference to Sheol.

Day 40　　Psalm 22:14-21

¹⁴ Poured out like water; bones all out of joint.
My heart within me melted, just like wax.
¹⁵ My strength is dried up, like an earthen pot.
My tongue just sticks and cleaves against my jaws.

By you I'm brought unto the dust of death,
¹⁶ For dogs surrounded and encompassed me.
A crowd of evil men are all around,
By them my hands and feet were pierced right through.

¹⁷ I count my bones. They look and stare at me.
¹⁸ They part my garments; cast lots for my clothes.
¹⁹ Do not be far away from me, O LORD.
You are my Strength. Come quickly to give aid!

²⁰ My soul - my life^a - deliver from the sword.
From the dog's grip^b, O save my precious life!^c
²¹ Give me salvation from the lion's mouth:
From the fierce oxen's horns. You've answered me!

^a My soul - my life] One word in Hebrew. The word is linked with the word for 'breath', Gen. 1:20,30, and hence 'life'.
^b Grip] Literally, 'from the hand of the dog'. This a Hebrew expression meaning 'from the power of the dog'. 'Grip' links the sense of both 'hand' and 'power'.
^c My precious life] AV 'my darling'. Literally, 'my only one'. The Septuagint translates here and 35:17 as 'my only begotten'. It is used in Judg. 11:34 of Jephthah's daughter. We translate 'precious life' in view of the parallel with the previous line, where he speaks of his soul, i.e. his life.

Day 41　　Psalm 22:22-31

²² Unto my brothers, I will tell your name.
In the assembly^a, I'll give praise to you.
²³ Give praise to him all you who fear the LORD.
Offspring of Jacob, glory give to him.　　　　→

All Israel's offspring, stand in awe of him.
²⁴ He did not scorn the humbling that he bore,
Did not abhor, nor hide his face from him.
But, when he cried to him for help, he heard.

²⁵ You'll be my praise in the great gathering.
I'll pay my vows before those who fear him.
²⁶ The meek ones eat, and they are satisfied.
And those who seek him, they shall praise the LORD!

Your heart will be alive for evermore.
²⁷ Earth's ends remember, and turn to the LORD!
Tribes of all nations shall before you bow.
²⁸ The kingdom is the LORD's for him to reign!

He rules the nations^b. He is over them.
²⁹ Earth's favoured ones^c shall eat and worship too^d.
All who go down to dust, before him bow!
Each one who cannot make his own soul live^e.

³⁰ There is an offspring that shall serve the LORD;
The generation for the LORD they'll be.
³¹ They shall come and proclaim his righteousness,
And tell an unborn people he did this.

ᵃ Assembly] Septuagint and Heb. 2:12 *ekklesia* (ἐκκλησια), the word used for
  Church in the New Testament.
ᵇ Rules the nations. He is over them] AV 'He is the Governor among the nations'.
  Hebrew *mašal* - מָשַׁל to rule or reign over. Compare Ps. 8:1.
ᶜ Favoured ones] Hebrew 'fat ones' *(dašen – דָּשֵׁן)* - those who are prosperous and
  successful.
ᵈ Too] i.e. together with the meek, v26.
ᵉ Each one who cannot ... live] 'Even he that cannot quicken (rather than 'keep
  alive' AV) his own soul' Geneva Bible (and see de Burgh, note). This is the
  usual meaning of this form of the verb. Those who 'go down to the dust', who
  cannot make their own soul live, shall indeed bow down (worship) before him.
  The reference is to resurrection not sustained life. See John 5:25.

Day 42   Psalm 23

¹ The LORD's my Shepherd. There's nothing I'll lack.
² For in fresh pastures he makes me lie down
He guides me where the restful^a waters flow.
³ He gives refreshment, and restores my soul.   →

He leads me in right paths for his name's sake.
[4] Though through a valley deathly dark[b] I go,
I fear no evil, for you are with me.
Your rod, your staff, they comfort and console.

[5] Before my foes, you set my table out.
Anoint my head, and my cup overflows.
[6] Goodness and mercy all my days attend[c],
In the LORD's house I shall dwell endless days[d].

---

[a] Restful] not 'still'. Waters of refreshments; streams where rest can be found.
[b] Deathly dark] Here and Ps. 107:10,14. AV 'the shadow of death'. A combination
of the words 'shadow' and 'death', indicating deep, dark, shadow, with 'death'
apparently used to indicate 'the darkest shadow'.
[c] Goodness and mercy all my days attend] Hebrew 'Surely, goodness and loving-
kindness (Hebrew ḥeṣedh - חֶסֶד. See Appendix 2 - Loving-kindness) shall
pursue me all the days of my life'.
[d] Endless days] Hebrew 'for length of days', generally taken to mean 'forever'

Day 43   Psalm 24

[1] The earth and all that fills it is the LORD's;
The world[a], and everything that dwells therein.
[2] For it was founded by him on the seas,
And he established it upon the floods.

[3] Who shall go up the mountain of the LORD?
And who shall stand within his holy place?
[4] The one who has clean hands and a pure heart:
Not vainly lifted up[b], nor telling lies.

[5] He shall receive the blessing from the LORD;
And righteousness have from his saving God.
[6] This is the generation who seek him,
Even the Jacob[c] - those who seek your face. ǂ

[7] Gates, raise your heads up! Be raised, ancient doors!
So that the King of Glory may come in.
[8] Who is this King of Glory? - It's the LORD!
The mighty LORD. Strong. Mighty in the fight!

⁹ Gates, raise your heads up! Rise up, ancient doors!
So that the King of Glory may come in
¹⁰ Who is this King, the King most glorious? ᵈ
The LORD of Hosts the King of Glory is! ⊹

ᵃ The world] The inhabited earth. *tebhel* - תֵּבֵל. See Appendix 2 - Earth.
ᵇ Not vainly lifted up] Hebrew 'who has not lifted up his soul to the vanity'.
ᶜ The Jacob] ESV, NIV, following the Syriac, add 'the God of' Jacob. We have
   translated 'Jacob' here in apposition to 'the generation'. 'The Jacobs' are the
   generation who seek God's face, i.e. the weak ones. See Rom. 11:26.
ᵈ King of Glory ... king most glorious] Hebrew 'king of the Glory', as 'King of Glory'
   throughout the Psalm.

Day 44   Psalm 25:1-7

¹ To you, O LORD, do I lift up my soul.
² My God in you I trust. Keep me from shame.
Don't let my enemies joy over meᵃ.
³ Let no-one be ashamed who waits on you.

They shall be shamed who, without cause, deceive.
⁴ Show me your ways, O LORD. Teach me your paths!
⁵ Cause me to tread your way of truthᵇ. Teach me!
I long for you all day, my saving God.

⁶ Your tender merciesᶜ call to mind, O LORD,
Rememberᵈ too your loving-kindnesses,ᵉ
For they have been for ever, from of old.
⁷ Remember not my sins and faults of youth.

Remember not my sins and faults of youth.ᶠ
My plea is that you will remember me
According to your loving-kindnesses,
And, LORD, because you are so very good.

ᵃ Joy over me] AV 'triumph over me'. *Statenvertaling* 'leap for joy over me'.
ᵇ Cause me to tread your way of truth] So the Hebrew.
ᶜ Tender mercies] Deep feelings of compassion aroused by the sight of weakness
   or suffering (Hebrew *rahamîm* - רַחֲמִים).
ᵈ Call to mind ... remember] One verb in the Hebrew.
ᵉ Loving-kindnesses] Plural. Hebrew *ḥeṣedh* - חֶסֶד. So too 'love' in the following
   verse. See Appendix 2 - Loving-kindness.
ᶠ We have repeated this line.

Day 45   Psalm 25:8-14

[8] The LORD is good and upright, and therefore,
He will instruct - teach sinners in the way.
[9] In judgment[a] he will make the meek to walk.
And to those who are meek he'll teach his way.

[10] All the LORD's ways are steadfast love[b] and truth
To those who keep his covenant and laws[c].
[11] Pardon my sin, LORD, for your own name's sake.
Forgive my very great iniquity.

[12] What man is this, the man who fears the LORD?
He will direct him in his chosen way.
[13] In good prosperity[d] his soul shall dwell.
The land[e] shall be his children's heritage.

[14] The secret counsel of the LORD will be
To those who fear him with a godly fear.
The LORD will cause such ones to understand.
He will make known his covenant to them.

---

[a] In judgment] Hebrew 'the judgment'. Motyer (1) 'according to what he has decided upon'; 'the authoritative decision of judge or king'.
[b] Steadfast love] Hebrew ḥeṣedh - חֶסֶד. See Appendix 2 - Loving-kindness.
[c] Laws] Hebrew 'edhâ - עֵדָה. See Appendix 2 - Law - Testimony
[d] In good prosperity] Literally, 'in good'. AV 'at ease'.
[e] The land] Hebrew 'eretṣ - אֶרֶץ. The Hebrew word may be translated either 'land' or 'earth'. See Appendix 2 - Earth.

Day 46   Psalm 25:15-22

[15] My eyes are ever, always, on the LORD,
For he will draw my feet out of the net.
[16] O turn to me. Have mercy upon me.
For I'm afflicted, desolate, alone.[a]

[17] The troubles of my heart are multiplied.
From my distresses, O do bring me out!
[18] Behold and see my trouble and my pain.
O do forgive my sins: bear them away.[b]   →

¹⁹ See how my enemies are multiplied,
And how they hate me with a cruel hate.
²⁰ O keep my soul! O do deliver me!
Keep me from shame. I put my trust in you.^c

²¹ Let my integrity and uprightness
Preserve and guard me, for I wait on you.
²² Redemption give to Israel, O God!
From his afflictions, O do set him free!^d

---

^a Desolate, alone] One word in Hebrew.
^b Bear away] This is the root meaning of the word usually translated 'forgive'.
^c Put my trust in you] The Hebrew verb is ḥaṣâ - חָסָה 'to flee to a refuge and a
    place of safety'. See Appendix 2 - Refuge.
^d Set him free] The word usually translated 'redeem' also means 'set free' (see
    Deut. 7:8). We have given both meanings in this verse.

Day 47   Psalm 26:1-7

¹ O vindicate! Give justice unto me.
For, LORD, I've walked in my integrity.
Upon the LORD I also put my trust.
I have not wavered, and I shall not slip^a.

² O prove me, LORD, and put me to the test.
My inner man and heart^b refine and try.
³ Your loving-kindness^c is before my eyes.
Therefore, I've walked the way your truth directs.

⁴ I do not stay or sit^d with false, vain men;^e
Nor will I go among the hypocrites
⁵ I hate the evildoers' company.
I will not stay or sit with wicked men.

⁶ To show my innocence I'll wash my hands.
So I will go about your altar, LORD.
⁷ So I'll proclaim with voice of thankfulness,
And tell the wondrous works that you have done

---

^a Wavered ... slip] The word can either be taken as applying to his 'trust', or as a
    stand-alone statement, 'I shall not slip'. We have given both senses.
^b Inner man and heart] 'Inner man' = Hebrew 'kidneys', AV 'reins'. See note on

7:9 where the order of these two is reversed.
^c Loving-kindness] covenant mercy. Hebrew *ḥeṣedh* - חֶסֶד. See Appendix 2 - Loving-kindness.
^d Stay or sit] The Hebrew verb can mean either, as also in v5.
^e Men] Hebrew *methîm* - מְתִימ - mortal, dying men. See Appendix 2 - Man.

Day 48   Psalm 26:8-12

⁸ LORD, I have loved the place where you reside:
That habitation is your house, O LORD.
I love the place, for there your glory is:
The tabernacle where your honour dwells.^a

⁹ With sinners do not gather up my soul,
Nor with blood-guilty men^b my life remove.
¹⁰ For in their hands there is a wicked plan.
Their right hand's full of gifts of bribery.

¹¹ But I will walk in my integrity.
Redeem me and be merciful to me!
¹² My foot stands on an even, level place.
In the assemblies I will bless the LORD.

^a We have expanded the second line of the verse. It is literally, 'the place of the dwelling of your glory'. We have repeated the verb (loved). The word the AV translates 'habitation' is especially used of the Tabernacle, and the word 'shekinah' *(šekhînâ* - שְׁכִינָה*)*, meaning God's Divine presence, is derived from it. The word translated 'glory' also means 'honour'.
^b Blood-guilty men] Hebrew 'men of blood'. 'Man' here is Hebrew *'enôš* - אֱנוֹשׁ - Frail, mortal man. See Appendix 2 - Man.

Day 49   Psalm 27:1-6

¹ LORD - Saviour - Light to me: Whom shall I fear?
Strength of my life. Who will make me afraid?
² When wicked men came up to eat my flesh -
My enemies and foes - they slipped and fell!

³ If against me an army should encamp^a,
My heart within me will not be afraid.
For, though a war should break out against me,
In spite of this I shall be confident.   →

⁴ One thing I asked, requested, of the LORD,
And for that thing I surely will enquire:
That all my life[b] I may dwell in his house[c],
Gaze on his beauty, in his Temple seek.

⁵ For he will hide me in the evil day.
He will conceal me in his sheltered place[d].
And secretly will hide me in his tent.
And he will lift me high upon a rock.

⁶ My head shall also now be lifted up
Above my foes who have surrounded me.
I'll sacrifice with joy[e] within his tent.[f]
Unto the LORD I'll sing; I'll sing with psalms.

---

[a] If against me an army should encamp] Hebrew, 'if against me an encampment
   shall camp'.
[b] All my life] Hebrew 'all the days of my life'.
[c] His house] Hebrew 'the house of the LORD'.
[d] Sheltered place] The word here is used of the booths of the Feast of Tabernacles
   (Succoth). AV 'pavilion'.
[e] I'll sacrifice with joy] Hebrew literally, 'I will sacrifice sacrifices of shouting'. The
   word 'shouting' is also used in Ps. 89:15. It is used of the shout that brought
   down the walls of Jericho (Josh. 6:4,20), and of the shout of joy when the
   foundation of the Second Temple was laid (Ezra 3:11-13).
[f] His tent] See 2 Sam. 6:17. AV 'tabernacle'.

Day 50   Psalm 27:7-14

⁷ LORD, answer me, for I cry with my voice.
Be gracious and give answer unto me.
⁸ 'Go seek my face' you said. My heart repeats,
'Your face, O LORD, I earnestly will seek'.[a]

⁹ Do not conceal, or hide, your face from me,
Nor put away your servant in your wrath.
O leave me not! For you have been my help
Do not forsake me, O my Saving God!

¹⁰ The LORD will take me in, though I should be
Forsaken by my father, mother too.
¹¹ Teach me your way, LORD. In a plain path lead,
Because of those who lie in wait for me[b]   →

54

¹² Don't give me up to my oppressors' will.^c
False witnesses rise up: breathe cruelty.
¹³ Unless I'd trusted that I yet would see -
His goodness in the land of those who live!^d

¹⁴ Wait^e on the LORD and take encouragement.
Your heart he'll strengthen. He will make it strong.
Again, I say 'Wait' - 'Wait upon the LORD'.
And wait for him in earnest, patiently.

---

^a Go seek ...seek earnestly] The same verb is used. In both cases it is the Hebrew
intensive (piel) - earnestly seek.
^b Those who lie in wait for me] Not just 'enemies'. 'Those who watch out for me
spitefully'. Compare Ps. 5:9. See de Burgh. Compare 'wait' v14.
^c Don't give me up to my oppressors' will] Literally, 'do not give me up to the soul
of my oppressors'. 'Soul' is here used of their inner passion, earnest desire, or
dearest wish. The word is likewise used in Ps. 17:9 and 41:2.
^d The land ... live] AV 'land of the living'. Compare Ps. 52:5; 116:9; 142:5. 'The
phrase "the land of the living" may fitly denote the future age', de Burgh. Verse
13 is an abrupt broken sentence - as if the consequences of the awful
possibility that he would not see life and God's goodness had just flashed
through his mind (cf. Gen. 31:42).
^e Wait] Hebrew *(qawâ - קָוָה)*. 'Look to'. 'Observancy of another whom we are
seeking to serve and to please', Newton (3) p288. We have expanded the
meaning of the Hebrew word in the last line. It is the Hebrew intensive (piel).

Day 51   Psalm 28

¹ I'll cry to you, O LORD. You are my rock.
Do not be deaf to me, nor silence keep,
Lest I be like those who go to the Pit.
² My pleas for mercy^a hear. I cry for help.

I lift hands to your Holy Inner Place^b.
³ With evildoers don't drag me away,
And with the workers of iniquity,
Who speak in peace with friends, with evil hearts.

⁴ Give them according to what they have done.
Give them according to their wicked deeds.
Repay them for the things their hands have done.
Return the recompense that they deserve.   →

⁵ They don't regard the things the LORD has done.
And don't regard^c the working of his hands.
He will destroy them and not build them up.
⁶ Blest be the LORD! He heard my cry for grace!ᵈ

⁷ The LORD's my strength and shield. I trust in him.
In him my heart trusts, and I have been helped.
Therefore, my heart is jubilant with joy,
And with my song I will give thanks to him.

⁸ Theireᵉ mighty strength is only in the LORD.
He's strong to save for his Anointed One.
⁹ O save your people! Bless your heritage!
Shepherd and carry them for evermore!

ᵃ My pleas for mercy] Hebrew 'the voice of my supplications'.
ᵇ Holy Inner Place] AV 'oracle' from the Hebrew word 'to speak'. This could be translated 'oracle of your sanctuary', or 'oracle of your holiness'. Others translate 'the inmost place', i.e. the Holy of Holies, as the word is used in 1 Kgs. 6:16 and elsewhere in Kings and Chronicles.
ᶜ Don't regard] We have repeated the verb from the previous line.
ᵈ My cry for grace] Hebrew 'the voice of my supplications'
ᵉ Their] i.e. the people's (v9). Some Hebrew MSS. read le'ammô - לְעַמּוֹ ('to his people') for lamô - לָמוֹ (to them), and this seems to have been the reading of the Septuagint and Syriac translators.

Day 52   Psalm 29

¹ Sons of the mightyᵃ give unto the LORD.
Give to the LORD the glory and the power.
² Give to the LORD the glory due his name.
In lovely holiness bow to the LORD.

³ Upon the waters the LORD's voice sounds out.
The thunders of the GOD of Gloryᵇ roar.
The LORD is on the mighty waters now.
The LORD is on the mighty waters now.ᶜ

⁴ Mighty and strongᵈ is the voice of the LORD.
Voice of the LORD! It's full of majesty.
⁵ Voice of the LORD! It breaks the cedars down.
Lebanon's cedars broken by the LORD!   →

⁶ He makes the Lebanon skip like a calf.
Sirion^e skips as if a wild young bull.
⁷ The LORD's voice is dividing flames of fire.
⁸ The LORD's voice makes the wilderness to shake.

The wilderness of Kadesh the LORD shakes,
⁹ And the LORD's voice now makes the deer give birth. ^f
The forests are laid bare at the LORD's voice.
Throughout his Temple 'Glory!' is declared.

¹⁰ The LORD has sat enthroned upon the flood.
He sits enthroned as King for evermore.
¹¹ The LORD will give unto his people strength.
The LORD will bless his people with his peace.^g

---

^a Sons of the mighty] i.e. the great ones of the earth. Because of the use of the
  Hebrew word *'elîm* - אֱלִים, some take it to mean 'angels', but see de Burgh's
  objection to this, and Girdlestone's comments.
^b The GOD of Glory] Literally, 'the GOD of *the* Glory'.
^c The LORD is on the mighty waters now] We have repeated this line.
^d Mighty and strong] One word in the Hebrew.
^e Sirion] Mount Hermon - cf. Deut. 3:9.
^f Makes the deer give birth] The verb twice translated 'shakes' is here translated
  differently. The word can mean writhing pains, as of giving birth.
^g His peace] Hebrew 'the peace' - the peace of God that passes all understanding.

Day 53   Psalm 30:1-5

¹ I will exalt you, LORD. You drew me up^a.
You did not let my foes rejoice at me.
² O LORD my God, I cried to you for help,
And you have been a healer unto me.

³ LORD, up from Sheol you have brought my soul:
Revived, and kept from falling in the Pit.
⁴ Those whom he loves^b, Sing psalms unto the LORD!
Give thanks when you recall his holiness^c

⁵ His anger lasts for just a moment long,
But his good favour lasts a whole life through.
Weeping may lodge, and for an evening stay,
But shouts of joy will be at break of day.

[a] Drew me up] As from a pit. See Exod. 2:16; Prov. 30:5. See Newton (5) p154.
[b] Those whom he loves] AV 'saints'. Hebrew ḥaṣîdhîm - חֲסִידִים, plural of Hebrew ḥaṣîdh - חָסִיד - one who is the object of God's loving-kindness and covenant love (ḥeṣedh - חֶסֶד). See Appendix 2 - Loving-kindness.
[c] When you recall his holiness] Literally, 'his holy memorial' or 'in commemoration of his holiness'. See Ps. 102:12 and 135:13.

Day 54   Psalm 30:6-12

[6] In my security and ease I said
'I shall be never shaken or be moved'.
[7] And 'LORD, your favour made my mountain[a] strong'.
You hid your face, and then I was dismayed[b].

[8] I cried to you, LORD, and your favour sought.
[9] What is the benefit of my shed blood
When I descend and go down to the pit?
Will dust give praise? Will it declare your truth?

[10] Please hear, O LORD. Have mercy upon me.
O LORD, do be a helper unto me.
[11] You turned my mourning into dance for me;
Took off my sackcloth and clothed me with joy,

[12] My glory[c] will praise you with psalms,
So that I'll not be silent any more.
O LORD my God I will give thanks to you –
Give thanks to you for ever, evermore.

[a] My mountain] Calvin and others understand 'my mountain' - David's mountain - as mount Zion, rather than regarding this as just a figurative expression.
[b] Dismayed] The word is a strong one 'denoting confusion and amazement caused by terror or calamity'. See 1 Sam. 18:21 and Job 4:5. See Newton (5) p 157.
[c] My glory] see note on 16:9. Dickson takes it to mean 'his tongue', as the means by which man, and no other creature, can sing, and glorify God.

Day 55   Psalm 31:1-8

[1] I put my trust in you for refuge[a], LORD,
Let me not be ashamed for evermore
But in your righteousness deliver me.
[2] Incline your ear and rescue speedily.   →

Be for me as a rock - a rock of strength
A fortress house[b] so that I may be saved,
[3] You are my stronghold, fortress of defence,
For your name's sake lead me and guide me through.

[4] Release me from the net they hid for me,
Because you are the one who gives me strength[c].
[5] Into your hand my spirit I commit.
You have delivered me[d], LORD, GOD of truth.

[6] I hate those who respect false empty things[e],
For in the LORD I place my confidence.
[7] I will be joyful in your steadfast love,
And in your loving-kindness[f] I'll be glad.[g]

For my affliction has been seen by you,
And you have known my soul in its distress.
[8] You did not give me into my foe's hand,
But in the roomy place you set my feet.

---

[a] I put my trust in you for refuge] Hebrew *ḥasâ* - חָסָה. See Appendix 2 - Refuge.
[b] A fortress house] Literally, 'a house of fortresses', where the plural emphasises strong defence. The word 'fortress' occurs again in v3, where we have translated 'fortress of defence'.
[c] The one who gives me strength] Hebrew 'my strength'. Septuagint 'the one who holds a shield over me', my protector.
[d] Delivered me] 'Redeemed me', or 'ransomed me'.
[e] False empty things] Hebrew 'emptiness of vanities', i.e. idols.
[f] Steadfast love ... loving-kindness] One word. Hebrew *ḥesedh* - חֶסֶד. See Appendix 2 - Loving-kindness.
[g] We have repeated the previous line with a different translation.

Day 56   Psalm 31:9-15

[9] Be gracious to me, LORD, for I'm pressed in:
My eye, my soul, my body, waste with grief.
[10] My life is spent with grief, my years with sighs:
Strength fails because of sin[a] and bones decay[b].

[11] For all my enemies I'm a reproach
And even more to those who dwell near me,
To my acquaintances a thing of dread.
And those who saw me fled when I went out.   →

59

¹² 'Dead and forgotten, mad, a broken pot!'
Thus I have heard the slander of the crowd.
¹³ Fear-all-around^c while they against me plot,
And seek somehow to take my life away.

¹⁴ But as for me, I trusted in you, LORD,
And do declare to you, 'You are my God'.
¹⁵ My times are in your hand - Deliver me!
Save from my foes, from those pursuing me!

---

^a Because of sin] Hebrew 'my sin' or 'my iniquity'. In reading the Psalm as the
   words of the Lord Jesus, it refers to our sin, imputed to him, which he bore for
   us.
^b Decay] The meaning of the word is uncertain. Koehler *Lexicon* 'decompose'.
^c Fear-all-around] The name Jeremiah that gave to Pashur in Jer. 20:3 = *Magor-
   missabib*, (מָגוֹר מִסָּבִיב). Horsley takes this to be a phrase in general use,
   meaning an object of general dread or aversion.

Day 57   Psalm 31:16-20

¹⁶ Upon your servant cause your face to shine,
And save me for your loving-kindness'^a sake.
¹⁷ Keep me from shame, LORD, for I called on you.
But shame the wicked. Hush them in the grave. ^b

¹⁸ Let lying lips be dumb that speak hard things
Against the righteous, proudly, with contempt.
¹⁹ For those who fear you, bounty^c is in store!
Prepared for those who trust you^d, before men.^e

²⁰ You hide them in your secret hiding place -
Hide in your presence^f from the schemes of man,
And in a shelter^g keep them secretly
From the contention of accusing tongues.   →

---

^a Loving-kindness] Hebrew *ḥeṣedh* - חֶסֶד. See Appendix 2 - Loving-kindness.
^b The grave] Hebrew *šeʾôl* - שְׁאוֹל. See Appendix 2 - Sheol.
^c Bounty] Hebrew, 'great [or much] good'.
^d Those who trust you] The Hebrew verb is *ḥaṣâ* - חָסָה 'to flee to a refuge and a
   place of safety'. See Appendix 2 - Refuge.
^e Before men] Hebrew 'before the sons of Adam', Hebrew *benê ʾadham* - בְּנֵי אָדָם.
   Man as a child of Adam. See Appendix 2 - Man.
^f In your secret hiding place ... in your presence] Hebrew literally, 'in the hiding
   place of your countenance'. We have expanded the meaning.

Day 58   Psalm 31:21-24

²¹ Blest be the LORD, who in a fortress townᵃ
With wonders showed his kindnessᵇ unto me
²² Though he did this, I spoke when I made haste,ᶜ
'I've been cut off before your very eyes!'

Yet nonetheless, you heard my pleading voice -
My supplications - when I cried to you
²³ O love the LORD, all who partake his grace,ᵈ
Those who are faithful are kept by the LORD.

The LORD will deal with those who act in pride.
The LORD will fully give to them their due.ᵉ
²⁴ Be of good courage! Let your heart be strong
All you who on the LORD wait patiently.

ᵃ A fortress town] AV 'strong city'; AV margin 'fenced city'; Calvin 'fortified city'. Modern translations render 'in a city under siege' and interpret the reference to events in David's life. It is better to keep the imagery without speculating regarding the circumstances under which it was written. The Geneva Bible's notes interpret the 'city' as the LORD himself. The expression is also used in 60:9.
ᵇ Kindness] Hebrew *ḥesedh* - חֶסֶד. See Appendix 2 - Loving-kindness.
ᶜ When I made haste] Not 'said in my haste' as implying moral failing. See Newton (6) p98.
ᵈ All who partake his grace] AV 'all ye his saints'. Plural of Hebrew *ḥasîdh* - חָסִיד. See Appendix 2 - Loving-kindness.
ᵉ Deal with ... give to them their due] One word in Hebrew.

Day 59   Psalm 32:1-6

¹ What *blessedness*ᵃ belongs to him who has
transgression pardonedᵇ - covering for sinᶜ!
² *Blest* man to whom the LORD imputes no sinᵈ! -
And in whose spirit there is no deceit.

³ When I kept silence, then my bones decayedᵉ
With cries of anguish I let out all day.
⁴ For day and night your hand weighed hard on me.
Gone is my moisture, as in summer drought. ‖   →

61

⁵ My sin I then acknowledged unto you,
And did not cover my iniquity.
Said, 'I'll confess my sins unto the LORD'.
'The guilt of sin you then forgave for me'. ⸶

⁶ All who you love^f shall pray because of this
Pray to you when it's time for finding you.
Be sure when floods of many waters come,
The waters shall not go as far as him.

---

^a What blessedness ...] and 'blest' in v2. Hebrew *'ašrê* - אַשְׁרֵי. See Appendix 2 -
Blessing.
^b Transgression pardoned] Literally, 'lifted off'.
^c Sin (1)] Hebrew, *ḥaṭ'â* - חֲטָאָה (fem. of חטא). This is the usual word for 'sin' - it
signifies a deviation from what is pleasing to God; missing the mark or goal
that God intends for man
^d Sin (2)] Vanity, iniquity or wrong - Hebrew *'awon* - עָוֹן. Cf. 2 Cor. 5:19.
^e Bones decayed] A different word to 'waste away' in 31:10.
^f All who you love] Hebrew *ḥaṣîdh* - חָסִיד. See Appendix 2 - Loving-kindness

Day 60   Psalm 32:7-11

⁷ You are for me a secret hiding place.
You will preserve me from adversity.
You will surround me with glad shouts of joy,
With celebration^a of deliverance ⸶

⁸ 'Yes, I'll instruct and teach the way to go,
And I'll advise you with my eye on you.
⁹ Be not like undiscerning horse or mule,
Unless they're bridled, they will not approach'.^b

¹⁰ The sorrows of the wicked one are great.^c
Mercy^d surrounds him who trusts in the LORD!
¹¹ Joy in the LORD! Be glad you righteous ones!
And shout for joy all you of upright heart!

---

^a Glad shouts of joy, celebration] We have extended the meaning of the word,
which is associated with singing or shouting for joy. The word is used again in
v11 where the AV translates 'shout for joy', and 33:1, where the AV translates
'rejoice'.
^b Unless ... they will not approach] Various translations have been offered. The
bridle and bit are to render the animal subservient, not (as the AV) to make it

go away. Calvin explains, 'you shall bind his jaw with a bit and bridle, lest they kick against (or become obstreperous against or obstinately disobey) you'.
[c] Great] Or 'many'
[d] Mercy] Hebrew *ḥeṣedḥ* - חֶסֶד. See Appendix 2 - Loving-kindness.

Day 61   Psalm 33:1-6

[1] You righteous, shout for joy[a] unto the LORD!
Praise is a thing that suits the upright well.
[2] Give praise unto the LORD upon the harp;[b]
Upon a ten-stringed lyre[c] sing psalms to him.

[3] Sing unto him a rare and choice new song.[d]
Play skilfully, and with a shout of joy.
[4] For the LORD's word is right; because it's true,[e]
And all his works are done in faithfulness.

[5] Justice and righteousness[f] are what he loves.
The mercy[g] of the LORD fills all the earth.
[6] By the LORD's word the heavens have been made
The breathing of his mouth made all their host.

[a] Shout for joy] AV 'rejoice', but the verb is usually 'shout for joy' or 'sing for joy'. The same word as used in 32:7.
[b] Harp] See Appendix 2 - *kinnôr* - כִּנּוֹר
[c] Upon a ten-stringed lyre] Literally, 'with a *nebhel* (נֶבֶל) ten', (AV 'the psaltery [and] an instrument of ten strings'). See Ps. 92:3, 144:9. Appendix 2 - Harps
[d] Rare and choice new song] 'Rare and choice' is one word in Hebrew = fresh, choice, polished.
[e] Right ... true] One word in Hebrew. The same word used in v1. We have extended the sentence 'For the word of the LORD is right'.
[f] Justice and righteousness] Hebrew 'righteousness and justice' (Cf. Ps.99:4). 'Justice' here is *mišpaṭ* - מִשְׁפָּט. See Appendix 2 - Law - Judgment.
[g] Mercy] Hebrew *ḥeṣedḥ* - חֶסֶד. See Appendix 2 - Loving-kindness.

Day 62   Psalm 33:7-11

[7] He heaped together waters of the sea,
And in the storerooms he laid up the deeps.
[8] All earth shall be afraid - shall fear the LORD.
All dwellers in this world[a] shall stand in awe.[b]   →

63

⁹ For he just spoke, and then it came to pass;
As he commanded it was set in place.
¹⁰ The nations' purposes the LORD makes naught,
And he frustrates what peoples planned to do.

¹¹ The counsel of the LORD forever stands.
Even the purposes his heart has planned
Unto all generations they shall be.
Unto all generations they shall be.ᶜ

ᵃ This world] The inhabited earth. *tebhel* - תֵבֵל. See Appendix 2 - Earth.
ᵇ Shall stand in awe] Hebrew 'shall stand in awe of him'.
ᶜ We have repeated the last line.

Day 63   Psalm 33:12-17

¹² *Blest*ᵃ be the nation whose God is the LORD –
The people chosen for his heritage.
¹³ The LORD has from the heavens looked about,
And all the sons of men he has beheld.

¹⁴ From where he dwells, he surveys all around,
He looks upon all those who dwell on earth.
¹⁵ He forms and fashions all their hearts alike,
And all the things they do he understands.

¹⁶ No king is saved by his great army's size;
No mighty manᵇ escapes by his great strength.
¹⁷ It's vain to trust for safety in a horse.
It can't deliver, though it has great strength.

ᵃ Blest] Hebrew *'ašrê* - אַשְׁרֵי. See Appendix 2 - Blessing.
ᵇ Mighty man] *gibbôr* - גִבּוֹר -Man as a mighty being. See Appendix 2 - Man.

Day 64   Psalm 33:18-22

¹⁸ See!ᵃ – The LORD's eye is on those who fear him.
On those who in his loving-kindnessᵇ hope.
¹⁹ To give their soul deliverance from death,
And in the famine to keep them alive.   →

²⁰ Our soul waits for the LORD - our Help and Shield.
²¹ Because of this, our heart will joy in him.
Trusting his holy name our heart is glad.
²² Your mercy's^c on us, LORD: we wait for you.

---

^a See!] Hebrew *hinneh* - הִנֵּה. See Appendix 2 - Behold!
^b Loving-kindness] Hebrew *ḥeṣedh* - חֶסֶד. See Appendix 2 - Loving-kindness.
^c Mercy] Hebrew *ḥeṣedh* - חֶסֶד. See Appendix 2 - Loving-kindness.

Day 65   Psalm 34:1-6

¹ In every season, I will bless the LORD.
His praise shall constantly be in my mouth.
² And in the LORD my soul will make its boast.
The humble ones will hear and will be glad.

³ O come and magnify the LORD with me.
Let us together lift his name on high.
⁴ I sought the LORD and he has answered me,
And out of all my fears he rescued me.

⁵ They looked to him and they were radiant.
Their faces shall not ever be ashamed^a.
⁶ This poor one cried: the LORD listened to him.
And out of all his troubles rescued him.

---

^a Shall not ever be ashamed] The Hebrew is emphatic, using an imperative as if to command what shall be. It expresses a certainty.

Day 66   Psalm 34:7-15

⁷ The angel of the LORD encamps around
The ones who fear him. He delivers them.
⁸ O taste and see, because the LORD is good.
Blest^a is the man^b who puts his trust in him.^c

⁹ O fear the LORD, you saints - his holy ones -
For there is nothing those who fear him need.
¹⁰ Young lions may have need, and long for food,
But those who seek the LORD lack nothing good. →

¹¹ O children come and listen unto me
And I will teach you how to fear the LORD.
¹² What man^d seeks life, and loves to see good days?^e
¹³ Then guard your tongue from wrong, your lips from lies.

¹⁴ Depart from evil, and do what is good.
Seek after peace and be pursuing it.
¹⁵ The LORD's eyes are upon the righteous ones,
Just as his ears are open to their cry.

---

^a Blest] Hebrew *'ašrê* - אֲשֶׁרֵי. See Appendix 2 - Blessing.
^b Man] Hebrew *gebher* - גֶּבֶר - a strong man. See Appendix 2 - Man.
^c Puts his trust in him] Hebrew *ḥaṣâ* - חָסָה. See Appendix 2 - Refuge.
^d Man] Hebrew *'îš* - אִישׁ -Man as an individual. See Appendix 2 - Man.
^e What man ... good days?] I Pet. 3:10-12 quotes v12-16. 1 Pet. 3:10a 'is curiously divergent from the Septuagint' (Alford) of v12 here.

Day 67   Psalm 34:16-22

¹⁶ But the LORD's face is set against all those
Who practice evil and do wickedly.
To cut off every memory of them
Even removing it from off the earth.

¹⁷ The righteous cry for help, and the LORD hears –
From out of all their troubles rescues them.
¹⁸ The LORD is near to those with broken heart;
Those with a contrite spirit he will save

¹⁹ The troubles of the righteous one abound
And yet he's rescued by the LORD from all
²⁰ He takes good care - protecting all his bones:
Not one is broken – not a single one!

²¹ Evil shall bring the wicked one to death.
Condemned^a are they who hate the righteous one.
²² Because the LORD redeems his servants' soul,
None are condemned who take refuge in him^b.

---

^a Condemned] 'Held guilty', AV margin 'guilty'. Here and v22. This verb is the root of the 'trespass' offering of Leviticus 5. Compare Gen 26:10.
^b Take refuge in him] AV 'trust in him' Hebrew *ḥaṣâ* - חָסָה. See Appendix 2 -

Refuge.

Day 68   Psalm 35:1-8

¹ LORD put on trial those who would try me;
Wage war on those who go to war with me.
² Take buckler and great shield[a]. Rise for my help!
³ Take out the spear. Stop[b] them pursuing me.

Say to my soul, 'I'm your deliverance'.
⁴ Confound, bring shame, to those who seek my soul.
Turn back, confuse them, who devise my hurt.
⁵ The angel of the LORD chase them like chaff[c].

⁶ O make their pathway dark and prone to slip –
The angel of the LORD pursuing them.
⁷ For, without cause, they hid their net for me,
And without cause dug for my soul a pit.

⁸ And let destruction come like this to him
As unexpected, when he does not know.
And let the net he hid entangle him;
Into that same destruction let him fall.

---

[a] Buckler and great shield] Two words for 'shield' are used here. *maghen* - מָגֵן, a
buckler, a small, round shield; and *tsinnâ* - צִנָּה the large body shield. The AV
translates the two words indiscriminately as 'shield', 'buckler', 'defence', and
here reverses their correct meaning. See Appendix 2 - Shields.
[b] Stop] Motyer (1) 'block the approach'; AV 'stop the way'. However, see Kimchi
and Perowne, who suggest the Hebrew means 'draw out the 'battle axe', or
'javelin', which is followed by modern versions. However, note the comment of
The Century Bible (Davison) and Gesenius *Lexicon*.
[c] Chase them just like chaff] Hebrew 'chase them as chaff before the wind'.
Compare Ps. 1:4.

Day 69   Psalm 35:9-16

⁹ My soul shall be so joyful in the LORD.
In his salvation shall my soul[a] delight
¹⁰ My bones all say, 'O LORD, who is like you?'
Who is like you, LORD, rescuing the poor?   →

67

You rescue him from one stronger than him.
The poor you rescue, and the one in need
From him who comes to plunder and despoil[b]
[11] The witnesses arise for violence[c].

They ask of me such things I do not know.
[12] Evil for good repay. My soul bereave.
[13] Yet I wore sackcloth when they were unwell,
And with the fasting I humbled my soul.

So may my prayer return unto my breast!
[14] I went as for my brother or a friend.
Bowed down as one who for his mother mourns,
[15] But, when I fell, they met to show their joy.

Yes, and the smiters gathered against me.
I knew them not[d] - they tore unceasingly.
[16] Like godless mockers, slandering for gain.[e]
Against me grinding, gnashing with their teeth.

---

[a] My soul] Hebrew 'it'.
[b] Plunder and despoil] One word in Hebrew - 'rob violently'.
[c] For violence] Intent on violence, AV 'false witnesses'. Hebrew as Exod. 23:1. Cf. 1 Kgs. 21:10,13, Matt. 26:59-61, and Acts 6:11,13.
[d] I knew them not] Literally, 'I did not know'. Compare Luke 22:64.
[e] Like godless mockers, slandering for gain] The AV 'with hypocritical mockers in feasts'. Jesters gaining their living [the word is 'cake', as 1 Kgs. 17:12] through their foolery at banquets. 'Speaking and doing anything to please and humour those that fill their panches [paunches]', *Dutch Annotations*. As Shakespeare 'trencher-friend'. The slander and scorn is that of Ps. 22:7.

Day 70   Psalm 35:17-23

[17] My Lord[a], how long will you just look and watch?
From their destructions, O restore my soul!
My precious life[b] save from the lions' young[c].
[18] I'll thank you in the great assembled throng.

Among much people I will give you praise.
[19] Keep my false foes[d] from being glad at me.
Let them not wink[e] that hate me without cause.
[20] They don't speak peace, but make deceitful plans,   →

Deceiving peaceful people in the land.
²¹ They opened up their mouth against me wide,
'Aha! Aha!', they said, 'our eye has seen'.
²² But you have seen, LORD. Do not silence keep!'

My Lord do not be far away from me.
²³ Awake! Rouse up yourself, as out of sleep.
Awake yourself to judgment, O my God:
My Lord, for vindication^f of my cause.

ᵃ My Lord] Hebrew *'Adhonay* - אֲדֹנָי. See Appendix 2 - Names of God. So too in v22 and 23.

ᵇ My precious life] AV 'my darling'. As 22:20.

ᶜ The lions' young] The Hebrew word is as in Ps. 34:10; Ezek. 19:6.

ᵈ False foes] i.e. those who are enemies for no good reason, and perhaps hide their enmity under a cloak of friendship. 'False' is parallel to 'without cause' in the following line.

ᵉ Wink] Hebrew 'bite the eye', i.e. suddenly close the eye in contempt or derision.

ᶠ To judgment ... to vindication] One word in Hebrew. *mišpaṭ* - מִשְׁפָּט. See Appendix 2 - Law - Judgment.

Day 71 Psalm 35:24-28

²⁴ Judge me according to your righteousness.
O LORD my God, give them no joy from me^a.
²⁵ Let not their heart say, 'We would have it so!'
Let them not say 'We have swallowed him up!'^b

²⁶ Make them ashamed, confound them every one
Who find their joy in my calamity.
And clothe them with dishonour and with shame^c
Who over me do magnify themselves.

²⁷ But those delighting in my righteousness –
Let them shout joyfully! Let them be glad!
Let them say always, 'Magnify the LORD!'
'For he has pleasure in his servant's peace'.

²⁸ My tongue will tell, and speaking, meditate,
And it shall talk about your righteousness.
And all the day it shall tell out your praise.
Your praise shall be its theme continually.^d

a Give them no joy from me. Let them not have cause to rejoice over, or gloat over, me - finding their joy in my calamity (v26). So also in v19.

b We have swallowed him] See Ps. 124:3.

c Dishonour ... shame] Hebrew, shame ... dishonour.

d We have expanded the meaning of the last verse.

Day 72   Psalm 36:1-4

¹ Thus spoke transgression[a] to the wicked one
(and it declared[b] to me within my heart[c])
'There is no fear of God before his eyes'.
² Self-flattery is all his eyes can see.

Self-flattery until his wickedness
has been found out, its hatefulness made known.
³ Words of his mouth are wicked and deceive.
He ceases to act wisely or do good.

⁴ When he is on his bed, he plots and plans,
Devising wickedness upon his bed.[d]
He sets himself a path that is not good,
And what is evil he does not refuse.

a Transgression] 'Rebellion' or 'covenant breaking' is the root meaning of this word, as 'rebelled' 2 Kgs 1:1; 3:5,7.

b Spoke ... declared] One word in Hebrew, ne'um - נְאֻם. Everywhere else this word refers to God giving revelation, an oracle. Perhaps we may say that God gives his 'oracle' of delusion to the ready acceptance of the wicked one (compare 2 Thess. 2:11, Isa. 10). See Ps. 110:1, the only other use of the word in the Psalms.

c Within my heart] We have taken this as a parenthesis. This is close to the Geneva Bible rendering. 'My heart' is the received text, but most modern versions overcome the difficulty of transgression 'speaking to the wicked within in my heart' by adopting the Syriac reading 'his heart'. It is better to take this as an aside, i.e. the wicked's transgression, though it emboldens the wicked, it also makes plain to the Psalmist's heart that the wicked has no fear of God. B.W. Newton, who interprets this portion of Antichrist, considers that he is identified to the believer by his very wickedness.

d When he is on his bed ... upon his bed] We have expanded this line.

Day 73   Psalm 36:5-12

⁵ Your steadfast love[a] is in the heavens, LORD:
Your faithfulness extends unto the clouds:
⁶ Like GOD's own mountains[b] is your righteousness:
Your judgments like unto a mighty deep.   →

O LORD, preserver of both man and beast,
⁷ How precious is your steadfast love^c, O God!
Therefore, the sons of men their refuge take,
And trust^d, beneath the shadow of your wings.

⁸ They feast on the abundance of your house.
You make them drink your river of delights.
⁹ For with you is the very fount of life,
And, in your light, we surely shall see light.

¹⁰ Prolong your mercy^e to those who know you;
Your righteousness to the upright in heart.
¹¹ The foot of pride, let it not come to me.
Nor let the wickeds' hand drive me away.

¹² There fell the workers of iniquity.
There they have fallen, and been overthrown.
They have been thrust down, and are cast away.^{f}
So that they can no longer rise again.

---

^{a} Steadfast love] Hebrew _ḥeṣedh_ - חֶסֶד. See Appendix 2 - Loving-kindness.
^{b} GOD's own mountains] 'The mountains of GOD' is the literal translation. AV 'great mountains'.
^{c} Steadfast love] As v6.
^{d} Their refuge take and trust] One word in Hebrew _ḥaṣâ_ - חָסָה. See Appendix 2 - Refuge.
^{e} Mercy] 'Steadfast love' as v5,7.
^{f} Fallen ... overthrown. Thrust down ... cast away] We have expanded the meaning of these two verbs.

Day 74   Psalm 37:1-6

¹ Don't fret yourself because of wicked men.
Do not have envy of those who do wrong.
² For they will soon be cut down like the grass,
And wither as the greenness of the herb.

³ Trust in the LORD and labour to do good.
Dwell in the land and surely you'll be fed.
⁴ Enjoy the LORD and make him your delight.
So he will give your heart's desires to you.   →

⁵ Roll your way over; cast it on the LORD^a.
Just trust in him and he will make it so.
⁶ He'll bring your righteousness out as the light.
He'll bring your judgment^b out like midday sun^c.

---

^a Roll your way over, cast it on the LORD] The Hebrew is literally, 'roll upon the LORD your way'. Cf. Ps. 22:8 (the same verb) and 1 Pet. 5:7.
^b Judgment] Hebrew *mišpaṭ* - מִשְׁפָּט. The same word is used in verses 6 and 28. See Appendix 2 - Law - Judgment.
^c Midday sun] At noon, the brightest part of the day. Gesenius Lexicon notes that the word is in the dual number, i.e. 'in double brightness'.

Day 75   Psalm 37:7-15

⁷ Rest in the LORD, wait patiently for him.
Fret not at one who makes his way succeed –
Because a man^a fulfils his evil plans.
⁸ Do not be angry. Go away from wrath.

Fret not yourself lest you do wickedly.^b
⁹ Those who do wicked things shall be cut off.
Those who, expecting, wait^c upon the LORD
They'll gain the earth^d as their inheritance.^e

¹⁰ In a short while the wicked shall not be.
You'll seek his place, but it will be no more.
¹¹ Those who are meek shall yet possess the earth,
Peace in abundance will be their delight.

¹² The wicked plots against the righteous one.
Gnashes his teeth at him – ¹³ but the Lord laughs!
For he foresees the coming of his day.
¹⁴ The wicked ones draw sword and bend their bow.

The poor and needy they seek to cast down –
To slay those who are upright in the way.
¹⁵ Their sword shall enter into their own heart.
Broken and ruined^f and shall their bows be too.

---

^a Man] Hebrew *'îš* - אִישׁ - Man as an individual. See Appendix 2 - Man.
^b Lest you do wickedly] Hebrew 'only to do wickedness'.
^c Expecting, wait] A different Hebrew word from the 'wait' of v7. We have

distinguished the meanings of the two words.

^d The earth] Hebrew *'erets* - אֶרֶץ. The Hebrew word may mean either 'earth' or 'land', as also the equivalent Greek word. See Ps. 25:13 and Matt. 5:5. See Appendix 2 - Earth.

^e Gain ... as inheritance] The principal meaning of the verb is 'to possess', as we have translated at v11.

^f Broken and ruined] One word in Hebrew. As v. 17.

Day 76   Psalm 37:16-22

¹⁶ Better the little of the righteous one^a
Than the great wealth of many wicked men.
¹⁷ Broken shall be the arms of wicked men,
Those who are righteous the LORD will uphold.

¹⁸ The LORD knows all the days of blameless men.
Their heritage shall be for evermore.
¹⁹ They will not be ashamed when evil comes.^b
In days of famine they will have their fill.

²⁰ As for the wicked^c, they will be destroyed;
And the LORD's enemies will pass away -
Just like the preciousness – the fat – of lambs,^d
For into smoke they shall consume away.

²¹ The wicked borrows but does not give back.
The righteous^e has compassion and he gives.
²² Those whom he blesses will possess the earth,^f
But those he curses, they shall be cut off.

^a The righteous one] Definite and singular.

^b When evil comes] Hebrew 'in the season of evil'.

^c The wicked] 'Wicked ones' (indefinite and plural).

^d Just like the ... fat of lambs] This would link the comparison with the next line, seeing it as a reference to the sacrifice of lambs on the altar. It may, however, be translated as 'the splendour of pastures' (see Isa 30:23 for this use of the word), i.e. their grass and flowers, making two separate comparisons. See the *Dutch Annotations* and Perowne.

^e Wicked ... righteous] Both indefinite and singular.

^f Shall possess the earth] They shall inherit the earth (or land) and so v9.

Day 77   Psalm 37:23-28

²³ A good man's[a] steps are ordered by the LORD;
And in his way he places his delight.
²⁴ Though he should fall, he will not be cast down,
Because the LORD upholds him with his hand.

²⁵ I was once young, but now I'm an old man.
I have not seen the righteous destitute,
Nor have I seen his children begging bread.
Nor have I seen his children begging bread.[b]

²⁶ All day he's merciful and freely lends.[c]
His offspring will give blessing and be blest.[d]
²⁷Depart from evil and do what is good
And then you will abide for evermore.

²⁸ The LORD loves judgment[e], and will not forsake.
The ones on whom he sets his steadfast love.[f]
For ever they will be kept and preserved.
The offspring of the wicked are cut off.

---

[a] A [good] man] The AV supplies 'good', but it is God's sovereignty, not his
'goodness' that establishes the elect. Hebrew *gebher* - גֶּבֶר - a strong man, a
warrior. See Appendix 2 - Man.
[b] We have repeated this line.
[c] He's merciful and freely lends] The AV translates 'all the day' by 'ever'. His
benevolence is constant, and (compare v25) it is not dependent on changing
circumstances. See v21 where we have translated 'merciful' as
'compassionate'. 'Freely lends', i.e. lends without usury. See Ps. 112:5, Deut.
15:6, Exod. 22:25
[d] Give blessing and be blest] The Hebrew is 'his seed is to blessing'.
[e] Judgment] Hebrew, *mišpaṭ* - מִשְׁפָּט. See Appendix 2 - Law - Judgment.
[f] The ones on whom he sets his steadfast love] AV 'saints'. Hebrew *ḥaṣîdhîm* -
חֲסִידִים. 'Those who are the object of God's loving-kindness *(ḥesedh* - חֶסֶד*)*'. A
different word than that used for 'love' in the previous line. See Appendix 2 -
Loving-kindness.

Day 78   Psalm 37:29-34

²⁹ Those who are righteous shall possess the earth[a],
And they will dwell in it for evermore.
³⁰ The righteous one speaks[b] wisdom with his mouth,
And, with his tongue, of judgment he will speak.   →

³¹ The Law of God abides within his heart,
None of the footsteps that he takes will slip.
³² The wicked waits to kill the righteous one,
³³ The LORD won't leave him in the wicked's hand.

The LORD will not condemn him when he's judged.
³⁴ Wait on the Lord, and keep upon his way!
He will exalt you to possess the earth^c.
You'll see the wicked when they are cut off.

---

^a The earth] Or 'land' as AV. As in verse 9.
^b Speaks] The root meaning of the word is 'meditates' (as Ps. 1:2 and 35:28).
Perhaps 'speaks thoughtfully'.
^c Earth] Hebrew '_erets_ - אֶרֶץ. See Ps. 37:9 and Appendix 2 - Earth.

Day 79   Psalm 37:35-40

³⁵ I've seen the wicked - ruthless, in great power,^a
Spreading just as a green and native tree.^b
³⁶ He passed away. Behold, he was no more!
I sought for him, but he could not be found.

³⁷ Mark him who's blameless. See the upright one.
For that man's destiny^c is one of peace.
³⁸ Together shall transgressors be destroyed:
The wicked's destiny - to be cut off!

³⁹ The righteous have salvation from the LORD.
He is their strength when trouble is at hand.
⁴⁰ The LORD will help and rescue from bad men:^d
Rescue and save them, for they trust^e in him.

---

^a Ruthless, in great power] Delitzsch 'a terror-inspiring tyrannical evil-doer'.
^b Green and native tree] One word in Hebrew. A tree that flourishes from never
having been moved or transplanted.
^c That man's destiny] Literally, 'that which comes after'. The 'end' or 'posterity' of
that man, as in v38. The word for 'man' here is '_îš_ - אִישׁ -Man as an individual.
See Appendix 2 - Man.
^d Bad men] Hebrew 'the wicked' - plural.
^e Trust] The Hebrew verb is _ḥasâ_ - חָסָה 'to flee to a refuge and a place of safety'.
See Appendix 2 - Refuge.

Day 80   Psalm 38:1-8

¹ O LORD, do not rebuke me in your wrath,
And in your anger do not chasten me -
² Because your arrows sink down deep in me -
Because your hand is pressing on me hard.

³ Your wrath has left no soundness in my flesh.
My bones are without rest because of sin.
⁴ Iniquities have gone over my head:
A heavy burden - far too much for me.

⁵ My wounds are stinking, and they are corrupt.
It is because of this - my foolishness.
⁶ I'm twisted up[a]. I'm brought down very low.
I go about a mourner all the day.

⁷ My loins are full of burning, searing heat[b],
And there is left no soundness in my flesh.
⁸ I am made feeble, crushed, and broken down,
Because of turmoil in my heart, I groan.

---

[a] Twisted up] The literal meaning. 'Bent', AV 'troubled'.
[b] My Loins ... searing heat] 'Loathsome disease' (AV) is an unfortunate and
inaccurate translation. Bodily and mental afflictions are connected with
indwelling sin, and this psalm is Messianic. See Newton (6) p.86. The word
here for 'loins' is only used here in the Book of Psalms. Gesenius *Lexicon*
defines it as 'the internal muscles of the loins, near the kidneys, to which the
fat adheres'. Motyer (1) 'my muscles'.

Day 81   Psalm 38:9-14

⁹ All that I long for is before you, Lord[a],
Also, my groaning is not hid from you.
¹⁰ My heart is beating fast, and my strength fails.
Light has gone from me, even from my eyes.

¹¹ My friends and loved ones stand back from my plague.
My neighbours and my kinsmen stand far off.
¹² And those who seek my life[b] lay snares for me.
Those who speak ruin plan deceits all day.   →

¹³ But I am like one deaf; I do not hear,
And as one dumb who opens not his mouth.
¹⁴ I have become as one who does not hear,
And in whose mouth there are no arguments.

---

^a Lord] My Lord. Hebrew *'Adhonay* - אֲדֹנָי. See Appendix 2 - Names of God.
^b Life] Hebrew 'soul'.

Day 82   Psalm 38:15-22
¹⁵ O LORD, I wait in patient hope^a for you.
You'll hear and answer^b me, My Lord^c, my God.
¹⁶ Because I said, 'Lest they rejoice at me,
Or, over me exalt, if my foot slips'.

¹⁷ I'm almost falling. I have constant pain!
¹⁸ I own my guilt. I'm sorry^d for my sin.
¹⁹ My enemies are full of life and strength,
And there are many hate me without cause.

²⁰ Evil for good my adversaries pay,
Because I follow after what is good.
²¹ Don't leave me, or be distant, LORD my God.
²² Lord^e, My Salvation, hurry for my help.

---

^a Wait in patient hope] Hebrew *yaḥal* - יָחַל.
^b You'll hear and answer] Hebrew *'anâ* - עָנָה. See Appendix 2 - Hear and Answer.
^c My Lord] Hebrew *'Adhonay* - אֲדֹנָי. David acknowledges God's lordship over him.
    See Appendix 2 - Names of God.
^d I'm sorry] 'Anxious', 'in anxious care over'. Hebrew *da'agh* - דָּאַג.
^e Lord] = My Lord, Hebrew *'Adhonay* - אֲדֹנָי. See Appendix 2 - Names of God.

Day 83   Psalm 39:1-6
¹ I said, I'll place a guard upon my ways,
So that I'm kept from sinning with my tongue.
I'll guard my mouth, and I will muzzle^a it,
While the ungodly are within my sight.

² So I kept silence; dumb from speaking good,
And pain and sorrow^b were stirred up in me.
³ My heart was hot; within me the fire burned.
After such thinking, I spoke with my tongue,   →

⁴ 'O LORD, cause me to know my mortal end.^c
Help me to know the limit of my days –
What is their measure, and how frail I am.
Help me to know how fleeting are my days.^d

⁵ 'See how^e, you've made my days so very short.
They are just like the handbreadths of a man.^f
For my whole life is nothing in your sight
Yes, even one who stands is but a breath' –

'And every man^g is wholly vanity^h ⧺
⁶ Man's going to and fro, a shadow cast.
Indeed, in vain they are disquieted.
They heap up wealth they know not who will gain'

---

^a Muzzle] So AV margin.
^b Pain and sorrow] The Hebrew word means both.
^c Mortal end] Hebrew 'my end'.
^d We have repeated and expanded the second line. The expression translated
'frail' in the AV means 'transitory'. Geneva Bible 'let me know how long I have
to live'.
^e See how] Hebrew *hinneh* - הִנֵּה. See Appendix 2 - Behold!
^f Very short ... man] Hebrew 'they are as handbreadths'.
^g Man] the Hebrew for 'man' here, and in the first line of v6, is Hebrew *'adham* -
אָדָם - Man as a child of Adam. See Appendix 2 - Man.
^h But a breath ... wholly vanity] We have expanded the last line of v5. The word
translated 'breath' and 'vanity' and 'vain' in verses 5,6 and 11 is the same
word, *hebhel* - הֶבֶל.

Day 84   Psalm 39:7-13

⁷ 'And now, what am I waiting for, My Lord^a?
My hope, my expectation, is in you.
⁸ From all of my transgressions rescue me.
Don't set me so a fool can mock at me'.

⁹ So I was dumb; I opened not my mouth,
Because the doer of this thing was you.
¹⁰ O take from me the plague that you have sent,
For I am wasted by your hostile hand.^b   →

¹¹ Rebukes from you correct a man for sin.
What he desires you melt just like a moth^c,
For a mere vanity^d is every man. ╫
¹² LORD, hear my prayer. Give ear unto my cry!

Answer my tears^e, for I'm your stranger^f here.
A sojourner as all my fathers were.
¹³ O spare me that I may recover strength^g,
Before I go away and am no more.

^a My Lord] Hebrew *'Adhonay* - אֲדֹנָי. See Appendix 2 - Names of God.
^b Hostile hand] Literally, 'the conflict of your hand', AV margin.
^c You melt just like a moth] 'Like as a moth fretting a garment' (PBV). Compare
   Hos. 5:12.
^d Vanity] Hebrew *hebhel* - הֶבֶל, as v5 and v6.
^e Answer my tears] Literally, 'unto my tear be not silent'.
^f Your stranger] Or 'a guest with you'. As Gen. 2:22, Hebrew *ger* - גֵּר.
^g O spare me that I may recover strength] The psalmist's plea is that the LORD will
   turn away his look of anger that he may recover his lost vigour and
   cheerfulness. The sentiment is the same as v10. The root meaning of the
   word translated 'strength' (*balagh* - בָּלַג) is 'to brighten'. BDB *Lexicon* is
   followed by the ESV = 'smile'. Motyer (1) 'Avert your gaze from me so I may
   brighten up'.

Day 85   Psalm 40:1-4

¹ I waited patiently^a upon the LORD.
He reached to me and listened to my cry –
² Brought from roaring pit^b, the mire and mud
My feet set on a rock – my steps made sure.

³ And he has put a new song in my mouth –
Even a song of praise^c unto our God.
Many will see, and will have godly fear,
And they will set their trust upon the LORD.

⁴ How *blesséd*^d is the man – the mighty man^e –
The one who sets his trust upon the LORD –
Who does not turn himself unto the proud –
Nor unto those who turn aside to lies

^a Waited patiently] Hebrew, 'waiting I waited'.
^b Brought from the roaring pit, the mire and mud] We have stayed with the literal

translation, 'roaring' pit, as supported by Calvin, rather than 'loathsome' (AV), or 'pit of ruin', 'pit of destruction' as suggested by others.
^c A song of praise] Hebrew simply 'praise'.
^d How blessed] Hebrew *'ašrê* - אַשְׁרֵי. See Appendix 2 - Blessing.
^e The mighty man] Hebrew *gebher* - גֶּבֶר - a strong man, a warrior. Here the strong man. See Appendix 2 - Man.

Day 86   Psalm 40:5-10

⁵ You've done so many things, O LORD my God –
Your wonders and the things you've planned for us –
They can't be set in order^a unto you
They're numberless if I should tell and speak

⁶ Sacrifice, offering, you don't desire.
(My ears you've dug and opened up for me:^b
even a body you've prepared for me)^c.
Burnt-, and sin-offering you don't require.

⁷ Then I said, 'Lo^d I come! Within the scroll –
Within the book - it is written of me.
⁸ I take delight to do your will my God.
Your Law is in the very midst of me'. ^e

⁹ Within the great assembly I proclaimed.
I did not put restraint upon my lips.
Behold, O LORD, these things you truly know.
¹⁰ Your righteousness I've not hid^f in my heart

For I have told of your sure faithfulness,
And your deliverance I did relate.
I haven't hid your mercy^g and your truth,
Even before the great assembled throng.

^a They can't be set in order] Literally, they are without order or value. De Burgh, 'surpassing all calculation'; Gesenius *Grammar* 'there is nothing to be compared'; Ewald *Syntax* 'nothing can be compared with Thee'; cf. Rom. 11:33.
^b My ears you've dug and opened up for me] Literally, 'pierced' or 'dug'. The suggested meaning is 'give me an ear to hear your instruction', or being given 'an obedient will'. It may also refer to the willing choice of a servant to serve his master forever (Exod. 21:6).
^c We have added the New Testament rendering (Heb. 10:5), which follows the Septuagint paraphrase. The Book of Hebrews may simply give an inspired

interpretation.

d Lo] Hebrew *hinneh* - הִנֵּה. So too 'Behold' v9. See Appendix 2 - Behold!

e In the very midst of me] Hebrew 'in my bowels' (as AV margin). The bowels as
the seat of the affections, as Song of Songs 5:4.

f Hidden ... hid] Two different words are used for 'hiding' in this verse. The first
(of righteousness) conveys more the idea of covering (Hebrew *kaṣâ* - כָּסָה). The
second (of kindness and faithfulness) has more the idea of denying, disowning
(kahadh - כָּחַד).

g Mercy] Hebrew *ḥeṣedh* - חֶסֶד. See Appendix 2 - Loving-kindness.

Day 87   Psalm 40:11-17

¹¹ Do not withhold your mercies[a] from me, LORD.
Your steadfast love[b], and truth my constant guard.
¹² Evils past counting have surrounded me.
My sins have gripped me so I can't look up.

My sins are more than hairs upon my head.
My heart fails in me - ¹³ O please help me LORD!
Make haste, O LORD, to come and give me help.
¹⁴ For some are seeking to destroy my soul.[c]

Let them together[d] be shamed and confused -
Those who would harm me - turn back - put to shame!
¹⁵ Let desolation[e] recompense their shame.
- All those who jeer at me, 'Aha!' 'Aha!'

¹⁶ But let all those who earnestly seek you -
Let them exult with joy - be glad in you.
Those who love your salvation, let them say -
Continually, 'The LORD be magnified!'

¹⁷ But as for me, I'm poor and I have need.
Yet, even so, My Lord[f] thinks upon me.
You are my Help and my Deliverer.
You are my God, so please make no delay.

a Mercies] Tender mercies. Deep feelings of compassion aroused by the sight of
weakness or suffering (Hebrew *raḥamîm* - רַחֲמִים).

b Steadfast love] Hebrew *ḥeṣedh* - חֶסֶד. See Appendix 2 - Loving-kindness.

c v14. We have changed the sequence of the clauses of this verse to link this and
the following stanza.

81

[d] Together] Hebrew 'as one'.

[e] Desolation] The word may either mean 'make desolate', or 'astonish', 'appal'. The root meaning is 'to be silent' and if this is the meaning to be taken here (as Perowne suggests), the psalmist wishes those who jeer at him to be struck dumb.

[f] My Lord] Hebrew 'Adhonay - אֲדֹנָי. See Appendix 2 - Names of God.

Day 88   Psalm 41:1-6

[1] He who attends[a] the poor one shall be *blest*![b]
The LORD will save him in an evil day. [c]
[2] The LORD shall keep him, and preserve his life,
He will have blessedness upon the earth.[d]

You will not leave him to his foes' ill-will.
[3] The LORD will strengthen when he's sick in bed.
And all his sickbed he will turn for him.
[4] I said, 'Be gracious unto me, O LORD!'

'Please heal my soul for I've sinned against you'.
[5] My enemies in malice speak of me,
'When will he die, and his name pass away?'
[6] And if he comes to me speaks emptiness.

Yes he speaks falsehood when he comes to me.[e]
His heart goes gathering iniquity,
Unto itself collecting wickedness.
When he goes out, he tells it in the street.[f]

[a] Attends] So Gesenius *Lexicon*. 'Deals wisely with', 'considers', perhaps 'is considerate to'.

[b] Blest] Hebrew *'ašrê* - אַשְׁרֵי. See Appendix 2 - Blessing.

[c] Evil day] i.e. a time of trouble.

[d] Upon the earth] The word may be translated 'earth' or 'land' - Hebrew *'erets* - אֶרֶץ. See Appendix 2 - Earth.

[e] Emptiness ... falsehood] We have expanded the meaning of the Hebrew word *hebhel* - הֶבֶל 'vanity', 'emptiness', 'lying'.

[f] He tells it in the street] Literally, 'he tells it outside'. The word 'outside' is translated 'street' by the AV 44 times, e.g. in Ps. 18:42 and 144:13. The English idiom 'behind my back' is close to the meaning here.

Day 89   Psalm 41:7-13

[7] All those who hate me join in whispering,
Devising ways how they can do me harm.
[8] 'A cursed thing[a] has taken hold on him'.
'Now he lies prostrate he shall rise no more!'

[9] My own familiar friend I trusted in –
Who ate my bread – against me raised his heel!
[10] LORD, will you please be merciful to me,
And raise me up to pay them back in full.

[11] By this I know that I am your delight.
My foe is not in triumph over me.
[12] But as for me – in my integrity –
You give me your support and hold me up.

You make me stand before your face always.
[13] The LORD be blest – the God of Israel!
From one eternity unto the next.
Amen. So be it, and again Amen!

---

[a] A Cursed thing] Literally, 'a thing of no-worth'. Hebrew *Belial (Beliya'al* - בְּלִיַּעַל).
It is also used more strongly as 'wickedness' and 'vileness' in Scripture. In later
use and in the New Testament it became a proper name for Satan, the Wicked
One. Also used in Psalms 18:4 and 101:3. Cf. 2 Cor. 6:15.

Book 2

Psalms 42 - 72

Day 90   Psalm 42:1-5

¹ Just as a deer pants for the water streams,
Likewise, my soul pants after you, O God!
² My soul is thirsting for the Living GOD.
When shall I come - be seen before God's face?

³ My tears have been my food both day and night.
They say to me all day, 'Where is your God?'
⁴ Recalling this I then pour out my soul,
For I once[a] travelled with the thronging crowd.

I went and led them to the House of God -
With shouts of gladness and with thankful praise -
A multitude of those who kept the feast -
The company of those on pilgrimage[b].

⁵ Why, O my soul, do you cast yourself down?[c]
Why so disturbed and troubled within me?
Wait. Hope[d] in God, for I shall praise him yet.
For his salvation, when he shows his face.[e]

---

[a] Once] Not 'on one occasion', but 'in a former time'.
[b] 'A multitude ... pilgrimage'] We have used two lines to express two words in
  Hebrew. The Hebrew may be translated 'the multitude going up to keep [or
  'celebrating'] one of the pilgrim feasts [Passover, etc] of Israel'. The Hebrew for
  such feasts is ḥaghagh - חָגַג cf. the Muslim (Arabic) Hajj.
[c] Cast yourself down] This is normally translated 'are cast down, but it is the
  hithpolel form of the Hebrew verb, indicating a reflexive / causative meaning.
  So too in v6,11, and 43:5.
[d] Wait. Hope] We have used two words to express one Hebrew word (yaḥal -
  יָחַל). The word means 'long, patient, waiting in hope'
[e] For his salvation when he shows his face] AV 'For the help of his countenance'.
  The plural Hebrew word is translated 'help' or 'salvation'. Calvin says, 'As soon
  as he is pleased to look on his people, he sets them in safety'.

Day 91   Psalm 42:6-11

⁶ My God, my soul is cast down within me,
So from the land of Jordan I'll recall;
From Hermon's peaks[a] and from the mount Mizar;
⁷ Deep calls to deep as noise of waterfalls.   →

Your rolling waves have all gone over me.
[8] His mercy[b] the LORD will command by day;
And in the night his song will be with me -
Even a prayer to the GOD of my life

[9] I'll say unto the GOD who is my rock,
'Why is it that you have forgotten me?'
'Why do I go out just as one who mourns,
Because the enemy oppresses me?'

[10] As if they put a sword into my bones;
As if they struck, so shattering my bones.[c]
My adversaries cast reproach on me.
They say to me all day 'Where is your God?'

[11] Why, O my soul, do you cast yourself down?
Why so disturbed and troubled within me?
Wait. Hope[d] in God: for I shall praise him yet.
He is my Saviour[e], and he is my God.

---

[a] Hermon's peaks. Hebrew 'the Hermons'.
[b] Mercy] Hebrew ḥeṣedh - חֶסֶד. See Appendix 2 - Loving-kindness.
[c] As if they put ... shattering my bones. We have given the two renderings
  suggested by the translators and commentators. AV, Horsley, etc, link it to the
  verb's usual use in the Old Testament - 'to kill' with the sword, as 'the
  instrument of slaughter'. Others take it as generic with an Arabic word 'to
  shatter', cf. Ps. 72:4. Also in Ezek. 21:22.
[d] Wait. Hope] We have used two words to express the one Hebrew word (yaḥal -
  יַחַל). The word means 'long, patient, waiting in hope'.
[e] My Saviour] Literally, 'the salvations of my face (countenance)', as v5. Ps. 104:15
  conveys the meaning, i.e. 'He makes my face to shine'!

Day 92   Psalm 43

[1] O vindicate me, God. Take up my cause,
Against a nation without godliness.[a]
Deliver from the unjust, crafty man.
[2] God of my strength, why have you cast me off?

Why do I go about as one who mourns
Through the oppression of the enemy?
[3] Send out your light and truth. Let them lead me,
To bring me where you dwell[b], your holy hill.   →

86

⁴ Then I will go unto God's altar there -
To God - the GOD of my exultant joy.
And I will offer thanksgiving to you
Upon the harp to God - to my own God.

⁵ Why, O my soul, do you cast yourself down?
Why so disturbed and troubled within me?
O hope in God, for I shall praise him yet.
He is my Saviour[c] and he is my God.

---

[a] Without godliness] As outside of God's covenant mercy. Literally, 'not ḥaṣîdh' -
לֹא־חָסִיד, i.e. not holy or gracious, nor affected by covenant love (ḥeṣedh - חֶסֶד).
See Appendix 2 - Loving-kindness.
[b] Where you dwell] Hebrew 'to your dwelling places'. It may perhaps be an
amplifying plural to express the dignity of the Temple.
[c] He is my Saviour] Literally, 'the salvation of my face (countenance)'. As 42:11.

Day 93   Psalm 44:1-8

¹ Our ears have heard, O God - our fathers told:
The work you worked in their days - days of old.
² You drove out nations, but did plant *them* in;
Afflicted peoples, but them you spread out[a].

³ They did not get the land by their own sword;
Their arm did not save them, but your right hand,
Even your arm, and the light of your face;
Because *you* showed your favour unto them.

⁴ You are the one who is my king, O God.
Command for Jacob your deliverance[b].
⁵ By you our adversaries we'll push down;
We'll trample down insurgents in your name.

⁶ My bow I will not trust - nor sword - to save.
⁷ From enemies[c] you saved. Shamed those who hate[d].
⁸ In God we'll boast and glory all day long,
Give thanks unto your name for evermore. ⫦

---

[a] Did plant them ... them you spread out] 'Them' is not in the Hebrew, but this
part of each line clearly refers to his 'fathers'. Planting and spreading out are
horticultural metaphors. The second word is applied to the shooting and

87

  spreading of branches. See Calvin.
^b Deliverance] Hebrew 'deliverances'. In the context perhaps rather 'victories'
  than 'salvation'.
^c Enemies] Hebrew 'our enemies'. The same word as 'adversaries' v5.
^d Hate] Hebrew 'hate us'.

Day 94   Psalm 44:9-19

⁹ But you have cast us off: made us ashamed,
And you do not go with our armies now.
¹⁰ You make us turn back from the enemy,
And those who hate us spoil us at their will.

¹¹ Like sheep for meat; among the nations strewn;
¹² You sell your people at such a low price.
Yes, you have sold them, without any gain.^a
¹³ You made us, to our neighbours, a reproach –

Scorn and derision to those round about.
¹⁴ A byword to the nations we've become –
Among the peoples – they just shake their head!
¹⁵ Confusion is before me all day long!

Covered with shame^b; ¹⁶ by taunts and blasphemies^c
Before the foe, and him who seeks revenge.
¹⁷ All this came on us; we did not forget.
Nor were we false unto your covenant.

¹⁸ Despite all this, our heart did not turn back:
Our step has not departed from your path,
¹⁹ But, where the jackals are^d, you've crushed us down,
And with the shade of death you've covered us.

^a Without any gain] 'For no wealth', or 'for no price'. Compare Jer. 15:13.
^b Covered with shame] Hebrew 'covered with shame of face'.
^c By taunts and blasphemies] Hebrew 'because of the voice of him who taunts
  and blasphemes'.
^d Where the jackals are] i.e. in a desolate wilderness. Compare Isa. 34:13; Jer.
  9:11.

Day 95   Psalm 44:20-26

²⁰ If the name of our God we had forgot –
If we'd spread out our hands to a strange GOD^a –
²¹ Would God not then be sure to find this out?
Because he knows the secrets of the heart.

²² But, for your sake, we're slain all the day long.
We are as sheep appointed to be slain.^b
²³ Awake, My Lord^c, why are you sleeping still?
Arise! Do not for ever cast us off.^d

²⁴ Why do you hide your face, and why forget?
We are afflicted, and we are oppressed.
²⁵ Our very soul is bowed down to the dust;
Our body is as fastened to the earth^e

²⁶ O do rise up for us, to be our help;
And do redeem us for your mercy's^f sake.
Yes, do rise up for us to be our help;
Yes, do redeem us for your mercy's sake.^g

---

^a A strange GOD] The Hebrew word '*El* -אֵל is used here of foreign gods, as also in
81:9. Compare Deut. 32:12.
^b As sheep appointed to be slain] Hebrew, literally, 'slaughter-sheep'. So too the
Greek Septuagint and Rom. 8:36.
^c My Lord] An acknowledgement of God's lordship even in the midst of apparent
abandonment. Hebrew '*Adhonay* - אֲדֹנָי. See Appendix 2 - Names of God.
^d Do not ever cast us off] The Hebrew word conveys the idea of permanency and
completeness.
^e Our body is as fastened to the earth] Hebrew 'belly is fixed to the earth'. See
note on Ps. 119:25
^f Mercy] Hebrew *ḥeṣedh* - חֶסֶד. See Appendix 2 - Loving-kindness.
^g We have repeated the two lines of the last verse.

Day 96   Psalm 45:1-8

¹ My heart boils over^a with a pleasing theme.
I speak the things that I've done for the king.
My tongue is as a ready writer's pen.
² 'Fair, fair^b are you, more than the sons of men!'   →

'Such graciousness is poured upon your lips!^{c}
Therefore has God blest you for evermore.
^{3} Gird your sword on your thigh, O mighty one.
Gird on your glory and your majesty'.

^{4} 'Yes, in your majesty, prosper - ride on!
For truth and meekness, and for righteousness.
Your right hand will teach you things that cause fear.
^{5} Sharp arrows pierce the heart of the king's foes^{d} -

'Therefore, the peoples fall down under him.
^{6} Your throne, O God, abides for evermore;
Your kingdom's sceptre is of uprightness^{e}.
^{7} You have loved justice: hated wickedness'.

'Therefore, has God, your God, anointed you -
More than your fellows - with the oil of joy.
^{8} All your clothes are myrrh - aloes - cassia,^{f}
Made glad from palaces of ivory'. ^{g}

---

^{a} Boils over] So the Hebrew.
^{b} Fair, fair] We have followed Perowne here. The reduplication in the verb form
  increases emphasis. See also Motyer (1).
^{c} Such graciousness ... your lips] Compare Luke 4:22.
^{d} Sharp arrows ... foes] Arrows - Hebrew 'your arrows'. We have changed the
  word order of this verse, following most versions. 'The peoples falling under
  him' is between the reference to the arrows being sharp, and their being in the
  heart of the king's enemies. The prophetic reference is to Christ bearing the
  bow, and going forth 'conquering and to conquer' (Rev. 6:2 and 19:11-16).
^{e} Your kingdom's sceptre is of uprightness] Literally, 'the sceptre of your kingdom
  is a just / fair / straight sceptre'.
^{f} Your clothes are... myrrh] Hebrew 'myrrh and aloes, cassia [are] all your clothes'.
^{g} Made glad from palaces of ivory] So AV and the Reformation translations. For
  'made glad by music of stringed instruments from ...' (most modern versions)
  see Perowne, note.

Day 97   Psalm 45:9-17

^{9} 'Daughters of kings are with your favoured ones.
At your right hand the queen^{a} in Ophir's gold.
^{10} O daughter, hear, consider, and give ear:
Forget your people and your father's house'.   →

90

¹¹ 'So will the king desire your beauty well.
He is your lord^b: Bow down yourself to him.
¹² There with a gift is the daughter of Tyre.
The richest of the people seek your face'.

¹³ 'Resplendent is the king's daughter within.
Her clothing is with gold embroidery.
¹⁴ With coloured robes she's brought unto the king.
The virgins, her companions, follow her'.

'In train to her, they will be brought to you.
¹⁵ They will be led with gladness and with joy,
They'll enter to the palace of the king.
¹⁶ In place of fathers shall your children^c be –

'You'll make them princes over all the earth.
¹⁷ I'll set your name as a memorial,^d
To every generation it shall be.
Peoples shall give you thanks for evermore!'

---

^a The queen] Not the usual word for 'queen'. Perhaps, 'royal bride'.
^b Lord] Hebrew *Adhôn* - אָדוֹן. Not the unique word used for God - *'Adhonay* - אֲדֹנָי.
 The word may also mean 'husband' cf. Gen. 18:12; 1 Pet. 3:6. See Appendix 2 -
 Names of God.
^c Children] Hebrew 'sons'.
^d I'll set your name as a memorial] Literally, 'I will cause your name to be
 remembered'. Compare Exod. 20:23 (AV 'make mention') and Exod. 20:24 (AV
 'record').

Day 98   Psalm 46

¹ God is to us our refuge and our strength:
A very present help in time of need.
² Therefore, we will not fear though earth be changed –
Though mountains be removed into the seas^a –

³ Although their waters foam, although they roar;
Though mountains tremble at its surging tide. ‖
⁴ There is a river whose streams will make glad
The holy dwelling place^b of the Most High^c.   →

⁵ God in the midst of it: it won't be moved.
And God will help it when the morning breaks.
⁶ The nations were in tumult; kingdoms moved.
The earth did melt when he raised up his voice.

⁷ The LORD of Hosts is present with us now.
The God of Jacob. He is our high tower. ╫
⁸ Come and behold the things the LORD has done.
He has made desolations in the earth.

⁹ To earth's remotest end he makes wars cease.
He breaks the bow, and cuts the spear in two.
The chariots he burns up in the fire.
¹⁰ 'Be still and surely know that I am God!'

'Among the nations I'll be lifted up.
I will be lifted up in all the earth'.
¹¹ The LORD of Hosts is present with us now.
The God of Jacob, he is our high tower. ╫

ᵃ The seas] Literally, 'to the heart of seas'.
ᵇ Dwelling place] Hebrew plural. The holy 'dwelling places' of the Most High. In
Exod. 25:9 it is the word (singular) used for the Tabernacle. It is derived from
the verb šakhan - שָׁכַן, from which comes the word 'shekinah' (šekhînâ -
שְׁכִינָה), meaning God's Divine presence that dwelt there (Exod. 25:8). Newton
(7) notes four 'dwelling places' of Divine glory; the Temple, Mount Zion, the
Heavenly City, and Heaven itself.
ᶜ The Most High] Hebrew 'Elyôn - עֶלְיוֹן. See Appendix 2 - Names of God.

Day 99   Psalm 47

¹ O all you peoples, join in clapping hands.
Shout out to God with a triumphant voice.
² Because the LORD Most Highᵃ is to be feared,
He is a great King over all the earth.

³ He makes the peoples subject unto us;
And he puts nations underneath our feet.
⁴ He chooses our inheritance for us:
The excellenceᵇ of Jacob whom he loves. ╫   →

92

⁵ God is gone up; ascended with a shout!
Even the LORD with sound of the shofar.^c
⁶ Sing psalms^d to God. Sing psalms of praise to him.
Sing psalms unto our king. Sing praise with psalms!

⁷ Because God is the King of all the earth.
Sing psalms with understanding, and with skill.^e
⁸ Over the nations, God now reigns as king.
God sits upon his throne of holiness.

⁹ The princes of the peoples^f gathered round
The people of the God of Abraham.^g
Because the shields^h of earth belong to God,
So he has been exalted very high.

---

^a LORD Most High] Hebrew 'LORD '*Elyôn*' - יהוה עֶלְיוֹן. See Appendix 2 - Names of God.

^b Excellence] 'excellency' or 'pride'. Apparently, a reference to the Holy Land (cf. Ezek. 20:6,15; Amos 6:8).

^c Shofar] The ram's horn blown at the year of Jubilee (Lev. 25:9), the New Year (*Rosh HaShannah*, Lev. 23:24), and on other occasions in Israel.

^d Sing psalms] Hebrew *zamar* - זָמַר. The word is used five times in v6 and v7. Even the NIV. translates 'sing ... a psalm of praise' in v7. See Appendix 2 - Sing Psalms.

^e With understanding and with skill] Hebrew *Maśkîl* - מַשְׂכִּיל (as in the title of Psalm 32 and elsewhere). It may refer to musical skill, but also, as Calvin says, 'singing with understanding'.

^f Princes of the peoples gathered round] Princes - see note on Ps. 118:9. 'Peoples' is plural here, not singular as the AV. They are therefore to be distinguished from the 'people' of the next line'. We understand this to be with hostile intent. Compare Psalm 48 (kings), Zech. 14:1-3, and Newton (8) p355.

^g The people of the God of Abraham] We have not added any joining words. The AV adds '*even*' the people [as if emphasising the identity of the peoples' with 'the people']; RV '*to be*' the people. The assumption of such versions is of a link to the promise to Abraham (Gen. 17:4), or even of a replacement theology. We are inclined to understand the verb ('gathered round') in the sense of 'brought into association with'; as BDB *Lexicon* on Miriam - Numb. 12:14,15. Compare v3.

^h Shields] AV translates the word 'shields' (*maghen* - מָגֵן) as 'rulers' in Hos. 4:18, as protectors of the general population. This is the generally accepted view of this verse. However, we believe it is rather the protection that God gives when he goes out in defence of his Israel (v7, Ps. 89:18, and Zech. 14). See E. Bendor-Samuel, *The Prophetic Character of the Psalms*, for an alternative interpretation of the verse. See Appendix 2 - Shields.

Day 100   Psalm 48:1-8

[1] Great is the LORD and greatly to be praised
In our God's city - on his holy hill!
[2] In beauty raised up[a], and the whole earth's joy
Is Zion's mount upon its northern sides.[b]

It is the city of the mighty King,
[3] And in its palaces, God is made known
As a high tower for refuge and defence.[c]
[4] Behold![d] - the kings joined! They passed by as one.

[5] They saw it[e], and therefore they were amazed.
They were astounded. They fled in alarm.
[6] For trembling fear took hold upon them there;
As anguish of a woman giving birth.

[7] You wrecked the ships of Tarshish with east wind.[f]
[8] Just as we heard, so we have seen it there –
The city of the LORD of hosts, our God, [g]
God will establish it for evermore. ⫪

---

[a] Jerusalem has a height of 800 feet on the edge of high tablelands. The Temple
was on the North of the city. But NB Isa. 2:4 etc.
[b] Zion's mount upon its northern sides] Compare Isa. 14:13, which Tregelles (2)
applies to Antichrist's ambition to supplant Christ.
[c] High tower for refuge and defence] This is the meaning of the word translated 'a
refuge' by the AV. The same word as in Ps. 46:7,11.
[d] Behold!] Hebrew *hinneh* - הִנֵּה. See Appendix 2 - Behold!
[e] They saw it] i.e. the holy city as it is exalted by God at the time spoken of by the
psalmist.
[f] You wrecked the ships of Tarshish with east wind] The ships of Tarshish were the
great ships (literally, 'vessels') that sailed to Spain (Jonah 1:3). 'Wrecked' -
literally, 'broke'. This is the same word as used of Assyria in Isa. 14:25.
[g] Seen it there - the city ... our God] Hebrew 'at the city of the LORD of hosts, at
the city of our God'.

Day 101   Psalm 48:9-14

[9] Upon your mercy[a] we have thought, O God,
Within your Temple, in its inner parts.[b]
[10] According to your name, so is your praise.
It reaches to the ends of all the earth.   →

Well-filled with righteousness is your right hand.
¹¹ Rejoice, Mount Zion, and be very glad!
Let Judah's daughters now exult with joy,
Because of the right judgments^c made by you.

¹² Walk about Zion. Circle it around.
Go and encompass it all round about.
And then the number of its towers count.
¹³ Set your heart on^d its ramparts and defence.

Mark well its palaces, so you can tell –
Recount to generations following –
¹⁴ That this is God, our God for evermore!
And he will guide us even unto death.^e

---

^a Mercy] Covenant mercy, loving-kindness. Hebrew *ḥeṣedh* - חֶסֶד. See Appendix 2 - Loving-kindness.

^b Inner parts] Hebrew *qerebh* - קֶרֶב. The word also used for 'the inner parts' of the victim in the sacrificial system, Lev. 1:9.

^c Right judgments] Plural. Hebrew *mišpaṭ* - מֶשְׁפָּט. See Appendix 2 - Law - Judgment.

^d Set your heart on] So the Hebrew. The disciples were once entranced with Zion's transient Herodian glory (Matt. 24:1), but this will be God's doing.

^e Even unto death] i.e. He will be our lifelong Guide. There is some difficulty with the last two words (or one word) of the Hebrew. By joining the words, as in many Hebrew manuscripts, the Septuagint, Syriac, and Vulgate translate this line parallel to the preceding one - 'he will guide us for ever'. See de Burgh.

Day 102   Psalm 49:1-5

¹ Hear all you peoples, and listen to this!
Give ear to this all dwellers in this world!^a
² Both common men and men of noble birth,^b
The rich man and the one who is in need.

³ My mouth will speak with words of wisdom now;
My heart will ponder on discerning things.^c
⁴ Unto a parable I'll turn my ear.
I'll open up my puzzle on the harp.

⁵ Why should I be afraid in evil days?
When I'm supplanted by my wicked foes;
When I'm surrounded by iniquity,
though it's behind me, even at my heels.^d

[a] This world] Hebrew *heledh* - חֶלֶד. The world as space-time. Tregelles (3) translates 'inhabitants of [this] age'. Girdlestone 'the transitory state of things in this world which passeth away'. See Appendix 2 - Earth.

[b] Common men ... men of noble birth] Hebrew 'sons of Adam' (Hebrew *'adham* - אָדָם - man as a child of Adam, human), and 'sons of ish' (Hebrew *'îš* - אִישׁ. Man as an individual. Man of higher rank). See Appendix 2 - Man.

[c] Words of wisdom ... discerning things] Both are plurals, 'wisdoms' and 'understandings'. Motyer (1) takes these as 'plurals of amplitude', i.e. the fullest possible wisdom and the fullest possible discernment.

[d] We have expanded the last line of the section. Commentators are divided as to whether iniquity encompasses the psalmist, or whether he sees himself as supplanted by the wicked (see Gen. 25:26; 27:36). The word translated 'foes' here may mean 'one who takes by the heel', or 'supplants'.

Day 103   Psalm 49:6-15

[6] They trust in wealth, of their great riches boast -
[7] And yet a man his brother can't redeem,
Nor give a ransom unto God for him -
[8] (Their soul is priceless. They cannot redeem)[a] -

[9] Redeem to[b] ever live; not see the Pit[c].
[10] For he must see it - wise men also die.
They, with the fool and stupid, pass away.
They leave their wealth to others after them.

[11] Their heart is[d] that their houses always last -
Dwellings for generations yet to come!
Therefore, they name their lands[e] after themselves.
[12] Yet man with honour will not stay for long.[f]

He's like the beasts. For they are cut off too.
[13] This is the way of those with foolish hope -
Their followers approve the things they say. [g] ╫
[14] As sheep for Sheol[h] they have set themselves.

And death shall be a shepherd[i] unto them.
By morning shall the just ones tread them down[j].
Their beauty[k] is for Sheol to consume
So they no longer have an honoured place. [l]   →

¹⁵ But God will make a ransom for my soul,
Redeem me from the grasp of Sheol's power.
For he will take and keep me in his care.
He will receive me so I am with him. ᵐ ‖

ᵃ They cannot redeem] The Hebrew is emphatic 'redemption fails (or 'is let
   alone') for ever'. This line may be read as a ransom failing, or of a person
   failing to redeem.
ᵇ Redeem to ...] This follows on from v7. 'A ransom so that he should live ...'. We
   have added the word 'redeem' in this line to make the connection with verses
   7 and 8 clear.
ᶜ The Pit] Hebrew ha-šaḥath - הַשָּׁחַת - the place of corruption, the grave. The
   definite article confirms this rendering. As Ps. 16:10.
ᵈ Their heart is] Literally, 'their inward part' is... (as Psalms 49:9 and 55:15), i.e.
   'inwardly thinking'.
ᵉ Lands] Hebrew 'adhamâ - אֲדָמָה. See Appendix 2 - Earth.
ᶠ Not stay long] Literally, 'sojourn'.
ᵍ Approve the things they say] Hebrew literally, 'take pleasure in their mouth'.
ʰ Sheol] Hebrew še'ôl - שְׁאוֹל. The place of the dead, here personified. See
   Appendix 2 - Sheol.
ⁱ Be a shepherd] He feeds them and tends them. The metaphor is extended. Not
   as the AV 'feed on them'.
ʲ Tread them down] 'Trample on them', 'putting their feet, as it were, upon the
   neck of prostrate foes' (Perowne). Septuagint 'to exercise complete dominion
   over them' (katakurieuo - κατακυριεύω)
ᵏ Beauty] The Hebrew word is wider, meaning the whole form of a man – 'all his
   outward show'.
ˡ An honoured place] A different word from 49:11. Here it literally means, 'a lofty
   abode'.
ᵐ He will receive me ... with him] We have expanded the meaning of this line into
   two lines. AV 'for he will receive me'. The Hebrew word may mean either
   'take' or 'receive'. See Psalms 18:16; 73:24; Gen. 5:24.

Day 104   Psalm 49:16-20

¹⁶ Be not afraid when someone becomes rich,
Or if the glory of his house increase.
¹⁷ For, when he dies, he takes nothing away.
His glory won't descend down after him.

¹⁸ Though, while he was alive, he blessed his soul
(And when you prosper, men will give you praise).
¹⁹ Yet he shall go to where his fathers are,ᵃ
And they shall never see the light again.   →

²⁰ The man who is in honour and admired

(If he is one who does not understand)
He may be likened to the senseless beasts.
They also perish, and they are cut off.

ᵃ Yet he shall go to where his fathers are] Literally, 'She [his soul] shall go down to the generation [or age] of his fathers'. We take 'generation' as meaning a class of people with certain moral characteristics (cf. Deut. 32:20; Matt. 24:34)

Day 105   Psalm 50:1-6

¹ The Mighty GOD of gods ᵃ, the LORD, thus spoke;
Called earth from sun's rise to its going down.
² From Zion - faultless beauty - God shined out.
³ Our God will come. He will not hold his peace.

A fire will go before him to devour.
Around him will a mighty tempest rage.
⁴ He'll call unto the heavens from above
And to the earth, to judge ᵇ his people's cause.

⁵ Assemble unto me those whom I love ᶜ,
Who made a covenant ᵈ by sacrifice.
⁶ The heavens shall declare his righteousness,
For it is God himself who is the Judge ᵉ. ⊹

ᵃ The Mighty GOD of gods] Hebrew *'El 'Elohîm* - אֵל אֱלֹהִים. Either 'the GOD of gods' or, taking *'El* - אֵל to mean 'might' here, 'The Mighty GOD' - as the AV. We have combined both thoughts.
ᵇ To judge] To determine or judge a cause in a legal sense. Hebrew *dîn* - דִּין. See Appendix 2 - Law - Judgment
ᶜ Those whom I love] Hebrew *ḥaṣîdhîm* - חֲסִידִים. Plural of Hebrew *ḥaṣîdh* - חָסִיד. See Appendix 2 - Loving-kindness.
ᵈ Made a covenant] Hebrew adds 'with me'.
ᵉ Judge] Hebrew *šôpheṭ* - שׁוֹפֵט. See Appendix 2 - Law - Judgment.

Day 106   Psalm 50:7-15

⁷ Hear, O my people, I will speak to you!
O Israel, I bring my charge to you!
For I myself am God, even your God
⁸ (Your sacrifices - I will not reprove   →

I'll not reprove for your burnt offerings
They also are before me constantly).
⁹ I would not take a young bull from your house,
Nor would I take the he-goats from your folds,

¹⁰ For every forest animal is mine,
Even the cattle on a thousand hills.
¹¹ The mountain birds are all well-known to me;
With me is every thing that moves ᵃ in fields.

¹² If I were hungry, I would not tell you.
The world ᵇ and all its fullness is for me.
¹³ Would I eat up the flesh of mighty bulls?
Or take the blood of he-goats for a drink?

¹⁴ Make sacrifice to God by giving thanks.
Perform your vows to Him who is Most High, ᶜ
¹⁵ And call on me in the day of distress. ᵈ
I'll rescue you, and you will honour me.

ᵃ Every thing that moves] We have translated literally - see Gesenius *Lexicon*, and
   BDB *Lexicon*. Koehler *Lexicon* 'locusts?' AV 'the wild beasts'. See note on
   80:13 where the same expression is used.
ᵇ The world] The inhabited earth. *tebhel* - תֵּבֵל. See Appendix 2 - Earth.
ᶜ Him who is Most High] Hebrew *'Elyôn* - עֶלְיוֹן. See Appendix 2 - Names of God.
ᵈ The day of distress] See Ps. 20:1.

Day 107   Psalm 50:16-23

¹⁶ God speaks these things unto the wicked one:
'What right have you repeating ᵃ my decrees?
Taking my covenant into your mouth?
¹⁷ You are the person who hates discipline',

'And you have put my words behind your back.
¹⁸ You saw a thief, and were well-pleased with him,
And with adulterers you cast your lot. ᵇ
¹⁹ Your mouth you have let loose in wickedness.   →

'Your tongue contrives to carry out deceit.
²⁰ You sit down[c] and against your brother speak.
You bring a slander on your mother's son.
²¹ Yet I kept silence when you did these things!'

'You thought that I was such a one as you![d]
I will reprove, set out[e] before your eyes!
²² You who forget <u>God</u>[f], Oh consider this,[g]
Lest I should tear, and none delivers you.

²³ The one who offers this for sacrifice -
Who offers thanks - will give glory to me;
And, to the one who orders his way well,
Salvation - God's salvation - I will show.

---

[a] Repeating] Literally, 'count up' as if to keep them more faithfully. Cf. the Talmud's 613 'precepts'. T&J Latin translates by *enarro* - 'to explain or relate in full'.
[b] And with adulterers ... your lot] Literally, 'you make your portion with adulterers'.
[c] Sit down] Sitting down to slander is reminiscent of Ps. 1:1.
[d] I was] This can be translated 'you thought the I AM was such a one as you' (cf. Exod. 3:14).
[e] Set out] Set out a charge. The verb is used of a row of the 'shew' bread.
[f] <u>God</u>] Hebrew *'Elôah* - אֱלֹהַּ. See Appendix 2 - Names of God.
[g] Oh consider] The Hebrew word of entreaty (*na'* - נָא) here emphasises the verb. The Geneva Bible translates 'Oh ...'. The AV translates 'now' (without reference to time - see SOED). See note on Ps. 118:2.

Day 108   Psalm 51:1-6

¹ According to your steadfast love[a], O God,
Be gracious - show your favour unto me;
According to your mercies[b], which are great,
Blot out the sins in which I have transgressed.

² O wash me well from my iniquity;
And purify - yes, cleanse me[c] from my sin.
³ For my transgressions are well-known to me;
Constantly I'm confronted by my sin.   →

⁴ Against you, and you only, have I sinned,
And I have done this evil in your sight:
So that you may be just when you declare:
So you are blameless when you act as judge.ᵈ

⁵ Yesᵉ, I was in iniquity when born;
I was in sin when my mother conceived.ᶠ

⁶ Yes, you delight in truth in inner parts; ᵍ
You'll teach me wisdom in the hidden part.ʰ

ᵃ Steadfast love] Hebrew *ḥeṣedh* - חֶסֶד. See Appendix 2 - Loving-kindness.
ᵇ Mercies] Tender mercies. Deep feelings of compassion aroused by the sight of
   weakness or suffering (Hebrew *raḥamîm* - רַחֲמִים).
ᶜ Purify ... cleanse me] We have expanded the meaning here. The verb is
   intensive (piel) in Hebrew. As well as meaning 'cleanse', it was used in a more
   specific sense for ritual purification (cf. Lev. 14:7,11, etc).
ᵈ Blameless when you act as judge] Rom. 3:4 translates 'might overcome (win)
   when you are judged (or 'go to law')'. Haldane notes that, in the case of
   Bathsheba, God was both prosecutor and judge in his own cause when Nathan
   convicted David of his sin (2 Sam.12:7,11). The word for 'judge' here is Hebrew
   dîn - דִּין. See Appendix 2 - Law - Judgment.
ᵉ Yes] Here and in v6. AV 'Behold'. Hebrew *hen* - הֵן. See Appendix 2 - Behold!
ᶠ Conceived] Hebrew, 'conceived me'
ᵍ Inner parts] The word is only used here and in Job 38:36. 'Thou lovest truth in
   the inner affections', Geneva Bible.
ʰ Hidden part] ESV 'the secret heart'.

Day 109   Psalm 51:7-15

⁷ You'll purge with hyssop that I may be clean;
You'll wash, so I'll be whiter than the snow.
⁸ Rejoicing, gladness, you will make me hear;
So bones that you have broken may rejoice.

⁹ O hide your face away from these my sins
And wipe awayᵃ all my iniquities.
¹⁰ A heart that's pureᵇ, create for me, O God;
A steadfast spiritᶜ make anew in me.

¹¹ Do not discard and cast me from your sight! ᵈ
Your Holy Spiritᵉ do not take from me!
¹² Give your salvation's joy to me again;
And with a willing spirit hold me up.   →

¹³ Then I'll instruct transgressors in your ways,
And sinners will return again to you.
¹⁴ Deliver from blood-guiltiness, O God.
You are the one who is my saving God[f].

My tongue will then shout loudly and will sing[g] –
With joy it will sing of your righteousness.
¹⁵ My Lord[h], will you just open up my lips,
Then my mouth also will declare your praise.

---

[a] Wipe away] The verb is used of wiping the face clean, 'obliterate', AV 'blot out'.
[b] A heart that's pure] Welsh Bible 'calon lân'.
[c] Steadfast spirit] Firm - so the *Statenvertaling* (*vasten geest*). As in Ps. 78:37; AV 'right spirit'.
[d] From your sight] Hebrew 'from before your face'.
[e] Holy Spirit] The third person of the Trinity; not 'holy spirit' - 'a Divine influence resting on man' (*The Century Bible* - Davison).
[f] My saving God] The God of my salvation.
[g] Shout loudly and will sing] the Hebrew word means both 'shout for joy' and 'sing'. It is used in Lev. 9:24.
[h] My Lord] Hebrew *'Adhonay* - אֲדֹנָי. See Appendix 2 - Names of God.

Day 110   Psalm 51:16-19

¹⁶ You do not take delight in sacrifice:
If that were so, I would give it to you.
You take no pleasure in burnt offering.
¹⁷ A broken spirit is God's sacrifice.

A broken spirit is God's sacrifice[a] –
A broken, contrite, heart you'll not despise.
¹⁸ Do good to Zion as it pleases you,
And build the walls up of Jerusalem.

¹⁹ Then with the sacrifices you'll be pleased –
Even with sacrifice of righteousness.
With sacrifices burnt, and offered whole,[b]
Bulls will be offered[c] on your altar then.

---

[a] We have repeated this line from the previous stanza of this version, as it is closely connected with the thought of both.
[b] With sacrifices burnt and offered whole] AV 'with burnt offering and whole burnt offering'. Two different words. 'Burnt offering' (Hebrew *'olâ* - עֹלָה) from a word meaning 'to go up', as the smoke of the burning did. This is the usual

word for 'burnt offering', as required in Lev. 1. Girdlestone considers the best rendering would be 'ascending offering'. 'Whole burnt offering' (Hebrew *kalîl* - כָּלִיל) is from a word meaning 'to be complete or perfect', indicating it was entirely consumed by the fire without any of the sacrifice reserved. Some (including Gesenius *Lexicon*) consider this to be parallelism, giving two aspects of the same sacrifice. The 'whole burnt offering' is referred to elsewhere in Lev. 6:20-23 (where it prefigured Christ as the priest who gave himself completely and entirely), Deut. 33:10; and 1 Sam. 7:9.
^c Bulls will be offered] Hebrew 'they will offer young bulls', as in Ps. 50:9.

Day 111   Psalm 52

¹ Why do you boast of evil, mighty man[a]?
GOD's loving-kindness[b] lasts all the day long.
² Your tongue devises such malicious things.
Like a sharp razor, you work your deceit.

³ You love what's evil, more than what is good;
And falsehood, more than speaking righteousness. ⸾⸾
⁴ Deceitful tongue; you love words that devour.
⁵ GOD also will destroy you evermore.

He'll seize you, and will tear you from your tent.
Uproot you from the land of those who live[c]. ⸾⸾
⁶ The righteous then shall see, and fear, and laugh.
⁷ 'Behold![d] The man[e] who made not God his strength!' [f]

'He put his trust in his abundant wealth,
And, in his malice, he made himself strong!'
⁸ But as for me, I'm like an olive tree
That flourishes within the house of God.

I trust God's steadfast love[g] for evermore.
⁹ Because you've done this, I'll give endless praise.
And I'll wait on your name, for it is good –
Before those who are your beloved ones.[h]

---

^a Mighty man] Hebrew *gibbôr* - גִּבּוֹר -Man as a mighty being. See Appendix 2 - Man.
^b Loving-kindness] Hebrew *ḥeṣedh* - חֶסֶד. See Appendix 2 - Loving-kindness.
^c The land of those who live] AV 'land of the living'. Compare 27:13; 116:9; 142:5
^d Behold!] Hebrew *hinneh* - הִנֵּה. See Appendix 2 - Behold!

103

[e] Man] Hebrew *gebher* - גֶּבֶר - a strong man, a warrior. This is one of the rare occasions where the word is used in a bad sense, perhaps here in mocking irony (as perhaps with *gibbôr* - גִּבּוֹר in v1). See Appendix 2 - Man.

[f] Strength] 'A place of strength' or 'a stronghold'.

[g] Steadfast love] Hebrew *ḥeṣedh* - חֶסֶד. See Appendix 2 - Loving-kindness.

[h] Beloved ones] AV 'saints'. Hebrew *ḥaṣîdh* - חָסִיד from *ḥeṣedh* - חֶסֶד. See Appendix 2 - Loving-kindness.

Day 112   Psalm 53

[1] 'There is no God!' the fool says in his heart.
They are corrupt, and what they do is vile.
No one does good[a], no not a single one,
[2] From heaven God looks on the sons of men.

He looks to see if any understand;
If there are those who will seek after God.
[3] They've turned away. They're all together foul.
No one does good, no not a single one.

[4] Do those who work such wickedness not know?
Who eat my people as a loaf of bread!
These are the ones who do not call on God.
[5] Great fear was on them – when there was no fear!

God scattered round about the bones of him
Who camped against you. You put them to shame.
They were rejected, and despised by God.
[6] O, please, grant that deliverance may come!

Israel's salvation shall from Zion come,
When God restores, and brings his people back.
He will return them from captivity.
Jacob will joy, and Israel be glad.

---

[a] No one does good] Rom. 3:10,12 develops this, under the inspiration of the Holy Spirit, as 'there is none righteous'. We have added 'not a single one', from the translation of the Septuagint and Rom. 3:10-12. Compare v3.

104

Day 113   Psalm 54

[1] Save me, O God. O save me by your name,
And by your strength give judgment on my cause[a].
[2] O be attentive to my prayer, O God,
And listen to the words[b] that my mouth speaks.

[3] Strangers rose up against me - ruthless foes[c]
Sought for my soul - had no regard for God[d]. ‖
[4] But surely[e] God's a helper unto me.
My Lord[f] is with those who support my soul.

[5] He will requite the evil of my foes[g].
O, in your truth, be sure[h] to cut them off!
[6] With willing heart[i] I'll sacrifice to you;
A freewill offering to you I'll bring.

I'll praise your name, O LORD, for it is good!
I'll praise your name, O LORD, for it is good![j]
[7] Because he rescued me from all distress.
My eye has looked upon my enemies.[k]

---

[a] Give judgment on my cause] In Hebrew one word, *dîn* - דִּין. See Appendix 2 -
Law - Judgment.

[b] Words] Spoken words. Hebrew *'emer* - אֵמֶר (from *'amar* - אָמַר, to say). See
Appendix 2 - Word.

[c] Ruthless foes] One word in Hebrew - as Ezek. 28:7 et al. AV 'the terrible (of the
nations)'.

[d] Had no regard for God] Literally, 'They did not set God before them'.

[e] But surely] Hebrew *hinneh* - הִנֵּה. See Appendix 2 - Behold!

[f] My Lord] Hebrew *'Adhonay* - אֲדֹנָי. See Appendix 2 - Names of God.

[g] Foes] 'Those that lie in wait, watching out for me spitefully' See 5:9

[h] In your truth, be sure ...] God's faithfulness will ensure the punishment of the
wicked. The word 'truth' here indicates something sure (cf. Prov. 11:18 'reward
of truth').

[i] With willing heart] Literally, 'with freewill offering'. See de Burgh.

[j] We have repeated this line.

[k] My eye has looked upon my enemies] We have given the literal translation. See
comment on the similar expression at Ps.112:8.

Day 114   Psalm 55:1-8

[1] Incline your ear unto my prayer, O God,
And from my supplication[a] do not hide.
[2] Take notice, and give answer unto me.
I mourn in my lament[b] and I'm distraught.[c]   →

³ Because the enemy is crying out;^d
Because the wicked are oppressing so.
For they would throw iniquity on me,
And in their anger keep their hate for me.

⁴ My heart writhes as in travail within me.
Terrors of death have fallen upon me.
⁵ Trembling and fearfulness^e have come on me,
And so with horror I am overwhelmed.

⁶ I said, 'O had I wings just like a dove
Then would I fly away and be at rest.
⁷ Yes!^f I would leave and wander far away,
And I would lodge within the wilderness'. ✚

⁸ 'I would make haste to find a sheltered place
I would make haste, and so make my escape
Far from the tempest and the stormy wind
Yes from the tempest and the stormy wind'.^g

---

^a Supplication: My prayer for grace] or 'my prayer for mercy'. This is the literal
  meaning. See Gesenius *Lexicon*. It is from the word meaning 'to be gracious
  to', 'to pity'. As in Ps. 6:9 and 119:170
^b Lament] Hebrew *śîaḥ* - שִׂיחַ. The word includes the meaning of meditating or
  musing. AV 'complaint', i.e. an expression of sorrow.
^c Distraught] AV 'make a noise'. The root meaning of the Hebrew word *hûm* (הומ)
  is 'to run around'. 'Used of one driven up and down by cares and solicitudes',
  Gesenius *Lexicon*.
^d Because the enemy is crying out] Hebrew 'because of the voice (or sound) of
  the enemy'.
^e Trembling and fearfulness] Hebrew 'fear and trembling'.
^f Yes!] Hebrew *hinneh* - הִנֵּה. See Appendix 2 - Behold!
^g In this stanza, we have expanded the meaning of the first line in the second, and
  have repeated the third line.

Day 115   Psalm 55:9-15

⁹ 'My Lord^a, destroy them, and divide their tongue!
For I have seen the city's savage strife'.
¹⁰ By day and night they go around its walls,
Iniquity and sorrow are within.   →

¹¹ Destruction^b is within the midst of it.
Deceit and guile do never leave its streets.
¹² It was no enemy brought me reproach,
For that is something that I then could bear.

He who rose up was not my hating foe,
For then I would have hid myself from him.
¹³ But it was you, a man^c, ranked just like me.^d
You, my companion, my familiar friend.

¹⁴ Together once we had sweet fellowship,
In company we walked unto God's house.
¹⁵ Death seize them! Take them down to Sheol^e live!
For wickedness^f is in their homes and heart.^g

---

^a My Lord] Hebrew *'Adhonay* - אֲדֹנָי. See Appendix 2 - Names of God.
^b Destruction] Hebrew 'destructions'. Motyer (1) 'a plural of amplitude', i.e. 'great destruction'.
^c Man] Hebrew *'enôš* - אֱנוֹשׁ - Frail, mortal man. See Appendix 2 - Man.
^d Ranked just like me] Calvin 'according to my own rank'. So too *Statenvertaling* and AV margin. T&J Latin *'par mihi'*. AV 'mine equal'. Compare 2 Kgs. 12:5 ('that every man is set at'), 2 Kgs. 23:35 ('according to his taxation').
^e Sheol] Hebrew *še'ôl* - שְׁאוֹל. See Appendix 2 - Sheol.
^f Wickedness] Plural, 'evils'.
^g In their homes and heart] Homes — see Motyer (1); Welsh Bible *'cartref'* (home). 'Heart' is Hebrew *beqerebh* - בְּקִרְבָּם - 'in their inner part'.

Day 116   Psalm 55:16-23

¹⁶ I'll call to God. The LORD will save me then.
¹⁷ I'll pray^a at evening, morning, and at noon.
I'll cry aloud, and he will hear my voice.
¹⁸ He has redeemed my soul to be at peace.

Saved^b from the battle that against me raged,
For there were many who stood on my side^c.
¹⁹ For GOD will hear, and he will answer them.
He is the one who sits enthroned^d of old. ⊬

Because their life continues without change^e;
Therefore, because of this, they don't fear God.
²⁰ This one^f laid hands on^g those at peace with him,
And he defiled and broke^h his covenant.   →

²¹ Mouth smooth as butter, yet war in his heart -
Soft oily words, yet they were like drawn swords.
²² Cast your lot on the LORD. He will sustain.
He will not let the righteous man be moved.

²³ But you, O God, will surely cast them down -
Thrown for destruction to the lowest pit. ⁱ
False, bloody men^j not living half their days.
But as for me, I'll put my trust in you.

---

^a Pray] Hebrew *śîaḥ* - שִׂיחַ. The word includes the meaning of meditating or musing. Horsley comments that, when it is used of prayer, it indicates private prayer, rather than public prayer.

^b Redeemed ... saved] We have repeated the verb in this line, linking it with 'the battle'.

^c Many who stood on my side] The Hebrew construction may mean either 'with' (as giving support) or 'against' (as the enemy). We have followed the AV and the older versions. Horsley 'Divine assistance described under the image of numerous auxiliaries'. See 2 Kgs. 6:16; 1 John 4:4.

^d Sits enthroned] Hebrew 'sits', but the verb frequently means 'sit as a king' - e.g. Ps. 2:4.

^e Because their life continues without change] Literally, 'whom there are no changes to them'. We have followed the Geneva Bible's notes 'but their prosperous estate still continueth', i.e. carnal security breeds atheism.

^f This one] The Hebrew is simply 'he', but the psalmist reverts back to the familiar friend of v13.

^g He laid his hands on] Hebrew 'he sent his hands against'.

^h Defiled and broke] Hebrew 'profaned'.

ⁱ Thrown for destruction to the lowest pit] Hebrew 'into the pit (1) of the pit (2)'. Delitzsch translates 'the abyss of the pit'. Different words are used for 'pit'. The second Hebrew word is translated 'destruction' when quoted in Acts 2:27 and 13:35.

^j False, bloody men] Hebrew 'men of bloods and deceit'. 'Man' here is *'enôš* - אֱנוֹשׁ - Frail, mortal man. See Appendix 2 - Man.

Day 117   Psalm 56:1-7

¹ O do be gracious unto me, O God,
For mortal man^a would hound and harry me.^b
He daily fights, and he oppresses me.
² My enemies^c would hound me all the day.

Against me many fight, O God Most High.^d
³ When I'm afraid I'll put my trust in you -
⁴ In God I'll praise his word - in God I trust.
I will not fear what flesh can do to me.   →

⁵ Yet all the day they twist and wrest[e] my words.
Against me are their thoughts - their evil plans.
⁶ They come together, and they hide themselves.
They mark my steps, when they wait for my soul.

⁷ Shall they escape by their iniquity?
Shall they escape by their iniquity?[f]
O in your anger make them to sink down.
In anger cast the nations down, O God.[g]

---

[a] Mortal man] Hebrew *'enôš* - אֱנוֹשׁ - Frail, mortal man; cf. v4 where he uses the
word 'flesh' to emphasise the frailty of man. See Appendix 2 - Man.
[b] Hound and harry] Hebrew, 'swallow', cf. Job 7:2. Perowne 'lit. Hath panted after
me, with open mouth ready to devour me, like a wild beast, thirsting for my
blood'. The same verb occurs in the next verse.
[c] My enemies] 'Those that lie in wait for me, watching me spitefully'. See 5:9.
[d] O God Most High] We have supplied 'God', as the Welsh Bible. The word used
here is *marôm* - מָרוֹם, what is high or lofty. De Burgh and modern versions take
it as 'an accusative used adverbially' here, and translate 'proudly' or 'haughtily'
- of David's enemies. Horsley would read [enemies] 'from on high' suggesting
that, in the application of the Psalm to the Messiah, there may be a reference
to 'spiritual wickedness in high places'. See Appendix 2 - Names of God.
[e] Twist and wrest] One word in Hebrew.
[f] We have repeated this line.
[g] Sink down ... cast ... down] We have extended this line. The word may either
mean 'to sink down' or 'to cast down'.

Day 118   Psalm 56:8-13

⁸ You keep a count of all my wandering.
Into your bottle put the tears I shed,
For are they not recorded in your book?
⁹ My foes will turn back in the day I call.

For this I know, that God is on my side.
¹⁰ In God I'll praise the word; The LORD's word praise[a].
¹¹ In God I put my trust, I'm not afraid,
For what then can a man[b] do unto me?

¹² Your vows are binding upon me, O God.
Thanksgivings I will render unto you.
¹³ You freed my soul from death. You kept my feet.
So in the light of life I'll walk with God.

a The refrain of v4 is repeated in a varied form. The Hebrew of this verse is
  literally, 'In God I will praise the word. In the LORD I will praise the word'. He
  trusts in God's sure word of promise.
b Man] Hebrew 'adham - אָדָם - Man as a child of Adam. Compare v1 and v4. See
  Appendix 2 - Man.

Day 119   Psalm 57:1-5

¹ Be gracious, God, be gracious unto me.
My soul has fled for refuge unto you.
In shadow of your wings I'll take refuge,ᵃ
Till these calamities have passed away.

² I will cry out unto the Most High God.ᵇ
GOD brings to pass his purposes for me.
³ He'll send from heaven, and he will save me.
The one who hounds me he will put to shame. ╫

God shall send forth his mercyᶜ and his truth -
His loving-kindness and his faithfulness.ᵈ
⁴ For roaring lions are all round my soul, ᵉ
And I lie down with those who flame with fire -

Menᶠ who have spears and arrows for their teeth -
With those whose tongue is like a sharpened sword.
⁵ High above heaven be exalted, God.
Above the whole earth let your glory be.

a Fled for refuge ... take refuge] The Hebrew verb ḥaṣâ - חָסָה 'to flee to a refuge
  and a place of safety' is used twice in this verse. See Appendix 2 - Refuge.
b Most High God] Hebrew 'Elohîm 'Elyôn - עֶלְיוֹן אֱלֹהִים. See Appendix 2 - Names of
  God.
c Mercy] Hebrew ḥeṣedh - חֶסֶד. See Appendix 2 - Loving-kindness.
d His loving-kindness and his faithfulness] We have in this line added the
  alternative meaning of the two words 'mercy' and 'truth'.
e For roaring lions are all round my soul] Hebrew 'My soul is in the midst of
  roaring lions'. 'Roaring lions' - Hebrew lebha'îm לְבָאִים. Gesenius Lexicon 'a
  lion, so-called for its roaring'.
f Men] Hebrew 'the sons of men' [Hebrew 'adham - אָדָם). Man as a child of
  Adam. See Appendix 2 - Man.

Day 120   Psalm 57:6-11

⁶ They have prepared a net for where I walk.
Because of this my soul has been bowed down.
In front of me they went and dug a pit,
But they have fallen into it themselves. ╫

⁷ My heart is fixed, O God, my heart is fixed.
And I will sing; with psalms I will give praise.
⁸ Awake my glory^a! Wake up lyre^b and harp!
Yes, I would even wake the morning dawn!

⁹ Among the peoples, I will thank you Lord;^c
Among the nations I'll sing psalms to you.
¹⁰ Your loving-kindness^d is so very great,
Even unto the heavens it extends.

Likewise, your truth extends unto the clouds.
¹¹ Above the heavens, be exalted, God!
Above the whole earth may your glory be.
Above the whole earth may your glory be.^e

---

^a My glory] See notes on Psalms 16:9 and 30:12.
^b Lyre] AV 'psaltery'. See Appendix 2 - *nebhel* - נֶבֶל.
^c Lord] My Lord, Hebrew *'Adhonay* - אֲדֹנָי. See Appendix 2 - Names of God.
^d Loving-kindness] Hebrew *ḥeṣedh* - חֶסֶד. See Appendix 2 - Loving-kindness.
^e We have repeated the refrain, which also occurs in v5.

Day 121   Psalm 58:1-5

¹ O congregation^a, do you speak what's right?
Do you judge uprightly, you sons of men?
² No^b. In your heart you work iniquities;
Your hands deal injury upon the earth.

³ The wicked are as strangers^c from the womb.
They go astray as soon as they are born.
And from the time they're born they speak a lie.
And from the time they're born they speak a lie.^d   →

⁴ For they have venom, venom like a snake;
Like the deaf cobra, shutting up its ear,
⁵ which does not hear the sound the charmers make
Though they should do their charming skilfully.

---

^a O congregation] The meaning of the word as it stands in Hebrew is 'dumbness' or 'silence'. See de Burgh, Perowne, and the major Hebrew lexicons. The Reformation translations, Kimchi, Calvin, and the AV, link this word to another root, translating 'congregation', which we have adopted. Most modern translations now assume different vowels, following Ewald and others, and so render the word as 'gods' or 'rulers'.

^b No] AV 'yea'. The Hebrew word ('aph - אַף). Compare Segond *loin de là* - 'far from it'. Welsh Bible *yn hytrach* - 'rather than that'. It is different from the word we have translated 'yes' ('akh - אַךְ) in v11, which adds emphasis, and is not always translated.

^c Strangers] The Hebrew word 'estranged' (zûr - זוּר) is used in connection with foreigners, but also of 'strange gods' - in opposition to the true God; and 'strange women' - i.e. harlots. The word also means, 'to be, or become, loathsome' - cf. Job 19:17.

^d We have repeated the line.

Day 122   Psalm 58:6-11

⁶ Shatter, O God, their teeth within their mouth!
Tear out the great teeth of young lions^a, LORD!
⁷ As water let them quickly flow away,
And blunt his arrows when he draws his bow.^b

⁸ Let them go like a snail that melts away;
Like one misborn who does not see the sun.
⁹ Before your pots can feel the heat of thorns,
Both green and burning, he'll sweep them away.^c

¹⁰ The just, when seeing vengeance, will rejoice,
And in the wicked's blood he'll wash his feet.
¹¹ A man^d will say, 'the just have a reward'.
'There is a God who judges^e in the earth!'

---

^a Young lions] The word is also used in Ps. 35:17. A different word for 'lion' is used in Ps. 57:4.

^b And blunt ... bow] 'When hee shooteth his arrows, let them be as broken', Geneva Bible. 'When he aims his arrows, let them be as headless shafts' NASB. 'Draws his bow' is literally, 'treads his bow'. See note on 7:12.

^c 'Some obscurity attaches to this verse', Calvin. It speaks of the sudden overthrow of the wicked. The picture is apparently of thorns, gathered to

provide tinder for cooking, which are blown away (in the desert) before they even heat the pot - so also Horsley, and Perowne.

[d] A man] Hebrew *'adham* - אָדָם, often used of mankind in general. See Appendix 2 - Man.

[e] Who judges] Hebrew *šôp̄het* - שׁוֹפֵט. The verb is plural, agreeing with *'Elohîm* - אֱלֹהִים, and therefore refers to his action rather than his position as judge (Compare 75:7 and 94:2).

Day 123   Psalm 59:1-9

[1] Deliver from my enemies, my God;
Defend[a] from those who rise up against me.
[2] Deliver from those who do wickedness;
And from bloodthirsty men[b], O do save me!

[3] For - See![c] - they lie in ambush for my soul.
The mighty ones are gathered against me,
For no offence or sin of mine, O LORD.
[4] They run, make ready, though I'm not at fault.

Stir up yourself up to help me - Look and see! -
[5] O LORD of hosts, the God of Israel -
To punish all the nations - rouse yourself!
Spare none of those who transgress wickedly. ╫

[6] Each evening they come back. Just like a dog
They howl. Around the city prowl about.
[7] See! - from their mouths such gushing talk flows out.[d]
Swords in their lips, they question 'Who will hear?'

[8] But you yourself, O LORD, will laugh at them;
And all the nations you will mock in scorn.
[9] (O his great strength![e]). For you I will keep watch,
Because God is my tower and my defence.[f]

---

[a] Defend] Literally, 'raise me up [to a secure place]'. See Calvin and *Statenvertaling*.

[b] Men] Hebrew *'enôš* - אֱנוֹשׁ - Frail, mortal man. See Appendix 2 - Man.

[c] See!] Hebrew *hinneh* - הִנֵּה. So too v7. See Appendix 2 - Behold!

[d] Gushing talk flows out] The Hebrew verb means 'to pour', or 'to flow out'. AV, following the Septuagint, 'utter'.

[e] O his great strength] The Masoretic text has 'his strength'. Some Hebrew MSS, the Septuagint, Targums, and the ancient versions generally, have 'my

strength', as v17 (cf. v16) - hence PBV. The change is a shortening of one of the Hebrew letters (עזו to עזי). The AV adds *because of* his strength' - i.e. Saul. We have followed Motyer (1) with the text as it stands, seeing 'his strength!' as an exclamation referring to the LORD, following his dismissal of the threat of the nations (v8). See also de Burgh and Bonar, and Calvin's objection to 'my strength'.

[f] My tower and defence] One word in Hebrew. Here and v16.

___

Day 124   Psalm 59:10-17

[10] God in his kindness[a] will come to meet me,
And let me look on those who wait for me.[b]
[11] 'Don't let them die, lest my people forget.
By power scatter, sink them, Lord[c], Our Shield'.

[12] 'For their sin of mouth, word of their lips
Let them be taken in their arrogance;
And for the curse and lie that they repeat
[13] Consume in wrath! Consume!' They are no more!

And let them know that God in Jacob reigns.
He rules[d] unto the very ends of earth. ╫
[14] Let them come back at evening like a dog –
They'll howl. Around the city prowl about.[e]

[15] Make them to wander round about for food,
And let them pass the night and not be filled.[f]
[16] But as for me, I'll sing about your strength.
At morning will I sing your love with joy.[g]

For you have been my tower and defence,
And, in the day of trouble, my refuge.
[17] I will sing psalms of praise to you, my Strength.
For God is my defence: my gracious God.[h]

___

[a] Kindness] Hebrew *ḥeṣedh* - חֶסֶד. See Appendix 2 - Loving-kindness.
[b] Those who wait for me] 'Those that lie in wait for me, watching me spitefully'. See 5:9.
[c] Lord] My Lord. Hebrew *'Adhonay* - אֲדֹנָי. See Appendix 2 - Names of God.
[d] Reigns ... rules] One word in Hebrew which includes both meanings.
[e] Each evening ... prowl about] The meaning is different from v6. Their sin has become their punishment. See Calvin. See Newton (8) p 366.
[f] And let them pass the night] We have followed the Geneva Bible 'thogh thei

tarie al night'. The meaning hinges on the Hebrew word *lûn* - לן. There are two verbs with the same spelling. The commonest verb means 'to lodge', or 'to pass the night'. The other means 'to grumble' or 'to growl' = AV 'grudge'. See Motyer (1).

[g] Sing your love with joy] AV 'sing aloud', but the verb usually means 'shout for joy' or 'sing for joy'. 'Love' here is Hebrew *ḥeṣedh* - חֶסֶד. See Appendix 2 - Loving-kindness.

[h] My gracious God] Hebrew 'God of my mercy'. Hebrew *ḥeṣedh* - חֶסֶד. See Appendix 2 - Loving-kindness.

Day 125   Psalm 60:1-5

[1] O God, you have cast off and scattered us.
You have been angry. Turn to us again!
[2] You caused the land[a] to shake. You broke it up.
Mend where it's broken. It's about to fall.[b]

[3] You've made your people to see what is hard.
The wine of shaking[c] you've made us to drink.
[4] You give a banner to those who fear you,
That it may be displayed because of truth. ╫

[5] For those who are so very dear to you –
For your beloved[d] – give deliverance.
O give salvation with your own right hand!
And please do hear, give answer[e] unto me.

[a] Land] Hebrew *'ereṣ* - אֶרֶץ. The word may mean land or earth. The context seems to indicate 'the land'. See Appendix 2 - Earth.

[b] It's about to fall] It has been shaken and is tottering.

[c] The wine of shaking] 'Reeling' or 'staggering'; Geneva Bible 'the wine of giddiness'. i.e. having drunk the cup of God's displeasure they stagger helplessly. It is described in Isa. 51:17 as 'the cup of my fury'. Compare Zech. 12:2 in relation to the Gentiles.

[d] Those who are so very dear to you ... your beloved] We have expanded this word, which is not *ḥeṣedh* - חֶסֶד, but a word meaning to love greatly. It formed the special name given to Solomon (2 Sam. 12:25).

[e] Hear, give answer] The Hebrew *'anâ* - עָנָה. See Appendix 2 - Hear and Answer.

Day 126   Psalm 60:6-12

[6] God has declared this in his holiness.
'I will rejoice, and Shechem I'll divide.
The valley of Succoth I'll measure out.
[7] Gil-e-ad and Manasseh are both mine.

[a] Ephraim's the strong defence unto my head.
Judah's my sceptre[b]; [8] Moab's my wash-pot.
And over Edom I will throw my shoe.
Shout out Philistia, because of me!'

[9] O who will bring me to the fortress-town?[c]
And who will guide me unto Edom's land?[d]
[10] Is it not you, O God, who cast us off?
For with our armies you no longer go.

[11] From out of tribulation[e] give us help.
Deliverance from man[f] is all in vain.
[12] Through God we will contend courageously.
For he himself will trample on our foes.

---

[a] The strong defence unto my head] Most modern versions render 'helmet', but
to speak of Ephraim as 'the LORD's helmet' seems odd. Bonar sees a reference
to Deut. 33:16,17 as 'Ephraim full of power, comes in as being able to push the
foe with his horns'. The word is also used of the LORD as a stronghold, a place
of safety (Nahum 1:7), so translated by T&J Latin here (robur). As the Hebrew
word 'head' (ro 'š - ראש) also means 'first' or 'chief' we could perhaps translate
'my chief defence'.
[b] Sceptre] As A.V. Gen. 49:10. The lawgiver's symbol of office.
[c] Fortress town] Hebrew as Ps. 31:21. See the note there.
[d] Edom's land] Hebrew, 'Edom'.
[e] Out of tribulation] Gill 'perhaps here is particularly meant that time of trouble
which will be a little before the destruction of Antichrist'.
[f] Deliverance from man] Hebrew 'the salvation of man'. This is human (Hebrew
'adham - אדם) rescue and deliverance, contrasted with Divine intervention.

Day 127   Psalm 61

[1] God, hear my cry[a]; attend unto my prayer:
[2] From the earth's utmost end I'll call to you.
Yes, I will call when my heart's overwhelmed.
Lead to the rock that is too high for me.   →

^{3} For you have been a refuge unto me,
A tower of strength before the enemy.
^{4} For ever I will dwell within your tent[b],
And I will trust[c] the cover of your wings. ǂ

^{5} You heard my vows, O God, and gave to me
The heritage of those who fear your name.
^{6} Days upon days yet add unto the king![d]
Let his years be as generations long!

^{7} He will abide for ever before God.
Set truth and mercy[e] to watch over him.
^{8} So I'll sing psalms for ever to your name,
As I perform my vows from day to day.

---

^{a} Cry] The word is usually associated with rejoicing, but may be associated with prayer and supplication, as here.
^{b} Your tent] The word may be translated 'tent' or (the) 'Tabernacle'.
^{c} Trust] The Hebrew verb is ḥaṣâ - חָסָה 'to flee to a refuge and a place of safety'. The word translated 'refuge' in the previous verse is derived from it. See Appendix 2 - Refuge.
^{d} Days upon days yet add unto the king: Literally, 'days upon the days of the king you will add'.
^{e} Truth and mercy] Hebrew 'mercy and truth'. The word 'mercy' is Hebrew ḥeṣedh - חֶסֶד. See Appendix 2 - Loving-kindness.

Day 128   Psalm 62:1-7

^{1} On God alone[a] my soul waits silently.
It is from him that my salvation comes.
^{2} My rock and my salvation - only him!
He's my stronghold, and I will not be moved.

^{3} 'How long will you rush in upon[b] a man?'
(You'll all be slain and you'll be broken down[c],
Just like a bowing wall, or shaky fence).
^{4} Though he be high[d] they plan to bring him down.

Though their mouth blesses, they delight in lies,
And, in their heart, they're cursing inwardly[e]. ǂ
^{5} My soul, in silence wait[f] for God alone,
Because my expectation is from him.   →

117

⁶ My rock and my salvation - Him alone!
He is my stronghold, and I'll not be moved -
⁷ On God my glory and salvation rest.ᵍ
Rock of my strength - my refuge is in God.

ᵃ Alone] The Hebrew particle ʾakh (אַךְ) occurs 6 times in this Psalm, in verses
2,4,5,6. The AV translates 'truly', 'only', 'surely'. It may be used to confirm
something (Motyer (1) translates 'yes, indeed' throughout) or to restrict the
meaning, i.e. 'alone' or 'only'. It could, perhaps, be translated 'yes, but this
one thing'.
ᵇ Rush in upon a man] See de Burgh for the difficulty of translating this unique
word ('rush in'). The word used for 'man' here is Hebrew ʾadham - אָדָם - Man
as a child of Adam. See Ps. 62:9. See Appendix 2 - Man.
ᶜ You'll all be slain and you'll be broken down] One word in Hebrew. The word
commonly means 'to slay', but here it seems to be used in its root meaning of
'to break down' (a wall, a fence). Most modern versions amend the text to
read 'that you may murder him'. See Motyer (1).
ᵈ High] Hebrew 'excellency' or 'height', here refers to his social status (as king).
ᵉ In their heart they're cursing inwardly] 'In their heart' and 'inwardly' are here
used to translate 'in the inner part' (beqerebh - בְּקֶרֶב). See AV margin.
ᶠ In silence wait] The Hebrew verb means 'to be dumb, quiet, and inactive (in
consequence of some strong affection of the mind)'; 'to wait silently upon the
LORD'.
ᵍ On God my glory and salvation rest] Hebrew is literally, 'upon (Hebrew ʿal - עַל)
God is my salvation and my glory'.

Day 129   Psalm 62:8-12

⁸ O people, put your trust in him always.
Pour out your heart to him - God's our refuge. ╫
⁹ Men are but breathᵃ - the best of menᵇ a lie -
Put in the scales, they are as light as breath.

¹⁰ Don't put your trust in what oppression gains,
Nor vainly hope in spoils of robbery.
And, if you find that riches do increase,
Let not your heart depend upon such things.

¹¹ Once God has spoken - and twice I have heard -
That power and great strengthᶜ belong to God.
¹² That steadfast loveᵈ belongs to you My Lord.ᵉ
Repaying every manᶠ for what he does.

ᵃ Breath] The Hebrew word hebhel - הֶבֶל means 'breath', 'vapour', or 'vanity'.
ᵇ Men ... best of men] Hebrew 'sons of ʾadham - אָדָם', and ''sons of - ʾîš - אִישׁ. As

Ps. 49:2. See the note there.

^c That power and great strength] The Hebrew word means both.

^d Steadfast love] Hebrew *ḥeṣedh* - חֶסֶד. See Appendix 2 - Loving-kindness.

^e My Lord] Hebrew *'Adhonay* - אֲדֹנָי. See Appendix 2 - Names of God.

^f Every man] Hebrew *'îš* - אִישׁ - Man as an individual. It is used in a generic sense here = 'every man individually'. See Appendix 2 - Man.

Day 130   Psalm 63:1-5

¹ I'll seek you early, God – you are my GOD.
For you my soul thirsts. My flesh longs for you
In a dry, weary land that's waterless.

² Thus in the Holy Place I gazed on^a you

I looked to see your glory and your power, ^b
³ For better is your love^c than life itself.
Therefore, my lips will utter praise to you.
⁴ Thus will I magnify you while I live

I'll bless you for as long as I shall live,^d
And, in your name, I will lift up my hands.
⁵ My soul is filled with fatness and with fat.
With joyful lips^e my mouth shall bring you praise.

^a Gazed on] This is not the usual word for 'seeing'. It is linked with vision (1 Sam. 3:1) or a 'seer'.

^b Your glory and your power] Hebrew 'your power and your glory'.

^c Love] Hebrew *ḥeṣedh* - חֶסֶד. See Appendix 2 - Loving-kindness.

^d I'll bless you for as long as I shall live] We have reworded and repeated the last line of the previous stanza here.

^e With joyful lips] Literally, 'with lips of shoutings for joy'.

Day 131   Psalm 63:6-11

⁶ When in my bed I do remember you;
In the night-watches meditate on you.
⁷ For you have been a helper unto me.
In your wings' shadow I will sing for joy.

⁸ My soul is clinging closely after^a you,
And by your right hand you do hold me up.
⁹ Those who are seeking to destroy my soul –
they shall go down into the depths of earth.^b

¹⁰ They shall fall by the power of the sword.^c
The jackals' portion is what they shall be.
¹¹ The king shall joy in God. And all shall praise^d
who swear by him^e; the mouths of liars stopped.

---

^a Clinging closely after] The Hebrew is 'to cling after', which conveys the ideas of both staying close to the LORD, and following him closely.
^b The depths of earth] A synonym for Sheol (Hades). Cf. Eph. 4:9. See Appendix 2 - Sheol.
^c The power of the sword] Hebrew 'the hand of the sword'.
^d Praise] Hebrew *halal* - הָלַל. Most versions translate 'glory' or 'boast in' here.
^e Swear by him] i.e. those who are his faithful subjects. See Deut. 6:13. The Hebrew may refer to either God or the king, who is the type of the Lord Jesus.

Day 132   Psalm 64:1-6

¹ O God, my voice hear in my private prayer.^a
And guard my life from terror of the foe.
² Hide me from what the wicked ones conspire –
From raging workers of iniquity

³ Who sharpen up their tongue, just like a sword,
And they, like arrows, aim^b their bitter word,
⁴ To shoot in secret at the blameless one.
Fearless they shoot to take him by surprise.

⁵ They make each other strong for what is bad.
They talk of hiding snares – 'For who will see?'
⁶ Plan evil. Say, 'We have a perfect plan!'
The inner man, the heart, is O so deep!^c   →

---

^a Private prayer] The translation of most versions is 'complaint', but that word, as currently used, includes the meaning of dissatisfaction, finding fault, grievance, injustice, which is evidently not the meaning here. The word can have the meaning 'meditation' (BDB *Lexicon*). It can mean 'speaking' in a range of senses. The translation 'prayer' (AV) follows the Septuagint and Vulgate. Horsley translates 'my-secret-prayer', and adds 'I think the word שִׂיחַ [*śiaḥ*] when it signifies prayer, denotes private prayer, as distinct from public'.
^b Aim ...] Literally, 'tread [their bows to shoot] their arrows'. See note on 7:12.
^c This verse has been translated and interpreted in a number of ways. The overall meaning is clear. Literally, the Hebrew is 'they devise [or 'search out'] iniquities. They say, 'We have perfected a device devised', 'a searching search', or 'a perfect plan'. Ewald, *Syntax*, 'repetition to express a high, or the highest, degree'. Finally the psalmist concludes, 'And the-inward-part of man [or 'of

each'] and the heart [is] deep'.

Day 133   Psalm 64:7-10

[7] But, with an arrow, God will shoot at them.
And then they will be wounded suddenly.
[8] They're made to stumble: their tongue makes them fall.[a]
All those who look on them will flee away.[b]

[9] All men shall fear, and shall declare God's work,
And they shall understand what he has done.
[10] The righteous one joys in the LORD, and trusts[c].
All those of upright heart shall offer praise.

---

[a] They're made to stumble: their tongue makes them fall] The Hebrew is difficult -
'and they make it [or 'him'] to stumble; against them [even] their tongue' -
Tregelles (3). 'They make it to stumble' is generally taken as 'the third person
indefinite' = 'they are made to stumble'. The reference to the tongue indicates
that what they have spoken (v3-6) is self-destructive (cf. Ps. 7:15; Prov.
18:7,12:15; Ahithophel). Some commentators [Horsley, de Burgh, etc] relate
this (in the prophetic aspect of this Psalm) to the judgments on the Jews
following their awful declaration rejecting their Messiah (Matt. 27:25).
[b] Flee away] Most modern versions have 'shake (the head)'. The lexicons
(Gesenius *Lexicon*, BDB *Lexicon*, Koehler, and Davies *Lexicon*) point towards the
AV translation.
[c] Trusts] Hebrew *ḥaṣâ* - חָסָה. See Appendix 2 - Refuge.

Day 134   Psalm 65:1-8

[1] Praise is awaiting you in Zion, God;
And unto you the vow will be performed.
[2] Hearer of prayer, all flesh shall come to you.
Hearer of prayer, all flesh shall come to you.[a]

[3] Iniquities[b] have been too strong for me.
Atone for our transgressions. Cover them![c]
[4] *Blest*[d] is the one you choose and cause to come;
He is the one who'll dwell within your courts.

We're filled with all the goodness of your house -
Even the Temple - your own holy place.
[5] By awesome things performed in righteousness,
God, our salvation, you will answer us.   →

121

You are the trust of all the ends of earth,
and of those who are distant on the sea.
^{6} Who firmly sets the mountains by his strength,
And who is girded round about with power.

^{7} He stills the roar of seas, the roar of waves,
And the disturbance that the peoples make.
^{8} Dwellers in distant lands will fear your signs.
The springs of dawn, and sunset, shout for joy.

---

^{a} Hearer ... you] We have repeated the line.
^{b} Iniquities] Literally, things [or words] of iniquity.
^{c} Atone ... cover them] One word in Hebrew - 'cover' (*kaphar* - כָּפַר). It is the verb
linked to atonement throughout the Old Testament (e.g. in Lev. 16). The
Hebrew word for the mercy seat of the ark derives from it.
^{d} Blest] Hebrew '*ašrê* - אַשְׁרֵי. See Appendix 2 - Blessing.

Day 135 Psalm 65: 9-13

^{9} You visit and give water to the earth:
It is abundantly enriched by you.
For God's own river^a is with water filled.
When you've prepared it, you prepare their corn.^{b}

^{10} Its furrows you do water copiously;
By this its ridges^c you do settle down;
By heavy showers you then make it soft;
You bless its increase and its springing up.^{d}

^{11} And with your goodness you have crowned the year.
Your paths with plenty and with fatness^e flow.
^{12} They flow to pastures of the wilderness,
The little hills do gird themselves with joy.

^{13} The meadows are arrayed and clothed^f with flocks.
The valleys also are decked out with corn.
They shout for joy, and they together sing.
They shout for joy, and they together sing.^{g}

---

^{a} River] The Hebrew word (*pelegh* - פֶּלֶג - normally in the plural) means a brook,
rivulet, or stream, as in Psalms 1:3 and 46:4 (AV 'streams').
^{b} When you've prepared it, you prepare their corn] We have followed the

Statenvertaling and the *Dutch Annotations*. See de Burgh. The verb is used
twice. 'It' (with a feminine ending) is taken to refer to the earth.
[c] Ridges] The 'lists', or 'ridges', between furrows in ploughing.
[d] Its increase and its springing up] one word in Hebrew.
[e] With plenty and with fatness] One word in Hebrew. 'Fat' and 'fatness' in the Old
Testament is used to indicate superabundance.
[f] Arrayed and clothed] One word in Hebrew.
[g] We have repeated the last line.

Day 136   Psalm 66:1-9

[1] All earth as one[a] shout joyfully to God!

[2] Sing out with psalms the glory of his name,
And celebrate his glory in his praise,

[3] Say unto God, 'How awesome are your works!'

For through the greatness of your strength and power[b]
Your enemies shall yield[c] themselves to you.

[4] All earth shall worship, and sing psalms to you;
Yes, they will sing with psalms unto your name. ╫

[5] Come and behold the things that God has wrought:
Fearful in deed toward the sons of men.

[6] He did convert the sea into dry land.
Through flood[d] they trod. There we rejoiced in him

[7] By his great power, he forever rules.
His eyes upon the nations will keep watch
So let the rebels not exalt themselves.
So let the rebels not exalt themselves.[e] ╫

[8] You peoples, bless the one who is our God!
And make the voice of his praise to be heard.

[9] He is the one who keeps our soul alive,
And he does not allow our feet to slip.

[a] All earth as one] Hebrew 'all the earth' (Hebrew *erets* - אֶרֶץ), but 'shout joyfully'
is plural. Hence, either 'all the inhabitants of the earth' or 'all things of the
earth' is intended. So also in v4. See Appendix 2 - Earth.
[b] Strength and power] One word in Hebrew.
[c] Shall yield] Hebrew 'to lie', or 'to deceive'. AV mg. 'yield feigned obedience to
Thee', as also in Psalms 18:44 and 81:16.
[d] Flood] We have followed the AV here. The psalmist evidently refers historically

to the crossing of the tribes through the Jordan into the Promised Land. The Hebrew (*nahar* - נָהָר) is a river, or flood, and 'the river' is an expression for the Euphrates (Isa. 7:20). The word usually refers to 'permanent natural watercourses' (Unger, *Expository Dictionary of the Old Testament*), although it is used more generally in Jonah 2:3 (cf. Isa. 43:2; 66:12).

[e] So let the rebels not exalt themselves] We have repeated the previous line, which is emphasised by the addition of *Selah*. See Appendix 3.

Day 137　　Psalm 66:10-15

[10] For you, O God, have proved and tested[a] us:
Refining us as silver is refined.
[11] You made us go into the hunter's net:
You laid affliction heavy on our loins.[b]

[12] You caused man[c] to ride roughshod on our heads;
Through fire, and through the waters, we did come.
Into abundance you have brought us out.
[13, 14] Burnt offerings I'll bring into your house!

The vows my lips expressed I'll pay to you,
Which my mouth spoke when I was in distress.
[15] I'll offer you fat beasts as offerings;
With smoke[d] of rams; I'll offer[e] bulls and goats. ⧘

[a] Proved and tested] One word in Hebrew.
[b] Loins] This word occurs here and at 69:23 in the Psalms. It differs from the word the AV translates 'loins' in Ps. 38:7. Gesenius *Lexicon* gives the meaning as 'the lower part of the back', and derives it from an unused root 'to be strong'. It is the location of pain for a woman in childbirth (Isa.21:3, so BDB *Lexicon* as the meaning here). Gesenius relates the expression here to bearing a burden (cf. ESV). Koehler *Lexicon* 'the outer lumbar region'.
[c] Man] Hebrew *'enôš* - אֱנוֹשׁ - Frail, mortal man. See Appendix 2 - Man.
[d] Smoke] AV 'incense'. 'The steam and smoke of the burnt sacrifices ascending as a cloud' (Perowne). 'The sweet smoke', JPS.
[e] Offer] Hebrew *'asah* - עָשָׂה. A very general 'doing' word. Especially used of offering or sacrifice.

Day 138　　Psalm 66:16-20

[16] Come here and listen, all you who fear God.
I will declare what he did for my soul.
[17] Unto to him with my mouth I cried aloud,
And his high praise was underneath my tongue[a].　　→

¹⁸ If, in my heart, I have regard for sin,
Then My Lord^b will not listen unto me.
¹⁹ But God has heard! He heard my prayer. ²⁰ Blest God!
Turned not away his mercy, or my prayer.^c

---

^a High praise was underneath my tongue] Literally, 'exaltation underneath my tongue'. See Ps. 149:6, where the AV translates 'high praises'.
^b My Lord] Hebrew '*Adhonay* - אֲדֹנָי. See Appendix 2 - Names of God.
^c Turned not away his mercy or my prayer] Hebrew 'who has not turned away my prayer and his kindness from me'. 'Mercy' Hebrew *ḥeṣedh* - חֶסֶד. See Appendix 2 - Loving-kindness.

Day 139   Psalm 67

¹ God shall^a bless and be gracious^b unto us;
And on us^c he will make his face to shine. ╫
² So shall your way be known upon the earth,
and your salvation to all nations then.

³ The peoples shall give thanks to you, O God;
Yes, all the peoples shall give thanks to you.
⁴ The nations shall rejoice and shout for joy.^d
The peoples you will judge with equity.

For you will govern nations on the earth,
And you will lead and be the nations' Guide^e. ╫
⁵ The peoples will give thanks to you, O God;
Yes, all the peoples shall give thanks to you!

⁶ The earth shall then deliver its increase.
God, even our own God, will bless us then.
⁷ We shall be blessed by God. He shall be feared
By all the ends of earth he shall be feared^f.

---

^a God shall] Calvin comments on this Psalm 'I have used the imperative mood throughout the Psalm … although the future tense, which is employed in the Hebrew, would suit sufficiently well'. Most translations vary the tense between optative (a wish or request - AV v1 - 4a, 5), and future (AV v 4b and v6,7). We have taken it as a declaration of God's future purposes throughout, rather than as a hopeful prayer.
^b Bless and be gracious] We have interchanged 'bless' and 'be gracious' to preserve the metre.
^c On us] Hebrew 'with us' (as AV mg.). Motyer (1) 'through being present with us'.

125

De Burgh 'denoting his constant presence'. This differs from the 'upon us' of
Numb. 6:25.
^d Shout for joy] The verb may also be translated 'sing for joy' as AV.
^e Govern ... lead ... Guide] The Hebrew word combines all these meanings and we
therefore have expanded the previous line. It is used in Ps. 23:3, and also of
God guiding Israel to the land of promise (Ps. 78:14).
^f He shall be feared] We have repeated this phrase.

Day 140   Psalm 68:1-6

¹ Let God arise!^a Scatter his enemies!
Let them that hate him flee before his face^b!
² As smoke is driven, so drive them away,
Like melting wax when put before the fire.

³ So let the wicked perish before God,
But let the righteous ones be filled with joy.
Let them exult before the face of God,
And in their joyfulness they will be glad.

⁴ Sing unto God. Sing psalms unto his name.
In deserts^c run a road for him who rides.
His name is JAH!^d Exult before his face!
⁵ Father to orphans, and the widows' judge^e

God is within his holy dwelling place.^f
⁶ God makes the lonely to dwell in a home;
Frees prisoners to great prosperity. ^g
But rebels shall dwell in an arid land.

^a Let God arise] The Hebrew of the first three verses can be read as a definite
statement, 'God shall arise ... the wicked shall perish', etc. Compare Ps. 67.
^b Before his face] 'Before the face of' occurs nine times in the opening eight
verses of the Psalm, in relation to God, the fire, and 'his people'.
^c In deserts] As Isa. 40:3. The word is applied to the plains around Israel.
Compare v7; Isa. 57:14. Only here is it translated 'heavens' by the AV.
^d JAH] Hebrew YAH - יָהּ. A shortened form of יהוה, the LORD, JEHOVAH. See Appendix
2 - Names of God.
^e Judge] Hebrew dayyan - דַּיָּן from the Hebrew dîn - דִּין. i.e. ensuring the fair
treatment of the most vulnerable and needy. See Appendix 2 - Law -
Judgment.
^f Holy dwelling place] The expression is used of the Temple.
^g Great prosperity] Hebrew 'the prosperities'. The word is only used here. See de
Burgh, and Gill. Orphans, widows, the lonely, and those who are bound, all see

improvement to their condition. Only (Hebrew *'akh* - אַךְ) for rebels is it otherwise. AV, and the older translations = 'which are bound with chains'.

Day 141   Psalm 68:7-14

[7] O God, before your people you went out.
When you were marching through the desert waste[a] ╫
[8] Earth quaked. The heavens poured out before God;
This Sinai[b] faced by God, by Israel's God.

[9] Abundant rain[c] you will send down, O God.
Establishing your weary heritage.
[10] Your company of people[d] lived in it,
Set[e] by your goodness for the poor, O God.

[11] My Lord[f] will give the word[g] - it is announced.
A mighty troop of women make it known.[h]
[12] The kings of armies flee; they surely flee,
And she that stays at home divides the spoil.

[13] Will you lie down among the cattle pens [i]
Silver-winged dove; feathers of yellow gold?
[14] In the Almighty's[j] scattering of kings,[k]
On dark Zalmon[l] you shall be white as snow. [m]

---

[a] Desert waste] Not the usual word for desert or wilderness. A different word from v4. Rather 'wasted land' or 'wasteland'. See Ps. 78:40 and 106:14.

[b] This Sinai] This is the literal Hebrew, 'Sinai indeed' or Sinai itself' would be possible translations. AV and others supply 'was moved', 'quaked', cf. Judg. 5:5.

[c] Abundant rain] Literally, 'a rain of gifts'. The word ('gifts') is the usual one for freewill offerings in Lev. 22 and elsewhere. See de Burgh.

[d] Company of people] AV 'congregation'. The word is derived from the verb 'to live' and could be translated 'living creatures'. It is also used of a 'company' of soldiers.

[e] Set] This is the same Hebrew word as we have translated 'establishing' (and the AV translates 'didst confirm') in the previous verse.

[f] My Lord] Hebrew *'Adhonay* - אֲדֹנָי. See Appendix 2 - Names of God.

[g] The word] the spoken word. Hebrew *'omer* - אֹמֶר (from *'amar* - אָמַר 'to say'). See Appendix 2 - Word.

[h] It is announced ... known] The participle is feminine = 'the women proclaiming are a numerous host' (so Geneva Bible). The deliverance of Israel was often celebrated by the women - Exod. 15:20; Judg. 5:1; 1 Sam. 18:6. See too v25.

[i] Cattle pens] So Tregelles (3). AV 'pots'. This word, in the dual number, has been variously translated. Newton (9) (following Keble), considers it 'the place

127

devoted to the preparation of sacrifices'. See Ezek. 40:43 (where the AV
translates the word 'hooks').
^j The Almighty] Hebrew *Šadday* - שַׁדַּי (Shaddai). See Appendix 2 - Names of God.
^k Scattering of kings] The Hebrew adds 'in it', i.e. the land.
^l Dark Zalmon] Zalmon is usually identified with the hill referred to in Judg. 9:48.
It is assumed that the whiteness of the snow is contrasted with the darkness of
the hill. Gesenius *Lexicon* gives the meaning of Zalmon as 'shady'. The Jewish
commentators Kimchi and Rashi give the meaning as 'darkness' or 'the shadow
of death'. The Jerusalem Bible translates 'Dark Mountain'; so too Newton.
Newton (10) suggests the symbolism is of the purified aspect of the land when
the LORD intervenes (Ps. 48:4,5); likewise de Burgh.
^m You shall be white as snow] We have followed Gesenius *Lexicon* for the meaning
of this verb. We follow the *Analytical Hebrew and Chaldee Lexicon* (Bagster) in
parsing this as hiphil future second person singular masculine.

Day 142   Psalm 68:15-23

¹⁵ A mighty mountain^a is the mount Bashan;
Mountain of high peaks is the mount Bashan.
¹⁶ Why look in envy, mountains of high peaks,
Upon the mount where God desired to dwell?

Truly the LORD will dwell there evermore.
¹⁷ Double ten thousand are God's chariots,
The number swelled, yes, many thousand times:^b
Among them is the One who is My Lord.^c

Sinai is now within the holy place.^d
¹⁸ You did go up - ascended up on high -
And you did lead captive captivity.
You have received and given gifts to man.^e

Yes, for the rebels he has given gifts,^f
That God whose name is JAH^g might dwell with them.
¹⁹ Blest be My Lord^h who bears usⁱ day by day -
The GOD^j who is salvation unto us. ✝

²⁰ GOD of deliverances is our GOD.
Ways out from death are from My Lord^k, the LORD.
²¹ But God will smite his foes upon the head -
His head of hair^l that goes on in his guilt.   →

²² My Lord has said, 'From Bashan I will bring –
And from the depths of sea I'll bring them back;
²³ So that your foot may paddle in the blood.
Your dogs' tongue finds its portion from your foes'.

ᵃ A mighty mountain] Literally, 'a mountain of God'. 'Of God' is frequently used in Scripture as an adjective describing greatness - e.g. Joel 3:3 literally, Nineveh was 'a city great unto God'. We have followed B.W, Newton (10) in v15 and v16. It is difficult to see how Bashan can be described as a 'hill of God' (AV) when it is frequently linked with insolence and earthly strength; cf. 'bulls of Bashan', Ps 22:12, etc.

ᵇ The number swelled, yes, many thousand times] Literally, 'thousands of repetition'. Perhaps 'thousands on thousands repeated'.

ᶜ My Lord] Hebrew 'Adhonay - אֲדֹנָי. See Appendix 2 - Names of God.

ᵈ Sinai is now within the holy place] We understand this to mean that the presence of God and holiness seen on Mount Sinai transfers to the Holy Place, God's sanctuary. See Newton (8).

ᵉ Received and given gifts to man] The Hebrew is 'received gifts to be in (or 'for') man'. The inspired quotation in Eph. 4:8 is the *giving* of gifts to man, which we have added to our translation. *The Dutch Annotations* comment 'Thou hast taken gifts (for to divide) among men [for such a use of the word 'to take' see Gen. 12:15; Hos. 14:3]'. Note the use of the word in Exod. 25:2; 35:5, meaning 'to bring an offering'.

ᶠ Yes, for the rebels he has given gifts] The Hebrew is simply 'Yes the rebellious'. Commentators differ as to whether 'yes the rebellious' should be connected with what has gone before (the giving of gifts), which is countenanced by the ancient versions and the majority of commentators, or with what follows ('that God might dwell with them).

ᵍ God whose name is JAH] Hebrew simply YAH 'Elohîm - יָהּ אֱלֹהִים - see v4.

ʰ My Lord] Hebrew 'Adhonay - אֲדֹנָי. See Appendix 2 - Names of God.

ⁱ Who bears us] the Hebrew verb means 'to put a burden on someone else' or 'to bear a burden'. AV and Calvin assume favourably putting 'benefits' on us. Modern translations assume bearing burdens. Jerome, Horne, and others translate 'carry us', which we have adopted; as the lost sheep was carried.

ʲ The GOD] literally, 'The *El*' ('*El* -אֵל)', emphasising both his uniqueness and his power. See Appendix 2 - Names of God.

ᵏ My Lord] Hebrew 'Adhonay - אֲדֹנָי. The unique word for the lordship of God. Here and v22. See Appendix 2 - Names of God.

ˡ His head of hair] Hebrew 'hairy scalp'. Here the rebellious sinner is personified. This is a mark of proud and arrogant sinners; cf. Absalom (2 Sam. 14:25,26).

Day 143   Psalm 68:24-35

²⁴ They've seen your ways of going forth, O GOD.
My God, My King's waysᵃ in the Holy Place;
²⁵ Singers before, musicians after them,
Among them young girlsᵇ beating tambourines.   →

26 In the assemblies, O bless God, My Lord! [c]
You who are from the fount of Israel!
27 There's little Benjamin, he who subdues; [d]
With Judah's princes and their company. [e]

Princes of Zebulun and Naphtali -
28 God gave you strength[f]. Make strong your work, O God! [g]
29 Your Temple[h] is found at[i] Jerusalem.
Therefore, a gift shall kings bring unto you.

30 Rebuke the living creature of the reeds,[j]
The herd of bulls, the peoples' calves[k] with them.
With gifts of silver they prostrate themselves.[l]
He scattered nations that delight in wars.

31 The foremost men[m] shall out of Egypt come,
And Cush shall haste to stretch its hands to God.[n]
32 O kingdoms of the earth, sing unto God,
And sing with psalms to him who is My Lord . [o] ╫

33 To him who on the highest heaven[p] rides -
The heavens which are from the ancient times.
See[q], he gives voice. It is a voice of strength.
34 Ascribe the strength and power[r] unto God.

His majesty is over Israel.
His strength is in the skies. 35 God to be feared!
'Out of your holy places - Israel's GOD!'
He gives the people strength and might. Bless God!

---

[a] Ways] Hebrew 'goings', as the previous line [ways of going forth].

[b] Young girls] Hebrew *'alamôth* - עֲלָמוֹת. Maidens, unmarried young women (as Isa. 7:14). See v11.

[c] My Lord] Hebrew *'A<u>dh</u>onay* - אֲדֹנָי. See Appendix 2 - Names of God.

[d] He who subdues] Hebrew, subdues or rules 'them'. There is obvious difficulty in taking Benjamin as ruling Israel, and better to understand this as Benjamin subduing Israel's enemies. So Newton (10).

[e] Their company] The Hebrew word means 'to bring together'; and 'to pile up', or 'cast' stones, 'to stone'. Newton (10) favours the latter, referring to Judah a judicial role in punishment - 'their minister of judgment'. See also Perowne, note.

[f] God gave you strength] Hebrew 'Your God commanded your strength'. Many

Hebrew manuscripts, Septuagint and Syriac read 'Command (summon) your
strength, O God'. This is followed by ESV, NIV, RSV, etc.
^g Make strong your work] Hebrew adds 'for us'. See Perowne, note.
^h Your Temple] Literally, 'your Palace' (Hebrew *hêkhal* - הֵיכָל), a word often used of
the Temple (cf. 5:7; 11:4; 79:1; 138:2).
ⁱ Found at] Hebrew is literally, 'over' ('*al* - עַל).
^j The living creature of the reeds] Literally, 'the living thing of the reeds'. "The
beast of the reed' evidently denotes Egypt or its head', Newton (10). So the AV
margin.
^k The herd of bulls, the people's calves] This is generally taken as the leaders
followed by the people (particularly the younger).
^l They prostrate themselves: So Gesenius *Lexicon*. Motyer (1) notes this is a
singular participle and therefore translates 'each humbling himself' (AV 'till
every one submit himself').
^m Foremost men] The meaning is uncertain. The ancient versions translate
'ambassadors', Gesenius *Lexicon* 'rich nobles'. AV 'princes'.
ⁿ Shall haste to stretch its hands] literally, 'its hands shall run'.
^o My Lord] Hebrew '*Adhonay* - אֲדֹנָי. See Appendix 2 - Names of God.
^p Highest heaven] Hebrew 'heaven of heavens'.
^q See] Hebrew - *hen* - הֵן See Appendix 2 - Behold!
^r Strength and power] As v28,33,35. One word in Hebrew.

Day 144   Psalm 69:1-5

¹ Save me, O God. The waters reach my soul.
² I sink in a deep mire. I cannot stand.
I have now come where the deep waters are:
The overwhelming flood sweeps over me.

³ I faint with crying out. My throat is dry.
My eyes have failed, while I wait for my God.
⁴ Those who have hatred for me without cause
Are more in number than hairs of my head.

My strong destroyers – lying enemies –
Though I stole nothing, yet I must repay.
⁵ You, O God, have known my foolishness;
My trespasses have not been hid from you.

Day 145   Psalm 69:6-12

⁶ Those who wait for you, My Lord^a - LORD of Hosts,
Let them not be ashamed because of me.
And those who seek you, God of Israel,
Let them not be perplexed because of me.   →

131

^{7} It's for your sake that I have borne reproach.
Shame and perplexity^b covered my face.
^{8} From my own brothers I am now estranged:
A foreigner unto my mother's sons.

^{9} The zeal for your house has consumed me so,
Reproaches cast at you now fall on me.
^{10} And so I wept, and my soul kept the fast,
And yet it brought reproaches upon me.

^{11} I put on sackcloth to show my remorse,
And I became a by-word unto them.
^{12} I am the talk of all those at the gate,^{c}
Yes, even drunkards make their song of me.

---

^{a} My Lord] Hebrew *'Adhonay* - אֲדֹנָי. See Appendix 2 - Names of God.
^{b} Shame and perplexity] One word in Hebrew – from the same root as the word
   we have translated 'perplexed' in v6.
^{c} I am the talk of all those at the gate] i.e. 'all those that sit in the gate talk about
   me'. The Hebrew word translated 'talk' here is *śiaḥ* - שִׂיחַ. It includes the
   meaning of complaint or displeasure. With the preposition that follows, it
   indicates 'against me'.

Day 146   Psalm 69:13-21

^{13} But, as for me, my prayer is to you, LORD,
At such a time as pleases you, O God.
In your great loving-kindness^a answer me -
Give answer in your saving faithfulness.

^{14} Rescue me from the mire (don't let me sink) -
From those who hate me - from the waters deep.
^{15} Let not the flood engulf me, nor the deep;
Let not the pit close up its mouth on me.

^{16} Give answer LORD - your steadfast love^b is good -
In your abundant mercies^c turn to me.
^{17} I am your servant. Do not hide your face.
I am in trouble. Answer speedily.   →

132

¹⁸ Draw near unto my soul and ransom it.
Deliver me from those who are my foes.
¹⁹ You know how I'm reproached, shamed and perplexed;
All those who trouble me are seen by you.

²⁰ My heart is heavy. Broken by reproach.
No one to pity or to comfort me.
²¹ They gave me bitter poison for my food;
They gave me vinegar to quench my thirst.

---

^a Loving-kindness] Hebrew *ḥeṣedh* - חֶסֶד. See Appendix 2 - Loving-kindness.
^b Mercy] As v16.
^c Abundant mercies] 'Great, tender mercies'. Deep feelings of compassion
aroused by the sight of weakness or suffering (Hebrew *raḥamîm* - רַחֲמִים).

Day 147   Psalm 69:22-28

²² As for their table, let it be a snare.
To those in peace^a cause it to be a trap.
²³ Darken their eyes so that they cannot see,
And make their loins to shake unceasingly.^b

²⁴ Pour out your indignation upon them,
And let your burning anger overtake.
²⁵ Make desolate the place in which they live;
Let no one dwell within their tents at all.

²⁶ For they pursue the one whom you did smite.
They tell the pain of those whom you did wound.
For they pursue the one whom you did smite.
They tell the pain of those whom you did wound.^c

²⁷ Add unto their iniquity yet more
Let them not enter to your righteousness
²⁸ Put them out of the book of those who live^d
And with the righteous do not write them down

---

^a To those in peace ...] The Septuagint and Rom. 11:9 render this Hebrew word by
'for a recompense' (*antapodoma* - ἀνταπόδωμα). This seems to indicate a
different reading and pointing of the Hebrew text, which would give 'for
retributions' (See BHS, Alford on the N.T., etc).
^b And make their loins to shake] The Septuagint and Rom. 11:10 translate 'and

bend their back'. See the note on Ps. 66:11
^c We have repeated this verse, which is the key to understanding the reason for
the judgment sought.
^d Put them out of the book of those who live: The Geneva Bible notes take this to
mean, 'let them be known as reprobate'. See too Dr Gill.

Day 148   Psalm 69:29-36

²⁹ But still I am afflicted and in pain.
O God, let your salvation lift me up.
³⁰ I will give praise unto God's name with song,
And magnify it with my grateful thanks.

³¹ This also is more pleasing to the LORD
Than is an ox, a bull with horns and hooves.
³² The humble ones shall see this and be glad.
Your heart shall live, who thus seek after God.

³³ The needy and the poor^a the LORD will hear.
He won't despise his people when they're bound.
³⁴ The heavens and the earth give praise to him,
The seas and every moving thing in them.

³⁵ For God saves Zion. Judah's cities builds
So they may stay and take possession there.
³⁶ His servant's seed shall then inherit it;
In it will dwell all those who love his name.

---

^a The needy and the poor] One word. The Hebrew word has both meanings.

Day 149   Psalm 70

¹ O God, to rescue and deliver me; ^a
O LORD, unto my help; Act speedily!^b
² Shame, and confuse, those who seek for my soul;
Turn back, disgrace, those who wish harm to me.

³ And may their shame cause them to be turned back -
All those who jeer at me, 'Aha!' 'Aha!'
⁴ Let all who seek you be glad and rejoice.^c
And let those who love your salvation speak.   →

'God be exalted' may they ever say.
⁵ I'm poor and needy. Hasten to me, God!
You are my Help and my Deliverer;
You are the LORD, so please make no delay.

ᵃ Rescue and deliver] One word in Hebrew.
ᵇ The grammar of v1 is unusual. We have translated literally, rather than supplying
   'make haste' as the AV in the first line.
ᶜ Rejoice] The Hebrew adds 'in you'.

Day 150   Psalm 71:1-8

¹ In you, the LORD, I've taken my refuge,ᵃ
So do not let me ever be ashamed.
² Deliver; rescue, in your righteousness.
O turn your earᵇ to me. Deliver me!

³ Be a strongholdᶜ where I may always go.
You gave commandment that I should be saved,
For you're a rock and fortress unto me.
⁴ Rescue me from the wicked's hand, my God.

Rescue meᵈ from the cruel and unjust,
⁵ Because you are my hope, My Lordᵉ - the LORD -
My trust from youth - ⁶ My mainstay from the womb.
You, from my mother's bodyᶠ, drew me out

My praise shall be of you continually.
⁷ To many I've become a prodigy,
You are my sure refuge - ⁸ my mouth is filled -
Filled with your praise, your honour, all day long.

ᵃ I've taken my refuge] AV 'I put my trust'. Hebrew ḥaṣâ - חָסָה. See Appendix 2 -
   Refuge.
ᵇ Turn your ear] Hebrew 'incline your ear'.
ᶜ Stronghold] Hebrew 'a rock of habitation'.
ᵈ Rescue me] We have repeated 'rescue me' from the previous line, which, in this
   translation, falls in the previous stanza. The Hebrew is 'from the grasp of an
   unjust and cruel one' (singular as 'the wicked' in the previous line).
ᵉ My Lord] Hebrew ʾAdhonay - אֲדֹנָי. See Appendix 2 - Names of God.
ᶠ Body] Literally, 'bowels'. The word is used of Abraham in Gen. 15:4, but may be
   taken here as a synonym for 'the womb'. 'That part of the body through which
   people come into existence' (!) Koehler Lexicon.

Day 151   Psalm 71:9-18

⁹ Don't cast me off in the time of old age;
When my strength fails, do not forsake me then.
¹⁰ Because my enemies against me speak,
And those who watch my soul confer as one.

¹¹ They say of me, that God's forsaken him,
'Pursue and seize him. None will rescue him!'
¹² O God, do not be far away from me.
My God, unto my help; Act speedily!

¹³ Shame, and consume, those who oppose my soul;
With scorn and shameᵃ clothe those who would harm me.
¹⁴ But as for me - I'll always wait in hope;
I'll add to all your praise yet more and more.

¹⁵ My mouth will tellᵇ about your righteousness,
And tell of your salvation all the day
For the numbers of them I don't know!
¹⁶ I'll come with My Lord'sᶜ strengthᵈ, even the LORD's.

I will commemorate your righteousness,
Even the righteousness of you alone.
¹⁷ O God, you have instructed me from youth;
Since then I have declared your wondrous works.

¹⁸ And to old age, as well (when I'm grey-haired).
O God, I ask, do not forsake me then!
Till to the generationᵉ I declare
Your armᶠ, your might, to all who are to come.

ᵃ Shame] This is a different Hebrew word from the word used in the first line of
   the verse. It includes dishonour, perplexity and disgrace.
ᵇ Tell] The Hebrew word is primarily used of giving a written account.
ᶜ My Lord] Hebrew *Adhonay* - יָנֹדֲא. See Appendix 2 - Names of God.
ᵈ Strength] Hebrew plural. Perhaps meaning 'mighty acts'. Otherwise, it may be
   the plural of magnitude - 'The LORD's great strength'.
ᵉ The generation] Most versions supply 'this', 'the next' etc, to 'generation'.
ᶠ Your arm] This is the Hebrew word. Most commentators avoid the metaphor
   and translate 'strength' or 'power.

Day 152   Psalm 71:19-24

¹⁹ Your righteousness, O God, is very high.
You've done great things. O God, who is like you?
²⁰ Great, grievous troubles you have made me see^a,
You will return and give me life again.

And from earth's depths you'll raise me up again.
²¹ You'll make me greater^b. Turn to comfort me.
²² I will give thanks to you upon the lyre^c,
And for your truth I'll thank you, O my God.

I will sing psalms unto you with the harp,
To you, the Holy One of Israel.
²³ My lips will sing for joy^d when I sing psalms^e
Together with my soul, which you've redeemed.

²⁴ My tongue will meditate^f all the day long
All day it will speak of your righteousness.
For they are put to shame, and are confused,
Who tried to find a way to do me harm.

---

^a Made me see] In this verse 'me' in the written text (*kethîbh* - כְּתִיב) is changed by
the Jewish Masoretes (*qerê* - קְרֵי) to 'us'. As the AV, we have followed the text
as written.
^b You'll make me greater] Literally, 'you will increase my greatness'.
^c Lyre] Hebrew 'with a vessel of a *nebhel*'. AV 'psaltery'; AV mg 'the instrument of
psaltery'. Hebrew *nebhel* - נֶבֶל. See Appendix 2 - Harps.
^d Sing for joy] The verb may also be translated 'shout for joy'.
^e Sing psalms] Hebrew 'sing psalms to you'.
^f Meditate ... speak] Koehler *Lexicon*, 'to mutter while meditating'. The Hebrew
word is used for 'meditate', and also to 'utter speech' (whilst doing so).

Day 153   Psalm 72:1-7

¹ Give your right judgments^a to the king, O God;
And give your righteousness to the king's son.
² Your people's cause he'll judge^b with righteousness,
Judge with right judgment your afflicted ones^c.

³ The mountains will bring to the people peace.
The hills will do the same by righteousness.^d
⁴ The poor ones of the people he'll judge right; ^e

The children of the needy[f] he will save.　　→

And the oppressor he will break and crush,
[5] They'll fear you just as long as there is sun.
While shines the moon; through generations long.[g]
[6] He shall come down as rain on the mown grass.

He'll come as showers watering the earth.
[7] So shall the righteous[h] flourish in his days;
Abundant peace shall then be multiplied,
Until the time the moon shall be no more.

[a] Right judgments] Hebrew *mišpaṭ* - מִשְׁפָּט. As in v2b. See Appendix 2 - Law - Judgment.
[b] Your people's cause he'll judge] Hebrew *dîn* - דִּין. See Appendix 2 - Law - Judgment.
[c] Afflicted ones] Or 'poor ones', as in v4.
[d] The mountains ... righteousness] We understand this to mean that *both* the mountains and hills will bring forth peace in (or through) righteousness (so the Geneva Bible).
[e] He'll judge right] Hebrew *šaphaṭ* - שָׁפַט, usually translated 'to judge', also conveys the meaning of vindicating or avenging.
[f] Needy] Hebrew singular.
[g] Through generations long] Hebrew 'generation of generations'.
[h] Righteous] Hebrew singular.

Day 154　　Psalm 72:8-11

[8] From sea to sea will his dominion be,
And from the River to the ends of earth.
[9] Before him shall the desert dwellers bow,
He'll make his enemies to lick the dust[a].

[10] The kings of Tarshish, and lands of the sea,[b]
Shall bring their gifts and tribute unto him.[c]
The kings of Sheba and Seba, likewise,
For, with their presents, they too shall draw near.

[11] All kings shall bow in reverence to him;
All nations shall unto him homage[d] pay.
Before him every king shall prostrate fall,[e]
And every nation shall his servant be.[f]

[a] Lick the dust] See Mic. 7:17. To be completely humiliated.

^b Lands of the sea] Hebrew 'coastlands'.
^c Gifts and tribute unto him] Hebrew 'shall return a gift'. The expression is used
   for bringing tribute (see 2 Kgs. 17:3).
^d Homage ... obey his command] The verb means 'service' of a servant or slave. It
   is used of worship, cf. Exod. 3:12; Deut. 4:19.
^e Shall prostrate fall] An intensive form of the Hebrew verb 'to bow' is used,
   indicating to lie prostrate on the ground. This is a type of the 'Greater than
   Joseph', cf. Gen. 42:6.
^f Before him every king ... and every nation shall his servant be] We have added
   this alternative translation of the first two lines.

Day 155   Psalm 72:12-14

¹² He'll save the needy when he calls for help.
And the afflicted, when no one gives aid.
¹³ He'll have compassion on the one who's weak^a.
And have compassion on the needy one.

And the souls of the needy ones he'll save,
¹⁴ For he will give a ransom for their soul
To free them from deceit and violence,
And their blood will be precious in his eyes.

^a 'Afflicted' (v12), 'weak' (v13)] Both of these words are translated 'poor' by the
   AV. We have given them their distinctive meanings.

Day 156   Psalm 72:15-20

¹⁵ He shall live^a, and be given Sheba's gold,^b
Prayer shall be made for him continually.
And they shall bless him throughout all the day.
¹⁶ Corn in abundance^c shall be in the land; ^d

It shall be even on the mountain top.^e
Its fruit shall shake like trees of Lebanon.^f
Those from the city shall flourish as grass.^g
¹⁷ So shall his name endure^h for evermore.

His name shall prosper while the sun still shines.ⁱ
And men shall count themselves as blest in him.^j
All nations shall declare his happiness.^k
¹⁸ Blest be the LORD God: God of Israel.   →

For he alone is doing wondrous things.
[19] Blest be his splendid[l] name for evermore.
His glory shall fill all the earth. Amen!
Amen. [20] The prayers of David[m] are fulfilled[n].

---

[a] He shall live] i.e. the king. cf. 'Long live the king!' (1 Kgs. 1:39).

[b] Be given Sheba's gold] The Hebrew is 'and he (or one) shall give gold of Sheba'.
It is not clear who is the giver, but commentators and versions are united in
identifying the one who receives with the one 'who shall live' in the first part of
the verse; as in v10.

[c] In abundance] *Hapax legomenon.* Kimchi, Calvin, AV, Hengstenberg, Tregelles
(1) 'a [small] handful of corn'. The Peshitta, Rashi, Luther, Gesenius *Lexicon*,
Jewish translations, Tregelles (3) translate 'abundance' from a different Hebrew
root. This is adopted by virtually all modern versions. But note Tregelles (1) 'A
handful of corn from which vast returns are obtained'.

[d] The land] Hebrew *'erets* - אֶרֶץ. We translate 'the land' (i.e. Israel) because the
word has the definite article, and is here compared with 'the Lebanon'. See
Appendix 2 - Earth.

[e] Even on the mountain top] Compare Isa. 7:25.

[f] Shall shake like trees of Lebanon] Hebrew, 'shall shake like Lebanon'.

[g] As grass] Hebrew, 'as the grass of the earth'.

[h] Endure] Hebrew, 'be'.

[i] While the sun still shines] Hebrew, 'before the face of the sun'.

[j] Men shall ... in him] Hebrew, 'they shall bless themselves in him'.

[k] Declare his happiness] Hebrew *'ašar* - אָשַׁר, as Psalm 1:1. A different word from
that used in the previous and following lines (*barakh* - בָּרַךְ).

[l] Splendid] 'Glorious' Hebrew *kabôdh* כָּבוֹד. From the same root as 'glory' in the
following line.

[m] David] Hebrew, 'David, the son of Jesse'.

[n] Fulfilled] 'Fulfilled', 'finished', or 'completed'. We take this to be a statement
that, when the things related in this Psalm shall come to pass, the prayers of
David shall reach their conclusion and fulfilment. See 2 Sam. 23:1-7. Most
metrical versions omit verses 19 and 20, but include the 'doxology' in other
'books' of the Psalms. See the Sandemanian psalter for another metrical
version of these verses.

Book 3

Psalms 73 - 89

Day 157   Psalm 73:1-12

¹ Yes, surely, God is good to Israel –
Even to such as are of a pure heart.
² But, as for me, my feet were almost gone.
The steps I took had nearly slipped away.

³ Because I envied vain and foolish men.ᵃ
I saw the wicked in prosperity;
⁴ For in their death there are not any pains,
And in their body they are fit and strong.ᵇ

⁵ They're not in trouble as are other men;ᶜ
Nor are they plagued and smittenᵈ as mankind.ᵉ
⁶ Therefore is pride a chainᶠ about their neck;
And with a robe of violence they dress.

⁷ Because of fatness their eye bulges out;
They overflow with all their heart could wish.
⁸ They scoff and speak with malice wickedly;
It is as from a high place that they speak.

⁹ They set their mouth within the heavens high;
It is as though their tongue struts through the earth.
¹⁰ Therefore his people turn back to this place,ᵍ
And a full measure shall be poured to them.

¹¹ And so they say, 'How can it be GOD knows?'
And 'Is there knowledge with the Most High God?'ʰ
¹² Take note of them!ⁱ – these are the wicked ones.
These alwaysʲ prosper and increase in wealth.

ᵃ Vain and foolish men] One word in Hebrew. We have supplied 'men'.
ᵇ In their body ... fit and strong] Hebrew, 'Fat is their strength'. Geneva Bible,
  'lustie and strong'] *Dutch Annotations*, 'healthy and lively'.
ᶜ Men] Hebrew *'enôš* - אֱנוֹשׁ - Frail, mortal man. See Appendix 2 - Man.
ᵈ Plagued and smitten] One word in Hebrew, especially used of Divine
  chastisement (see v14; Isa. 53:4).
ᵉ Mankind] Hebrew *'adham* - אָדָם - Man as a child of Adam. See Appendix 2 -
  Man.
ᶠ Chain] We may take this as a necklace. Compare the reference to clothing in the
  next line. Pride is their adornment (cf. Prov. 1:9). It is nevertheless true that
  pride also enchains them.
ᵍ To this place] Newton (1) takes this as a reference to the attraction of the Jews

[h] The Most High God] Hebrew *Elyôn* - עֶלְיוֹן. See Appendix 2 - Names of God.
[i] Take note of them!] AV 'behold'. Hebrew *hinneh* - הִנֵּה. See Appendix 2 - Behold!
[j] Always] In Hebrew a word meaning 'of long or perpetual duration'. AV 'in the world'.

Day 158   Psalm 73:13-22

[13] Surely, it is in vain I've cleansed my heart.
And that I washed my hands in innocence.[a]
[14] Because I have been stricken[b] all day long,
And every morning brought my chastisement.

[15] If I had said that I will speak like this,
Truly[c], I'd be a traitor to your sons.[d]
[16] So, when I pondered how I might know this,
It was a thing of trouble, in my eyes –

[17] Till I went in the Holy Place[e] of GOD;
Till I considered what their end will be.
[18] Yes, surely, you've put them where they will slip![f]
In utter ruins[g] you then cast them down.

[19] How suddenly they are made desolate!
They are consumed with terrors utterly.
[20] As when one wakes up from a dream, My Lord,[h]
When you rise up, their shadow[i] you will scorn.

[21] For my heart was embittered and was grieved,[j]
My feelings hurt, as pierced right through my side. [k]
[22] For I was brutish, and I did not know:
Toward you I was even like a beast.

---

[a] Washed my hands in innocence] See Ps. 26:6; Isa. 1:15-17; Matt. 27:24.
[b] Stricken] Literally, 'plagued'.
[c] Truly] Hebrew *hinneh* - הִנֵּה. See Appendix 2 - Behold!
[d] To your sons] Hebrew 'to the generation of your sons', i.e. as in Ps. 14:5.
[e] Holy Place] The Sanctuary (Hebrew *miqdaš* - מִקְדָּשׁ), used of the Tabernacle (Exod. 25:8) and the Temple (1 Chr. 22:19).
[f] Where they will surely slip] Literally, 'in slippery places'. The word is related to the smooth stone used as a lot (see v26 AV 'portion'), by which land was divided. This is their portion.

^{g} Utter ruins] The word only occurs again in Ps. 74:3.

^{h} My Lord] Hebrew *'Adhonay* - אֲדֹנָי. See Appendix 2 - Names of God.

^{i} Shadow] Hebrew 'image'. De Burgh 'shadowy form'.

^{j} Was embittered and was grieved] One word in Hebrew. Literally, 'was soured', as of leavened bread or vinegar.

^{k} My feelings ... side] Literally, 'I was pierced in my kidneys'. In Biblical Hebrew the kidneys are the seat of the emotions. We have paraphrased, as it is difficult to otherwise convey the meaning. See notes on 7:9 and 16:7.

Day 159   Psalm 73:23-28

^{23} In spite of that I am always with you.
You've taken hold of me by my right hand.
^{24} So by your counsel you will lead me on,
To glory you'll receive me afterward.

^{25} Who is there in the heavens on my side?
Beside you I have no delight on earth.
^{26} And, though my flesh and heart should waste away,
God's my heart's strength and portion evermore.

^{27} Those far from you will surely^a be destroyed.
You put an end to all who whore from you.
^{28} It's good that I draw near to God^b. My Lord^c -
The LORD's my refuge^d; All your works I'll tell.

---

^{a} Surely] Hebrew *hinneh* - הִנֵּה. See Appendix 2 - Behold!

^{b} It is good that I draw near to God] This could be translated 'nearness to God is my good', i.e. access, approach. Cf. Isa. 58:2. It is essential to his wellbeing; in contrast to the wicked in v27.

^{c} My Lord] Hebrew *'Adhonay* - אֲדֹנָי. The unique word used of God's lordship. This follows on the next line 'My Lord the LORD'. See Appendix 2 - Names of God.

^{d} My refuge] Hebrew *Maḥseh* - מַחְסֶה, from the verb *ḥasâ* - חָסָה. See Appendix 2 - Refuge.

Day 160   Psalm 74:1-4

^{1} O why, O God, have you rejected us?
Why have you cast us off continually?^{a}
Why does your anger fume and smoke^b against -
Against the sheep, those in your shepherd care?^{c} →

² Remember your own gathered company^d –
Even the people you have bought^e of old;
The rod^f to you assigned, which you redeemed;
This mount of Zion in which you did dwell.

³ Unto the utter ruins^g turn your steps.
The enemy wrecked^h all the holy place.
⁴ Your foes have roared within your meeting place.
They have replaced the signs by their own signs.ⁱ

---

^a Rejected ... cast us off continually] We have expanded this one line. The Hebrew
  may mean 'rejected' or 'cast off'. We have translated 'continually' rather than
  'for ever' (AV). The idea is permanence rather than endless duration (cf. Lam.
  3:33 where a different word is used for 'forever'): perhaps the meaning is
  'altogether cast us off' see Gesenius *Lexicon* and Girdlestone (v3 would then
  mean utter ruin).
^b Fume and smoke] One word in Hebrew. This is the literal meaning. . See Ps.
  80:4 (Hebrew).
^c Shepherd care] shepherding. It refers to their relation to the shepherd rather
  than to a place, a pasture.
^d Gathered Company ... people] The community of Israel (Exod. 12:3,6).
^e Bought] The word can mean 'got' in a general sense (Exod. 15:16).
^f Rod] Modern translations render the word as 'tribe', which the word can mean,
  but which is never applied to all Israel. See de Burgh on why 'rod' is preferable.
^g Utter ruins] 'Devastations'. 'perpetual desolations', 'ruined for ever'. As Ps.
  73:18.
^h Wrecked] 'Laid waste'. The word (r'a'- רעע) here may mean 'did evil in'.
ⁱ Signs] Literally, 'they have set up their signs as signs'. We understand this to
  relate to religious symbols, or worship, rather than military ensigns (as AV).
  The word is used again in v9. However, see Numb. 2:2ff.

Day 161   Psalm 74:5-11

⁵ Once one was known as he who chopped down trees
As one who raised up axes in the wood.^a
⁶ And now they break all its carved work at once;
With axes and with hammers break it down.

⁷ And they have set your Holy Place^b on fire;
Brought to the dirt^c the place where your name dwells.
⁸ For they have spoken thus within their heart,
'Let us together crush^d them utterly!'   →

145

They have burned all GOD's meetings[e] in the land.
[9] We see no signs! No prophet anymore!
And there is none of us who knows how long,
[10] O God, for how long shall the foe reproach?

Will those who hate you ever scorn your name?
[11] What is the reason you hold back your hand?
Why is it that you hold back your right hand?
O draw your hand forth[f], and then make an end!

---

[a] Once one was known … wood] The meaning of the Hebrew is difficult. See
Perowne, de Burgh. AV '[A man] was famous'. 'Men used to work to build
God's Temple. *Then* they will work for its destruction' Newton (1).
[b] Holy Place] The Sanctuary (Hebrew *miqdaš* - מִקְדָּשׁ), used of the Tabernacle
(Exod. 25:8) and the Temple (1 Chr. 22:19).
[c] Brought to the dirt] Literally, 'profaned to the earth'.
[d] Crush] 'Suppress', 'utterly subdue'.
[e] God's meetings] Meeting places, or places of assembly. AV (following T&J Latin,
and Geneva Bible) 'synagogues', but, if this is a historical allusion, it probably
predates synagogues as we know them.
[f] Draw your hand forth] Literally, 'draw it out of your bosom'.

Day 162   Psalm 74:12-17

[12] Yet nonetheless, God is my king of old.
Working deliverances in the earth.
[13] You - you[a] divided the sea by your might,
Upon the waters broke the monsters' heads.

[14] The heads of the leviathan[b] you crushed:
Gave it as food for people of dry lands.
[15] You did divide both water-spring and brook,
And you dried up the ever-flowing streams

[16] Yours is the day - yours also is the night.
You have established the light[c] and the sun.
[17] You have set all the borders of the earth.
Summer and winter have been formed by you.

---

[a] You, you] 'You yourself'. The Hebrew emphasises God as the agent here and in
the following verses.
[b] Leviathan] See Ps. 104:26. This verse refers symbolically to Pharaoh and Egypt's
armies.

146

Day 163   Psalm 74:18-23

¹⁸ Remember, LORD, the enemy's contempt!
A foolish people have blasphemed your name.
¹⁹ Give not the soul of your dove to the beast: ^a
Your poor one's ^b life do not always forget.

²⁰ Regard your covenant: The land's ^c dark parts
Are habitations full of violence.
²¹ O let not the oppressed return in shame.
The poor and needy – they shall praise your name.

²² Arise, O God! Arise, defend your cause!
Mind how the fool reproaches you all day.
²³ Do not forget your adversaries' voice.
The rebels' tumult ^d goes up constantly.

^a Beast] Geneva Bible = 'beast'. *Statenvertaling* 'wild beasts'. Compare the
Hebrew of Ps. 79:2. See *Dutch Annotations* on Ps. 68:11. See De Burgh. The
word properly signifies 'living' or 'alive' and from that 'animals', particularly
wild beasts. AV translates 'multitude [of the wicked]'. We believe this is the
only time the AV translates the word by 'multitude'. The same word occurs in
the next line, where it is translated 'life'. YLT translates the word by 'company'
both times in this verse.
^b Poor one] Or 'afflicted' one (as translated in 72:12). Also in v21.
^c Land] The Hebrew word *'erets* - ארץ can mean land or earth. Appendix 2 - Earth.
^d Rebels' tumult] Hebrew 'the tumult of those who rise up against you'.

Day 164   Psalm 75:1-6

¹ We give you thanks, O God. We give you thanks.
Your name is near ^a - your wondrous deeds do tell.
² 'When I shall take the set, appointed, time, ^b
I, even I ^c, will judge with equity'

³ 'The earth and all that dwell therein shall melt
I am the one who made its pillars firm ✚
⁴ I told the boasters, "Do not make your boast".
And told the wicked, "Do not lift the horn"'.   →

147

⁵ See that you do not lift your horn on high,
And do not speak with a proud outstretched neck.
⁶ For neither from the east, nor from the west,
Nor from the desert^d, is the lifting up.^e

---

^a Your name is near] Compare Deut. 4:7.
^b When I shall take the set, appointed time] The LORD becomes the speaker.
Geneva Bible 'a convenient time'. *Statenvertaling* 'when I shall have received
the appointed' - the *Dutch Annotations* add 'kingdom'. 'The AV translates
'when I shall receive the congregation'. The Hebrew word (*mô'edh* - מוֹעֵד)
means something fixed, whether of time or place (and hence of people in a
place). The AV elsewhere translates as 'appointed time' (see Ps. 102:13; Hab.
2:3; Dan. 8:19; 11:27,35).
^c I, even I] The pronoun is emphatic.
^d The desert] AV 'from the South'. The Hebrew word is *midhbar* - מִדְבָּר, usually
rendered 'wilderness' (as in Numb. 1:1). The reference here is evidently to the
barren desert toward the South (in relation to the east and west).
^e Lifting up] The metaphor occurs here and in verses 4,5,7,10. The lifting up of
the head, or horn, is a picture of strength, relief, and deliverance. The word for
'lifting up' here (Hebrew *harîm* - הָרִים) may be translated 'the mountains', and
the sentence would then read 'nor from the wilderness of the mountains'. This
is the reading of the ancient versions, which is favoured by Newton (11).

Day 165   Psalm 75:7-10

⁷ For God is judge^a; so this man he brings down,
And yet another man, he raises up.
⁸ For in the LORD's hand there's a cup of wine,
The wine is foaming and is mixed right up.

And from that cup of wine^b the LORD pours out –
Surely, the very dregs they shall drain out.
Yes, all the wicked of the earth shall drink;
⁹ And I will tell of it^c for evermore

Unto the God of Jacob I'll sing psalms.^d
¹⁰ The horns of all the wicked I'll cut off.
Not so for him who is the righteous one
His horns shall be exalted – lifted high!

---

^a Judge] *šôphet* - שׁוֹפֵט. See Appendix 2 - Law - Judgment.
^b From that cup of wine] Hebrew 'from it'.
^c I will tell of it] We have taken the verb to be transitive, referring to the downfall
of the wicked, which is, of course, the source of praise in the following line.
^d Sing psalms] Hebrew *zamar* - זָמַר. See Appendix 2 - *zamar* - זָמַר.

Day 166   Psalm 76:1-6

¹ It is in Judah that God is made known: ᵃ
In Israel his name is very great.
² It is in Salem that his tentᵇ is set:
And Zion is the place in which he dwells.

³ There - thereᶜ he broke the arrowsᵈ of the bow.
The shield, the sword, and weapons of the war. ᵉ ⫲
⁴ You are resplendent. You are excellent.
As you come from the mountains of the prey.

⁵ The braveᶠ have been despoiled. They slept their sleep.
None of the mighty menᵍ could use their hands.
⁶ At your rebuke (you who are Jacob's God),
Both chariot and horse fell fast asleep.

ᵃ Made known] 'Revealed'. See BDB *Lexicon*.
ᵇ Tent ... the place in which he dwells] The words may be translated 'covert' and 'lair', symbolising the LORD as a lion going down to the prey (cf. Amos 1:2 and Isa. 31:4).
ᶜ There, there] 'There' is emphasised.
ᵈ Arrows] Literally, 'lightnings', 'fiery shafts', 'flashings'.
ᵉ The weapons of war] AV, and frequently, 'battle'. Gesenius *Lexicon* takes this as 'weapons of war' by metonymy; following on from the breaking of bow, shield, and sword. Compare Hos. 1:7 and 2:18.
ᶠ Brave] Hebrew 'strong of heart', 'stout hearted', perhaps 'stubborn'.
ᵍ Men] Hebrew *'enôš* - אֱנוֹשׁ - Frail, mortal man. Although appearing to be 'mighty' and skilled to fight, they were helpless at the LORD's word of rebuke. See Appendix 2 - Man.

Day 167   Psalm 76:7-12

⁷ But you indeed, are the One to be feared;
When you are angry who stands before you?
⁸ You, from the heavens, made the judgmentᵃ heard;
The earth was then afraid, and it was still.

⁹ When God arises to give judgment out,ᵇ
All the afflicted of the earth to save. ⫲
¹⁰ The wrath of man will yield its praise to you.ᶜ
All that remains of wrathᵈ you will gird on. ᵉ   →

149

¹¹ Make vows – perform them to the LORD your God.
All those around God-to-be-feared^f bring gifts.
¹² The spirit of the princes he'll cut off.
He is a terror to the kings of earth.

---

^a Judgment] The words translated 'judgment' by the AV in v8 and v9 are different.
The word in v8, *dîn* - דִּין, may be rendered 'sentence', it is a judgment declared.
The word in v9 (*mišpaṭ* - מִשְׁפָּט) means rather judgment executed. See
Appendix 2 - Law - Judgment and (2).
^b To give judgment out] Hebrew *mišpaṭ* - מִשְׁפָּט. See note on v8.
^c The wrath of man] The Hebrew is 'Certainly, the wrath of man'.
^d All that remains of wrath] Hebrew 'the remainder of wraths'. The wrath of man
is made to bring God praise, and, when it is expended, God's wrath follows (cf.
Ps. 45:3). See de Burgh.
^e You will gird on] This, not 'restrain' (AV), is the usual meaning of the word.
^f God-to-be-feared] Literally, 'the Fear' - the proper object of all fear (cf. Isa.
8:12,13; and also Gen. 31:42,53 - though a different word for fear is used
there). Segond *'Dieu Terrible'*. Welsh Bible *'Yr Ofnadwy'*.

Day 168   Psalm 77:1-6

¹ With my voice I cried out aloud^a to God;
My voice to God! And he gave ear to me.
² I sought My Lord^b the day of my distress
My outstretched hand was not weary by night.

My soul would not take comfort from its grief.
³ I would remember God, and I would sigh.
I think on this, and then my spirit faints. ⧺
⁴ You have held back the watches of my eyes.^c

I am so troubled that I cannot speak.
⁵ I thought upon the days that were of old
Upon the years that were of ages past.
⁶ I will recall what I sang in the night!

I will commune and ponder^d with my heart,
And with my spirit I will search out well.
I will commune and ponder with my heart,
And with my spirit I will search out well.^e

---

^a Cried out aloud] This is a strong word, applied to Esau (Gen. 27:34), and Shiloh
crying out for the loss of the Ark (1 Sam. 4:14).
^b My Lord] Hebrew *'Adhonay* - אֲדֹנָי. See Appendix 2 - Names of God.

^c You have held back the watches of my eyes] 'Guards' or 'watches' is only used
here. It may mean (1) the eyelids = kept me from sleeping, or (2) The night
watches (one letter different) = you have held my eyes in the night watches (cf.
Ps. 63:6).
^d Commune and ponder] One word in Hebrew - as v3b and v12b.
^e I will commune ... search out well] We have repeated the previous two lines.

Day 169   Psalm 77:7-15

⁷ So will My Lord^a reject for evermore?
Will he not show his favour anymore?
⁸ And has his kindness^b reached a final end?
Has his word^c failed for ages yet to come? ^d

⁹ Has GOD forgotten to act graciously?
Has he in anger shut his mercies up? ⊹
¹⁰ I said that 'This is my infirmity.
The years of the Most High's^e right hand are these'.^f

¹¹ I will recall the deeds of JAH - the LORD. ^g
Your wonder^h I'll remember from of old.
¹² I'll meditate on all that you have done,
Speak with myself about your mighty deeds.

¹³ O God, your pathway is in holiness.
The way of God is in the Holy Place.ⁱ
Who is a GOD who's great as is the God?^j
¹⁴ You are the GOD^k who's done this wondrous thing.

Among the peoples you've made your strength known.
¹⁵ You have redeemed your people with your arm,
You bought them back by your own mighty power^l -
You brought them back^m, Jacob and Joseph's sons. ⊹

^a My Lord] Hebrew *'Adhonay* - אֲדֹנָי. See Appendix 2 - Names of God.
^b Kindness] Hebrew *ḥeṣedh* - חֶסֶד. See Appendix 2 - Loving-kindness.
^c Word] the spoken word. The word he spoke to Abraham, Isaac, and Jacob, and
indeed from Sinai. Hebrew *'omer* - אֹמֶר (from *'amar* - אָמַר to say). See
Appendix 2 - Word.
^d For ages yet to come] Literally, 'to generation and generation'.
^e The Most High] Hebrew *'Elyôn* - עֶלְיוֹן. See Appendix 2 - Names of God.
^f The years ... are these] We take this as a new thought that comes to his troubled
mind. See Bonar, and de Burgh who links the phrase with the following verse.
The Hebrew word 'years' may be translated 'changing', hence the translation of

the LXX, Vulgate, T&J Latin, *Statenvertaling*, YLT, etc ['this is his trouble - that the right hand of the Most High has changed']. See Motyer [1] for a summary of the difficulty of translation.

^g JAH - the LORD] Hebrew *YAH* - יָהּ is a shortened form of 'LORD', frequently used in connection with the Exodus. See Appendix 2 - Names of God.

^h Wonder] The word is singular, and is the same as 'wondrous thing' in v14. The entire redemptive work of God is viewed as one marvellous work.

ⁱ Holiness ... Holy Place] we have given the alternative reading given by the *Dutch Annotations* as well as that relating it to a place (as the AV 'the Sanctuary').

^j Who is a GOD ... the God] The Hebrew is 'Who is a great *El* like *Elohim*?' See Appendix 2 - Names of God. AV follows the Septuagint and the Syriac in reading 'our God'.

^k The GOD] Hebrew *'El* - אֵל with the definite article, emphasising both God's uniqueness and his power. See Appendix 2 - Names of God.

^l You bought them ... arm] We have repeated this line with a different translation. 'Redemption' is used in the sense of 'buying back' (as in the case of Boaz and Ruth), and 'arm' is often used figuratively of might and power.

^m You brought them back] We have repeated these words.

Day 170   Psalm 77:16-20

¹⁶ The waters saw you - they saw you, O God -
The waters saw you, and they were in pain.
The very depths did tremble and did quake;^a
¹⁷ The clouds poured water; skies gave out a sound.

Your arrows also went out round about;
¹⁸ Noise of your thunders in the whirling wind.
Lightnings lit up the world^b - earth shook and quaked.
¹⁹ And your highway, it was within the sea.

In mighty waters were the paths you took,
And yet your footprints were not traceable.
²⁰ You led your people like a flock of sheep,
Even by Moses' and by Aaron's hand.

^a Tremble ... quake] One word in Hebrew, as v18.
^b The world] The inhabited earth. *tebhel* - תֵּבֵל. See Appendix 2 - Earth.

Day 171   Psalm 78:1-8

¹ My people, give your ear unto my Law;^a
Incline your ear unto words^b of my mouth.
² My mouth I'll open in a parable;
I will pour forth dark sayings from of old.   →

³ Things we have heard, and things that we have known,
Things which our fathers have declared to us,
⁴ We'll not conceal nor hide^c them from their sons:
And tell^d the generation yet to come.

To tell to them the praises of the LORD;
Tell of his strength, and wonders he has done.
⁵ In Jacob he a Testimony^e raised;
In Israel a Law^f he did appoint.

These he commanded to our fathers then,
So they should make them known unto their sons.
⁶ To let the future generation know,
Even the sons that should be born to them.

They should rise up to tell^g them to their sons,
⁷ So they might put their confidence in God,
That they might not forget the deeds of GOD,
And that they might observe what he commands.^h

⁸ So they might not be as their fathers were:
A stubborn generation that rebelled,
A generation with unsettled heart, ⁱ
Whose spirit was not faithful unto GOD.

---

^a Law] instruction or teaching. Hebrew *tôrâ* - תּוֹרָה. See Appendix 2 - Law - Law.
^b Words] 'Spoken words', Hebrew *'emer* - אֶמֶר (from *'amar* - אָמַר, to say). See
  Appendix 2 - Word.
^c Conceal ... hide] One word in Hebrew.
^d Telling] 'Relating', 'recounting'. As in v3b - 'our fathers related to us'.
^e Testimony] The word used of the Ark of the Testimony, and sometimes of the
  law itself. Hebrew *'edhâ* - עֵדָה. See Appendix 2 - Law - Testimony.
^f Law] Instruction or teaching. As in v1.
^g Tell] 'Relate', 'recount'. As in 3b and 4b.
^h What he commands] His commandments. The plural of Hebrew *mitswâ* - מִצְוָה.
  See Appendix 2 - Law - Commandment.
ⁱ Unsettled heart] As v37.

Day 172   Psalm 78:9-16

⁹ The sons of Ephraim, armed and bearing bows,^a
Retreated in the day the battle raged.
¹⁰ They did not keep the covenant of God;
Refused to walk according to his Law.^b   →

153

¹¹ And they forgot the things that he had done -
His wondrous works that he showed unto them.
¹² He did a marvel^c, in their fathers' sight,
In Egypt's land, even in Zoan's field.

¹³ He parted sea, and made them to pass through.
He made the waters stand up like a heap.
¹⁴ By day he also led them with a cloud,
And, all night long, led^d with the light of fire.

¹⁵ Rocks he split open in the wilderness,
And gave them drink, as if from the great deeps.
¹⁶ He brought forth flowing waters from the rock,^e
And he made waters flow as rivers do.

---

^a Armed and bearing bows] Perhaps 'equipped as archers'. Geneva Bible
'shooting with the bowe', as T & J and the Welsh Bible.
^b Law] Instruction or teaching. Hebrew *mitswâ* - מִצְוָה. See Appendix 2 - Law -
Commandment.
^c Marvel] Hebrew singular. As Ps. 89:5.
^d Led] We have supplied the word 'led' as Exod. 13:21.
^e Rock] This is a different word to that used in v15, and may perhaps be translated
'cliff'. The first word refers to Exod. 17:6. The second word (here) perhaps
refers to Numb. 20:11, where both words occur.

Day 173   Psalm 78:17-29

¹⁷ They still went on to sin against him more -
Provoked the Most High^a in the arid land.
¹⁸ And, in their heart, they put GOD to the test -
Demanding food, the food that their soul craved.

¹⁹ They contradicted God, 'Can GOD' they said
'Prepare a table in the wilderness?'
²⁰Behold!^b He struck the rock^c and waters gushed;
Streams overflowed. 'Can he give bread also?'

'Can he supply his people yet with meat?'
²¹ Therefore the Lord heard. He was full of wrath.
A fire was kindled against Jacob then,
Anger ascended against Israel.   →

²² Because they did not put their faith in God -
On his salvation they did not depend.
²³ The clouds he had commanded from above.
Had opened up the doors of heaven then.

²⁴ He had rained manna down on them to eat,
And gave to them of heaven's wheaten grain.ᵈ
²⁵ Man then did eat the bread of mighty ones.ᵉ
Food in abundance he sent them to eat.

²⁶ In heaven went the East wind, which he drove,
And the South wind was guidedᶠ by his power.
²⁷ And he rained flesh upon them, as the dust.
And birds with wings, like to the sand of seas.

²⁸ He made them to fall down within their camp,
Even around the places where they dwelt.
²⁹ So they did eat, and so they were well-filled.
And so he gave to them what they desired.

ᵃ The Most High] Hebrew *'Elyôn* - עֶלְיוֹן. Compare v35 and v56. See Appendix 2 -
   Names of God.
ᵇ Mark this!] Hebrew - *hen* - הֵן. See Appendix 2 - Behold!
ᶜ Rock] The same word as in v16.
ᵈ Wheaten grain] The word means the fully developed ear of the cereal, typically
   wheat (see Geneva Bible and BDB *Lexicon*). The word used in the Septuagint
   translation, and in John 6:31 is *arton* - ἄρτον 'a cake or loaf of wheat bread'
   (Liddell and Scott).
ᵉ Mighty ones] So AV mg. Although the Septuagint and Vulgate here translate
   bread of 'angels', Scripture nowhere uses this word (*'abîrîm* - אַבִּירִים) as a
   synonym for angels, although they are described as 'mighty' (Ps. 103:20 - using
   a different word for 'mighty').
ᶠ Drove ... guided] See Perowne and Welsh Bible. Both words are used of God
   guiding Israel like a flock in v52. The metaphor is of God leading and guiding
   the winds, which are under his power. The first word is used in Numb. 11:31,
   and the second in Exod. 10:13.

Day 174   Psalm 78:30-39

³⁰ They were not yet estranged fromᵃ their desire -
But - when their food was still within their mouth -
³¹ The anger of God rose against them then.
He slew their finestᵇ; smote Israel's young men.   →

155

³² And yet, in all this, they sinned even more.
Despite his wonders, they did not believe.
³³ He made their days to vanish like a breath;
Their years in sudden terror^c passed away.

³⁴ But when he slew them, they sought after him.
Turned back again and sought GOD earnestly.^d
³⁵ And they remembered that God was their rock,
That GOD Most High^e was their redeemer too.

³⁶ Still they would yet deceive him with their mouth;
And they dissembled to him with their tongue.
³⁷ Their heart was not steadfast and sure^f with him.
Nor were they faithful in his covenant.

³⁸ But he in tender mercy hid the sin.
Forgave iniquity^g. Did not destroy.
His anger, many times, he did turn back,
Not stirring up full measure of his wrath.

³⁹ And he remembered that they were but flesh -
A wind that passes and comes not again.
Yes, he remembered that they were but flesh -
A wind that passes and comes not again.^h

---

^a Estranged from] 'Strangers to', i.e. while they were still enjoying the food.
^b Finest] Hebrew 'fattest'.
^c Sudden terror] One word in Hebrew. The word conveys the meaning of
   'hastening' (Septuagint, Vulgate, Geneva Bible), as well as terror (AV).
^d Sought GOD earnestly] A different word for 'sought' in the first part of the verse.
   The word we have translated 'earnestly' is related to the Hebrew word for the
   dawn - hence an eager, early, diligent seeking.
^e GOD Most High] Hebrew 'El 'Elyôn - עֶלְיוֹן אֵל. See Appendix 2 - Names of God.
^f Steadfast and sure] One word in Hebrew - 'right', 'set', 'firm', 'steadfast', as v8.
^g Hid the sin. Forgave iniquity] we have repeated and expanded the expression.
   The word (Hebrew kaphar - כָּפַר) means 'a covering of iniquity', 'a propitiating
   of sin'. It is linked to atonement. The word for the mercy seat of the ark
   derives from it.
^h Yes ... again] We have repeated the last two lines.

Day 175   Psalm 78:40-51

[40] How often they rebelled against him there –
In wilderness; grieved him in desert waste.[a]
[41] Repeatedly they turned and tested GOD,
And vexed the Holy One of Israel.

[42] It was *his* hand; but they remembered not
The day that he redeemed them from the foe.
[43] How he had worked his signs in Egypt's land[b] –
The wonders that he did in Zoan's field.

[44] He turned their watercourses[c] into blood –
Their flowing waters[d] so they could not drink.
[45] He sent devouring swarms of flies to them[e]
And sent the frogs that devastated them.

[46] To caterpillar he gave their increase[f],
And to the locust the fruit of their toil.
[47] Their vines he caused to die[g] by sending hail;
Also their sycomores he killed by frost.

[48] He gave their livestock also to the hail;
He gave their flocks to fiery thunderbolts[h].
[49] He let his burning anger loose on them –
Wrath, indignation, and adversity.

They were a band of hurtful messengers
Of evil angels sent to do great harm.[i]
[50] He prepared a way[j] for his anger to go.
He did not spare or keep[k] their soul from death.

But he gave up their life unto the plague.
[51] All the firstborn in Egypt he struck down.
He struck down the first issue of their strength.
And killed their firstfruits[l] in the tents of Ham.[m]

---

[a] Desert waste] Not the usual word for desert or wilderness. Rather 'wasted land' or 'waste land'. See Ps. 68:7 and 106:14.
[b] In Egypt's land] Hebrew 'in Egypt'.
[c] Watercourses] The Hebrew word here is an Egyptian loan word used almost exclusively of the Nile and, in the plural, of its tributaries and canals. See

157

Gesenius, and BDB *Lexicons.* As Exod. 7:19.

[d] Flowing waters] Participle of 'to flow' - as also in v16.

[e] To them] Hebrew 'among them'.

[f] Their increase] The Egyptians' crops, fruit.

[g] Caused to die, Killed, gave, etc.] In these, and some following verses, we have
   supplied the verb of the first line to the second line, where it equally applies.

[h] Fiery thunderbolts] The same word as used in Ps. 76:3 (where AV 'arrows of the
   bow').

[i] They were a band ... to do great harm] We have expanded the reference to 'evil
   angels' (AV) as there are several ways of understanding this short phrase. The
   'band' may mean a 'mission', a 'sending'. 'Angel' is the same word in Hebrew
   as 'messenger'. The word translated by 'evil' does not necessarily mean
   morally evil, but may mean 'hurtful', 'injurious'. 'Evil' is plural, indicating 'much
   evil'. Most commentators do not think evil spirits are referred to here.

[j] He prepared a way] Literally, 'levelled a way', 'made a way smooth'. As Prov.
   4:26; 5:6.

[k] Spare or keep from] One word in Hebrew, 'restrain'

[l] First issue ... firstfruits] Hebrew 'beginning of strengths'. We have extended the
   line to convey the meaning. The Hebrew verb means to 'strike down' with the
   effect of killing.

[m] Ham] i.e. Egypt, so-called from the son of Noah;. 'Egypt' in Hebrew is usually
   Mitsraîm - מִצְרַיְמָ, as in the first part of the verse, from the son of Ham (Gen.
   10:6).

Day 176   Psalm 78:52-57

^{52} Then his own people he led out like sheep.
The flock he guided in the wilderness.
^{53} He led them safely, so they did not fear.
Their enemies were covered by the sea.

^{54} Unto the border of his holy place,
He brought them: even to this mountain here -
The mountain that his right hand had obtained,
^{55} And he drove out the nations from their face.

He portioned out their heritage by line,[a]
And in their tents made Israel's tribes to dwell.
^{56} In spite of this, they tested and provoked -
Tested, provoked against, the Most High God.[b]

His testimonies they did not observe,
^{57} But they turned back and acted faithlessly.
Just like their fathers, turned back faithlessly:
Changing direction like a faulty bow. [c]   →

ª Their heritage by line] Hebrew 'them as an inheritance by line'. Having just
spoken of the nations, the psalmist evidently refers to their land. The land
(their inheritance) was marked out by measuring line to be apportioned to the
children of Israel.
ᵇ The Most High God] Hebrew *'Elohîm 'Elyôn* - אֱלֹהִים עֶלְיוֹן. See Appendix 2 -
Names of God.
ᶜ Faulty bow] Or 'deceitful bow'. The reference is to a warped bow that will not
fire arrows straight and cannot be relied upon.

Day 177   Psalm 78:58-64

⁵⁸ With their high places they moved him to wrath.
They made him jealous with their images –
Moved him to jealousy with their carved stonesª.
⁵⁹ God heard this, and then he was full of wrath.

He forcibly rejected Israel,
Concerning Israel he felt disgustᵇ.
⁶⁰ The tabernacle of Shiloh he left –
The tent that he had pitched to dwell with menᶜ.

⁶¹ His strengthᵈ he gave up to captivity.
He gave his glor‿eᵉ into the foe's hand.
⁶² He gave his people over to the sword,
And he was angry with his heritage.

⁶³ Their choice young men were then consumed by fire,
And so their virgins had no marriage song.ᶠ
⁶⁴ Their priests fell by the sword, and were laid low.ᵍ
Their widows shed no tears – did not lament.ʰ

ª Images ... carved stones] We have expanded one line to two here. The graven
images were carved stones.
ᵇ Rejected ... disgust] We have again expanded one line to two to give both
meanings of the Hebrew word, which may be translated as both 'reject', and
'abhor', 'feel disgust towards', 'despise', 'hate'. The same word is used in v67.
The ESV 'utterly rejected' and NIV 'completely rejected' overstates the adverb
used, and contradicts the remainder of the Psalm.
ᶜ Pitched to dwell with men] The Hebrew word here (*šakhan* - שָׁכַן) is frequently
used of pitching a tent. It is the root of the word 'shekinah' (*šekhînâ* - שְׁכִינָה),
meaning God's Divine presence. 'Men' here is Hebrew *'adham* - אָדָם - Man as
a child of Adam, which is used collectively for mankind or the human race (cf.
Rev. 21:3). See Appendix 2 - Man.
ᵈ His strength] The ark is called this as it was the place where God's power was

159

manifested (1 Sam. 4:3; Ps. 132:8).

[e] His glory] Compare 1 Sam. 4:21.

[f] Had no marriage song] *Statenvertaling* and Geneva Bible 'their young daughters were not praised'. *Dutch Annotations* 'viz. with nuptial songs' – the word 'praised' is *halal* - הָלַל from which 'Hallelujah' is derived.

[g] Fell ... were laid low] The Hebrew word conveys both of these meanings.

[h] Shed no tears – did not lament] The Hebrew word primarily means 'to weep', here in mourning and lamentation.

Day 178   Psalm 78:65-72

[65] My Lord[a] then woke as one who wakes from sleep
Just like a mighty man[b], shouting[c] from wine.
[66] He smote his foes, and so he drove them back.
And he gave to them everlasting shame.

[67] The tent of Joseph he rejected then,
And did not choose the tribe of Eph-ra-im.
[68] It was the tribe of Judah that he chose –
even the mount of Zion which he loved.

[69] He built his Holy Place[d] like heights sublime[e],
And as the earth, established evermore.
[70] His servant David he also did choose,
And from the sheepfolds he then took him out.

[71] From following the ewes that nursed their young,
He brought him out to shepherd and to rule:[f]
To shepherd Jacob - people who are his:
To shepherd Israel - his heritage.

[72] And so he shepherded, and pastured them,
According to his heart's integrity.
He led them out, just as a shepherd does,[g]
And guided with his skilful, prudent, hands.[h]

[a] My Lord] Hebrew *'Adhonay* - אֲדֹנָי. See Appendix 2 - Names of God.

[b] A mighty man] *gibbôr* - גִּבּוֹר - Man as a mighty being. Appendix 2 - Man.

[c] Shouting] The word is associated with joy - 'joyfully shouting'.

[d] Holy Place] The Sanctuary (Hebrew *miqdaš* - מִקְדָשׁ), used of the Tabernacle (Exod. 25:8) and the Temple (1 Chr. 22:19).

[e] Heights sublime] Hebrew 'heights'. Translations add [high] 'palaces' (AV), 'heavens' (ESV), mountains, etc

[f] To shepherd and to rule] Literally, 'to shepherd', or 'pasture' and 'feed', but figuratively 'to rule' or 'to govern' (see 1 Chr. 17:6, Mic. 5:4; 2 Sam. 5:2; Compare Rev. 2:27 etc.
[g] Led ... as a shepherd does ... Guided] One word in Hebrew. AV 'guided'. We have expanded the meaning of the word to show the continuation of the metaphor. The same word is used in Ps. 23:3 of the LORD 'leading'.
[h] Hands] A different word for 'hand' is used here from Ps. 77:20, and it is here plural (dual). There it is the hand as the instrument of power, here it is the palm of the hands. Compare the comfort of both rod and staff (Ps. 23:4).

Day 179   Psalm 79:1-4

[1] O God, the Gentile nations[a] have come in.
They have invaded your inheritance.
Your Holy Temple[b] is by them defiled.
They made Jerusalem just ruined heaps.

[2] Your servants' corpses they have given up
As food for birds of heaven to devour.[c]
The flesh of your beloved[d] they gave up
Unto the wild beasts of the earth to eat[e].

[3] Around Jerusalem they poured their blood –
Poured out like water – with none burying![f]
[4] We are unto our neighbours a reproach;
Scorn and derision to those round about.

[a] Gentile nations] AV 'heathen'. Hebrew *gôyîm* - גּוֹיִם, always used of the Gentile, or non-Jewish, nations.
[b] Your Holy Temple] Literally, 'the Palace (Hebrew *hêkhal* - הֵיכַל) of your holiness'.
[c] To devour] We have added these words to complete the sense.
[d] Beloved] Plural. Hebrew *ḥasîdhîm* - חֲסִידִים from *ḥesedh* - חֶסֶד. See Appendix 2 - Loving-kindness.
[e] To eat] We have added these words to complete the sense.
[f] Around Jerusalem ... no burying] Compare 1 Macc. 7:17, and see Tregelles (4) on Daniel 11.

Day 180   Psalm 79:5-9

[5] How long, LORD? Will your anger always last?
And will your jealousy burn just like fire?
[6] O let your burning anger be poured out[a]
On nations that do not acknowledge you.   →

161

O let your burning anger be poured out[b]
On kingdoms that do not call on your name.
[7] Jacob's devoured; His pasture they laid waste.[c]
[8] Do not recall against us our past faults![d]

Let your kind mercies[e] meet us speedily,
For we have been brought down so very low.
[9] Help us, our Saving God, for your name's praise;[f]
For your name, rescue, cover our sins up.[g]

---

[a] Burning anger be poured out] The word for 'anger' is associated with heat. 'Poured out' parallels v3.

[b] We have repeated this line to precede the second half of Asaph's request in this verse.

[c] Devoured ... laid waste] The first verb is in the singular [he has devoured], the second in the plural. In quoting this psalm, Jeremiah (10:25) puts both verbs in the plural and applies them to his time. We suspect this verse refers to Antichrist. In Dan. 9:27 the same verb is used for 'desolating' as here translated 'laying waste'. The word 'pasture' is the word for the dwelling place of sheep or shepherds.

[d] Past faults] 'Former iniquities'. Some translate 'sins of our forefathers', literally, 'of those who were at the first'. Compare the Hebrew of Lev. 26:45. See Dan. 9:16, particularly with reference to this verse and v4.

[e] Kind mercies] Or 'tender mercies'. Hebrew *rahamîm* - רַחֲמִים.

[f] Praise] Glory, honour, esteem.

[g] Cover our sins up] The word 'cover' (Hebrew *kaphar* - כָּפַר) is linked to atonement. The word for the mercy seat of the ark derives from it.

Day 181   Psalm 79:10-13

[10] Why should the nations say, 'Where is their God?'
Make known before the nations in our sight
The vengeance for your servants' outpoured blood!
[11] The captive's sighs - let them come unto you.

According to the greatness of your power[a]
Spare those who are appointed unto death.[b]
[12] Return unto our neighbours sevenfold[c]
The taunts with which they taunted you, My Lord.[d]

[13] So we, who are your people and your flock,
And are the object of your shepherd care[e] -
We will give thanks to you for evermore -
To endless ages[f] we'll recount your praise.

^a Power] Hebrew 'arm'.

^b Those who are appointed unto death] Hebrew literally, 'the sons of death'. As
Ps. 102:20.

^c Sevenfold] Hebrew 'sevenfold into their bosom (AV) or lap (other translators)'.
This may be taken either as seven measures into the lap or fold of the garment
(as Ruth 3:15) and therefore meaning abundance; or, as of retribution. See the
reference to the 'head' in Ps. 7:16, etc. See J.A. Alexander on Isa. 65:7.

^d My Lord] Hebrew 'Adhonay - אֲדֹנָי. See Appendix 2 - Names of God.

^e Shepherd care] 'Shepherding'. It refers to their relation to the shepherd rather
than to a place, 'a pasture'. As Ps. 74:1.

^f Endless ages] Hebrew 'to generation and generation'. 'From generation to
generation'.

Day 182   Psalm 80:1-3

¹ O Israel's Shepherd, do incline your ear,
You who have guided Joseph like a flock.
The One enthroned upon the cherubim -
Dwelling between the cherubim^a - Shine forth!

² In Ephraim's sight stir up your mighty strength -
In sight of Benjamin, Manasseh too.
And come and save us! ³ O God, turn us back!
Make your face shine, and then we will be saved.

^a Enthroned ... dwelling ... cherubim] We have given two suggested translations.
The verb with the root meaning 'to sit' may also mean 'to be enthroned', and
'to dwell'. Compare Exod. 25:22; 1 Sam. 4:4; Ps. 99:1; Ezek. 1: 5,26-28. See
Baron (1).

Day 183   Psalm 80:4-7

⁴ How long, O LORD the God of Hosts? Till when?
Your anger fumes^a against your people's prayer.
⁵ For you have fed them with the bread of tears,
And in full measure gave them tears to drink.

⁶ Unto our neighbours you make us a strife;
Our enemies just laugh among themselves.
⁷ O God of hosts, restore us, turn us back.^b
Shine with your face, and then we will be saved.

^a Fumes] This is the literal meaning in Hebrew, i.e. 'is angry against'. See Ps. 74:1
(Hebrew). David Baron (1) comments that it is God, not his anger, who is said

Day 184   Psalm 80:8-14

⁸ From out of Egypt you have brought^a a vine.
You drove out nations, and you planted it.
⁹ You cleared the ground to make a space for it.
You made it take deep root. It filled the land.

¹⁰ By it the mountains were cast in the shade,
And, by its branches^b, the cedars of GOD^c.
¹¹ It sent its branches even to the Sea,
And to the River^d it sent out its shoots.

¹² Why have you broken her enclosures down?
So, all the passers-by do pick her fruit.
¹³ The boar out of the wood tears it apart.
The wild beast of the field devours it up.^e

¹⁴ O God of hosts return again, we pray.^f
Oh, turn again, from heaven look and see!
Oh, come and visit, take care of this vine.
Oh, come and visit, take care of this vine.^g

^a Brought] The Hebrew word can mean 'brought', or 'pluck up'. Gesenius *Lexicon* gives the root meaning as 'to pull up', 'to pluck out ... especially the stakes of a tent when a camp moves' as in the Exodus 12:37, etc. This suggests 'transplanted', as v15.
^b Branches] Different words for 'branches' are used in this and the following verse. The first especially indicates covering, and the second is usually used collectively, and in relation to harvest (= 'vintage'?).
^c The cedars of GOD] Hebrew 'the cedars of *'El* -אֵל -. Baron (1) takes this to be the extent of Israel northward, i.e. to Lebanon (cf. v11, eastward and westward). Some translate 'the mighty (AV 'goodly') cedars'. See Appendix 2 - Names of God *'El* - אֵל.
^d Sea ... River] i.e. from the Mediterranean Sea to the Euphrates River (see Deut. 11:24).
^e The wild beast of the field devours it up] Literally, 'that which moves in the field' as Ps. 50:11 (see note). Baron (1) refers this to the 'restless activity' of the last beast of Daniel's vision. The word 'devour' may relate to grazing animals, but it is used in a much stronger sense as well (see Mic. 5:6 - AV 'waste').
^f We pray] The Hebrew word of entreaty (*na'* - נָא) in this verse emphasises the verb. The word applies to all the verbs in the verse, which we have then

164

[g] Come and visit, attend to] We have extended the meaning of the verb, which
   includes the idea of 'paying careful attention to'. We have repeated this line.

Day 185   Psalm 80:15-19

[15] Prepare what your right hand has set in place[a]
Also the son[b] you made strong for yourself.
[16] See[c], it is burned with fire. It is cut down.
You look in anger[d] and they are destroyed.

[17] Your hand be on the man of your right hand,[e]
The son of man[f] you made strong for yourself.
[18] Then we shall not backslide away from you.
Revive us and we shall call on your name.

[19] LORD God of hosts, restore us, turn us back.[g]
Make your face shine, and then we shall be saved.
LORD God of hosts, restore us, turn us back.
Make your face shine, and then we shall be saved.[h]

---

[a] Prepare what your right hand has set in place] The interlinear Hebrew is given as
   'this *shoot* which has planted your right hand' [Jay Green, Tregelles (3) 'stock'].
   The AV has 'vineyard' instead of 'shoot' (following on from verses 8-14), but
   the word for 'vine' is not in this verse. Baron (1) notes that the word translated
   'shoot' or 'vineyard' is not a substantive, but an imperative, as translated by
   the Septuagint ['prepare', the same verb is used in Heb. 10:5]. The primary
   meaning of the second Hebrew verb translated 'planted' is 'set in place'.
[b] Son] This is the word used in Hebrew. See Baron (1), and compare v17. *The
   Dutch Annotations* say 'understand here the Son of God'. Many (extending the
   metaphor of the vine in verses 8-14 and from their translation of v.25)
   translate 'branch'.
[c] See] We have added this word. The psalmist returns to considering the plight of
   the LORD's vine. We understand this verse as an aside.
[d] You look in anger] Literally, 'because of the rebuke of your face'.
[e] The man of your right hand] The Hebrew word used for 'man' here is *'îš* - אִישׁ -
   man as an individual. See Appendix 2 - Man.
[f] Son of man] The Hebrew word for 'man' here is *'adham* - אָדָם - Man as a child of
   Adam. See Appendix 2 - Man.
[g] Restore us, turn us back] One word in Hebrew (as v3 and v7).
[h] LORD God of Hosts ... saved] We have repeated the last two lines of the final
   verse.

Day 186   Psalm 81:1-5

¹ Sing out with joy to God who is our strength;
Unto the God of Jacob raise a shout.
² Take up the psalm[a]! Bring here the tambourine!
Sweet harp with lyre[b]! ³ Blow shofar at new moon.[c]

At the full moon[d], for the day of our Feast[e].
⁴ For this decree was made for Israel.
It is an ordinance that should be kept –
A right arrangement[f] made by Jacob's God.

⁵ To be a witness, he appointed this.
A Testimony he in Joseph set.
When against[g] Egypt he was going forth;
When I heard speech that was unknown to me.[h]

---

[a] Psalm] Hebrew *zimrâ* - זִמְרָה from *zamar* - זָמַר. See Appendix 2 - *zamar* - זָמַר.

[b] Lyre] AV 'psaltery'. See Appendix 2 - Harps.

[c] Blow shofar at new moon] The ram's horn was blown at Rosh Hashana at the new moon of the seventh month (Lev. 23:24) which is followed 15 days later by Tabernacles (full moon), as Perowne notes. The regular new moon was ushered in by the sound of silver trumpets (Numb. 10:10), not the shofar. However, de Burgh favours the reference being to the Passover.

[d] At the full moon] So Gesenius *Lexicon*, Perowne, Bonar, and Delitzsch. The word occurs only here and Prov. 7:20; AV (which follows the Jewish sage Rashi) translates 'at the appointed time'.

[e] Feast] the Hebrew word is *ḥagh* (חַג) cf. Arabic (Moslem) *Hajj*. One of the solemn pilgrim festivals of Israel. Tabernacles is pre-eminently referred to as 'the feast' (1 Kgs. 8:2,65; 12:32; Neh. 8:14; Hos. 7:9; Ezek. 45:25, etc). See Gill's comments.

[f] Ordinance ... right arrangement] AV 'law'. One word in Hebrew, *mišpaṭ* - מִשְׁפָּט, which is usually translated 'judgment'. Here the core meaning of the word is apparent, cf. Ps. 119:132. See Appendix 2 - Law - Judgment.

[g] Against] So Bonar, *Statenvertaling*, and T&J Latin. See Horsley, de Burgh, and Perowne on the difficulty of translating the preposition by 'out through' (AV). 'He' therefore refers to the LORD, not to Israel.

[h] I heard ... that was unknown to me] The switch to 'I' is explained by Kimchi as Israel 'beginning to hear ['the proper force of the tense in the original' Soncino] God, whom it had not yet learned to know as the self-revealing God of redemption. 'I' reverts to God in the next verse.

Day 187   Psalm 81:6-10

[6] 'I took his shoulder from the burden then.
Likewise, his hands were from the basket freed.
[7] You called in trouble, and I rescued you.
I gave you answer from the thunder cloud'. [a]

'I proved you at waters of Meribah. [b] ╫
[8] My people, Hear. I'll testify to you.
O Israel, if you'll listen to me,
[9] There will not be among you a strange GOD'.

'You won't bow down to any foreign GOD, [c]
[10] For it is I, the LORD, who is your God –
The One who brought you up from Egypt's land.
'Open your mouth wide and I'll fill it up'.

---

[a] From the thunder cloud] Literally, 'the covering of thunder' - so Gesenius
   Lexicon and de Burgh. See Exod. 14:24 and compare v8-10 and Exod. 19:18,19
   and 20:18. The word translated 'answered' often simply means 'speak'.
[b] Meribah] Hebrew 'strife' Exod. 17:7; Numb. 20:13.
[c] Strange GOD ... Foreign GOD] The Hebrew word *'El* - אֵל is here used of the
   heathen gods. Cf. Ps. 77:13. Strange GOD = Ps. 44:20, Foreign GOD = Deut.
   32:12. See Appendix 2 - Names of God.

Day 188   Psalm 81:11-16

[11] 'My people would not listen to my voice,
And Israel would not submit to me.
[12] I gave them up to their own stubborn heart,
That they might walk in counsels they devised.

[13] O that my people would listen to me,
That Israel would walk within my ways.
[14] Then I would soon subdue their enemies,
And I would turn my hand against their foes.

[15] The haters of the LORD would yield[a] to him.
Their time[b] should then endure for evermore.
[16] He'd feed them with the finest of the wheat[c]
'I'd fill[d] you with the honey from the rock'

---

[a] Yield] Hebrew 'tell a lie'. AV mg. 'yielded feigned obedience'. See also at Psalms

167

18:44 and 66:3.
^b Their time] *Statenvertaling*, Perowne, and de Burgh agree that 'their time' refers
to God's people, continuing on from v14, not to the 'haters' of the first part of
the verse; that they should endure for evermore if they would but listen and
follows his ways, v13. Compare Acts 3:19-21.
^c Finest of the wheat] Hebrew 'fat of the wheat', as Ps.147:16.
^d Fill] i.e. 'satisfy'. Compare v10 where a different word is used for filling.

Day 189　　Psalm 82:1-4

¹ God stands up in the Gathering of GOD,^a
And he holds judgment^b in the midst of gods.
² 'How long will you give judgment that is wrong?'
'How long show favour to the wicked ones?' ╫

³ 'Give judgment to the weak and fatherless;
Maintain the right of the oppressed and poor;
⁴ Rescue the weak, the one who is in need;
Deliver from the hand of wicked men^c'.

---

^a The Gathering of GOD] Literally, 'the assembly of 'El -אֵל. See Appendix 2 - The
Names of God. AV translates 'the congregation of the mighty'. Bonar and
Newton (11) consider those assembled in v1 and 6 (AV 'gods') to be earth's
judges, those who have been given the delegated power of government.
Motyer (1) argues this strongly from John 10:34-36 and other Scriptures, but
see Isa. 3:13,14; and Numb. 27:17 (Israel = 'the congregation of the LORD')
^b Holds judgment] We have translated the verb *šaphaṭ* - שָׁפַט 'hold judgment', or
'give judgment' in v1-3. See Appendix 2 - Law - Judgment.
^c Wicked men] Hebrew 'wicked ones'.

Day 190　　Psalm 82:5-8

⁵ 'They neither know, nor do they understand,
And they in darkness wander round about.
All the foundations of the earth do shake.
⁶ I said, 'You're gods. All sons of the Most High'.^a

⁷ 'But you will die just like all other men,^b
And as one of the princes you will fall.
⁸Arise, O God, give justice to the earth,
For all the nations are your heritage.

---

^a The Most High] Hebrew '*Elyôn* - עֶלְיוֹן. See Appendix 2 - Names of God.
^b All other men] Hebrew 'as man' - *'adham* - אָדָם - Man as a child of Adam,

Day 191   Psalm 83:1-8

¹ O GOD, please do not stay in silence now.
Hold not your peace, and be not still, O God!
² For - See!ᵃ - the uproar of your enemies;
Those who hate you have lifted up the head.

³ Against your people they plot craftily,
And they conspire against your hidden ones.
⁴ And they say, 'Come, the nation we'll wipe out;
No more remembered will be Israel's name'

⁵ For they consulted as with one accord;
Against you they have made a covenant.
⁶ The tents of Edom and the Ishmaelites,
The tents ofᵇ Moab and the Hagarenes.

⁷ The tents of Gebal, Ammon, Amalek,
Philistia, and those who dwell at Tyre.
⁸ Assyriaᶜ has also joined with them.
They give support untoᵈ the sons of Lot. ⫟

ᵃ See!] Hebrew *hinneh* - הִנֵּה. See Appendix 2 - Behold!
ᵇ The tents of] We have repeated these words in this and the following line. This seems to be an encampment of these nations against Israel. See Dan. 11:45.
ᶜ Assyria] Hebrew *'aššûr* - אַשּׁוּר - Assyria or 'the Assyrian'. It may be taken to mean the empire of Assyria. De Burgh notes the word as 'a frequent appellation of Antichrist'. We could read 'They have been joined by the Assyrian'.
ᵈ They give support unto] Literally, 'they are the arm of'.

Day 192   Psalm 83:9-12

⁹ Do unto them as unto Midian,
As unto Sisera and to Jabin
(When they were at the Kishon torrent streamᵃ),
¹⁰ At Endor they were cut off and destroyed. ᵇ   →

169

For they became as dung upon the ground.[c]
[11] Their nobles make like Oreb and Ze'eb;
Their princes[d] as Zeba and Zalmunna,
[12] Who said 'Let's take God's pastures for ourselves!'

---

[a] Torrent stream] One word in Hebrew, *nahal* - נַחַל.
[b] Cut off and destroyed] One word in Hebrew.
[c] Ground] Hebrew *'adhamâ* - אֲדָמָה. See Appendix 2 - Earth.
[d] Their princes] Hebrew 'all their princes'.

Day 193   Psalm 83:13-18

[13] My God, make them just like the whirling dust,[a]
And as the stubble blown before the wind;
[14] Just as the fire that burns the forest up;
And as a flame that sets mountains on fire.

[15] Just so, pursue them with your storm of wind,
And terrify them with your hurricane.
[16] And make their faces to be full of shame,
So they may come to seek your name, O LORD.

[17] Make them ashamed and troubled evermore.
Yes, let them be confounded and destroyed.
[18] And let them know that you, your name - the LORD[b] -
Alone are over all the earth, Most High.[c]

---

[a] Whirling dust] Literally, 'rolling thing'. AV and ancient versions, 'wheel'. Others, 'whirlwind'. See the parallel passage, Isa. 17:13, where AV mg gives 'thistle down'; others similarly give 'tumbleweed'.
[b] You, your name] The sentence structure is a little unusual. It has two subjects, 'you', and 'your name', making the 'you' emphatic. See Calvin. We might translate 'that you alone bear the name of JEHOVAH, the self-existent one', in contrast to all false gods (see also Ewald *Syntax*).
[c] The Most High] Hebrew *'Elyôn* - עֶלְיוֹן. See Appendix 2 - Names of God.

Day 194   Psalm 84:1-7

[1] How lovely are your dwellings, LORD of hosts.
[2] My soul both longs – even faints - for the LORD's courts.
My heart and flesh cry[a] to the living GOD,
[3] Just as the sparrow has secured a home,   →

170

The swallow has secured itself a nest –
A nest in which it may lay down its young –
A place that's near[b] your altars, LORD of hosts –
Your altars, LORD of hosts[c], my King, my God.

[4] *Bléssêd*[d] are those who dwell within your house.
They shall continually give praise to you. ⧾
[5] *Bléssêd* the man who has his strength in you,
Who has your highways set within his heart.[e]

[6] When through the valley of Baca[f] they pass,
They turn it to a place of water springs.
The autumn rain thus covers it with pools;
Clothes it with blessings of the early rain.[g]

[7] Onward they go, increasing strength to strength, [h]
Each shall be seen in Zion before God. [i]
Onward they go, increasing strength to strength,
Each shall be seen in Zion before God. [j]

---

[a] Cry] The word signifies crying out in joy and with rejoicing.
[b] A place that's near] The Hebrew word that starts this line (*eth* - אֶת) may be a
    preposition meaning 'near' or 'by', or the (untranslated) sign of the accusative
    (hence AV *'even'*). See Perowne (note).
[c] Your altars, LORD of Hosts] We have repeated this phrase from the previous line.
[d] Blessed] Hebrew *'ašrê* - אַשְׁרֵי. Here and v5. See Appendix 2 - Blessing.
[e] Who has your highways set within his heart] Literally, 'the highways [are] in their
    heart'. It may be taken: (1) morally - walking in God's paths (compare Prov.
    16:17; Isa. 40:3; (2) literally, - of the pilgrim highways to Zion (v7), where God's
    dwellings, courts, and altars were (compare 2 Chr. 9:11 - see Horsley, and
    modern versions, which supply 'to Zion'); prophetically - of Israel's final return
    (compare Isa. 11:16; 49:10-13). In all the verses quoted the Hebrew word
    translated 'highways' is used. It denotes 'a made road, cast up, or embanked',
    de Burgh.
[f] Baca] All the ancient versions translate this word, or name, by 'weeping' - the
    valley of weeping thus becomes a valley of joy. Compare the valley of Achor,
    Hos. 2:15.
[g] The autumn rain ... early rain] We have given an alternative translation in the
    second line. The Hebrew word (*môreh* - מוֹרֶה) is the early (as opposed to the
    latter) rain, that fell in the autumn (as Joel 2:23). The covering is with
    'blessings' - so the German (Luther), Dutch (*Statenvertaling*), Latin (T&J)
    translations, and Gesenius *Lexicon*. The AV translates 'pools', with the change
    of one of the vowels of the text.
[h] Increasing strength to strength] Or 'from company to company' (AV mg).
[i] Each shall be seen in Zion before God] Hebrew 'appears unto God'. As Motyer
    (1) comments in Exod. 23:17, 'to appear before (or 'unto', אֶל *-el)* God' meant

171

[j] Onward ... before God] We have repeated the last two lines.

Day 195　　Psalm 84:8-12

[8] O LORD, the God of hosts, do hear my prayer!
O God of Jacob, Do give ear to me! ╫
[9] O God, behold our shield[a], and do regard –
Regard the face of your anointed one.

[10] Because a day spent in your courts is good,
Far better than a thousand spent elsewhere.
I'd rather keep the door in my God's house,
Than dwell among the tents of wickedness.

[11] Because the LORD God is both sun and shield.
The LORD gives grace and glory – Won't withhold –
A good thing from those who walk blamelessly.
[12] The man[b] who trusts you, LORD of hosts, is *blest!* [c]

---

[a] O God, behold our shield] We may either read 'shield' as referring to God as our
shield ('O God our Shield', in which case it is repeated in v11) or, as we have
taken it, of the Anointed one (of the next line).
[b] Man] Hebrew *'adham* - אָדָם - Man as a child of Adam, human. Used collectively
for mankind or the human race. An ordinary member of mankind is raised to
blessedness by his trust in the Lord. See Appendix 2 - Man.
[c] Blest] Hebrew *'ašrê* - אַשְׁרֵי. See Appendix 2 - Blessing.

Day 196　　Psalm 85:1-7

[1] You have shown favour to your land, O LORD;
You have turned back[a] Jacob's captivity.
[2] You've covered over all your people's faults,[b]
And you have lifted, pardoned[c], all their sin. ╫

[3] You have entirely set aside your wrath; [d]
From your hot anger you have turned away.
[4] O God of our salvation turn us back;
And end the grief that you have over us. [e]

[5] Will you be angry with us evermore?
And will your anger ever be prolonged –
To every generation yet to come? [f]
[6] Will you not give new life to us again?　　　→

Will you not give new life to us again[g] –
So that your people may rejoice in you?
[7] Your loving-kindness[h] show to us, O LORD,
And grant us the salvation that you give.

---

[a] Turned back] Or 'brought back'. The verb occurs in v1,3,6,8 of this Psalm.
[b] You've covered over all your people's faults] See Psalms 32:1 and 78:38.
   'Iniquities' in most versions.
[c] Lifted, pardoned] The word usually translated 'pardoned' also means 'lifted'. In
   this verse we have a 'covering over' and a 'lifting off' of sin.
[d] Entirely set aside your wrath] All your wrath you have turned away.
[e] End the grief that you have over us] The Hebrew verb here means 'turn away' or
   'dissipate'. It is the vexation we have caused him, as of grieving the Spirit of
   God, rather than 'anger' that the Psalmist prays about here. The word the AV
   translates 'anger' here is different from the word in v5, and is more commonly
   translated 'grief'.
[f] To every generation yet to come] Hebrew 'to generation and generation'.
[g] We have repeated this line to keep continuity with the previous stanza.
[h] Loving-kindness] Hebrew ḥesedh - חֶסֶד. See Appendix 2 - Loving-kindness.

Day 197   Psalm 85:8-13

[8] I'll listen to what GOD[a] the LORD will speak,
Because unto his people he speaks peace.
Yes, he speaks peace unto those whom he loves,[b]
But let them not turn back to foolishness.

[9] His saving help is near[c] those who fear him,
So that the glory may dwell[d] in our land.
[10] Mercy[e] and truth have now together met;
Yes, righteousness and peace together kissed.

[11] Truth, faithfulness[f], have sprung up from the earth,
And out of heaven righteousness looks down.
[12] the LORD will truly give that which is good,
And so our land will yield its harvest home.[g]

[14] Before his face shall righteousness go forth,
And will establish his steps in the way.[h]
Before his face shall righteousness go forth,
And will establish his steps in the way.[i]

---

[a] GOD] Hebrew 'El - אֵל. See Appendix 2 - Names of God.

^b Those whom he loves] We have repeated 'he speaks peace' from the previous line. AV 'saints'. Hebrew *ḥaṣîdhîm* - חֲסִידִים. Those who are the objects of God's loving-kindness and covenant love. See Appendix 2 - Loving-kindness.

^c His saving help is near] The Hebrew emphasises the 'nearness'. AV 'Surely his salvation is nigh'. The word 'near' applies to time, place, and relationship. 'Saving help' - 'salvation' is the same word as 'Jesus' (Yeshua) in Hebrew. See also Ps. 118:14.

^d The glory may dwell] Hebrew *liškkon kabhodh* - לִשְׁכֹּן כָּבֹד. The first word 'to dwell' (*šakhan* - שָׁכַן) is the root word of the shekinah (*šekhînâ* - שְׁכִינָה) - God's Divine presence. It is frequently used of God 'dwelling' with his people.

^e Mercy] Hebrew *ḥesedh* - חֶסֶד. See Appendix 2 - Loving-kindness.

^f Truth, faithfulness] One word in Hebrew (*'emeth* - אֱמֶת). The AV usually translates the word by 'truth', as in v11, but Gesenius *Lexicon* considers the primary meaning to be 'faithfulness', which the AV generally reserves for the kindred word (*'emûnâ* - אֱמוּנָה). See Neh. 7:2, where the AV translates *'emeth* as 'faithful'.

^g Harvest home] Its increase, produce, or fruit.

^h Will establish ... way] De Burgh 'righteousness shall direct his going in the way - all his proceedings'.

ⁱ We have repeated the last two lines.

Day 198   Psalm 86:1-5

¹ Incline your ear, O LORD, and answer me;
Because I am afflicted and in need.
² Preserve my soul, for I am loved by you.^a
Your servant save, who trusts in you, my God!

³ O please, My Lord^b, be gracious unto me;
For unto you I cry out all the day
⁴ Make the soul of your servant to be glad;
For unto you, My Lord, I lift my soul.

⁵ For you, My Lord, are good and pardoning.
Yes, you are good, and ready to forgive.^c
You are abounding in your steadfast love^d
Unto all those who call on you for help.

---

^a I am loved by you] Hebrew *ḥaṣîdh* - חָסִיד - one who is the object of God's loving-kindness and covenant love. *Statenvertaling* 'I am [thy] favourite'. AV 'I am holy' is an unfortunate translation. See Appendix 2 - Loving-kindness.

^b My Lord] Hebrew *'Adhonay* - אֲדֹנָי. So also in v4,5,8,9,12,15 of this Psalm. See Appendix 2 - Names of God.

^c We have repeated the previous line, extending its meaning.

^d Steadfast love] Hebrew *ḥesedh* - חֶסֶד. See Appendix 2 - Loving-kindness.

Day 199 Psalm 86:6-13

⁶ LORD, hear[a] my prayer. My supplications heed.
⁷ I'll call on you in my day of distress;
Because you will then hear and answer[b] me.
⁸ There's none like you among the gods, My Lord.

There are not any works like unto yours.
⁹ All of the nations - made by you - shall come,
And they shall worship before you, My Lord,
And they shall greatly glorify[c] your name.

¹⁰ For you are great, and you do wondrous things.
You're God alone! ¹¹ LORD, teach your way to me;
And I will walk in your sure, faithful, truth.[d]
Make my heart one, that I may fear your name.

¹² I'll thank you Lord[e], my God, with my whole heart.
I'll glorify your name for evermore;
¹³ Because your steadfast love[f] is great to me.
From depths of Sheol[g] you've rescued my soul.

---

[a] Hear] 'Incline your ear to'.
[b] Hear and answer] The word in Hebrew carries both meanings.
[c] Greatly glorify] Hebrew intensive (piel).
[d] Sure, faithful, truth] One word in Hebrew ('emeth - אֱמֶת), which conveys the meaning of 'truth', 'faithfulness', 'reliability'.
[e] Lord] My Lord, Hebrew 'Adhonay - אֲדֹנָי. See Appendix 2 - Names of God.
[f] Steadfast love] Hebrew ḥeṣedh - חֶסֶד. See Appendix 2 - Loving-kindness.
[g] Sheol] Hebrew še'ôl - שְׁאוֹל. See Appendix 2 - Sheol.

Day 200 Psalm 86:14-17

¹⁴ O God, the proud have risen against me.
A band of ruthless men have sought my soul,
And they have not kept you before their eyes -
¹⁵ My Lord, the merciful[a] and gracious GOD.

You're slow to anger, very kind[b] and true.
¹⁶ O turn to me, be gracious unto me.
Grant to your servant your strength and your power.[c]
Give your salvation to your handmaid's[d] son.   →

175

¹⁷ O make a sign, a sign with me for good^e
That those who hate me may see and be shamed.
For LORD you helped, and gave comfort to me.
For LORD you helped, and gave comfort to me.^f

---

^a Merciful] 'Compassionate', 'showing pity'. As Exod. 34:6.
^bKind] 'Showing loving-kindness'. Hebrew ḥeṣedh - חֶסֶד. See Appendix 2 - Loving-kindness.
^c Strength … power] One word conveying both meanings in Hebrew.
^d Handmaid] A female servant or slave. A slave by birth had a greater claim on his master than one bought.
^e Make a sign … sign with me for good] AV 'show me a token of good'. 'Token' has been devalued in meaning. The Hebrew word means 'a sign', or even 'a proof'. The word we have translated 'make' is a very general one that could mean 'show'. 'Work' is its commonest meaning. The Hebrew word 'with' is used in 'Immanuel' – 'God with us'.
^f For LORD you helped … to me] We have repeated the last line.

Day 201   Psalm 87

¹ His place is founded on the holy hills.^a
² The LORD has greater love for Zion's gates –
Than all the places in which Jacob dwells.
³ City of God your glories are foretold! ⫪

⁴ Unto remembrance to those who know me
Rahab^b and Babylon I'll call to mind
Note this^c – Philistia and Tyre, with Cush.^d
This is the one, the one who was born there.

⁵ But unto Zion it will be declared
That every one of them^e is born therein.
The Most High^f will establish it himself.
The Most High will establish it himself.^g

⁶ The LORD shall count - the peoples he'll write down –
He will record that 'This one was born there', ^h ⫪
⁷ And they will sing, and they will dance for joy.ⁱ
'The fountain-head of all my springs is you!'^j

---

^a His place is founded on the holy hills] Literally, 'his foundation is upon'. Geneva Bible Notes 'God did chose that place among the hills to establish Jerusalem and Temple'.
^b Rahab] The Hebrew word refers to a fierce animal (crocodile?) that is

emblematic of Egypt (see Hebrew of Ps. 89:10 and Isa. 30:7 and 51:9). Newton
   (8) 'Egypt morally'; Bonar 'proud Egypt'.

c Note this] Hebrew *hinneh* - הִנֵּה. See Appendix 2 - Behold!
d Cush] So the Hebrew. AV 'Ethiopia'.
e Every one of them] Hebrew 'man and man' (*'îš ve 'îš* - אִישׁ וְאִישׁ). Perowne 'one
   after another'.
f The Most High] Hebrew *'Elyôn* - עֶלְיוֹן. See Appendix 2 - Names of God.
g We have repeated this line.
h The Lord will count ... born there] Bonar notes the connection of thought with
   Numb. 1:18, where God conducts a census of his Israel.
i They will sing ... dance for joy] Taking the participles as finite verbs. See Perowne
   (notes) following Hupfeld.
j The fountain-head of all my springs is you] Literally, 'All my springs in you'. Cf. Ps.
   36:9; Isa. 12:3; Rev. 21:6.

Day 202   Psalm 88:1-8

¹ O Lord, the God of my deliverance, ᵃ
Both day and night I've cried out in your sight.
² O let my prayer come in before your face;
To my entreaty ᵇ do incline your ear.

³ My soul is full of troubles to excess;
Unto Sheol ᶜ my life is drawing near.
⁴ I'm counted with those sinking to the Pit.
I have become a man ᵈ who has no strength.

⁵ I am a castaway among the dead. ᵉ
I'm like the slain ones lying in the grave -
Those who you don't remember any more -
Like those who have been cut off from your hand.

⁶ You put me down into the deepest pit,
And in dark places, regions dark and deep.
⁷ Your burning anger presses hard on me.
You have afflicted me with all your waves. ╫

⁸ You have removed my best friends ᶠ far from me;
You made me as a loathsome thing to them.
I am shut up and I have no way out.
I am shut up and I have no way out. ᵍ

a Deliverance] 'Salvation'.

177

^b Entreaty] The word is usually linked with joy, but may, as here, be associated
   with prayer and supplication.
^c Sheol] Hebrew *še'ôl* - שְׁאוֹל. The place of the dead. See Appendix 2 - Sheol.
^d A man] Hebrew *gebher* - גֶּבֶר - a strong man, a warrior. See Appendix 2 - Man.
^e A castaway among the dead] Luther 'abandoned among the dead'. See
   Perowne note.
^f Best friends] As v18. See note there.
^g We have repeated the last line.

Day 203   Psalm 88:9-12

⁹ Through my affliction my eye wastes away.
LORD, I have called upon you every day;
LORD, I have called on you all through the day,^a
And unto you I have stretched out my hands.

¹⁰ Will you show wonders to those left for dead? ^b
The mighty ones^c - shall they rise and praise you? ☩
¹¹ And shall your mercy^d be told in the grave?
Your faithfulness told where Destruction^e is?

¹² Or will your wonders be known in the dark?
Your righteousness, shall it indeed be known?
Shall it be known in the forgotten land?^f
Shall it be known in the forgotten land?^g

^a LORD, I have called ... all through the day] We have repeated the line giving the
   two meanings of the Hebrew expression - a calling on God 'all the days' or 'all
   the day'.
^b Those left for dead] Horsley translates 'a person left for dead, under his wounds,
   upon the field of battle ... and incapable of rising to defend himself'. Cf.
   Septuagint *traumatian* (τραυματιαν). 'We have no corresponding word in the
   English Language'. 'Wonders' is singular in Hebrew.
^c Mighty ones] Hebrew *repha'îm* - רְפָאִים, as Gen. 14:5, where it refers to a race of
   giants. De Burgh here translates 'the mighty dead'. We follow Newton (12)
   here. He considers the translation 'shades' (ESV) or *'manes'* to be a
   contradiction of New Testament teaching.
^d Mercy] Loving-kindness, covenant mercy. Hebrew *ḥeṣedh* - חֶסֶד. See Appendix
   2 - Loving-kindness.
^e Destruction] Hebrew *'Abhaddôn* - אֲבַדּוֹן. In the Old Testament the word is
   referred to as the place of destruction. In the New Testament (Rev. 9:11) it is a
   name to Satan, the Destroyer.
^f A forgotten land] Almost universally translators give 'land of forgetfulness'
   (Geneva Bible 'oblivion'). The Lord's story of the rich man and Lazarus makes
   clear that the dead do not lose their memory, whether through supposed 'soul
   sleep' or annihilation. We believe that the Septuagint is correct in translating

178

'being forgotten', either in a natural sense that the dead fade from memory, or that there should be no remembrance of them or their place when believers enter into glory. We cannot defend the usual translation on the grounds of the imperfect understanding of the writer. These are the words of the Holy Spirit.
[8] We have repeated the last line as a solemn question. In adverse providences we should long that God's covenant mercy, faithfulness, wonders and, righteousness should be vindicated in our lives before our death.

Day 204   Psalm 88:13-18

[13] But as for me - I've cried to you, O LORD,
And in the morning my prayer meets with you.
[14] Why is it, LORD, that you reject my soul?
Why do you turn your face away from me?

[15] Afflicted, close to death from my youth up,
I bear your terrors, everywhere I turn.[a]
[16] Fires of your wrath[b] have gone right over me;
Your dreadful terrors, they have cut me off.

[17] Like waters, they've come round me all day long;
Together they enclosed me round about.
[18] Lover and friend you've put far off from me,
And my best friends[c] are put in a dark place.

---

[a] Everywhere I turn] The word is of uncertain meaning and only occurs here. We have followed the Jewish Publications Society *Tanakh*, which in turn follows Gaon Saadia (882-942), who wrote explanatory notes on the *hapax legomena* of the Hebrew Bible. AV 'I am distracted'.
[b] Fires of your wrath] 'God's burning wrath'. The word is plural.
[c] Best friends] Literally, 'those who know me well' Pual (intensive passive participle). A different word from the previous line. The word is plural.

Day 205   Psalm 89:1-5

[1] I'll ever sing the mercies[a] of the LORD,
And with my mouth I'll tell your faithfulness,
Unto all generations[b] I'll make known
[2] Mercy[c], I said, 'shall be built evermore!'

In heaven[d] you will set your faithfulness.
[3] 'I've covenanted with my chosen one;
And to my servant, David, sworn an oath
[4] Your offspring I'll establish evermore'.   →

179

'I'll build your throne through generations long'.^e ✝
⁵ So shall the heavens praise your wonder^f, LORD!
Indeed, your faithfulness shall be praised too,
In the assembly of your holy ones.

---

^a Mercies] Loving-kindnesses (plural). As Isa. 55:3. Hebrew *ḥeṣedh* - חֶסֶד. See Appendix 2 - Loving-kindness.
^b Unto all generations] Hebrew 'to generation and generation'.
^c Mercy] As v1.
^d Heaven] Hebrew 'the heavens'
^e Through generations long] Hebrew 'generation and generation' – 'for ever continuously', as the covenant with Noah (Gen. 9:12). See too 2 Sam. 7:11-16.
^f Wonder] Singular in Hebrew; *pele* '- פֶּלֶא. It is an attributive – 'wonderfulness', 'wondrousness'. 'Wonderful' in Isa. 9:6, which Saphir translates as 'enigma'.

Day 206   Psalm 89:6-14

⁶ Who in the sky^a compares unto the LORD?
Who of the sons of might^b are like the LORD?
⁷ GOD to be held in awe, and to be feared,^c
Even in session^d with the holy ones.

Above all those about him to be feared
⁸ LORD, God of hosts, who is like you - strong LORD!^e
Your faithfulness encircles you around.
⁹ You are the one who rules the raging sea.

When waves rise up, it's you who makes them still.
¹⁰ You have crushed Rahab^f, as one that is slain;
With your strong arm, scattered your enemies.
¹¹ Yours are the heavens. Yes, the earth as well.

The world^g, and all its fullness, you set up.^h
¹² You have created both the north and south.
Tabor and Hermon shall joyⁱ in your name.
¹³ Your arm is mighty and your hand is strong.

Your right hand is exalted up on high
¹⁴ Founded^j on judgment and on righteousness. ^k
Your throne's established, and is fixed and firm -
Mercy and truth shall be before your face.^l

^a In the sky] 'Other peoples worship heavenly bodies as deities: but how can these be compared unto God!', Soncino. This is not the usual word for 'heaven'. Apart from here and v37 the AV translates the word as 'clouds' or 'skies'.

^b Sons of might] Hebrew *'elîm* - אֵלִים is used here. Some take these to be angels, but see de Burgh's objection to this, and Girdlestone's comments. See Hebrew *'El* - אֵל, Appendix 2 - Names of God.

^c To be held in awe and to be feared] One word in Hebrew. The presence of God is cause of terror and trembling.

^d In session] See note on 111:1, where the AV again translates 'assembly'. Gesenius *Lexicon* 'a seated gathering'.

^e LORD] Hebrew *YAH* - יָהּ. The name of God used in many of the Psalms, and in the transliterated expression Hallelujah. Compare Exod. 15:2 and 11.

^f Rahab] Egypt. See note on Ps. 87:4.

^g The world] The inhabited earth. *tebhel* - תֵּבֵל. See Appendix 2 - Earth.

^h Set up] Literally, 'founded', 'laid the foundations of'.

ⁱ Shall joy] The verb is usually rendered 'shout for joy' or 'sing for joy'.

^j Founded ... established and is fixed and firm ...] We have expanded the meaning. All of these words describe the settlement and foundation of the LORD's throne

^k Judgment and righteousness] Hebrew 'righteousness and judgment'. 'Judgment' here is *mišpaṭ* - מִשְׁפָּט. Appendix 2 - Law - Judgment.

^l Mercy and truth ... your face] 'Mercy' is God's loving-kindness. Hebrew, *ḥeṣedh* - חֶסֶד. The word translated 'truth' may also mean 'faithfulness'. Compare v24. See Appendix 2 - Loving-kindness.

Day 207   Psalm 89:15-18

¹⁵ *Blest*^a be the people who know the glad sound^b!
They walk, LORD, in the brightness of your face.
¹⁶ They will rejoice in your name all day long.
And through your righteousness they're lifted up.

¹⁷ Because you are the glory of their strength,
And through your favour you exalt our horn.
¹⁸ Because, our shield belongs unto the LORD -
The Holy One of Israel - our King.

---

^a Blest] Hebrew *'ašrê* - אַשְׁרֵי. See Appendix 2 - Blessing.

^b Glad sound] See note on 27:6. It is literally, 'the shouting'. The word is also used in Numb. 10:5,6, where the AV translates 'alarm'. The NIV translation is wholly unsatisfactory.

Day 208   Psalm 89:19-29

¹⁹ You spoke in vision to the One you love: ^a
And said 'I gave help to a mighty man', ^b
One chosen from the people I've raised up
²⁰ 'David my servant has been found by me'; ^c   →

181

Him I've anointed with my holy oil'.
²¹ My hand will be enduringly with him;
My arm shall also give strength unto him.
²² The enemy shall have no claim on him,

The son of wickedness shall not afflict.ᵈ
²³ I will beat down his foes before his face;
Those hating him I'll strike down, and will plague!ᵉ
²⁴ My faithfulness and loveᶠ shall be with him,

In my name shall his horn be lifted up.
²⁵ And I will set his hand upon the sea,
And on the rivers will set his right hand.
²⁶ 'You are my Father', he will call to me.

'The Rock of my salvation and my GOD'
²⁷ I will appoint him as the firstborn one,
And make him Most Highᵍ of the kings the earth.
²⁸ I'll keep my mercyʰ for him evermore;

My covenant shall stand fast unto him.
²⁹ His offspring I'll establish evermore;
As long as heaven's days shall his throne be.
As long as heaven's days shall his throne be.ⁱ

ᵃ To the One you love] Hebrew *ḥasîdh* - חֲסִיד from *ḥeṣedh* - חֶסֶד. See Appendix 2 -
Loving-kindness. There is a difference in the Hebrew texts and the versions on
whether this word is here singular or plural. AV has singular, but the Trinitarian
Bible Society Hebrew text has the plural! See note by de Burgh who favours
the singular, which is a title of Christ. See Ps. 16:10 where the same issue of
singular and plural occurs.
ᵇ A mighty man] Hebrew *gibbôr* - גִּבּוֹר - Man as a mighty being. Used of Christ.
See Appendix 2 - Man.
ᶜ Found by me] See 1 Sam. 13:14 where the LORD speaks of 'seeking a man after
his own heart'.
ᵈ Afflict] Hebrew, 'afflict him'.
ᵉ Strike down ... plague] One word in Hebrew.
ᶠ Love] Hebrew *ḥeṣedh* - חֶסֶד. See Appendix 2 - Loving-kindness.
ᵍ Most High] Hebrew *'Elyôn* - עֶלְיוֹן. The word is most frequently used as a name
for, or title of, God –'the Most High'. See Appendix 2 - Names of God. Here, in
this Messianic Psalm, it has a double application to him who is Emmanuel (Isa.
7:13-15), and King of Kings (Ps. 72:11; Rev. 1:5; 19:16).
ʰ Mercy] Hebrew *ḥeṣedh* - חֶסֶד. See Appendix 2 - Loving-kindness.
ⁱ We have repeated the last line.

Day 209   Psalm 89:30-37

³⁰ If my Instruction^a his sons should forsake:
If in my judgments they decline to go: ^b
³¹ Or my decrees^c, if they make them profane:
If my commandments they should fail to keep –

³² Their sin^d will I then visit with the rod;
With scourging, visit their iniquity.
³³ Yet I'll not take my steadfast love^e from him;
Nor will I let my faithfulness to fail.

³⁴ My covenant I will not violate
Nor alter what has gone out from my lips.
³⁵ For I have once sworn by my holiness;
Surely to David I will not be false!

³⁶ His offspring shall endure for evermore.
Before me, as the sun, his throne shall be.
³⁷ It shall be fixed for ever, as the moon;
As steadfast as the witness in the sky^f ╫

---

^a Instruction] Hebrew *tôrâ* - תּוֹרָה. See Appendix 2 - Law - Law.

^b Decline to go] The form of the Hebrew verb used properly means 'to make themselves go' another way (see Davies *Lexicon*). The verb is literally, 'to walk'. It is the reverse of Ps. 1:1.

^c Decrees] Here it is the feminine form of Hebrew *ḥoq* - חֹק. It may be significant that 'profane' is used in connection with this form, as 'profane' is also associated with the violation of women (Gen. 49:4; Lev. 19:29), as well as being associated with breaking the Sabbath, etc. See Appendix 2 - Law - Decree. The word is used again in v34 (AV 'break').

^d Sin] This properly means 'transgression'.

^e Steadfast love] Hebrew *ḥeṣedh* - חֶסֶד. See Appendix 2 - Loving-kindness.

^f Witness in the sky] Either (parallel to the first line of the verse) the moon; or, perhaps, God himself. AV translates 'heaven', but this is not the word usually translated 'heaven'. See note on v6.

Day 210   Psalm 89:38-45

³⁸ But it is you who cast off and reject;
You've been enraged with your anointed one!
³⁹ Your servant's covenant you have made void;
You have defiled his crown unto the ground.   →

^{40} All his defensive walls you've broken down;
You've made a ruin of his fortresses.
^{41} All who pass by the road have plundered him,
And to his neighbours he's been a reproach.

^{42} You've lifted up the right hand of his foes;
And all his enemies you have made glad.
^{43} And his sword's sharpened edge you've turned away;
And in the battle have not let him stand.

^{44} You've made the splendour that he had to cease,
And you have hurled his throne down to the ground.
^{45} The days he was a young man you've cut short,
And (as a garment) covered him^a with shame. ⸭

---

^{a} (As a garment) covered him] One word in Hebrew. This is the usual word for 'clothed' rather than just 'covered'.

Day 211   Psalm 89:46-52

^{46} How long, O LORD? Will you forever hide?
For how long will your wrath burn just like fire?
^{47} Recall how short a time I have to live –
Are all sons of man^a made all in vain?

^{48} What man^b is he who lives, and won't see death?
Can he set his soul free from Sheol's hand? ⸭
^{49} My Lord^c, where are your mercies^d as of old?
You swore to David in your faithfulness.

^{50} Take note^e, My Lord, the taunt your servants bear,
For, in my bosom, I bear the reproach.
That all the great and many^f peoples make –
^{51} With which your enemies reproach, O LORD

For they discredit your anointed thus,
Reproach the footsteps your anointed takes.^{g}
^{52} Blest be the LORD for ever, evermore.
Amen, and yet again, Amen. Amen.

---

^{a} Man] Hebrew *'adham* - אָדָם - Man as a child of Adam. See Appendix 2 - Man.

^b Man] Hebrew *gebher* - גֶּבֶר - a strong man, a warrior. See Appendix 2 - Man.

^c My Lord] Hebrew *'Adhonay* - אֲדֹנָי. So also in v50. See Appendix 2 - Names of God.

^d Mercies] God's acts of loving-kindness or covenant love. Hebrew *hesedh* - חֶסֶד. See Appendix 2 - Loving-kindness.

^e Take note] The usual translation given is 'remember', but the word also means 'call to mind', be mindful of', which is clearly the meaning here.

^f Great and many] The Hebrew may mean either.

^g The footsteps your anointed takes] We could translate 'for the delays of every step he takes'. The Jewish commentators (Kimchi, Targum) agree that this refers to the tarrying of Messiah (the Anointed One), and so also Bonar, Newton, de Burgh, Perowne, Horne, etc (cf. 2 Pet. 3:4, and perhaps, in a different sense, Song of Solomon 1:8)

Book 4

Psalms 90 - 106

Day 212   Psalm 90:1-6

^{1} My Lord^a, you've been a dwelling place^b for us,
In every age^c, ^{2} before mountains were born
Before you brought the earth and world^d to birth.
Yes, you are GOD for ever, evermore.

^{3} O, how you turn frail man^e back to the dust!^{f}
You say 'Go back again^g, you sons of man!'
^{4} Even a thousand years are, in your eyes,
A day that's past, and a watch in the night.

^{5} They're swept away by you^h. They are as sleep!
At morning^i, they sprout up like fresh green grass;
^{6} It flourishes at morning, and sprouts up;
When evening comes it's cut and withered dry.

---

^{a} My Lord] '*Adhonay* - אֲדֹנָי. See Appendix 2 - Names of God.
^{b} Dwelling place] This word may mean either 'dwelling place' or 'refuge'. It is
used in Deut. 33:27. See Ps. 71:3 where 'habitation' is used in connection with
a place of refuge, and also Deut. 33:27. The LORD's 'dwelling place' is spoken of
as being in Zion (Ps. 76:2), and the Temple (Ps. 26:8).
^{c} In every age] Hebrew 'in generation and generation'.
^{d} Earth and world] The first word is the general Hebrew term *('erets* - אֶרֶץ*);* the
second word is the populated earth *(tebhel* - תֵּבֵל*).* See Appendix 2 - Earth.
^{e} Frail man] Hebrew *'enôš* - אֱנוֹשׁ - Frail, mortal man. See Appendix 2 - Man.
^{f} Turn back to the dust] As in Gen. 3:19 - crushed and reduced to dust. AV
'destruction'. Jerome translates *contritionem*, hence some have taken the
word metaphorically to mean 'turning in contrition and repentance'. Motyer
(1) notes that the verb is jussive - it is an exclamation.
^{g} Go back again] Return (to dust), as the first clause of the verse.
^{h} They're swept away by you] Literally, 'you have flooded them away'.
^{i} At morning ... evening] Hebrew 'in *the* morning ... in *the* evening'. The definite
article emphasises the singularity of the morning and evening. So too v14.

Day 213   Psalm 90:7-11

^{7} For by your anger we have been consumed;
By your hot anger^a we are terrified.
^{8} You've set before you our iniquities;
Our secret sins in the light of your face.

^{9} For all our days decline under your wrath;
We've spent our years just as a passing thought^b.
^{10} Our days, in years, are only seventy^c;
Perhaps, because we're strong, it's eighty years.   →

But their pride[d] is just toil and vanity,
For it soon passes, and we fly away,
[11] The power of your anger who can know?
As your wrath is, so ought we thus to fear.[e]

---

[a] Hot anger] AV 'wrath'. A different word from 'anger' in the first clause. It is here
linked to the meaning 'heat'.
[b] Passing thought] Geneva Bible 'thought', Perowne, and Gesenius *Lexicon*.
Others translate 'murmur' or 'sigh'. AV 'as a tale that is told'.
[c] Our days, in years, are only seventy] Hebraism. Literally, 'the days of our years -
in them are seventy years' (Perowne).
[d] Pride] Or by metonymy 'source of pride', 'all in which men make their boast'. So
Perowne and Gesenius *Lexicon*.
[e] As your wrath is, so ought we to fear you] Hebrew 'according to your fear your
wrath'. We have followed the *Dutch Annotations* on the meaning.

Day 214   Psalm 90:12-17

[12] Teach us to count the number of our days –
So that a heart of wisdom we may gain.
[13] Turn back, O LORD, for how long will it be?
Show your compassion[a] on your servants now.

[14] At morning satisfy us with your love[b];
So all our days we'll joy[c], and we'll be glad.
[15] For days that you've afflicted, make us glad –
The years that we have seen adversity.[d]

[16] Show to your servants the thing you have done;
And show your majesty[e] upon their sons.
[17] The beauty[f] of the LORD our God give us[g];
The work our hands have done establish sure.[h]

---

[a] Show your compassion] AV 'repent thee'. The word has the wider meaning of
'being sorry', 'showing compassion', or 'relenting'.
[b] Love] Hebrew *ḥeṣedh* - חֶסֶד. See Appendix 2 - Loving-kindness.
[c] We'll joy] The verb is usually rendered 'shout for joy' or 'sing for joy'.
[d] The days ... afflicted ... years ... adversity] Hebrew 'make us glad according to the
days ...' i.e. may the length of our time of joy match that of our past afflicted
days and sorrowful years. Cf. Joel 2:25.
[e] Majesty] The word used here means 'splendour', 'Divine majesty'.
[f] Beauty] The same word is used in Ps. 27:4.
[g] Give us] Hebrew 'put on us'.
[h] The work our hands have done establish sure] The Hebrew is 'and the work of
our hands establish upon us, and the work of our hands establish it'.

Day 215   Psalm 91:1-7

¹ The dweller in the Most High's[a] secret place
In the Almighty's[b] shadow will abide.
² 'He is my refuge', I'll say of the LORD,
'My fortress and my God - in whom I trust'.

³ He, from the fowler's snare, will rescue you,
and from the devastating pestilence.
⁴ For with his feathers he will cover you;
You'll flee for refuge[c] underneath his wings.

His truth's a great shield; armour round about.[d]
⁵ You will not fear the terror of the night;
Nor fear the arrow that flies in the day;
⁶ Neither the pestilence that stalks at dark;

Nor yet destruction that lays waste at noon.
⁷ For, though a thousand may fall at your side,
And though ten thousand fall at your right hand,
It won't approach or come near[e] unto you.

---

[a] The Most High] Hebrew 'Elyôn - עֶלְיוֹן. See Appendix 2 - Names of God.
[b] The Almighty] Hebrew Šadday - שַׁדַּי (Shaddai). See Appendix 2 - Names of God.
[c] You'll flee for refuge] The Hebrew verb is ḥasâ - חָסָה 'to flee to a refuge and a place of safety'. The word translated 'refuge' in v2 and v9 is derived from it. See Appendix 2 - Refuge.
[d] A great shield; Armour round about] The first word here is tsinnâ - צִנָּה. The second word, ṣoḥerâ - סֹחֵרָה (AV 'buckler') means 'what goes around'. See Appendix 2 - shields.
[e] Approach or come near] One word in Hebrew.

Day 216   Psalm 91:8-16

⁸ For you will only look on with your eyes,[a]
And you will see the wicked's[b] recompense.
⁹ Because you've made the LORD (who's my Refuge)
Even the Most High[c] for your dwelling place.[d]

¹⁰ So shall no harm or evil[e] come to you;
Neither shall any plague come near your tent.
¹¹ He will command his angels about you,
So that they'll keep and guard[f] in all your ways.   →

189

^{12} For they will carry you upon their hands,
Lest you should strike your foot against a stone.
^{13} On lion and on adder you will tread;
The lion's young and serpent^g you'll tread down.

^{14} 'Because his love to me is very great,^{h}
I will give unto him deliverance.
I will exalt him, for he knows my name.
^{15} He'll call on me and I will answer him'.

'I'll be the one^i who's with him in distress.
I will deliver, and I'll honour^j him.
^{16} I'll give to him a long fulfilling life,^{k}
And my salvation I will show to him'.

---

^{a} For you will only look on with your eyes] i.e. 'you will be physically untouched in
the time of the LORD's judgment'.

^{b} The wicked] Hebrew plural.

^{c} The Most High] Hebrew 'Elyôn - עֶלְיוֹן. See Appendix 2 - Names of God.

^{d} My Refuge] The change of person in this verse ('my refuge') has led to a range of
different translations. We have taken the words 'my Refuge' to be an aside and
the words of the Psalmist (as v2), not the words of the LORD. This, we think, is
the best explanation of the Hebrew. So Tregelles (3) and The Dutch
Annotations, 'the Prophet's words unto himself'; cf. AV. See Perowne
(introduction and note on v2).

^{e} Harm or evil] The Hebrew word means both.

^{f} Keep and guard] One word in Hebrew.

^{g} Serpent] A poetical word. The same word is used in Ps. 74:13 and Exod. 7:9ff.
Elsewhere it may mean 'a crocodile'.

^{h} His love to me is very great] Literally, 'on me he set love'. Compare the Hebrew
in Gen. 34:8, Deut. 21:11 for the meaning, and see Motyer (1).

^{i} I'll be the one] The Hebrew emphasises 'I'.

^{j} Honour] The word used, Hebrew kabhadh - כָּבַד, may be translated 'glorify'.

^{k} I'll give ... fulfilling life] Hebrew 'with length of days I will satisfy (fill, fulfil) him'.

Day 217   Psalm 92:1-4

^{1} It's a good thing to give thanks to the LORD,
And to sing psalms to your name, O Most High.^{a}
^{2} By morning to proclaim your steadfast love,^{b}
And then your faithfulness with every night.^{c}

^{3} With ten-stringed-instrument, and with the lyre^d,
Even with meditation^e on the harp.
^{4} By what you've done, LORD, you have made me glad.
For what your hands have wrought I'll sing for joy^f.

^a O Most High] Hebrew *'Elyôn* - עֶלְיוֹן. See Appendix 2 - Names of God.

^b Steadfast love] Hebrew *ḥeṣedh* - חֶסֶד. See Appendix 2 – Loving-kindness.

^c With every night] Hebrew 'in the nights' (as AV margin).

^d With ten-stringed-instrument and with the lyre: Literally, 'upon the ten, and upon the *nebhel* (נֶבֶל) (AV 'psaltery'). Compare Psalms 33:2 and 144:9 where there is no 'and'. See Appendix 2 - Harps.

^e Meditation] AV 'with solemn sound', Hebrew *higgaion* - הִגָּיוֹן. The word is also used at Ps. 9:17. See Appendix 3, Psalm Titles, Selah (סֶלָה), and Higgaion (הִגָּיוֹן)

^f I'll sing for joy] AV 'triumph'. The verb is usually rendered 'shout for joy' or 'sing for joy'.

Day 218   Psalm 92:5-9

⁵ How great, LORD, are the things that you have done!
The things that you devise are very deep.

⁶ The carnal, brutish^a man just cannot know,
And he who is a fool can't understand.

⁷ When wicked flourish, and spring up as grass,
And when all evil doers are in flower;
It is so that they they'll ever be destroyed.^b

⁸ But you are God Most High^c, LORD, evermore.

⁹ For - See! - Behold! - your enemies, O LORD;
For - See!^d - your enemies shall be wiped out.
So likewise those who do iniquity
Scattered and separated they shall be.^e

^a Carnal, brutish man] Hebrew 'brute-man'. A man who does not rise above mere animal concerns. As Ps. 73:22. The ESV and NIV abandon the metaphor.

^b When the wicked flourish ... shall ever be destroyed] Compare Dan. 8:24,25. See Tregelles (4).

^c God Most High] Hebrew *Marôm* - מָרוֹם. Literally, 'height'. We take this to be a title of God. See Appendix 2 - Names of God.

^d See! Behold! ... See!] Hebrew *hinneh* - הִנֵּה. See Appendix 2 - Behold!

^e Scattered and separated] We have given the shades of the meaning of the Hebrew word.

Day 219   Psalm 92:10-15

¹⁰ You've lifted up my horn as a wild ox.
With fresh green^a oil you have anointed me
¹¹ My eye has viewed my watchful enemies.^b
My ears have heard the wicked who assailed.^c   →

¹² The righteous one shall flourish like the palm,
And as a cedar grows in Lebanon.
¹³ Those who are planted into^d the LORD's house
Shall flourish well in the courts of our God.

¹⁴ And, in old age^e, they shall still bring forth fruit;
They will be full of sap, and verdant green.
¹⁵ This is to show^f the LORD is just and right.^g
My rock, in whom is no unrighteousness.

---

^a Fresh green] Hebrew 'green'. The expression indicates the best and freshest type of olive oil. The same word is translated 'flourishing' by the AV in v.14 ('green' AV mg.).
^b My watchful enemies] 'My enemies, those who are against me and watch me in a cunning treacherous way'. See Perowne, and BDB *Lexicon* which considers the meaning of the *hapax legomenon* uncertain.
^c The wicked who assailed] Hebrew 'the evil-doers who rise up against me'. Most commentators assume that the psalmist is here 'viewing' and 'hearing' the rout and discomfiture of his enemies.
^d Planted into] The word may mean plant or transplant – cf. Ezek. 17: 8,10,22,23.
^e In old age] Literally, 'in the greyness'. *Statenvertaling* 'in the gray age'
^f Show] 'To present something prominently or meaningfully before someone' Koehler *Lexicon*.
^g Just and right] The Hebrew word means both. Its root meaning is 'to be straight'.

Day 220   Psalm 93

¹ The LORD now^a reigns! He's robed in majesty!
The LORD is robed with strength, which he's put on.
The world's^b established so it won't be moved.
² Your throne's established, even from that time.^c

You are the one from all eternity.^d
³ The floods of waters are raised up, O LORD;
The floods of waters have raised up their voice;
The floods of waters raise their pounding waves.

⁴ More than the sounds that many waters make –
Yes, than the mighty breakers of the sea –
The LORD on high is mighty, excellent!^e
The LORD on high is mighty, excellent!^f   →

⁵ Your testimonies are extremely sure.^g
The beauty of your house is holiness
And holiness is fitting for your house,^h
O LORD, for length of days, for evermore.ⁱ

---

^a Now] We have added the word 'now' to convey the meaning of the expression, as used in 2 Sam. 15:10; 1 Kgs. 1:11; 2 Kgs. 9:13 of the accession of a king to the throne (Perowne), and, as de Burgh notes (quoting Hengstenberg), Psalms 96:10; 97:1; and 99:1, which all refer to the coming of the LORD in his Kingdom. The reference is not to the eternal kingship of God, or his providential reign, but to a new event, which could be translated 'has become king'.

^b The world] The inhabited earth. tebhel - תֵּבֵל. See Appendix 2 - Earth.

^c Even from that time] Hebrew 'from then' (AV mg.). See the use of this word in Gen. 39:5; Exod. 5:23; 9:24. See de Burgh.

^d You are the one from all eternity] Literally, 'from everlasting - you'. 'You' is therefore emphatic, and there is no verb.

^e Mighty, excellent] One word in Hebrew. The same word is used in the previous line (mighty) of the sea's waves. It may mean both 'excellent' (Psalms 8:1; 76:4), and 'excelling'.

^f The LORD ... excellent] We have repeated this line.

^g Sure] Or 'faithful'.

^h The beauty of your house is holiness. And holiness is fitting for your house] The Hebrew word ('beauty' or 'fitting') may be translated either way. See Horsley. It is used in S. of S. 1:5, and 1:10 (AV 'comely'). We have given both meanings.

ⁱ For length of days, for evermore] Hebrew 'for length [or 'duration'] of days', as in Ps. 23:6.

Day 221   Psalm 94:1-7

¹ Avenging GOD^a, O LORD, avenging GOD!
Shine forth! ² Be lifted up, Judge^b of the earth!
Return a recompense upon the proud.
³ Till what time^c shall the wicked be, O LORD?

Till what time shall the wicked ones rejoice?
⁴ They bluster and in arrogance they speak;
The evildoers all act boastfully.
⁵ They crush and break your people down^d, O LORD!

They humble and afflict^e your heritage;
⁶ The widow and the sojourner^f they slay;
They kill the orphan, ⁷ say, 'the LORD^g won't see',
'Nor will the God of Jacob come to know'.

---

^a Avenging GOD] Literally, (as AV margin) 'GOD of vengeances'. The word for God

193

here is *'El* - אֵל. See Appendix 2 - Names of God.

^b Judge] Hebrew *šôp̄ẹṭ* - שֹׁפֵט. See Appendix 2 - Law - Judgment.

^c Till what time?] This is nearer the original than 'How long?' It looks forward asking 'until when', rather than seeking to know the duration.

^d Crush ... break down] One word in Hebrew.

^e Humble and afflict] One word in Hebrew.

^f Sojourner] A special term for a foreigner in Israel, who was in a dependent or vulnerable position (Ps. 39:12; Gen. 23:4; 1 Chr. 29:15). Also, a stranger Gen. 2:22. Hebrew *ger* - גֵּר.

^g The LORD] Hebrew *YAH* - יָהּ, a shortened form of 'the LORD' or 'JEHOVAH'. The name of God used in many of the Psalms, and in the transliterated expression 'Hallelujah'. Compare Exod. 15:2 and 11.

Day 222   Psalm 94:8-15

⁸ You stupid^a of the people, think on this;
You fools, when will you come to understand?
⁹ He who has planted ears, shall he not hear?
He, who formed eyes^b, shall he not look and see?

¹⁰ The nations' Tutor^c, shall he not chastise?
- The One who teaches knowledge to mankind.^d
¹¹ The thoughts of man are known unto the LORD.
They are just vanity, only a breath.^e

¹² *Blest^f* is the worthy man^g you chasten, LORD,^h
Even the one you teach out of your Law,
¹³ It is to give him restⁱ in adverse days,
Till for the wicked one^j the pit is dug.

¹⁴ Surely, the LORD won't give his people up;^k
Neither will he forsake his heritage.
¹⁵ For unto righteousness judgment shall come,^l
All those of upright heart shall follow on.

---

^a Stupid] Hebrew plural. 'Brutish'. Those who act on mere animal understanding and thinking. As Psalms 73:22; 92:6.

^b Ears ... eyes] Singular in Hebrew.

^c The nations' Tutor] He who instructs, corrects, or chastises the nations. The Septuagint translates this Hebrew word with the word used in Heb. 12:6,7,10 (AV 'chasten'), which derives from the word for a child. The Hebrew word is used in Deut. 8:5; Prov. 19:18; 29:17. It means to educate in the right way, to discipline, to chastise.

^d Mankind] Hebrew *'adham* - אָדָם - Man as a child of Adam. So too in v11. See

Appendix 2 - Man.
e Just vanity, only a breath] One word. Hebrew *hebhel* - הֶבֶל.
f Blest] Hebrew *'ašrê* - אַשְׁרֵי. See Appendix 2 - Blessing.
g Worthy man] Hebrew *gebher* - גֶּבֶר - a strong man, a warrior. In contrast to
    'mankind in general' v10,11. See Appendix 2 - Man.
h LORD] Hebrew *YAH* - יָה. As v7.
i To give him rest] 'Set his mind at rest' Horsley. Ewald *Syntax* comments on the
    use of this and other verbs that they 'express a change into a [new] condition,
    caused by the action of another from without'.
j The wicked one] Hebrew 'the wicked' - singular.
k Give ... up] The word is used of a field left fallow.
l Judgment] Hebrew *mišpaṭ* - מִשְׁפָּט. See Appendix 2 - Law - Judgment. This line
    means 'right principles executed aright'.

Day 223   Psalm 94:16-23

¹⁶ Who rises for me against wicked men?^a
Who stands for me against those that do wrong?
¹⁷ Unless the LORD had been a help to me,
My soul would soon have dwelt in silent death.^b

¹⁸ When I had said, 'My foot falters and slips',^c
Your loving-kindness^d, O LORD, held me up.
¹⁹ When I have many anxious thoughts and doubts,^e
Your consolations then delight my soul.

²⁰ Will evil's throne have fellowship with you?
Which frames and causes^f trouble by decree.
²¹ Against the righteous one^g they join in league,
The guiltless one^h they wickedly condemn.

²² Yet nonetheless the LORD is my high tower;
My rock of refuge is my God to me.
²³ He's turned their evil back upon themselves.
The LORD our God will cut them down in sin!

---

a Wicked men] Hebrew 'the ones doing evil'.
b Silent death] Hebrew 'dwelt in silence'. The Hebrew word (silence) is used twice
    in the Psalms (here and 115:17) of the place of death - Sheol, where a person
    is silenced (Ps. 31:18), and there is no voice of praise. The Septuagint
    translates 'Hades' here. See Appendix 2 - Sheol.
c Falters ... slips] One word in Hebrew which conveys both meanings.
d Loving-kindness] 'Hebrew *ḥesedh* - חֶסֶד. See Appendix 2 - Loving-kindness.
e Anxious thoughts and doubts] One word in Hebrew.

195

g The righteous one] Hebrew 'the soul of the righteous one'.
h The guiltless one] Hebrew 'innocent blood'. Compare Gen. 4:10 and Matt. 27:4, where Bloomfield takes the meaning to be 'an innocent person'. The frequent references to 'shedding innocent blood' in the Old Testament may also point to a condemnation of an innocent person to death here, as RSV, NASB, ESV, and NIV assume. However, the Hebrew word translated 'condemn' here does not strictly mean a judicial condemnation. It means literally, 'to make wicked', and hence 'to deal with as wicked' (Girdlestone).

Day 224   Psalm 95:1-5

¹ O come, let's sing unto the LORD with joy!
The rock of our salvation give loud praise!
² Let's come before his face in giving thanks!
Let's make a joyful noise to him with psalms!ᵃ

Let's come before his face in giving thanks!
Let's make a joyful noise to him with psalms!ᵇ
³ Because the LORD's a great and mightyᶜ GOD,
He's a great king, who is above all gods.

⁴ The very depths of earth are in his hand;
The summits of the mountains are his too.
⁵ The sea belongs to him - it is his work -
The dry land he then fashioned with his hands.

ᵃ Psalms] Hebrew *zemîr* - זְמִיר, from the verb *zamar* - זָמַר. See Appendix 2 - Sing Psalms.
ᵇ We have repeated the last two lines of the previous stanza at the beginning of this one.
ᶜ Great and mighty] One word in Hebrew, as 'great' king in the next line.

Day225   Psalm 95:6-11

⁶ O come and let us worship and bow down.
Before the LORD, our Maker, let us kneel.
⁷ For he's our God. We're in his shepherd care,ᵃ
A people who are sheep under his hand.ᵇ

Today - today! - if you would hear his voice,
⁸ Be not hard-hearted,ᶜ as at Meribah.
As in the desertᵈ - the day of Massahᵉ -
⁹ Your fathers tried me. Proved me. Saw my work. →

196

¹⁰ That generation grieved me forty years;
Said 'It's a people who err in their heart'.
They do not know my ways, ¹¹ I therefore vowed –
Swore in my wrath – 'They shall not have my rest'.^f

---

^a In his shepherd care] 'Shepherding'. The words refer to Israel's relation to the
shepherd rather than to a place, 'a pasture'.

^b Under his hand] Motyer (1) "'Hand' is his particular care of the individual sheep,
as each passes under his hand each night into the safety of the fold".

^c Be not hard-hearted] Hebrew 'do not harden your heart'. The word for
hardening is used of Pharaoh (Exod. 18:26). Girdlestone explains it as
'restlessness, impatience, and irritability', differentiating it from other words
used for hardening of the heart.

^d Desert] Hebrew *midhbar* - מִדְבָּר, usually translated 'wilderness', a wild
uncultivated place, but it also means such a barren desert land as Sinai.

^e Meribah ... Massah] The reference is to Exod. 17:1-7. The words are translated
by the Septuagint, and so quoted in Heb. 3:8 - 'provocation ... temptation'

^f They shall not have my rest] Hebrew, 'if they shall come to my rest', Hebraism
(see Ewald *Syntax*) in relation to swearing of an oath, meaning 'they shall
certainly not enter into my rest.

Day 226   Psalm 96:1-6

¹ O sing unto the LORD a brand-new^a song;
O let the whole earth sing unto the LORD.
² O sing unto the LORD, and bless his name.
From day to day make his salvation known.

³ Among the nations tell his glory forth;
Among all peoples tell his wondrous works.
⁴ The LORD is great. He should be greatly praised.
He should be held in fear above all gods.

⁵ For, all the peoples' gods are empty things.^b
The one who made the heavens is the LORD.
⁶ Before him majesty and honour dwell;^c
Beauty and strength^d are in his holy place.

---

^a Brand-new] The Hebrew word means 'fresh', 'choice', 'polished'.

^b Empty things] 'Vanities', 'things of nought'. A word that is also translated 'idols'.
Compare 1 Cor. 8:4; Acts 14:15.

^c Dwell] We have supplied the verb. There is no verb in the two lines of this
verse.

^d Beauty and strength] Hebrew 'strength and beauty'.

Day 227   Psalm 96:7-13

⁷ Let peoples' families give to the LORD –
Give to^a the LORD the glory and the strength
⁸ Give to the LORD the glory of his name,
And with an offering, enter his courts.

⁹ In lovely holiness bow to the LORD.
Before him shake with trembling^b all the earth!
¹⁰ Among the nations say, 'The LORD is king!'^c
The world^d is fixed that it shall not be moved.

In uprightness he shall the peoples judge.^e
¹¹ The heavens shall be glad – the earth rejoice.
The sea and all its plenitude shall roar;
¹² The field, and all that's in it, shall rejoice.

Then all the forest trees shall shout for joy
¹³ Before the LORD. He comes, he comes!^f
To judge^g the earth^h; The worldⁱ with righteousness,
And comes to judge the peoples with his truth.^j

---

^a Give to] 'Ascribe to', 'assign to', by declaring him glorious and strong, and his name glorious. In Hos. 8:13 a derived word is translated 'offerings' by the AV (i.e. things that are given).

^b Shake with trembling] AV 'fear'. RV, NASB, NKJV, ESV 'tremble'. The principal meaning of the word in Hebrew is 'to twist', 'to dance', 'to whirl', hence to writhe (in pain?). Gesenius *Lexicon* says 'tremble ... probably from the leaping or palpitation of the heart'. So again in Ps. 97:4.

^c The LORD is king] Perowne; literally, 'has become king'. See Septuagint and note on Ps. 97:1.

^d The world] The inhabited earth. *tebhel* - תֵבֵל. See Appendix 2 - Earth. Compare v13.

^e He shall ... judge] In this and the following verses we have translated the Hebrew as a future prediction (as Delitzsch), rather than as an exhortation. The word for 'judge' here is Hebrew *dîn* - דִין. See Appendix 2 - Law - Judgment. Compare Ps. 9:8.

^f He comes. He comes!] There is strong emphasis by repetition and by the use of the Hebrew word here (*kî* - כִּי), which we take, not in its usual meaning - 'because', but as an emphatic stress – 'certainly', 'surely', (he comes); as Gen. 18:20 = 'certainly great'; Ps. 141:8 = 'certainly my eyes are toward you'. See Koehler *Lexicon*.

^g To judge] 'To justly rule', *šaphat* - שָׁפַט twice in v13. The meaning is more that of ruling and ensuring justice than delivering a sentence. A different word (*dîn* - דִין) is used in v10. That word signifies passing judgment and making

[h] The earth] Hebrew 'erets - אֶרֶץ. See Appendix 2 - Earth.
[i] The world] The inhabited earth. tebhel - תֵּבֵל. See Appendix 2 - Earth.
[j] Truth] Or rather, 'faithfulness'.

Day 228   Psalm 97:1-6

[1] The LORD is king![a] The earth shouts out for joy![b]
The many islands and the coasts[c] are glad!
[2] Cloud and thick darkness circle him about.
His throne's by righteousness and judgment[d] fixed!

[3] Before his face is going out a fire;
And it burns up his foes on every side.
[4] His lightnings flash, and bathe the world in light;[e]
The earth looks on, and trembling is afraid.[f]

[5] Like wax, the mountains melt before the LORD -
Before him who is Lord of all the earth.
[6] The heavens do declare his righteousness,
And all the peoples do his glory see.   →

[a] The LORD is king] Rather 'the LORD has become king'. Davidson Syntax, notes this
    as an example of the inchoative or inceptive perfect, denoting the beginning of
    an action. So too Delitzsch and others. It looks forward prophetically to a
    future event. So too in Ps. 99:1.
[b] 'Shouts out for joy', etc] Versions change tense confusingly in this Psalm. We
    have generally followed Delitzsch in keeping it in the present tense.
[c] Islands and the coasts] The Hebrew word includes both. Perhaps 'maritime
    regions'.
[d] Judgment. Hebrew mišpaṭ - מִשְׁפָּט. Appendix 2 - Law - Judgment.
[e] His lightnings flash and bathe the world in light] His lightnings lit up the
    inhabited earth - tebhel - תֵּבֵל. See Appendix 2 - Earth.
[f] Trembling is afraid] As Ps. 96:9.

Day 229   Psalm 97:7-12

[7] Carved-image worshippers will all be shamed;
All those who serve such will be put to shame[a] -
Those who take pride in idols (worthless things[b])!
You gods, bow down and worship before him!   →

⁸ Zion, with joy, heard. Judah's daughters danced ᶜ
At the just judgments ᵈ that you made, O LORD.
⁹ Above all earth you are the LORD Most High; ᵉ
You are exalted far above all gods.

¹⁰ O you who love the LORD, hate wickedness!
He guards and keeps ᶠ the souls of those he loves. ᵍ
He from the wicked one delivers them –
Recovers them out of wicked's hand. ʰ

¹¹ He, for the righteous, sows the light as seed, ⁱ
And he sows joy for the upright in heart.
¹² You who are righteous, be glad in the LORD,
With thanks commemorate his holiness. ʲ

ᵃ Carved image worshippers … will be put to shame] We have expanded the
sentence. AV 'they that serve graven images'. Those who are engaged in
religious duties (worship) are said to be in servitude to the false god. The
Hebrew word is also used of the service of the LORD (Numb. 8:23-26), and
sacrifice (Exod. 10:26; Isa. 19:21). 'Carved image' is singular. Horsley
translates 'the carved image'. We have expanded the Hebrew to two lines.

ᵇ Idols (worthless things)] We have expanded the meaning. The word for 'idol' in
Hebrew is 'a thing of nought', 'a nothing-ness', something of no value.

ᶜ Danced] The root of the word is to go around in a circle, hence to leap or exult
for joy (Gesenius *Lexicon*). As in Ps. 48:11.

ᵈ Just judgments] Hebrew *mišpaṭ* - מִשְׁפָּט. See Appendix 2 - Law - Judgment.

ᵉ LORD Most High] Hebrew 'LORD *Elyôn*' - יהוה עֶלְיוֹן. See Appendix 2 - Names of
God.

ᶠ Guards and keeps] One word in Hebrew.

ᵍ Those he loves] AV 'saints'. Hebrew *ḥasîdhîm* - חֲסִידִים - those who are the
object of God's loving-kindness and covenant love. See Appendix 2 - Loving-
kindness.

ʰ He from the wicked one … out of the wicked's hand] We have extended the
translation in these two lines. Literally, 'He delivers them out of the hand of
the wicked one'.

ⁱ For the righteous sows the light as seed] The Hebrew word *zara'* - זָרַע means 'to
sow as seed'. We take the Hebrew preposition, which we translate 'for' in the
sense of 'on account of', 'in behalf of' (see Gesenius *Grammar*). Thus, light is
disseminated on behalf of the righteous one. Compare Isa. 60:1; John 1:9;
Matt. 5:16. In v11 'righteous' is singular. In v12 it is plural (as are the 'upright
in heart' of v11). Horsley (*Nine Sermons*) considers that, in many of the
Psalms, 'The Just One' is 'an appellation which exclusively belongs to Christ in
his human character' (e.g. Ps. 34:19,21). We have repeated the verb ('sows')
in the second line.

ʲ With thanks commemorate his holiness] Literally, 'Give thanks for his holy
memorial'. 'Give thanks at the remembrance of his holiness' AV. Many

versions 'translate' 'memorial' as 'his holy name'. The phrase is the same as in Ps. 30:4. It is assumed that this is a reference to Exod. 3:15, 'this is my name for ever, and this is my memorial to all generations'. We have followed Horsley - 'thankfully commemorate his holiness' (compare Calvin and Segond).

Day 230   Psalm 98:1-3

¹ O sing unto the LORD a brand-new [a] song!
For wondrous are the things that he has done.
He has procured salvation to himself, [b]
By his right hand, and by his holy arm.

² The LORD caused his salvation to be known;
Before the eyes of nations he has shown -
He has revealed to them his righteousness;
He has revealed to them his righteousness. [c]

³ His loving-kindness [d] and his faithfulness
He's called to mind concerning Israel's house.
And the salvation that our God has wrought [e]
All the remotest ends of earth have seen.

[a] Brand-new] The Hebrew word means 'fresh', 'choice', 'polished'.
[b] Salvation to himself] i.e. 'not deliverance of him, as if God had been himself in danger or distress; but that is done *for* anyone, which is done agreeably to his wishes and intentions, and at his instigation', Horsley. See Ps. 59:16,17. It is the usual word for 'to save' and links with 'salvation' in the following two verses. This is the only time the AV translates the word by 'got the victory'.
[c] We have repeated the last line of v2.
[d] Loving-kindness] Hebrew *ḥesedh* - חֶסֶד. See Appendix 2 - Loving-kindness.
[e] The salvation that our God has wrought] Hebrew, 'the salvation of our God'.

Day 231   Psalm 98:4-9

⁴ The whole earth, shout with joy [a] unto the LORD!
Break out, and shout for joy, yes, and sing psalms!
⁵ Sing psalms [b] unto the LORD, sing with the harp
With harp and with the sound of psalmody. [c]

⁶ With trumpets and the sound of the shofar [d] -
Shout in the presence of the LORD, the King!
⁷ Let the sea roar, and all its plenitude;
The world [e] as well, and those who dwell therein.   →

⁸ Let floods applaud - Let mountains shout as one -
⁹ Before the LORD: He comes to judge the earth!
For he will judge the world with righteousness,
And he will judge the peoples uprightly.

ᵃ Shout with joy] AV 'rejoice', but the verb is usually 'shout for joy' or 'sing for joy'.
ᵇ Sing Psalms] Hebrew *zamar* - זָמַר. Here and the previous verse. See Appendix 2
  - Sing Psalms.
ᶜ Sound of psalmody] AV 'the voice of a psalm'. Psalmody = Hebrew *zimrâ* - זִמְרָה.
  See Appendix 2 - Sing Psalms.
ᵈ Shofar] The ram's horn blown at the year of Jubilee (Lev. 25:9), the New Year
  (*Rosh HaShannah*, Lev. 23:24), and on other occasions in Israel.
ᵉ The world] The inhabited earth. *tebhel* - תֵּבֵל. Here and verse 8. Motyer (1) 'the
  world of people'. See Appendix 2 - Earth.

Day 232   Psalm 99:1-5

¹,² The LORD is King!ᵃ The peoples tremble now!ᵇ
He sits enthroned upon the cherubim.ᶜ
Great is the LORD in Zion. The earth quakes.ᵈ
Above all peoples he's exalted high.

³ Praise your great, fearful name! Holy is he.ᵉ
⁴ Justiceᶠ is loved by the strength of the king
And now you have established equity;
In Jacob you've made justice, righteousness.

⁵ Exalt and lift the LORD our God on high
And worship at the footstool of his throne.ᵍ
Holy is he. He is the Holy One!
Holy is he. He is the Holy One!ʰ

ᵃ The LORD is king] Rather 'the LORD has become king'. See note on Ps. 97:1.
ᵇ Tremble now] The word may mean either in fear or excitement. We have
  avoided defining it more closely, e.g. 'with fear', but have added 'now' showing
  it is a response to the LORD's declared rule. A different word is used in Ps. 97:4.
ᶜ Enthroned upon the cherubim] See Ps. 80:1. The verb with the root meaning 'to
  sit' may also mean 'to be enthroned', and 'to dwell'. Compare Ps. 80:1; Exod.
  25:22; 1 Sam. 4:4; Ezek. 1: 5,26-28. See Baron (1).
ᵈ The LORD ... quakes] We have reversed the order of these two sentences for the
  sake of the metre.
ᵉ Holy is he!] AV 'It [i.e. 'the name'] is holy'. Either is possible, but 'he is holy'
  parallels the phrase in v5 and v9. Compare Isa. 40:25 for the use of the
  Hebrew word *qadhôsh* - קָדוֹשׁ - 'holy' of the LORD, 'the Holy One'.
ᶠ Justice] Right judgment. Hebrew *mišpaṭ* - מִשְׁפָּט. Twice in this verse. See

202

Appendix 2 - Law - Judgment.

[g] Worship at the footstool of his throne] The 'footstool' was the lower step of the throne (Isa. 66:1; Ezek. 43:7). In Ps. 132:7 it is used of the sanctuary as the place of worship. Compare also Matt. 5:35. The word used for 'to worship' (šaḥâ - שָׁחָה) literally means, 'to bow down', 'to prostrate oneself', in worship, honour or submission. Compare the Greek *proskunein* - προσκυνειν.

[h] Holy is he. He is the Holy One] We have expanded and repeated 'Holy is he' (as v3), which is the theme of this section.

Day 233   Psalm 99:6-9

⁶ Moses and Aaron were among his priests;
Samuel with those who call on his name.
They called upon the LORD. He answered them.
⁷ In the cloud-column he spoke unto them.

They kept the testimonies that he gave –
Kept the decree that he gave unto them.
⁸ O LORD, our God, you heard and answered[a] them;
For GOD Propitious[b] you were then to them.

Yet you took vengeance upon their misdeeds[c].
⁹ Exalt and lift the LORD our God on high!
Bow down in worship at his holy hill.
Holy, yes, holy is the LORD our God.

[a] Heard and answered] One word in Hebrew. Hebrew 'anâ - עָנָה. See Appendix 2 - Hear and Answer.

[b] GOD Propitious] We have followed Calvin here. The Hebrew verb is used of forgiveness (Ps. 32:1). It is also used of the substitutionary bearing away of sin (Lev. 10:17, Isa. 53:12; hence Calvin 'a God propitious', a God who was propitiated for their sakes. See Calvin's commentary and footnote, and Motyer (1). 'GOD' here is 'El - אֵל - See Appendix 2, Names of God.

[c] Their misdeeds] This 'their' appears to refer to the people, rather than Moses, etc. De Burgh is of the view that the second 'them' of v7, but not the first, also refers to the people. However, it may be better to consider 'them' and 'their' throughout these two verses to refer to the people.

Day 234   Psalm 100

¹ All earth, shout joyfully[a] unto the LORD!
² With glad delight[b] give service to the LORD.
Come, with a joyful song[c], before his face.
³ Know and acknowledge[d] that the LORD is God.   →

He made us, for we did not make ourselves;[e]
We are his people; the sheep in his care.[f]
[4] With a thanksgiving come into his gates;
O enter, go into his courts with praise.

O give your thanks to him, and bless his name.
[5] Because the LORD is good. The LORD is good![g]
His loving-kindness[h] is for evermore;
All generations-long[i] his faithfulness.

---

[a] Shout joyfully] As Ps. 98:4,6.

[b] Glad delight] One word in Hebrew. AV 'gladness'.

[c] Joyful song] We have translated this verb as 'shout joyfully' in v1.

[d] Know and acknowledge] One word in Hebrew, which includes both meanings.

[e] He made us... ourselves] So the AV, Septuagint, Vulgate, and the Hebrew text as it stands. The rabbinic correction (qerê - לוֹ) reads 'He has made us, and we are his' (as the AV margin). This is favoured by de Burgh, Horsley, Perowne, and many others and is adopted by the modern translations, and Jewish translations.

[f] His care] AV 'pasture'. The Hebrew word means 'shepherding'. It refers to the relation to the shepherd rather than to a place, 'a pasture'.

[g] The LORD is good] We have repeated 'the LORD is good'.

[h] Loving-kindness] Hebrew ḥeṣedh - חֶסֶד. See Appendix 2 - Loving-kindness.

[i] All generations-long] There is no verb in the Hebrew in the last two lines. 'All generations' (Hebrew: 'from generation to generation') is not just a measure of time, but expresses the experience of his loving-kindness (Hebrew, ḥeṣedh - חֶסֶד, covenant love) by every generation of his elect people.

Day 235   Psalm 101:1-4

[1] Of mercy[a], and of judgment, I will sing.
Yes, unto you, O LORD, I will sing psalms.
[2] I will act wisely in a blameless way.
When is the time when you will come to me?

I will walk with integrity of heart
The times when I'm indoors within my house.[b]
[3] I will not put, or set, before my eyes
A thing of uselessness and wickedness.[c]

I hate the work of those who turn aside,
And it will not attach itself to me.
[4] A crooked heart will thus depart from me;
A wicked person I'll refuse to know.[d]

[a] Mercy] Hebrew *ḥeṣedh* - חֶסֶד. See Appendix 2 - Loving-kindness.

[b] Indoors, within my house] We have rendered this somewhat idiomatically. The Hebrew word 'within' is a strong word that is used for the internal parts of an animal, or the inmost part of a person. We judge the meaning to be 'I will act with integrity even when I'm alone in the secrecy of my own house'

[c] A thing of uselessness and wickedness] Hebrew *Belial (Beliya'al* - בְּלִיָּעַל), literally, 'without-profit'. It is used more strongly as 'wickedness' and 'vileness' in Scripture. In later use and in the New Testament it became a proper name for Satan, the Wicked One. Also used in Psalms 18:4 and 41:8, cf. 2 Cor. 6:15.

[d] A wicked person I'll refuse to know] Literally, 'A wicked I will not know'. This could be translated 'an evil or wicked thing', but the parallel with the previous line 'crooked heart' favours a person rather than a thing.

Day 236   Psalm 101:5-8

[5] He who, in secret, slanders with his tongue
against his neighbour. I will cut him off![a]
The one with haughty eyes[b], and a proud heart;
I will not suffer and I cannot bear.[c]

[6] My eyes are on the faithful of the land,
So they may stay and they may dwell[d] with me.
The one who's walking in an upright way.
He is the one who'll minister[e] to me.

[7] The one who acts in order to deceive;
He shall not dwell or stay within my house.[f]
The one who speaks with falsehoods, and tells lies;
He shall not be established in my sight.

[8] When every morning comes[g] I will destroy,
And silence[h] all the wicked of the land.
So that all evildoers are cut off,
And severed[i] from the city of the LORD.

[a] Cut him off] There are cognate forms of the Hebrew word used here in Arabic and Syriac that mean 'to make speechless', 'to silence' (see BDB *Lexicon*). The word more commonly has the meaning 'to exterminate', 'to destroy'.

[b] Haughty eyes] AV 'a high look'. A superior, disdainful, way of looking down on others. See Ps. 131:1.

[c] I will not suffer and I cannot bear] We have expressed the meaning of the verb more fully.

[d] May stay ... may dwell] One word in Hebrew. The root of the word is 'to sit', hence to stay settled in a place.

[e] Minister] The word is used of Joshua (Josh. 1:1) and of the ministry of the priests (Numb. 18:2).

[f] Dwell or stay within my house] As in v. 7. 'within' as v2 ('indoors').

[g] When every morning comes] Hebrew 'at the mornings': perhaps 'each morning'. Judicial decisions were made in the mornings (Jer. 21:12; Zeph. 3:5; 2 Sam. 15:2; Luke 22:66). The Targum relates it to the morning of 'the world to come'. See Gill; so too Newton (1).

[h] I will destroy and silence] One word in Hebrew. The same word as in v5. Here it clearly means 'reduce to silence by extermination'.

[i] Cut off. And severed] One word in Hebrew, used of extermination and cutting.

Day 237   Psalm 102:1-5

[1] LORD, hear my prayer. Let my cry come to you.
[2] And in the day when my distress shall come,
Do not then hide your face away from me.
Incline your ear and listen unto me.

Answer me quickly in the day I call,
[3] For all my days have disappeared like smoke.[a]
My bones have burned as hot as[b] in a hearth,
[4] My heart is smitten, and withered like grass.

I have forgotten I should eat my bread,
[5] Because of the loud groans my voice lets out,[c]
It is as though my bone sticks to my flesh.
It is as though my bone sticks to my flesh.[d]

[a] Disappeared like smoke] Hebrew 'in smoke'. We might say 'all my days have gone up in smoke'.

[b] Burned as hot as] The verb means 'to be hot' (see Delitzsch, and Welsh Bible), and also 'to burn'.

[c] Because ... voice] Hebrew 'on account of the voice [or sound] of my groaning'.

[d] It is as though ... flesh] We have repeated the last line.

Day 238   Psalm 102:6-11

[6] I'm like a pelican[a] of the wild land; [b]
And I am as an owl of desert wastes.
[7] Sleepless, I watch[c], and so I have become
Just like a lonely sparrow on the roof. [d]   →

⁸ My enemies reproach me all the day;
Those raging at me use me as a curse.^e
⁹ For I have eaten ashes, just like bread;
My tears are also mingled with my drink.

¹⁰ Your wrath and indignation was the cause.^f
You took me up, and then cast me away.
¹¹ My days are like a shadow that declines,
And I am withered - withered like the grass.

---

^a Pelican ... owl ... sparrow] There have been numerous attempts to identify these
birds from the Hebrew words. With the pelican and the sparrow it is usually
now assumed that the AV is incorrect, as these are out of their natural scene -
either away from water, or away from their natural habit of being in flocks.
However, the writer, in expressing his loneliness and isolation, may have been
deliberate in using this imagery. We have retained the words used in the
Authorised Version.
^b Wild land] Hebrew *midhbar* - מִדְבָּר, usually translated 'wilderness', a wild
uncultivated place.
^c Sleepless, I watch] The Hebrew word conveys both watchfulness and
sleeplessness.
^d Sparrow on the roof] The Welsh word for 'sparrow', *'aderyn y to'* literally, *'roof
bird'* makes some difficulty for translators of the Welsh Bible.
^e Use me as a curse] Horsley, 'make me their standard of execration'; 'to swear
by', rather than 'to swear at'. Perowne - as if they said 'God do to me [to you]
as God has done to this man', cf. Isa. 65:15; Jer. 29:22.
^f Your wrath and indignation was the cause] Literally, 'from the face of your
indignation and your wrath', i.e. 'because of your ...'

Day 239   Psalm 102:12-17

¹² But you, LORD, are enthroned^a for evermore;
For ever you will dwell, and will remain.
Throughout all generations^b it shall be
That your memorial shall still abide.

¹³ You will arise, and will share Zion's grief,^c
The time for pity on her now has come.
For now the set, appointed, time has come.
For now the set, appointed, time has come.^d

¹⁴ For in its stones your servants take delight,
And they have pity, even on its dust.
¹⁵ And the LORD's name the nations then will fear.
Your glory will make all earth's kings afraid.   →

¹⁶ For now the LORD has built^e Zion again.
He now appears in glory, and is seen!
¹⁷ He turns unto the destitute one's^f prayer –
Does not despise or disregard their prayer.

---

^a Enthroned ... dwell ... remain ... endure] The Hebrew verb may have each of
these meanings. 'Enthroned', in our view, conveys the meaning in the context,
following Psalms 92-100. We have added the extended meaning in the
following line.
^b Throughout all generations ... endure] Hebrew 'your memorial to generation
and generation'. We have supplied the verb ('abide'). Compare Ps. 30:4. It is
assumed that this is a reference to Exod. 3:15, 'this is my name for ever, and
this is my memorial to all generations', intimating his covenant relation with his
people. See Psalms 30:4 and 135:13.
^c Share ... grief] Be compassionate towards. 'A deep and tender feeling of
compassion, such as is aroused by the sight of weakness or suffering in those
that are dear to us, or in need of help' - Girdlestone. See Hos. 1:6 and 2:23.
^d We have repeated this line, which marks a pivotal point in the psalm.
^e Has built] The verbs in v16 and v17 are in the present tense. The psalmist, as a
prophet, spoke in the present of things yet future. See Delitzsch.
^f The destitute one] The word is singular and with the definite article, contrasting
with the second half of the verse, which is plural.

Day 240   Psalm 102:18-22

¹⁸ This shall be written for a future time;
Yes, for a generation yet to come.
A new-created people shall bring praise;
A people yet unborn^a will praise the LORD.^b

¹⁹ Because he looked down from his holy height^c;
And, from the heavens, looked upon the earth
²⁰ To hear the sighing of the prisoner:
To let the very sons of death^d go free.

²¹ That the LORD's name they may in Zion tell,^e
And in Jerusalem declare his praise –
²² When peoples come and meet with one accord,
The kingdoms too, that they may serve the LORD.

---

^a A new created people ... a people yet unborn] We have expressed the Hebrew in
two ways. It is an unusual construction (see Gesenius *Grammar*). Cf. Ps. 22:31.
^b The LORD] Hebrew Y*AH* - יָהּ. A shortened form of יהוה, the LORD, JEHOVAH. First
used in connection with the redemption deliverance of the Exodus (Exod.
15:2).

208

^c Holy height] Or 'height of his sanctuary'.
^d Sons of death] So the Hebrew, as Ps. 79:11. AV 'those that are appointed to death'. Compare Jer. 40:4. We might keep the personification of death and paraphrase 'to make Death let go of his children'.
^e To tell] 'To declare'. It is the same word used in v18 for 'writing', and the Hebrew word for 'book' derives from it. We have repeated the verb in the next line.

Day 241   Psalm 102:23-28

²³ My strength he weakened and broke^a in the way.
'My days have been cut short by him', ²⁴ I said,
'My GOD, don't take me halfway through my days,
Throughout all generations are your years'.

²⁵ In the beginning^b, you founded the earth;
The heavens also are your handiwork.
²⁶ Though they will perish, you yourself remain.
All, as a garment, will wear out with age.

Like clothing you will change them. They'll be changed!^c
²⁷ You are the same^d. Your years will never end.
²⁸ Your servants' children will securely dwell.^e
Their offspring in your presence fixed and sure.^f

^a He weakened and broke] One word in Hebrew. It is generally used with the meaning 'to afflict', 'to humble', but it is agreed that the meaning 'to weaken' or 'to break' is intended here.
^b In the beginning] AV 'of old', but the Hebrew can bear the meaning 'in the beginning', as the Septuagint and Heb. 1:10. Compare Gen. 1:1; John 1:1.
^c Change ... changed] The Hebrew uses the same word each time, meaning 'to change' (one's clothes) or 'to alter' (something). The Septuagint and Heb. 1:12 use different words 'roll up ... be changed'.
^d You are the same] Hebrew 'you (are) he'. Horsley translates 'but thou [still art] he [that was before]'. Compare Isa. 41:4.
^e Securely dwell] AV 'continue', but it usually translates the verb as to 'dwell', 'abide', 'remain'. De Burgh assumes 'in the land' is meant (so too Segond). Compare Ps. 37:29.
^f Fixed and sure] 'Established'. As noted by Calvin, and expressed in the following Psalm, the covenant extends to future ages.

Day 242   Psalm 103:1-5

¹ O my soul, give your blessing to the LORD,
And all within me bless his holy name.
² O my soul, give your blessing to the LORD;
And all his benefits do not forget.   →

209

³ He who forgives^a all your iniquities;
The one who heals all your infirmities.^b
⁴ He who redeems your life out of the Pit,
From going down to the destroying Pit.^c

He is the one who puts a crown on you –
Yes, loving-kindness^d - tender mercies too!
⁵ He gives your mouth its fill of what is good,
So, like an eagle, you renew your youth.

---

^a Forgives] Hebrew *ṣalaḥ* - סָלַח. The word is only used of God's forgiveness. It is usually translated by the Septuagint with words that mean 'be propitious to'; as Luke 18:13 'God *be merciful* to me a sinner'.
^b Infirmities] We have avoided the usual translation 'diseases' as it is usually linked to contagion and infection, whereas the intent here is an individual's infirmities, particularly bodily infirmities.
^c Going down ... Pit] We have expanded this line to bring out the meaning of the word 'Pit'. The word in Hebrew (*šaḥath* - שַׁחַת) is bound up with the idea of destruction (AV), corruption and dissolution. It derives from a verb meaning 'to go down'. See Girdlestone, and note on Ps. 16:10 (AV 'corruption'). Acts 2:27 makes the meaning of Ps. 16:10 clear. Compare Isa. 52:14 and Jonah 2:6, where the same Hebrew word is used.
^d Loving-kindness] Hebrew *ḥeṣedh* - חֶסֶד. See Appendix 2 - Loving-kindness.

Day 243   Psalm 103:6-13

⁶ The LORD works out his deeds of righteousness,
And judgments^a for all those who are oppressed.
⁷ To Moses he gave knowledge of his ways;
To Israel's children made his actions known.

⁸ The LORD shows pity^b, and is gracious^c too;
He's slow to anger and is very kind.^d
⁹ He will not endlessly contend, or chide;^e
Nor will he store his anger up^f always.

¹⁰ He's not repaid us^g as our sins deserve;
Nor dealt in line with our iniquities.
¹¹ As heavens' height is stretched above the earth
His mercy's^h strong above those fearing him.

¹² As far apart as East is from the West
He has removed our wilful sinsⁱ from us.
¹³ Just as a father is toward his sons,
The LORD shows pity on those who fear him.

a Works out his deeds of righteousness ... judgments] Literally, 'working righteousnesses and judgments'. We take these to mean the LORD's various acts. It is possible to take the plurals here as intensive singulars - '[great] righteousness ... [great] judgment', as AV and many versions.

b Shows pity] Having deep feelings of compassion aroused by the sight of weakness or suffering (Hebrew *raḥûm* - רחם). Here and v13.

c Gracious] Showing kindness freely to one who has no claim on it or means to repay. Hebrew *ḥannûn* - חנן.

d Kind] Hebrew *ḥeṣedh* - חסד. See Appendix 2 - Loving-kindness.

e Contend, or chide] One word in Hebrew.

f Store his anger up] The Hebrew is simply 'guard' or 'keep' ('anger' is supplied by translations). As Calvin comments, the LORD is not like 'the man who cannot forgive the injuries he has received, cherishes secret revenge in his heart, and waits for the opportunity of retaliation'. Perhaps, 'will not bear a grudge'. Compare Lev. 19:18.

g Repaid us] Literally, 'done to us'

h Mercy] Hebrew *ḥeṣedh* - חסד. See Appendix 2 - Loving-kindness.

i Wilful sins] AV 'transgressions'. The Hebrew word means something greater than the usual word for 'sin' - see Job 34:37.

Day 244   Psalm 103:14-18

¹⁴ Because he knows how we are formed and made,
And he is mindful that we are but dust.
¹⁵ As for frail man[a], his days are as the grass.
He blossoms as a flower of the field.

¹⁶ The wind blows over it, and it is gone.
And where it was is then no longer known.
¹⁷ But the LORD's mercy[b] is from ages past
To endless ages[c] - on those who fear him.

To children's children is his righteousness;
¹⁸ This is to those who keep his covenant.
Who, so that they may do what he commands,
Recall his precepts, and keep them in mind.

a Frail man] Hebrew *'enôš* - אנוש - Frail, mortal man. See Appendix 2 - Man.

b Mercy] Hebrew *ḥeṣedh* - חסד. See Appendix 2 - Loving-kindness.

c From ages past to endless ages] Literally, 'from everlasting and unto everlasting'.

Day 245   Psalm 103:19-22

^{19} The LORD, in heaven^a has set up his throne;
His kingdom's government is over all.
^{20} O bless the LORD, his angels of great strength,
Who do his bidding^b, heeding his word's call.

^{21} O bless the LORD, all you his army hosts –
You ministers^c who do what pleases him!
^{22} All his works, bless the LORD! In every place
Of his dominions! My soul, bless the LORD!

---

^{a} Heaven] Hebrew 'heavens'. It is the throne that is set up in the heavens, not
  'the LORD who is in heaven ...'
^{b} Do his bidding] Hebrew literally, 'do his words'.
^{c} Army hosts ... ministers] This refers to angels. Compare Luke 2:13 and Heb.
  1:14. Our God in his might and power is 'the LORD of hosts'.

Day 246   Psalm 104:1-5

^{1} O my soul, give your blessing to the LORD
O LORD my God, for you are very great.
You're clothed with honour, and with majesty.
^{2} Wrapping yourself in light as with a robe.

Like a tent curtain^a spreading heaven^b out,
^{3} Who, on the waters, frames his upper rooms.^{c}
Making the clouds to be his chariot.
And who goes forth upon^d the wings of wind.

^{4} Who makes his angels spirits, like the wind.^{e}
Who makes his ministers a blazing fire.
^{5} Who sets the earth in its established place.^{f}
So that it never ever shall be moved.^{g}

---

^{a} Tent curtain] As with Bedouin tents. The word (AV 'curtain') is used in
  connection with the Tabernacle. See too Isa. 54:2.
^{b} Heaven] Hebrew 'the heavens'.
^{c} Upper rooms] Apparently referring to the clouds, as in v13.
^{d} Goes forth upon] Hebrew 'walks on'.
^{e} Spirits like the wind] There is difficulty in translating the Hebrew word (rûaḥ -
  רוח), which may mean either 'spirit' or 'wind', as also the New Testament Greek
  word (pneuma - πνευμα) - See John 3:8. We accept John Brown's translation
  and interpretation here (Commentary on Hebrews, on Heb. 1:7), rather than

that of modern versions. The Psalm is largely concerned with creation, and the statement is not about wind and fire being like angels, but about the creation of angels. The psalm declares 'they are created beings who in their qualities bear a resemblance to the winds and the lightning'. Heb. 1:7 supplies the exegesis, 'he says of the angels ...'

[f] Who sets ... place] Literally, 'who founded [or 'established'] the earth upon its foundations [or 'bases'].

[g] Never ever shall be moved] 'The motion of the earth is not denied; but the power of any to disturb it out of its appointed place in the universe, or prevent its answering the purpose for which it was created', de Burgh

Day 247   Psalm 104:6-9

[6] You clothed the earth[a] with sea[b], as with a robe.
Over the mountain tops the waters stood.
[7] Because of your rebuke they took to flight.
Your thunder sounded. They hasted away!

[8] The mountains rose, and valleys did subside
Unto the place which you had set for them.
[9] You've set a limit that they cannot cross,
So that they shall not cover earth again.

[a] Earth] Hebrew 'it'; following on from the previous verse.
[b] Sea] Hebrew 'the deep' as in Gen. 1:2. This day's portion is an expansion of Gen. 1:9.

Day 248   Psalm 104:10-15

[10] He sends out springs into the torrent beds,[a]
Between the mountains they go on their way.[b]
[11] To all the wildlife of the field give drink,
And the wild donkeys there do quench their thirst.

[12] Near them the birds of heaven[c] have their home;
Among the branches they give out their song.
[13] He waters[d] mountains from his upper rooms[e]
Your fruitful work[f] thus satisfies the earth.

[14] To feed the livestock, he makes grass to grow.
He makes the green herb grow to serve man's[g] needs;
So that he may bring bread[h] out of the earth.
[15] And he gives wine so it may cheer the heart.   →

213

The wine to cheer the heart of mortal man; [i]
Also, the oil to cause his face to shine;
And then the bread to make a man's heart strong;
Even the heart of a frail mortal man. [j]

---

[a] Torrent beds] Perowne's translation. This is a different word to 'valleys' in v8, which may be rendered 'plains'. It is rather the deep cuts made by intermittent streams of the desert - ravines, wadis.

[b] Go on their way] Hebrew 'walk', as v3.

[c] Heaven] Hebrew 'heavens'.

[d] Waters] Hebrew 'gives drink to' - as v11. See Deut. 11:11.

[e] Upper rooms] As in v3.

[f] Fruitful work] Hebrew 'the fruit of your work'. Apparently referring to rain as the product of God's purposeful working, paralleling the previous line.

[g] Man's] Hebrew 'adham - אָדָם - Man as a child of Adam. It is here 'the man's'. See Appendix 2 - Man.

[h] Bread] Often used of food in a general sense. Here and v15.

[i] He gives wine ... mortal man] We have expanded the first line of the verse into two. The Hebrew is 'and that wine may make glad the heart of man'. The word for 'man' in the previous verse is 'adham - אָדָם, 'man' in the general sense, but here it is man in his frailty ('enôš - אֱנוֹשׁ); weak, mortal man. We are inclined to think that wine, like divorce, was given to man in his weakness (compare Matt. 19:8), in view of the sorrow of his labour after the Fall. Compare the remainder of the verse with Gen. 3:19. For the spiritual man wine, oil, and bread are but shadows and types of God's better provision to the renewed heart. See Appendix 2 - Man.

[j] Man's ... mortal man] Man in his frailty ('enôš - אֱנוֹשׁ). In the last line of this portion we have expanded the word 'man' to reflect the change in the Hebrew word between v14 and v15.

Day 249   Psalm 104:16-19

[16] The LORD's trees have a bountiful supply [a] -
Cedars of Lebanon - planted by him;
[17] And there the little birds [b] prepare their nests;
As for the stork, the fir trees are its home.

[18] The lofty mountains are for the wild goats;
The rocky cliffs give conies [c] a refuge.
[19] He made the moon for the appointed times;
He made [d] the sun, which knows where it should set.

---

[a] Have a bountiful supply] Hebrew 'are filled' or 'satisfied' as v13. AV 'are full (of sap)'.

[b] Little birds] A generic term for smaller birds. Different from the word used in v12.

^c Conies] This is the animal declared unclean in Lev. 11:5. Wyclif translated the Hebrew word (*šaphan* - שָׁפָן - literally, 'hider') as 'cony' - an English word for rabbit ('rabbit' was originally the young animal), following the Vulgate and perhaps Jewish tradition. It is generally agreed the animal is the Syrian hyrax or 'rock badger', but 'cony' has persisted in Bible translations.
^d He made] We have repeated the verb from the previous line.

Day 250   Psalm 104:20-24

²⁰ You make the darkness, and then it is night,
In which the forest beasts^a all prowl around.^b
²¹ Then the young lions roar after their prey,
Seeking that they may get their food from GOD.

²² The sun comes up, and then they get away,
And in their dwelling places they crouch down.
²³ To his employment, man^c goes out to work,
and to his labour, until evening comes.

²⁴ How many are the things you've done, O LORD!
With skill and wisdom^d you achieved them all.
The earth is full of riches you possess.^e
The earth is full of riches you possess.^f

^a Beasts] Literally, 'living things'.
^b Prowl around] The Hebrew word generally applies to reptiles and fishes (Gen. 1:21). It expresses stealthy movements.
^c Man] Hebrew *'adham* - אָדָם - Man as a child of Adam. See Appendix 2 - Man.
^d Skill and wisdom] One word in Hebrew.
^e The earth is full of riches you possess] AV, 'full of thy riches'; Horsley 'the whole contents of the earth is your property'. We reject the translation 'the earth is full of your creatures', which most modern translations adopt. Here, in Prov. 8:22 (AV 'possessed'), and in Gen. 14:22 the Hebrew word (*qanâ* - קָנָה) is translated 'create' or 'creature' by the Septuagint. Prov. 8:22 thereby became a 'proof text' of the Arians in their denial of Christ's uncreated and eternal Sonship. This has been followed by Rashi, and Jewish commentators and translations. Tregelles (1) states, 'There does not appear to be any sufficient ground for ascribing the sense of 'to create' to this verb; in all the passages cited for that sense, 'to possess' appears to be the true meaning'.
^f The earth ... possess] We have repeated the last line.

Day 251   Psalm 104:25-30

²⁵ There is the sea - that great and wide expanse[a]!
And countless moving creatures are in it;
In it are living things both small and great;
²⁶ And there the vessels go upon their way.

Leviathan[b], you formed to play in it!
²⁷ All these in hope wait on you anxiously.
That you may give them food when it is due;
²⁸ You give it to them, and they gather it.

Your hand you open. They're well satisfied.
²⁹ You hide your face, and then they are dismayed:
You take away their spirit[c] and they die: [d]
They then go back again unto their dust.

³⁰ You send your Spirit out and they are made.[e]
So you renew the face of earth[f] again.
You send your Spirit out and they are made.
So you renew the face of earth again.[g]

---

[a] Wide expanse] Literally, 'wide of hands'.
[b] Leviathan] A great, sea-creature. It is used as of a literal creature, and also
    symbolically (See note at Ps. 74:14, and compare Isa. 27:1 and Rev. 20:2). It is
    only elsewhere referred to at Job 3:7 (Hebrew and AV margin); 41:1,31, 32; Ps.
    74:14; Isa. 27:1.
[c] Spirit] As in Greek, the Hebrew word may mean 'breath' or 'spirit'. Also in v30.
[d] Die] Not the usual word for 'dying'; it is rather 'expire', or 'breathe out their life'.
    So too in Gen. 6:17. Cf. Luke 23:46. See Girdlestone.
[e] Made] This Hebrew word is usually translated 'created'. As Gen. 1:1.
[f] Earth] Hebrew 'adhamâ - אֲדָמָה, 'ground'. See Appendix 2 - Earth.
[g] We have repeated the last two lines.

Day 252   Psalm 104:31-35

³¹ The glory of the LORD forever lasts.
The LORD will joy in things that he has done.
³² He looks upon the earth, and then it quakes;
He touches mountains, causing them to smoke.

³³ I'll sing unto the LORD while I yet live;
Sing psalms unto my God while I shall be.
³⁴ O Let my inmost thoughts[a] be sweet[b] to him,
And, as for me, I'll be glad[c] in the LORD.   →

³⁵ Let sinners be consumed out of the earth,
And let the wicked people be no more.
O my soul, give your blessing to the LORD.
O Hallelujah, give praise to the LORD.^d

---

^a Inmost thoughts] 'Meditation', 'musing'. The same word is translated 'talk' by
   AV in Ps. 105:2, i.e. 'talk to oneself'.
^b Be sweet] 'Be pleasing' or ' be acceptable'. As Ps. 19:15. The verb is used of the
   sacrifice that is acceptable to God (Jer. 6:20; Hos. 9:4).
^c Be glad] The same word used of the LORD rejoicing over his works in v31.
^d Hallelujah ... LORD] The last line is simply 'Hallelujah'. We have added the English
   translation.

Day 253   Psalm 105:1-7

¹ Give thanks unto the LORD! Proclaim^a his name!
Make known among the peoples what he's done!^b
² Sing unto him! O, yes, sing psalms to him!
And meditate^c on all his wondrous works.

³ O let your boast be in his holy name.
The heart of those that seek the LORD be glad!
⁴ O seek the LORD, and seek after his strength;
His face seek constantly for evermore.^d

⁵ Recall his wondrous works, which he has done;
His wonders, and the judgments of his mouth.
⁶ O offspring of his servant Abraham -
Children of Jacob - You his chosen ones!

⁷ He is the LORD our God. The LORD our God!^e
In all the earth his judgments^f are set forth.
He is the LORD our God. The LORD our God!
In all the earth his judgments are set forth.^g

---

^a Proclaim] AV 'call upon'. Horsley, de Burgh, and Baron (2) favour the *publishing*
   of the LORD's name in view of the mighty works which the psalmist goes on to
   relate. 'The phrase ... is not adequately rendered in our English versions by the
   words, "call upon His Name"'.
^b What he's done] 'His deeds', or 'his doings'.
^c Meditate] AV 'talk of'. The Hebrew word is translated 'muse' by AV in Ps. 143:5,
   and 'meditate' in Ps. 119:15.
^d Constantly ... for evermore] One word in Hebrew, which means something done

continually or ceaselessly, and in perpetuity, as the shewbread was to be
displayed (Exod. 25:30).
^e The LORD our God] We have repeated the phrase.
^f Judgments] The word 'judgment' (Hebrew *mišpaṭ* - מִשְׁפָּט.), also used in v5,
refers to governmental justice as well as 'judicial decisions'. See Appendix 2 -
Law - Judgment.
^g We have repeated the last two lines.

Day 254   Psalm 105:8-15

⁸ He ever keeps his covenant in mind –
The word that he commanded and confirmed.^a
Yes, to a thousand generations on –
⁹ The covenant he made with Abraham.

To Isaac gave it as his solemn oath –
¹⁰ To Jacob made it stand as a decree,
And for an everlasting covenant –
the covenant he gave to Israel.

¹¹ He said, 'To you I will give Canaan's land,
The measured lot^b of your^c inheritance'.
¹² In number they were only a few men^d –
Yes, very few, and sojourners^e in it.

¹³ From nation unto nation they walked on,
From kingdom to another people went.
¹⁴ He let no man^f oppress, or do them wrong,^g
And for their sakes brought punishment on kings.

¹⁵ He said, 'Do not touch my anointed ones,
And to my prophets see you do no harm'.
He said, 'Do not touch my anointed ones,
And to my prophets see you do no harm'.^h

^a Commanded and confirmed] AV 'commanded'. The word in Hebrew *(tsavâ* -
צִוָּה*)* means both (Exod. 18:23; Numb. 27:19 the meaning is 'confirmed').
Girdlestone 'set up' or 'appoint'. See the further description of the covenant in
v10, 'established', or 'made to stand'. See Appendix 2 - Law - Commandment.
^b Measured lot] Hebrew '(measured) line'. As in Ps. 78:55. See note on Ps. 16:6.
^c You ... your] The first 'you' is singular - the word given each individual. The word
'your' is plural - the inheritance given to all their offspring.
^d Men] Hebrew *methîm* - מְתִים - mortal, dying men. See Appendix 2 - Man.

218

^e Sojourners] '"New-comers" without any hereditary rights or claims in the land where they sojourned', David Baron (2).

^f Man] Hebrew *'adham* - אָדָם - Man as a child of Adam. See Appendix 2 - Man.

^g Oppress or do them wrong] One word in Hebrew.

^h We have repeated v15.

Day 255   Psalm 105:16-23

¹⁶ And then he called a famine on the land:
He broke all staff of their support - their bread.^a
¹⁷ He sent ahead of them a certain man:^b
Joseph it was, who was sold for a slave.

¹⁸ His feet were put in chains so that they hurt;
His very soul went into iron bands.^c
¹⁹ Until the time that his word came to pass,
The thing the LORD spoke^d tried and tested him.

²⁰ The king then sent to set at liberty:
The ruler of the peoples set him free.
²¹ He set him up as master of his house,
And ruler over all that he possessed.

²² To bind his princes as he chose to do,^e
And to teach wisdom unto his old men.^f
²³ Then Israel came into Egypt too:
And Jacob sojourned in the land of Ham.^g

^a He broke ... bread] Hebrew 'all the staff of bread he broke'. 'Feeble man is dependent on "bread", even as the lame or cripple upon his "staff", and it is *God* who provides this means of support for him, and who can "break" it' - Baron (2).

^b A certain man] Hebrew *'îš* - אִישׁ -Man as an individual. See Appendix 2 - Man.

^c His ...iron bands] Hebrew 'into iron went his soul'. Baron (2) 'his whole being, his mind and spirit, as well as his body, was in the "iron"'. 'An iron collar around his neck' - adopted by versions (RSV onwards) seems to us a speculative dumbing down of the meaning.

^d The thing the LORD spoke] It refers to what God told him in his dreams. 'Word' in the previous line (Hebrew *dabhar* -דָּבָר) is a more general term. See Appendix 2 - Word.

^e As he chose to do] AV 'at his pleasure'. Hebrew 'with his soul', i.e. from the seat of his emotions and passions (cf. Ezek. 16:27, AV 'to the will of').

^f Old men] So the Hebrew literally. AV 'senators'. Most versions 'elders'.

g Land of Ham] Egypt, so-called from the son of Noah; Egypt is usually referred to
in Hebrew as *Mitsraîm* (מִצְרַיִם), as in the first part of the verse, from the son of
Ham - Gen. 10:6.

Day 256   Psalm 105:24-36

²⁴ He gave his people great fertility,ᵃ
And made them stronger - stronger than their foes.
²⁵ He turned their heart to hate his people then -
To act against his people cunningly.

²⁶ Moses and Aaron were the ones he sent -
Moses his servant, Aaron whom he chose.
²⁷ They set among them the words of his signsᵇ -
His stunning wonders in the land of Ham.

²⁸ He sent the darkness: Caused it to be dark
(And theyᶜ did not rebel against his words).
²⁹ To blood he turned their waters: Killed their fish.
³⁰ With frogs their land swarmed, even their kings' rooms.

³¹ He spoke the word, and there came swarms of flies.
In all the margins of their land were gnats.ᵈ
³² He made their heavy showers to be hail,ᵉ
Along with flaming fire within their land.

³³ Their vines and fig trees he also did smite:
In all the margins of their landᶠ broke trees.
³⁴ He spoke the word, and then the locusts came,
And caterpillarsᵍ, more than one can count.

³⁵ They ate up all the green plants in their land,ʰ
And ate up all the produce of their ground.ⁱ
³⁶ He struck down all the firstborn in their land.
The firstfruits of all their virility.ʲ

ᵃ Gave his people great fertility] Hebrew 'He made his people very fruitful'.
ᵇ The words of his signs] So the Hebrew. Perhaps as prophetic utterances spoken
before they happened (so Perowne). Compare 'words', v28,31. Compare Ps.
145:5.
ᶜ They] i.e. Moses and Aaron submitted to their difficult mission, so Baron (2).
They delivered 'the words of his signs' without question, v27.

220

[d] Gnats] The word is of uncertain meaning. AV 'lice'. Possibly linked to a word meaning 'to buzz' = mosquitoes? The Septuagint, Vulgate, and Douay Version simply transliterate the Hebrew word (cinifes). Wycliffe, Perowne, and many modern versions translate 'gnats'. NEB 'maggots'. See BDB *Lexicon*.

[e] He made their heavy showers to be hail] The word 'showers' indicates 'heavy showers' in contrast with another Hebrew word for 'showers'.

[f] In all the margins of their land] Hebrew 'in their borders', i.e. 'in every part'. As in v31.

[g] Caterpillars] A form of locust seems to be meant. See Joel 1:4, where it has been suggested that it means locusts in different forms of development. In Joel the AV translates the word here as 'canker worm'. The Septuagint translates it by a word meaning a locust in an early stage of its development. It was bristly (Jer. 51:27) and had (or developed) wings, so it could fly away (Nahum 3:16 - Hebrew).

[h] Land] Here and v30, Hebrew *'erets* - אֶרֶץ. See Appendix 2 - Earth.

[i] Ground] Hebrew *'adhamâ* - אֲדָמָה. See Appendix 2 - Earth.

[j] Firstfruits of all their virility] The expression is also used in Gen. 49:3 of Reuben, in Ps. 78:51. The word means 'manly strength' - a different word 'fertility' used in v24.

Day 257   Psalm 105:37-45

[37] He brought them out, with silver and with gold.
No one among his tribes was faltering.
[38] Egypt was glad as they were going out,
Because their fear had fallen upon them.[a]

[39] He spread a cloud out for a covering,
Along with fire to lighten up the night.
[40] They[b] made request, and he brought quail to them:
Gave them the bread of heaven to the full

[41] He opened up the rock: Waters gushed out,
Which, in dry places, as a river flowed.
[42] For he was mindful of his holy word,
And mindful of[c] his servant Abraham.

[43] He brought his people out with joyfulness -
His chosen ones with song and shout for joy.[d]
[44] The nations' homelands he gave unto them.
What peoples toiled for, they inherited.

[45] That they might keep the things that he decrees,[e]
And might observe the things that he directs.[f]
O Hallelujah, give praise to the LORD.[g]
O Hallelujah, give praise to the LORD.[h]   →

[a] Their fear ... upon them] The fear of the Israelites upon the Egyptians.

[b] They] Hebrew 'he' - the people collectively (as AV). We have added 'to them' as implied in 'brought'.

[c] Mindful of] We have repeated the verb. 'This was the twofold motive which actuated Him in all the marvellous works which he did on their behalf', Baron (2). God's 'friendship' with Abraham was a motivating factor; see 2 Chr. 20:7; Jas. 2:23.

[d] With song and shout for joy] One word in Hebrew, encompassing shouting, singing, and joy. Compare Exod. 15 and Isa. 35:10.

[e] Things that he decrees] His decrees or laws. Hebrew ḥoq - חֹק. See Appendix 2 - Law - Decree.

[f] The things that he directs] God's 'Laws'. Plural of Hebrew tôrâ - תּוֹרָה. See Appendix 2 - Law - Law.

[g] Hallelujah ... LORD] The last line of the Psalm is simply 'Hallelujah'. We have added the English translation.

[h] We have repeated the last line.

Day 258   Psalm 106:1-5

¹ O Hallelujah, give praise to the LORD!^a
Give thanks unto the LORD, for he is good!
His loving-kindness^b is for evermore.
² Who can express the LORD's great mighty works?^c

And who shall cause all his praise to be heard?
³ Those who keep judgment^d, they are truly *blest*^e
He who, at all times, acts in righteousness.
⁴ Your people's favour^f, LORD, recall for me.^g

With your salvation help and visit^h me
⁵ So I may see the good your chosen have:ⁱ
So I may share your nation's joyfulness:^j
So I may glory with your heritage.

---

[a] Hallelujah ... LORD] The first line is simply 'Hallelujah'. We have added the English translation.

[b] Loving-kindness] Hebrew ḥeṣedh - חֶסֶד. See Appendix 2 - Loving-kindness.

[c] Great mighty works] Hebrew 'the mights'. Motyer (1) '(military) prowess'.

[d] Keep judgment] 'To receive, respect and entertain the word of God, as a decree wisely given forth by him', Dickson. 'Judgment' = Hebrew mišpaṭ - מִשְׁפָּט. See Appendix 2 - Law - Judgment.

[e] Truly blest] Hebrew 'ašrê - אַשְׁרֵי. Plural 'O the blessings of those ...'. See Appendix 2 - Blessing.

[f] Your people's favour] i.e. the favour the LORD bears to his people, in which the psalmist seeks to be included. The word 'favour' more widely means 'acceptance' and 'taking pleasure in' (Hebrew ratṣôn - רָצוֹן).

^{g} Recall for me] 'Keep in mind'. AV 'remember'. He desires the privileges of the
    LORD's people to extend to him also.
^{h} Help and visit] One word in Hebrew.
^{i} The good your chosen have] cf. Jere. 29:32. The general word 'good' in Hebrew,
    as in English, takes on the extended meanings of 'weal', 'benefit', 'prosperity'.
    The Psalmist desires to see the good of his people, following from right
    judgment and deeds of righteousness (v3).
^{j} To share your nation's joyfulness] Hebrew 'to be glad in the gladness of your
    nation'.

Day 259   Psalm 106:6-12

^{6} Together with our fathers we have sinned;
We've been perverse, and acted wickedly.
^{7} Our fathers did, in Egypt, not discern;
Your wondrous works they did not understand.

Your many mercies^a they did not recall
But at the sea - the Red Sea^b - they rebelled.
^{8} Yet, nonetheless he saved, for his name's sake,
That he might make his mighty power known.

^{9} The Red Sea he rebuked, and it dried up:
He led them through the depths as a dry land.^{c}
^{10} Saved from the hand of him who hated them;
And ransomed them from out of the foe's hand.

^{11} The waters overspread their enemies,
And not a single one of them was left.
^{12} In his words they believed, and sang his praise.
In his words they believed and sang his praise.^{d}

^{a} Mercies] Hebrew 'loving-kindnesses', 'acts of steadfast, covenant love'. Hebrew
    hesedh - חֶסֶד. See Appendix 2 - Loving-kindness.
^{b} Red Sea] Hebrew 'the Sea of Reeds', or 'the Sea of Suph', as Exod. 10:19 and
    Deut. 1:1. So too in v9,22; 136:13,15.
^{c} Dry land] The Hebrew word (AV 'wilderness'; Hebrew _midhbar_ - מִדְבָּר, also used
    in v14 and 26) does not necessarily mean desert, but may mean 'a plain' (de
    Burgh) or pasture land. In Hos. 2:3 it is in parallel with 'dry land'.
^{d} We have repeated the last line of the section.

Day 260   Psalm 106:13-23

¹³ They very soon forgot^a the things he did;
They did not wait until he gave advice.
¹⁴ They craved intensely^b in the wilderness;
And in the desert waste^c they tested GOD.

¹⁵ He gave to them what they requested him,
Yet, with it, he sent leanness^d to their soul.
¹⁶ They envied Moses where they were encamped,
And envied Aaron, the LORD's holy one.

¹⁷ The earth then opened; swallowed Dathan up;
Abiram covered, and his company.
¹⁸ A fire was kindled in their company!
And so the flame burned up the wicked ones.

¹⁹ In Horeb they then fashioned a bull-calf:
Before a metal image^e bowed themselves.
²⁰ So they exchanged the glory of their God,^f
For likeness of an ox that eats the grass.

²¹ So they forgot GOD, who delivered them –
He, who in Egypt had done mighty things;
²² The things of wonder^g in the land of Ham;
Even, the fearful things by the Red Sea.

²³ Therefore he said that they should be destroyed,
Had not his chosen, Moses, then stood up:
He stood up in the breach^h, before his face,
To turn his deadly wrath away from them.ⁱ

---

^a Very soon forgot] Hebrew 'made haste to forget'.
^b Craved intensely] Hebrew 'craving they craved' or 'desiring they desired'.
^c Desert waste] Not the usual word for 'desert' or 'wilderness'. Rather 'waste land'. So too at Psalms 68:7 and 78:40.
^d Leanness] It is possible to take the word to mean 'wasting away of the body', in which case viewing 'soul' as the whole person.
^e Metal image] We have avoided the traditional expression 'molten image' (AV). 'Molten image' is difficult to understand, and the image may not have been of solid gold (see Delitzsch on Exod. 32:4). Horsley suggests 'overlaid image' or 'metalline shell', but these make assumptions regarding the process used to make the image, and are prolix. The Jerusalem Bible conveys the contempt implicit in the Psalm, and translates 'performed prostrations to a smelted

thing', although this is also prolix.

^f The glory of their God] Hebrew 'their glory'. It is evident that 'their glory' is metonymy for God himself, in whom alone they should have gloried. See Jer. 2:11.

^g Things of wonder] The verb used in Hebrew is *pal'a* - פָּלָא. The name 'Wonderful' attributed to Christ in Isa. 9:6 derives from it. Saphir translates that word as 'enigma'.

^h Stood up in the breach] The metaphor is of one who, when a gap appears in an army's defensive line, takes his stand in that gap, so that others might not be exposed to the consequences. Alternatively, of the same response to a breach made in the wall of a besieged city. See Ezek. 22:30.

ⁱ To turn his deadly wrath away from them] Literally, 'to turn away his wrath from slaughtering'. The word 'destroy' is used for two different words in this verse in the AV and most versions. The word used here is used of Abraham's near slaying of Isaac (Gen. 22:10), and of the slaying (AV killing) of the Passover lamb (Exod. 12:6). The word translated 'destroy' in the first part of the verse always means 'to destroy' or 'to annihilate', and is always used in connection with the vengeance and judgment of God. See Girdlestone, and *Theological Wordbook*.

Day 261   Psalm 106:24-31

²⁴ Then they despised the pleasant, longed-for^a land,
And in his word they did not place their trust;
²⁵ But, in their tents, they murmured and repined,^b
They did not listen unto the LORD's voice.

²⁶ He raised his hand and swore an oath^c to them -
To make them fall down in the wilderness,
²⁷ Among the nations to make their seed fall,
And in the countries, he would scatter them.^d

²⁸ They put themselves in yoke with Baal Pe-or,
And sacrifices of the dead did eat;
²⁹ Stirred up his anger with the things they did,
And then the plague broke in upon them there.

³⁰ In righteous vengeance^e Phineas stood up.
Because of this, the plague was then held back.
³¹ It was accounted to him righteousness
Unto all generations, evermore.

^a Pleasant, longed for] One word in Hebrew, ('land of desire' AV margin). The root of the word is translated 'covet' in Exod. 20:17. See Zech. 7:14.
^b Murmured and repined] One word in Hebrew. As Deut. 1:27.

[c] Raised his hand and swore an oath] 'Raised his hand' in Hebrew. The raising of the hand was used when an oath was sworn. See Exod. 6:8; Deut. 32:40; Rev. 10:5,6.

[d] And in the countries ... them] See Ezek. 20:23. The 'falling' of the 'seed' [offspring] of that generation in the wilderness was not threatened in Numb. 14. The scattering among the nations did not occur at that time. Perhaps the oath and prophecy relating to their unbelief was in mercy referred to the later time, when these things did occur to Israel, as threatened in Lev. 26 and Deut. 28.

[e] In righteous vengeance] There is some uncertainty regarding the precise meaning of the intensive form of the common Hebrew word 'to pray' (palal - פָּלַל), which is used here. Gesenius Lexicon gives 'to execute judgment in punishing'. Calvin 'executed justice'. AV 'executed judgment'. The Septuagint translates by a word meaning 'to propitiate', apparently on the basis of Numb. 25:13. Modern versions generally weaken the nature of his actions to 'intervene', etc, as if a man can 'intervene', or 'arbitrate', and so break up a quarrel between a people and their God! We have been guided by the passage in Numbers as to the meaning here. Phineas was 'the minister of righteous vengeance, turning away wrath' (Perowne).

Day 262   Psalm 106:32-40

32 At waters of Meribah they caused wrath
Moses fared badly on account of them.
33 Because, against his Spirit they rebelled,
And he in haste spoke rashly with his lips.

34 The peoples they did not wipe fully out,
Which was the word the LORD had said to them.
35 They mixed themselves up with the peoples then,
And also learned to do the things they did.

36 They served their idols, and they were a snare;
37 To demons sacrificed daughters and sons.[a]
38 The blood of innocents they then poured out! -
Blood of their sons, and of their daughters, shed.

To Canaan's idols they were sacrificed;
The land was thus polluted with the blood.
39 And by their works they made themselves defiled,
And played the harlot by the things they did.

40 And so the anger of the LORD blazed up -
His anger then against his people burned.
His heritage became a thing he loathed,
And he abhorred his own inheritance.[b]   →

226

^a Daughters and sons] Hebrew 'their sons and their daughters'.
^b His heritage ... inheritance] We have repeated this line of the verse in different
   words.

Day 263   Psalm 106:41-48

⁴¹ He then gave them into the nations' hand,
And those who hated them ruled over them.
⁴² Their enemies oppressed them – They were crushed;^a
Under their hand they were brought to their knees.

⁴³ Many a time he did deliver them,
Yet nonetheless, they purposed to rebel.
They were brought low for their iniquity.
⁴⁴ He saw them in distress. He heard their cry.^b

⁴⁵ He brought to mind for them his covenant.
In his great mercy^c he relented then.^d
⁴⁶ He caused compassion to be shown to them
By^e all who held them in captivity.

⁴⁷ Salvation give to us, O LORD our God!
And from the nations truly gather us!^f
So to your holy name we shall give thanks,
And so our glory shall be in your praise.

⁴⁸ Blest be the LORD, the God of Israel,
From everlasting and for evermore.^g
Let all the people say 'Amen', 'Amen'.^h
O Hallelujah, give praise to the LORD!ⁱ

---

^a Oppressed ... crushed] One word in Hebrew. The word is used of the crushing of
   Balaam's foot (Numb. 22:25), although it is usually used metaphorically, as
   here.
^b Cry] The word is usually associated with rejoicing, but it is also linked to prayer
   and supplication.
^c Mercy] Hebrew ḥeṣedh - חסד. See Appendix 2 - Loving-kindness.
^d Relent] AV 'repent'. The word has a wide meaning of being sorry, showing
   compassion, or relenting.
^e By] Hebrew literally, 'in the face of'; 'before' or 'in the presence of'.
^f Truly gather us] The verb is in the intensive (piel) - fully and completely gather
   us.

227

^g From everlasting and for evermore] Hebrew 'from everlasting to everlasting' i.e. from ages past to ages to come.

^h 'Amen'. 'Amen'] Only one 'Amen' in the Hebrew.

ⁱ Hallelujah ... Lord] The last line is simply 'Hallelujah'. We have added the English translation.

Book 5

Psalms 107 - 150

Day 264   Psalm 107:1-9

[1] 'Give thanks unto the LORD, for he is good;
His loving-kindness[a] is for evermore!'
[2] Let them say this, those ransomed by the LORD,
Those he has ransomed out of the foe's hand.

[3] For he has gathered them out of the lands –
From East and West, from North, and from the sea.[b]
[4] Some roamed in wilderness – a desert[c] way.
They found no settled town in which to dwell.[d]

[5] Hungry and thirsty, their soul failed within,
[6] Then in their trouble they cried to the LORD.
From their afflictions he delivered them,
[7] He led them straight unto a settled town.

[8] For loving-kindness[e] let them thank the LORD,
And for his wonders to the sons of men.
[9] He satisfies the longing soul's desire,
And fills the hungry soul with what is good.

---

[a] Loving-kindness] Hebrew *ḥeṣedh* - חֶסֶד. The AV translates with strange
   inconsistency in this Psalm. Here it translates 'mercy', and in v43 'loving-
   kindness'. Elsewhere (4x) it translates 'goodness'. However, it translates a
   different word by 'goodness' in v9. See Appendix 2 - Loving-kindness.
[b] From the sea] AV 'from the South'. 'From the sea' is the reading of the Hebrew,
   which normally indicates West when referring to a direction. Assuming the
   writer is referring to the four points of the compass, versions and translators
   suggest various 'solutions' to make the reading 'South'. E.g. (1) 'The [South]
   sea' (so the Targum). E.g. (2) Speculatively reconstructing the text (ימין for ימים)
   to read 'South'. We consider it is best to translate the text as it stands. Isa.
   11:11 indicates a gathering from the coasts and islands of the (Mediterranean)
   sea. See also Isa. 49:12, which does not give the points of the compass, and
   where 'the sea' in Hebrew is generally translated 'West'.
[c] Desert] The word indicates 'a waste' or 'wasteland'.
[d] Settled town in which to dwell] Or 'city of habitation'.
[e] For loving-kindness] Hebrew 'for his loving-kindness'. See Appendix 2 - Loving-
   kindness.

Day 265   Psalm 107:10-16

[10] Some sat in darkness and in deathly shade,[a]
Bound in affliction and by iron bands.[b]
[11] For they rebelled against the words[c] of GOD;
They spurned the counsel of the Most High God.[d] →

¹² Therefore, with labour he brought their heart down.
They stumbled, and there was no-one to help.
¹³ Then, in their trouble, they cried to the LORD,
From their distresses he delivered them

¹⁴ He brought from darkness and from deathly shade;
The chains that bound them^e he asunder broke.
¹⁵ For loving-kindness^f, let them thank the LORD,
And for his wonders to the sons of men.

For loving-kindness, let them thank the LORD,
And for his wonders to the sons of men.^g
¹⁶ The doors of brass he utterly broke down;
The bars of iron he has hacked^h apart.

---

^a Deathly shade] The expression occurs here, v14, and Ps. 23:4. AV 'the shadow
   of death'. A combination of the words 'shadow' and 'death', indicating deep,
   dark, shadow, with 'death' apparently used to indicate 'the darkest shadow'.
^b Iron bands] Hebrew 'iron'.
^c Words] 'Spoken words'. Hebrew *'emer* - אֵמֶר (from *'amar* - אָמַר - to say). See
   Appendix 2 - Word.
^d The Most High God] Hebrew *'Elyôn* - עֶלְיוֹן. See Appendix 2 - Names of God.
^e The chains that bound them] 'Their bands'. A different word from that used in
   v10 (AV 'iron'), although the verb is used there (bound).
^f For loving-kindness] Hebrew *ḥeṣedh* - חֶסֶד. See Appendix 2 - Loving-kindness.
^g For loving-kindness ... men] We have repeated these two lines of v8 at the start
   of this stanza.
^h Utterly broke down ... hacked apart] Both of these verbs are in the intensive in
   Hebrew (as the verb in v14), and mean more than just 'broke' and 'cut'. The
   verb 'cut', in this form, is used of the hewing down of trees.

Day 266   Psalm 107:17-22

¹⁷ Because the foolish went their sinful way -
Their empty things^a - they brought themselves down low
¹⁸ And so their soul loathed any kind of food,
And they drew near unto the gates of death.

¹⁹ Then, in their trouble, they cried to the LORD;
From their distresses he delivered them.
²⁰ He sent his word. He healed them and restored.^b
He rescued them out of their pits of death.^c   →

²¹ For loving-kindness^d, let them thank the LORD.
And for his wonders to the sons of men.
²² Offer the sacrifice^e of grateful thanks;
Declare what he has done with shouts of joy.

---

^a Empty things] AV 'iniquities'. The word is used of vain, empty, and futile things that are wrong, and self-harming.
^b Healed ... restored] One word in Hebrew. Not just a cure, but a restoration. See Ps. 60:2.
^c Pits of death] One word; Hebrew *šeḥîth* - שְׁחִית. The word is only used here and Lam. 4:20. The Hebrew verb it comes from (*šaḥath* - שָׁחַת) is bound up with the idea of destruction (AV), corruption, and dissolution. See Girdlestone and note on Ps. 16:10 (AV 'corruption'). Compare Isa. 52:14 and Jonah 2:6. Geneva Bible 'their graves'.
^d For loving-kindness] Hebrew *ḥesedh* - חֶסֶד. See Appendix 2 - Loving-kindness.
^e Offer the sacrifice ...] Hebrew 'sacrifice sacrifices ...'

Day 267   Psalm 107:23-32

²³ Some others go in ships down to the sea,
And in great waters are engaged in trade.
²⁴ They too have seen the works the LORD has done
And saw^a his works of wonder in the deep.

²⁵ He spoke^b, and made the stormy wind to rise.
It made the swelling waves to surge up high.
²⁶ Which soared to heaven, and dropped to the deeps.
Their soul was melted in their troubled state.

⁷ They reeled and staggered, like a drunken man,
At their wits end – their wisdom swallowed up.^c
²⁸ Then, in their trouble, they cried to the LORD,
From their anxieties he rescued^d them.

²⁹ He stilled^e the tempest to a quiet hush,
So that its waves were silently at rest;
³⁰ Because the waves^f calmed down, they were then glad:
He led them to the haven they desired.

³¹ For loving-kindness^g, let them thank the LORD,
And for his wonders to the sons of men,
³² Exalt him in the people's gathering,^h
And let them praise him in the elders' seat.

[a] Saw] We have repeated the verb from the previous line.

[b] Spoke] So the Hebrew. Most versions interpret this as 'commanded'. Compare 'God said ...' Gen. 1:3 etc, and the Saviour's words - Mark 4:39.

[c] At their wits end - their wisdom swallowed up] We have given the meaning and the metaphor. The Hebrew expression is literally, 'all their wisdom [or 'skill'] swallows itself up'. The meaning is that their seafaring skills were no longer of use to them in the storm. A different verb with the same spelling would translate as 'is confused', see Koehler *Lexicon*.

[d] Rescued] Literally, 'he caused to go out from', as Joseph being brought out from prison (Gen. 40:14).

[e] Stilled] The usual meaning of the verb is 'to rise up'. Davies *Lexicon* indicates here 'to bring to a standstill'.

[f] The waves] Hebrew 'they'. We take this as a continuation of the previous line.

[g] For loving-kindness] Hebrew 'for his loving-kindness' steadfast love, covenant mercy. Hebrew *ḥeṣedh* - חֶסֶד. See Appendix 2 - Loving-kindness.

[h] Gathering] The word is used particularly of Israel's assembly for religious purposes (see Deut. 31:30).

Day 268   Psalm 107:33-43

33 He caused the rivers to be desert land[a]
And springs of waters to be thirsty ground.
34 A fruitful land became a salty waste[b] –
Because the people living there were bad.

35 He turned the barren land into a pool;[c]
And a dry land he turned[d] to water springs;
36 Those who were hungry he caused to dwell there,
And there they made themselves a settled town.

37 They sowed the fields; the vineyards they did plant;
A fruitful increase they did therefore yield.
38 He blest them, so they greatly multiplied;
He didn't let their cattle to decrease.

39 And yet they were decreased. They were bowed down
Under oppression, evil times[e], and grief.
40 Upon the princes[f] he poured out contempt.
He made them wander in the trackless waste.

41 Out of affliction he exalts the poor,[g]
And makes his families just like a flock.
42 The upright ones shall see, and will be glad,
And all unrighteousness shall shut its mouth.   →

⁴³ He who is wise, and will observe these things,
They will discern the mercies^h of the LORD.
He who is wise, and will observe these things,
They will discern the mercies of the LORD.ⁱ

---

^a Desert land] Hebrew *midhbar* - מִדְבָּר, usually translated 'wilderness', a wild uncultivated place, but it can mean a barren desert land - a wilderness for a reason. Compare Ps. 106:9.

^b Salty waste] Hebrew 'saltness', as AV margin. Like the plain of Sodom.

^c Pool] Hebrew 'pool of waters'. 'Pool' = 'a place where water collects', or a place of reeds (Davies *Lexicon*).

^d Turned] We have repeated the verb from the first line.

^e Evil times] A general term for "badness" or "sorrow". Geneva Bible 'evil', AV 'affliction', RV 'trouble'. The word is used in v26 ('troubled state') and v34 ('evil').

^f Princes] This does not necessarily mean those of royal birth. See Ps. 118:9, where we have translated 'the great and the good'.

^g The Poor] Singular, 'the poor one' or 'the afflicted one'.

^h Mercies] Plural, 'loving-kindnesses'. Motyer (1) 'plural of amplitude' i.e. 'great mercy'. Hebrew *ḥeṣedh* - חֶסֶד. See Appendix 2 - Loving-kindness.

ⁱ We have repeated the last two lines.

Day 269   Psalm 108:1-6

¹ My heart is fixed, O God, and I will sing!
I will sing psalms^a, yes, with my glory^b too.
² Awake the lyre^c! Awake the harp as well!
Yes, I would even wake the morning dawn!

³ Among the peoples, I will thank you LORD;^d
Among the nations, I'll sing psalms^e to you.
⁴ Your loving-kindness^f is so very great,
Over above the heavens it extends.

Likewise, your truth extends up to the clouds.
⁵ High over heaven be exalted, God!
Above the whole earth may your glory be.
⁶ For your beloved give deliverance.

For those who are so very dear to you,^g
O give salvation, with your own right hand.
And please do hear, give answer^h unto me;
And please do hear, give answer unto me.ⁱ

^a I will sing psalms] Hebrew *zamar* - זָמַר. See Appendix 2 - Sing Psalms.
^b My glory] See notes on Psalms 16:9 and 30:12.
^c Lyre] AV 'psaltery'. See Appendix 2 - Harps.
^d LORD] In the parallel passage, Ps. 57:9, the reading is 'My Lord' - *'Adhonay* - אֲדֹנָי.
   See Appendix 2 - Names of God.
^e I'll sing psalms] As v1.
^f Loving-kindness] Hebrew *ḥeṣedh* - חֶסֶד. See Appendix 2 - Loving-kindness.
^g Your beloved ... those who are so very dear to you ...] We have expanded
   (repeated) this description making clear that 'beloved' is plural.
^h Hear, give answer] One word in Hebrew - *'anâ* - עֲנָה. See Appendix 2 - Hear and
   Answer.
ⁱ We have repeated the last line.

Day 270   Psalm 108:7-13

⁷ God has declared this in his holiness,
'I will rejoice, and Shechem I'll divide;
The valley of Succoth I'll measure out;
⁸ Gilead and Manasseh are both mine'.

'Ephraim's the strong defence unto my head;^a
Judah's my sceptre^b,   ⁹Moab's my wash-pot;
And over Edom I will throw my shoe;
Over Philistia I'll shout for joy'.

¹⁰ O who will bring me to the fortress-town?^c
And who will guide me unto Edom's land?^d
¹¹ Have you not spurned and cast us off^e, O God?
For with our armies you no longer go.

¹² From out of tribulation^f give us help:
For man's deliverance^g is all in vain.
¹³ Through God we shall contend courageously,
For he himself will trample on our foes.

^a The strong defence unto my head] See Ps. 60:8.
^b Sceptre] as Gen. 49:10 AV. The lawgiver's symbol of office.
^c Fortress town] Hebrew as Ps. 31:21.
^d Edom's land] Hebrew, 'Edom'.
^e Spurned and cast us off] One word in Hebrew.
^f Out of tribulation] See Gill on Ps. 60:11. He connects this 'tribulation' with that
   of Matthew 24.
^g Man's deliverance] Hebrew 'the salvation of man'. This is human (Hebrew
   'adham - אָדָם - Man as a child of Adam.) rescue and deliverance contrasted
   with Divine intervention.

Day 271　　Psalm 109:1-5

¹ Do not be silent, O God of my praise.
² Against me they have opened up their mouth –
A wicked mouth and a deceitful mouth.ᵃ
Against me with a lying tongue they spoke.

³ With words of hatred they surrounded me,
And they have fought against me without cause.
⁴ They are my adversariesᵇ for my love.
They stand against meᶜ – but I pray, I pray!ᵈ

⁵ They have repaid me evil for the good;
And recompensedᵉ me hatred for my love'
They have repaid me evil for the good;
And recompensed me hatred for my love.ᶠ

ᵃ Against me ... deceitful mouth] This line is literally, 'because a mouth of the
  wicked [singular] and a mouth of deceit against me they have opened'.
ᵇ Adversaries] Or 'accusers', as v20.
ᶜ They stand against me] 'The ones standing against me', 'my adversaries'. A
  participle as a substantive in Hebrew. This form occurs again in v20 and v29,
  and the noun in v6. The verb here (šaṭan - שָׂטַן, from which 'Satan' is derived)
  means 'to oppose', 'to withstand', and 'to accuse'.
ᵈ I pray, I pray!] Literally, 'but I - prayer', i.e. 'I am the very embodiment of prayer',
  'nothing but prayer'. Perowne interprets 'having recourse to no other means
  of defence'. Compare Ps. 120:7 'I am peace'.
ᵉ They have repaid ... recompensed] The same word. We have repeated the verb
  in the second line.
ᶠ We have repeated the last two lines of the verse.

Day 272　　Psalm 109:6-15

⁶ The Wicked One shall be set over him;
And so, shall Satanᵃ stand at his right hand.
⁷ When he is judged he shall go out condemned.ᵇ
Even his prayer, it shall be reckoned sin!

⁸ His days shall be in number but a few;
Another take the charge given to him.
⁹ Orphaned and fatherlessᶜ shall be his sons,
And she who was his wife a widow too.　　　→

236

 ^{10} His sons shall ever wander round and beg;
Out of their ruins they shall go and seek.^{d}
^{11} The moneylender seize all that he has,
And all he laboured for shall strangers spoil.

^{12} No-one shall keep up kindness^{e} unto him.
No one show pity on his orphaned sons.^{f}
^{13} And his posterity shall be cut off:
Within a generation^{g} their name gone.

^{14} His fathers' folly^{h} shall the LORD recall;
His mother's sin shall not be blotted out;
^{15} They shall remain before the LORD always;
And his remembrance cut off from the earth.

---

^{a} Satan] We have retained the AV translation. The word means 'an adversary' or 'an accuser'. In the book of Job it is used, with the definite article, of the Evil One. The Septuagint translates 'Devil' - Διαβολος here, which is followed by the Vulgate (juxta LXX *Diabulus*; juxta Hebr. *Satan*). Compare Zech. 3:1, and see comment on v4. The translation 'Wicked One [not 'man'] is consequently used in the previous line.
^{b} Condemned] The form of the Hebrew verb means 'accounted guilty', in the same manner that the believer is said to be 'accounted righteous'.
^{c} Orphaned and fatherless] Hebrew 'orphans', which in Job 24:9 means bereft of father only.
^{d} Out of their ruins they shall go and seek'. Most translations supply 'ruined homes' and 'seek food'. This appears unnecessary to us. The curse is surely as the curse of Cain (Gen. 4:14). They depart from their blasted former privileged condition as vagabonds and beggars.
^{e} Kindness] Hebrew *ḥesedh* - חֶסֶד. See Appendix 2 - Loving-kindness.
^{f} His orphaned sons] 'His orphans' (masculine).
^{g} Within a generation] The Hebrew may mean 'in another generation' or 'in the generation following'. The Septuagint evidently had אֶחָד for אַחֵר (*'eḥad* for *'aḥer*) in their Hebrew manuscript, which would give the meaning as 'in a single generation', which Horsley and some modern translations favour.
^{h} Folly] AV 'iniquity' - empty foolishness.

Day 273   Psalm 109:16-21

^{16} For he did not remember to be kind,^{a}
He persecuted the poor, needy man;
The broken-hearted he set out to kill.
^{17} As he loved cursing, it shall come to him.   →

He disliked blessing; it shall be far off.
¹⁸ He clothed himself with cursing as his coat,
As water it went to his inner parts,
And just like oil it went into his bones.

¹⁹ Just like a garment[b] he wraps round himself;
And like a belt that he always puts on.
²⁰ To my accusers this – the LORD's reward![c]
To those who speak bad things[d] against my soul.

²¹ But you, LORD – My Lord[e], work on my behalf;
On my behalf do work, for your name's sake.
Because your loving-kindness is so good.
Your steadfast love[f] is good. Deliver me.[g]

---

^a To be kind] Literally, 'to work loving-kindness' [Hebrew, *ḥeṣedh* - חֶסֶד].
^b Just like a garment] Hebrew 'may it be as his garment'.
^c To my accusers this - the LORD's reward!] or 'This is the LORD's reward to my
   accusers'. 'Accusers' is the word we have translated 'adversaries' in v4.
^d Speak bad things against] Literally, 'speak evil against'.
^e LORD, My Lord] Hebrew, JEHOVAH *'Adhonay* - יהוה אֲדֹנָי. See Appendix 2 - Names
   of God.
^f Loving-kindness ... steadfast love] Hebrew *ḥeṣedh* - חֶסֶד. See Appendix 2 -
   Loving-kindness. One word here in Hebrew. We have reworded and repeated
   the line.
^g In this verse we have repeated several phrases in different ways, as they are
   interlinked.

Day 274   Psalm 109:22-31

²² For I'm afflicted, and I am in need.
Also, my heart is wounded within me.
²³ Like a declining shadow I depart,
And as a locust I am shaken off.

²⁴ Because of fasting, my knees are now weak;
My flesh is failing and is lank and lean.[a]
²⁵ I've been to them[b] an object of reproach,
And, when they look on me, they shake their head.

²⁶ Give help to me, O LORD. You are my God;
Save me according to your steadfast love;[c]
²⁷ And they shall then know that this is your hand;
That you yourself, O LORD, have done this thing. →

²⁸ They'll curse, but you will bless. Though they rise up
They'll be ashamed: Your servant shall rejoice.
²⁹ So my accusers^d will put on disgrace;
Array themselves with shame as with a robe.^e

³⁰ My mouth shall^f give great thanks unto the LORD.
Among the many, I will give him praise.
³¹ For at the poor one's right hand he shall stand
To save him from the judges^g of his soul.

---

^a Is lank and lean] Literally, 'for want of oil'. The word translated 'fat' here by the
AV is 'oil', as in v18. Only here does the AV translate it as 'fat'. Kirkpatrick
notes that anointing with oil was not used during fasting and mourning (2 Sam.
14:2), and the consequences of this may be what is intended. See de Burgh.
See also Davidson *Syntax* regarding the use of the Hebrew preposition (*min -*
מִן) expressing the absence of something.
^b I've been to them] The Hebrew emphasises the contrast between the 'I' and
'them'.
^c Steadfast love] Hebrew *ḥeṣedh* - חֶסֶד. See Appendix 2 - Loving-kindness.
^d Accusers] Or 'my adversaries', as v6 and v20.
^e As with a robe] The 'robe' was the outer garment. Josephus indicates it reached
down to the ankles. De Burgh 'from head to foot'.
^f My mouth shall] Hebrew 'with my mouth I shall'.
^g The judges] Participle from Hebrew verb *šaphaṭ* - שָׁפַט = 'those that judge'. It is
the only place where the AV translates *šaphaṭ* by 'condemn'. 'Judges' is the AV
margin. See Appendix 2 - Law - Judgment.

Day 275   Psalm 110:1-3

¹ The word the LORD declared^a unto my Lord^b -
'Sit down at my right hand until the time^c -
Until I shall have set your enemies -
Till they've been set a footstool for your feet'.

² The LORD shall send the sceptre of your power,
from Zion. 'Rule among^d your enemies!
³ Your people shall be freewill offerings,^e
When in your day of strength you shall make war.^f

When in your day of strength you shall make war,^g
They shall be^h beautiful in holiness,ⁱ
As issuing out of the morning's womb^j.
Your offspring shall be as the morning dew.^k

^a Word ... declared] The word translated by the AV simply as 'said' (*ne'um* - נְאֻם) is almost exclusively used of Divine revelations. We could translate 'the oracle of the LORD ...'. YLT translates 'the affirmation of JEHOVAH'. It was the claim of the false prophets that 'he said ...' (the word used here) in Jer. 23:31. It is used almost exclusively in prophetic contexts - 'thus saith the LORD'. Note Mark 12:36, quoting this verse, says that David spoke *'by the Holy Spirit...'.*

^b My Lord] This is not *'Adhonay* - אֲדֹנָי, the unique word for the lordship of God, although that word occurs at v6. The word here is *'adhôn* - אֲדוֹן. 'My lord' is frequently a form of address to a person of superior rank in the Old Testament. We have used a capital letter for 'Lord' here, as the New Testament frequently indicates that this was a word to Christ. See Appendix 2 - Names of God.

^c Until the time] The meaning of 'until' in this verse is defined by its quotation in Heb. 10:13. It does not mean 'while', including the interval till its fulfilment (although the Hebrew word may mean this), but it denotes the time limit after which the prophecy will be fulfilled. In Hebrews, where the Greek word for 'until' (*heos* - ἕως) followed by the subjunctive is used, that always conveys this meaning. See de Burgh, and Gesenius *Lexicon* on *'adh* - עַד.

^d Rule among] Rule - Literally, 'to tread down', or 'subjugate' (49:14; 72:8 AV 'have dominion over'). 'Among' - The word used is a strong word in Hebrew. Horsley 'in the very midst of'.

^e Freewill offerings] Literally, 'willingnesses' (intensive plural substantive of 'to will'). This is the usual word for 'freewill offerings' in Lev. 22; Ps. 119:108, and elsewhere. See de Burgh. Luther 'shall offer willingly'. *Statenvertaling* 'shall be very willing'. The meaning is that they shall give unconditional and unconstrained service, Rom. 12:1.

^f When in your day of strength you shall make war] The Hebrew word '(AV 'power' - different from the word of v2) may mean either 'strength' or 'army' (see Exod. 14:28; 2 Kgs. 6:15). Geneva Bible 'Thy people shall come willingly at the time of assembling thine armie in holy beautie: the youth of thy wombe shal be as the morning dewe' See Perowne, Kirkpatrick, and Tregelles (1). *Statenvertaling* 'in the day of thy warlike power'.

^g We have repeated this line from the previous stanza.

^h They shall be] We have supplied the verb as this refers back to 'your people'.

ⁱ Beautiful in holiness] Hebrew 'beauties of holiness'. 'Holy attire' or 'priestly garments' may be intended.

^j As issuing out of the morning's womb] 'Out of the womb of the dawning day' *Statenvertaling*. Compare Job 38:8.

^k Your offspring shall be as the morning dew] We have adopted the understanding of Geneva Bible, Lowth, Horsley, and Gill of this line. 'Offspring' is singular and in Eccles. 11:9,10 is used of youthfulness. B.W Newton (11) refers the 'offspring' to Israel who 'shall at last be willing in the day of his power - the first-born of the millennial day, fresh in the youth-time of that morning of joy'.

Day 276   Psalm 110:4-7

⁴ The LORD has sworn, and he will not repent:

'You are a priest - a priest for evermore,

After the order of Melchizedek'

⁵ My Lord at your right hand^a; he'll shatter^b kings.   →

He'll shatter kings in the day of his wrath.
⁶ He'll sit in judgment[c] on the nations then;
He'll fill them with the bodies of the dead;
He'll crush the head of an extensive land;[d]

⁷ He shall drink from the wayside rushing stream,
Because of this he will lift up his head.[e]
He shall drink from the wayside rushing stream,
Because of this he will lift up his head.[f]

---

[a] My Lord at your right hand] We understand these words as addressed to the
    Father concerning David's (and our) Lord at his right hand. 'My Lord' Hebrew
    'Adhonay - אֲדֹנָי. See Appendix 2 - Names of God.
[b] Shatter] Or 'crush'.
[c] Sit in judgment] Hebrew *dîn* - דִּין. See Appendix 2 - Law - Judgment (2). In the
    parallel references (Isa. 2:4; Joel 3:12; Mic. 4:3) the other word for 'to judge
    (*šaphaṭ* - שָׁפַט) is used.
[d] Head of an extensive land] So literally. See Calvin. In Hebrew 'head' and 'land'
    are singular, not plural as the AV.
[e] His head] Hebrew 'the head'.
[f] We have repeated these two lines.

Day 277   Psalm 111:1-6
¹ O Hallelujah, give praise to the LORD[a]!
I'll give thanks to the LORD with the whole heart,
In fellowship of just and upright men,[b]
Even among the gathered company.[c]

² Great are the works and doings[d] of the LORD,
Sought out by all who have delight in them.
³ His work has splendour and has majesty.
His righteousness stands fast for evermore.

His work has splendour and has majesty.
His righteousness stands fast for evermore.[e]
⁴ He's made his wonders a memorial;
The LORD is gracious and compassionate.

⁵ To those who fear him he's supplied their food;[f]
Forever keeps his covenant in mind.
⁶ His works[g] of power to his people showed,
In giving them the nations' heritage.

[a] Hallelujah ... LORD] The first line is simply 'Hallelujah'. We have added the English translation.

[b] Just and upright men] One word in Hebrew 'the upright'.

[c] Fellowship ... gathered company] There is a distinction between the two words used (AV 'assembly' and 'congregation'). The first implies a closer, intimate gathering (See Jer. 23:18-22, AV 'counsel'; Ps. 25:14 'secret'; 55:14 'counsel'; 64:2 'secret counsel'; 83:3 'counsel'; 89:7 'assembly' - see note], the second the public assembly (frequently as 'the congregation of the children of Israel' in the book of Numbers). PBV 'secretly among the faithful, and in the congregation'.

[d] Acts and doings] One word in Hebrew. Different from 'work' in v3, but a close synonym.

[e] We have repeated the last two lines of the previous stanza.

[f] Food] The word strictly means 'prey', or metaphorically 'the spoil of war'. In late use it means simply 'food' and conveniently supplies the appropriate Hebrew letter for this alphabetical psalm.

[g] Works] The same word as in v2 'works and doings'.

Day 278   Psalm 111:7-10

7 Judgment and truth[a] are the works of his hands
All things that he appoints are fixed and sure;[b]
8 They are established ever, evermore;
They're done in faithfulness and uprightness.

9 He sent a ransom for his people's sake.
For ever is his covenant ordained.
His name is holy, and is to be feared –
10 The start of wisdom is to fear the LORD.

His name is holy and is to be feared –
The start of wisdom is to fear the LORD.[c]
Good understanding have all who do this.[d]
Established is his praise for evermore.

[a] Judgment and truth] Hebrew, 'truth and judgment'. Judgment = *mišpaṭ* - מִשְׁפָּט. See Appendix 2 - Law - Judgment.

[b] Fixed and sure] One word in Hebrew, of the same root as 'amen'.

[c] We have repeated the last two lines of the previous stanza.

[d] Do this] We have taken this to mean 'fearing his name', 'fearing the LORD'. The word is plural (these). The AV supplies 'his commandments'.

Day 279   Psalm 112:1-4

[1] Hallelujah![a] Blest man[b] who fears the LORD!
In his commandments he takes great delight;
[2] His offspring shall be mighty upon earth.
The issue of the upright[c] shall be blest;

[3] And wealth[d] and riches shall be in his house.
His righteousness stands fast for evermore.
[4] For upright men light rises when it's dark.[e]
He's gracious, merciful, and righteous too.[f]

---

[a] Hallelujah] 'Praise the LORD!' In Hebrew simply 'Hallelujah!'.

[b] Blest man] 'O the blessings of the man'. Hebrew 'blessings' *ašrê* - אַשְׁרֵי. See Appendix 2 - Blessing. 'Man' Hebrew *'îš* - אִישׁ - man as an individual. See Appendix 2 - Man.

[c] The issue of the upright] Literally, 'the generation of upright ones'. This is in parallel to 'offspring' in the previous line, and we may understand it as being the progeny, or the rising generation that follows after righteous parents (compare Psalms 14:5; 24:5; Luke 1:50).

[d] Wealth] The Hebrew word means 'plenty', 'substance', 'sufficiency'.

[e] We have repeated this line from the last line of the previous stanza.

[f] He's gracious, merciful, and righteous too] The Hebrew of this line is simply the three adjectives in the singular (no verb). They may refer to the 'man' of v5, or (as the *Dutch Annotations* prefer) to the LORD, as in Ps. 111:4.

Day 280   Psalm 112:5-10

[5] It's well for that man[a] who acts graciously
Who lends and justly[b] deals with his affairs;[c]
[6] Because he'll never stagger or be moved;[d]
The righteous is remembered evermore.

[7] He will not be afraid to hear bad news;
His heart is steadfast, trusting in the LORD.
[8] His heart's upheld. He will not be afraid.
Until the time he looks upon his foes.[e]

[9] He's open-handed[f] - He gives to the poor;
His righteousness will stand for evermore.
With glory will his horn be lifted up;
[10] The wicked one will see and will be grieved.   →

The wicked one[g] will gnash and grind[h] his teeth,
And then he will just melt and pine[i] away;
What wicked men desire will all be lost.[j]
What wicked men desire will all be lost.[k]

---

[a] It's well for that man] Literally, 'the good man'. *Dutch Annotations* 'well to, or happie is the man'. This parallels verse 1 of the Psalm. Hebrew *'îš* - אִישׁ -Man as an individual. See Appendix 2 - Man.

[b] Justly] AV 'with discretion', Motyer (1) 'thoughtful right decision making'. However, this is the only time the AV translates the word by 'discretion', and de Burgh translates 'he will act with uniform justice and integrity'. Yet again, as noted by the *Dutch* Annotations it may be taken as 'maintaining his cause in judgment' (so NASB). The key word is Hebrew *mišpaṭ* - מִשְׁפָּט. See Appendix 2 - Law - Judgment.

[c] Affairs] Literally, 'words', which is the sense that Motyer (1) adopts.

[d] Stagger or be moved] One word in Hebrew.

[e] Until the time he looks upon his foes] We have translated the Hebrew literally. If Ps. 91:8 is taken as the interpreter of this idiom, it is not so much 'his desire' as 'the LORD's recompense' for which he waits.

[f] Open-handed] Literally, 'he disperses', or 'he scatters'.

[g] The wicked one will] Hebrew 'he will'. We have supplied this to maintain the continuity with the previous stanza and to make clear that this refers to the wicked person.

[h] Gnash and grind] One word in Hebrew.

[i] Melt and pine] Hebrew simply 'melt'. We have given the metaphor and the meaning.

[j] Will all be lost] Most translations give 'will perish'. The root meaning of the verb is, however, 'to be lost', as 'a lost sheep' - Ps. 119:176. What the Psalm indicates is the loss of all that wicked men desire. This is generalised from 'the wicked person' (singular) at the beginning of the verse to 'wicked ones' (plural) at the end.

[k] We have repeated the last line.

Day 281   Psalm 113

[1] O Praise the LORD![a] Praise, servants of the LORD!
Praise the LORD's name! [2] The LORD's name will be blest
from now, for ever. [3] From the rising sun
to where it sets. The LORD's name will be praised!

[4] High over all the nations is the LORD;
His glory is above the heavens too![b]
[5] Who's like the LORD our God, who dwells[c] on high;
[6] Who stoops to view the heavens and the earth.[d]   →

244

^{7} He raises up the poor one from the dust;
He lifts the needy from the rubbish heap,
^{8} That he among the princes may be sat,^{e}
Among his people's princes he will be.
^{9} He sets the barren woman in a home,^{f}
And as a joyful mother of her sons.
O, Hallelujah, give praise to the LORD!^{g}
O, Hallelujah, give praise to the LORD!

---

^{a} O Praise the LORD!] Hebrew = 'Hallelujah'.
^{b} His glory is above the heavens too!] As Ps. 148:13.
^{c} Dwells] The Hebrew word may also mean 'is seated' or 'enthroned'.
^{d} Who stoops ... earth] Literally, 'who makes himself low to see in the heavens and in the earth'.
^{e} Be sat] The Hebrew word may mean either 'set' or 'sat', and is in the causative verb form. The LORD causes the person to be sat among princes [or 'the great and the good'] (see Ps. 118:9).
^{f} Sets ... in a home] Literally, 'causes to dwell in a house'. The word 'house' here clearly means more than bricks and mortar, and the word is often translated 'home'. See, for example, Deut. 24:5.
^{g} Hallelujah ... LORD] This line is simply 'Hallelujah'. We have added the English translation. We have repeated this line.

Day 282   Psalm 114

^{1} When out of Egypt Israel came forth,
From foreign people^a Jacob's house went out.
^{2} Judah became a holy place^b for him,
And Israel the place where he did rule.^{c}

^{3} The sea beheld, and then it fled away;
The Jordan turned around, and it went back.
^{4} The mountains skipped about like they were rams;
The hills as though they were just little sheep.^{d}

^{5} What's wrong with you, O sea, to flee away?
You Jordan, that you turned and you went back?
^{6} You mountains, why did you skip round like rams?
You hills, that you should act like little sheep?

^{7} Tremble, and shake^e before the LORD, O earth
Yes, tremble from the face of Jacob's <u>God</u>!
^{8} Who changed the rock into a water pool;
The stone of flint into a water spring.

[a] Foreign people] Literally, 'people of a strange [or unintelligible] language'.
[b] Holy place] AV 'Sanctuary'.
[c] The place where he did rule] Hebrew plural, 'places', 'realms' - indicating an extensive dominion.
[d] Little sheep] Hebrew 'sons of sheep'
[e] Tremble and shake] One word in Hebrew. 'To writhe as a woman in childbirth'. We have repeated the verb in the following line.

Day 283   Psalm 115:1-8

[1] Not unto us, O LORD, not unto us;
But no, instead[a], give glory to your name.
Both for your mercy[b], and for your truth's[c] sake
[2] Why should the nations say, 'Where is their God?'[d]

[3] Our God's in heaven[e]. He does what he will,[f]
[4] Their grievous idols[g] are silver and gold,
No more than workmanship of human hands:[h]
[5] They have a mouth, and yet they do not speak;

Yes, they have eyes, and yet they do not see;
[6] And they have ears, and yet they do not hear;
They have a nose and yet they cannot smell;
[7] As for their hands, they do not handle things;

As for their feet, with them they do not walk;
And with their throat they cannot make a sound.[i]
[8] And those who make them are the same as them!
And everyone who puts their trust in them.

[a] But no, instead ...] The word usually translated 'but' (*kî* - כִּי) here gives emphasis to what follows. The psalmist rejects any suggestion that we should receive glory. We have therefore expressed this more strongly than a simple 'but'.
[b] Mercy] Hebrew *ḥeṣedh* - חֶסֶד. See Appendix 2 - Loving-kindness.
[c] Truth] The word may also mean 'faithfulness'.
[d] Where is their God?] This is evidently a taunt, indicated by Hebrew *na' *- נָא), which may indicate a taunt or an entreaty - see Perowne. The 'now' of the AV is not a reference to time. See note on Ps. 118:2.
[e] In heaven] Hebrew 'in the heavens'.
[f] What he will] AV 'whatsoever he hath pleased'. Geneva Bible 'what so euer he will'. In the Greek Septuagint the Hebrew word is usually translated by a word that means 'to will' (*thelo* or *boulomai* - θελω or βουλομαι).
[g] Grievous idols] One word in Hebrew. The word used here for idol indicates that

which causes labour or grief.
^h Human hands] Literally, 'the hands of man'. The word for 'man' here is Hebrew
  'adham - אָדָם - Man as a child of Adam. See Appendix 2 - Man.
ⁱ Cannot make a sound] The verb may mean 'speak', but the root of the verb
  relates to inarticulate speech (as indicated by Jewish commentators). It is
  therefore used of animal sounds - Isa. 31:4 and 38:14. The idol is incapable of
  even such communication (but see Rev. 13:15). Horsley translates 'grumble
  with the throat'!

Day 284   Psalm 115:9-14

⁹ Put your trust in the LORD, O Israel
For he's their helper, and he is their shield.
¹⁰ Put your trust in the LORD, O Aaron's house
For he's their helper, and he is their shield.

¹¹ You who do fear the LORD, trust in the LORD,
For he's their helper, and he is their shield.
¹² The LORD's been mindful of us. He will bless -
Yes, he will bless the house of Israel!

¹³ He will give blessing unto Aaron's house -
Bless them that fear the LORD, both small and great.
¹⁴ The LORD will add to you and give increase^a -
Increase you more and more - your children too!

^a Add to you and give increase] One word in Hebrew.

Day 285   Psalm 115:15-18

¹⁵ You are the ones who are blest^a of the LORD -
The LORD who made the heavens and the earth.
¹⁶ The heavens, yes, the heavens, are the LORD's -
He gave the earth unto the sons of man.

¹⁷ The dead do not give praise unto the LORD,^b
None who sink to the silence of the grave.^c
¹⁸ But we will bless the LORD^d now, evermore!
O Hallelujah, give praise to the LORD!^e

^a Blest] Hebrew *barakh* - בָּרַךְ. See Appendix 2 - Blessing.
^b Do not give praise unto the LORD] Literally, 'not … praise JAH' (*lo … hallelu YAH* - -

247

יְהַלְלוּ־יָהּ ... לֹא). We might translate 'the dead do not give hallelujahs'!

c None who sink to the silence of the grave] Hebrew 'not all those who descend to silence'. The Hebrew word (silence) is used twice in the Psalms (here and 94:17) of the place of death - Sheol, where a person is silenced (Ps. 31:18). The Septuagint translates 'Hades' - ᾅδης.

d The LORD] Hebrew JAH - יָהּ a shortened form of יהוה, the LORD, JEHOVAH. See Appendix 2 - Names of God.

e Hallelujah ... LORD] The line is simply 'Hallelujah'. We have added the English translation.

Day 286   Psalm 116:1-9

¹ I love the LORD because the LORD has heard –
He heard my voice, and my imploring cries;
² Because he has inclined his ear to me,
Therefore, I, all my days ᵃ, will call on him.

³ The cords of death encircled me around;
The pains of Sheol had closed in on me.ᵇ
I found distress, and I found anguish too –
⁴ I called upon the LORD's name [and I said].

'LORD, I implore you ᶜ, let my soul escape!'
⁵ The LORD is gracious, and is righteous too,
Tender compassion ᵈ is shown by our God.
⁶ The simple-hearted are kept by the LORD.

I was brought low, and he delivered me.
⁷ And now, my soul, go back and have your rest; ᵉ
The LORD will yet complete his work in you.ᶠ
⁸ You surely have rescued my soul from death.

You have relieved my eyes from shedding tears;
And you have kept ᵍ my feet from stumbling too.
⁹ In the LORD's presence I will go about
And walk around the lands of those who live.ʰ

---

a All my days] Literally, 'in my days' (AV margin). AV and most versions 'as long as I live'.

b Pains of Sheol had closed in on me] Sheol, šeʼôl - שְׁאוֹל. See Appendix 2 - Sheol. Literally, 'the confines of Sheol found me'. The root word ('pains' or 'confines') means narrowing or confining, but also means the distress and anguish caused by such circumstances. It is used of the emotional distress of a woman in

248

childbirth (Jer. 48:41 and 49:22).

^c I implore you] The psalmist uses a word of entreaty that emphasises the verb (Hebrew *na'* - נָא, and *'anna'* - אָנָּא) in verses 4,14,16,18 of this psalm. The AV renders 'I beseech thee', 'O ... truly' and 'now' in these verses. 'Now' is used without reference to time - see SOED. We have used 'I implore', 'let it be', and 'I'm pleading'. See note on Ps. 118:2.

^d Tender compassion] One word in Hebrew. As in Ps. 103:13.

^e Go back and have your rest] Hebrew 'return unto your rests'. 'Rests' is plural for emphasis.

^f Complete his work in you] See note on Ps. 142:7.

^g Rescued ... relieved ... kept] We have expanded these three examples of deliverance, supplying the sense of the verb in each line.

^h The lands of those who live] Hebrew 'the lands of the living'. Compare Psalms 27:13; 52:5; 142:5.

Day 287   Psalm 116:10-15

¹⁰ I have believed, and therefore I did speak,^a
Yet I^b have been afflicted very much.
¹¹ So I spoke in my haste, and so I said
That 'all mankind are liars, every one'.^c

¹² O how can I repay unto the LORD
For all the ways he has looked after me.^d
¹³ The cup of full salvation I will take^e
And I will call on the name of the LORD.

¹⁴ So I'll fulfil my vows unto the LORD –
In sight of all his people, let it be.^f
¹⁵ The death of those on whom he sets his love^g
Is in the LORD's eyes a most precious thing.^h

^a I have believed ... speak] The AV adopts the Septuagint translation used by Paul in 2 Cor. 4:13. Most modern translations translate otherwise. Perowne writes 'the Hebrew will not admit of such a rendering'. De Burgh evidently disagrees. We have retained the New Testament translation.

^b Yet I] The Hebrew doubles the emphasis on 'I', as is also done in v11 where we have been able to translate 'I myself'.

^c All mankind are liars, every one] We have expanded this line as it speaks of universality and inclusiveness. The word for 'man' here is Hebrew *'adham* - אָדָם, - man in the general sense (see Ps. 115:16, compare Rom. 3:4). However, as Horsley notes, it is here *ha-'adham* -הָאָדָם referring collectively to the whole race. The Hebrew word includes more than telling lies, and means being deceitful in a wider sense. They are literally, 'a lie' (cf. Jere. 17:9). See Appendix 2 - Man.

^d All the ways he has looked after me] AV 'all his benefits'. Derived from the verb used in v7. See Koehler, *Lexicon* and note on Ps. 142:7.

^e The cup of full salvation I will take] Hebrew 'cup of salvations'; Motyer (1) = 'plural of amplitude'; See de Burgh. The only repayment we can make to God (we have none) is to accept his cup full of blessings.

^f Let it be] The psalmist again uses a word of entreaty. See note on v4. The AV translates 'now' (not in the temporal sense - see SOED).

^g Those on whom he sets his love] Hebrew *ḥaṣîdhîm* - חֲסִידִים. We understand these to be the objects and recipients of his mercy, loving-kindness, covenant love (*ḥeṣedh* - חֶסֶד). See Appendix 2 - Loving-kindness.

^h A most precious thing] Hebrew 'precious', a word frequently used in connection with precious stones, and evidently conveying the loving care and value in which the LORD holds his elect, and views their final trial.

Day 288   Psalm 116:16-19

¹⁶ Ah, yes indeed^a, I am your servant, LORD –
I am your servant and your handmaid's^b son.
You loosed my shackles, and you set me free!^c
¹⁷ So unto you I'll offer sacrifice.

A sacrifice of thanks I'll give to you!^d
And I will call on the name of the LORD;
¹⁸ My vows I will fulfil unto the LORD –
In sight of all his people let it be!^e

¹⁹ Let it be in the courts of the LORD's house,
And in the midst of you, Jerusalem.
O Hallelujah, give praise to the LORD!^f
O Hallelujah, give praise to the LORD!^g

^a Ah, yes indeed] The psalmist uses a word of entreaty and affirmation (Hebrew *'anna'* - אָנָּא). AV expresses this by 'O ... truly'. See note v4.

^b Handmaid] Female servant or slave. A slave by birth had a greater claim on his master than one bought.

^c You loosed my shackles and you set me free] The verb is in the intensive mood. His bonds were not merely loosened, but completely loosened - removed.

^d A sacrifice of thanks I'll give to you] Literally, 'to you I will sacrifice the sacrifice of thanks(giving)'.

^e May it be] AV expresses this word (*na'* - נָא) by 'now'. See note on v4.

^f Hallelujah ... LORD] The line is simply 'Hallelujah'. We have added the English translation.

^g We have repeated the last line.

Day 289   Psalm 117

¹ All nations give praise to the LORD alone!ᵃ
And all the peoples celebrate his praise!ᵇ -
² Because his mercyᶜ has prevailed on us.ᵈ
The LORD's truth lasts forever. Praise the LORD!ᵉ

ᵃ Praise to the LORD alone] This is not the usual 'praise the LORD' - 'Hallelujah', as
   at the end of this Psalm. An untranslated word ('eth - אֵת) is put before 'the
   LORD' which directs to, and emphasises, the word that follows. This only occurs
   elsewhere in Ps. 148:1,7; and Jer. 20:13. We might simply say with emphasis
   'praise ... the LORD!'
ᵇ Celebrate his praise] One word in Hebrew (šabhah - שַׁבְּחוּ). Barely
   distinguishable in meaning from 'give praise' in the first line, but perhaps a
   more exuberant expression.
ᶜ Mercy] Hebrew ḥeṣedh - חֶסֶד. See Appendix 2 - Loving-kindness.
ᵈ Has prevailed on us] This is the literal meaning. See Gesenius, Baron, de Burgh.
ᵉ Praise the LORD!] 'Hallelujah!' Literally, 'give praise to JAH' (YAH - יָהּ). See
   Appendix 2 - Names of God.

Day 290   Psalm 118:1-6

¹ Give thanks unto the LORD for he is good,
'His loving-kindnessᵃ is for evermore'.
² Ah, yes indeedᵇ: let Israel now say,
'His loving-kindness is for evermore'.

³ Ah, yes indeed: let Aaron's house now say,
'His loving-kindness is for evermore'.
⁴ Indeed: let those who fear the LORD now say,
'His loving-kindness is for evermore'.

⁵ I was shut inᶜ and I cried to the LORD,ᵈ
With the wide placeᵉ the LORD has answered me.
⁶ The LORD is on my sideᶠ, I will not fear,
What can my fellow manᵍ do unto me?

ᵃ Loving-kindness] Hebrew ḥeṣedh - חֶסֶד, and so in v2,3,4. See Appendix 2 -
   Loving-kindness.
ᵇ Ah, yes indeed] The Hebrew includes a word of entreaty and affirmation (na' -
   נָא), here and in verses 2,3,4,25(2) - AV translates 'now' (without the temporal
   sense - see SOED). See note on Ps. 116:4.
ᶜ I was shut in] Literally, 'in my strait' or 'confinement'. See note on Ps. 116:3.
   This contrasts with 'the wide place'.
ᵈ LORD] The word translated 'LORD' twice in this verse is JAH (YAH - יָהּ). In view of
   the use of the Hallel in the Passover (Ps. 14:2, etc) this is particularly suited, as

251

JAH is first used at the Exodus (Exod. 15:2). It is also used in verses 18 and 19 of
this Psalm, where we have translated 'LORD'. See Appendix 2 - Names of God
[e] With a wide place] The AV supplies 'set me in a ...', which is unnecessary here -
see de Burgh. See Ewald *Syntax*, in reference to the use here of the Hebrew
preposition usually translated 'in'. So too Baron (3).
[f] On my side] Literally, 'for me' (AV margin). Heb. 13:6, following the Septuagint,
translates 'the LORD is my helper' - (Greek *boethos* - βοηθός) the one
supporting, or succouring me.
[g] My fellow man] The Hebrew word for 'man' here (Hebrew *'adham* - אָדָם) is the
generic word for mankind. The contrast is with the first line of the verse - 'if
the LORD is on my side ...'. So too v8. See Appendix 2 - Man.

Day 291   Psalm 118:7-14

⁷ The LORD is on my side to be my help; [a]
I'll look upon those who are hating me. [b]
⁸ It's better to take refuge [c] in the LORD,
Than to rely upon your fellow man.

⁹ It's better to take refuge in the LORD
Than to rely upon the great and good. [d]
¹⁰ All of the nations circled me around;
In the LORD's name I'll surely cut them off.

¹¹ They closed me in, yes, closed me round about;
In the LORD's name I'll surely cut them off.
¹² They were around [e] me like a swarm of bees; [f]
They were extinguished, like a fire of thorns.

In the LORD's name I'll surely cut them off.
¹³ You thrust against me hard [g] to make me fall;
The LORD helped me   ¹⁴ JAH is my strength and song, [h]
And he's become salvation unto me. [i]

[a] To be my help] Literally, 'among them' or 'with them that help me' (as AV). We
have followed Baron (3) here, and the AV translation of the same idiom at Ps.
54:4. We take this as an emphatic expression, i.e. There might be others 'for
us', but the whole dynamic is changed 'if God be for us'. The LORD is not merely
one, among other, helpers.
[b] I'll look upon those who are hating me] Most translations seek to make up the
sense by making the 'seeing' 'in triumph', 'in pleasure', 'the downfall of'. We
have translated literally. E. Bendor-Samuel in *The Prophetic Character of the
Psalms*, suggests that this is rather 'fearlessly to face the enemy' (Compare 2
Kgs. 14:8).

^c Take refuge] Here and in v9. AV 'trust'. The Hebrew verb is Hebrew *ḥaṣâ* - חָסָה.
See Appendix 2 - Refuge.

^d The great and good] The Hebrew word (*nadhîbh* - נָדִיב) is translated 'princes' in
most versions. It means those of an 'exalted material and social position'
(Theological Wordbook) and those who give liberally (the root of the word).
We have used the English idiom, which is usually used ironically. See too
Psalms 47:9 and 107:40.

^e Were around] The same word as we have translated 'enclosed' [around] in the
previous lines.

^f A swarm of bees] Hebrew 'like bees'.

^g Thrust against me hard] Literally, 'thrusting you thrusted'. This (infinitive
absolute) form conveys a violent thrust.

^h Song] Hebrew *zimrath* - זִמְרָת. See Appendix 2 under *zamar* - זָמַר. Translated
'psalm' by the Dutch *Statenvertaling*.

ⁱ Salvation unto me] i.e. 'my salvation'. The Hebrew may be expressed as
salvation 'to' or 'for' me. As David Baron (3). The very name 'Jesus' in Hebrew
is here used - transliterated *Yeshua* - salvation. So too in v21.

Day 292   Psalm 118:15-21

¹⁵ The sound of joy and of deliverance^a
Is now within the tents of righteous men!^b
The right hand of the LORD works mightily –
¹⁶ The right hand of the LORD is lifted high.

The right hand of the LORD works mightily;
¹⁷ I shall not die, but, rather^c, I shall live!
I shall declare the works the LORD has done.
I shall declare the works the LORD has done.^d

¹⁸ The LORD has chastened me so very much,^e
But he has not delivered me to death.
¹⁹ Open to me the gates of righteousness,
Through them I'll enter in. I'll thank the LORD!

²⁰ This is the gate – the gate that's for the LORD;^f
The righteous ones will enter in through it.
²¹ Because you answered me, I will give thanks;
You have become salvation unto me.

^a The sound of joy and of deliverance] Literally, 'the voice of joyful shouting and
salvation'.

^b Righteous men] Hebrew 'the righteous', plural. The same as v20.

^c But, rather] The preposition used leads to a strong opposite statement. Literally,

253

'I will not die - because I will live'! Compare Dan. 9:18 ('not ... but for your great mercies')
^d We have repeated this line.

^e Chastened me so very much] Hebrew 'chastening he has chastened me'.

^f The gate. The gate that's for the Lord] literally, 'to' or 'for' the LORD. Compare Ps. 24:7-10

Day 293   Psalm 118:22-29

²² The stone that was refused by those who built^a
Has now become the chief head-cornerstone.
²³ The LORD did this. In our eyes - Wonderful!
²⁴ This is the day, the day the LORD has worked.^b

Let us rejoice and in this day^c be glad.
²⁵ Hosanna!^d Save! O LORD, for this we plead!
We plead, O LORD. Oh give us good success!
²⁶ Blest^e is the one who comes in the LORD's name.

'We bless you all^f, from out of the LORD's house';
²⁷ The LORD is GOD^g and he has shined on us!^h
The pilgrim-sacrificeⁱ bind up with cords,
Even unto the very altar's horns.^j

²⁸ You are my GOD, and I will give you thanks;
You are my God, and I will lift you up.
²⁹ Give thanks unto the LORD for he is good,
His loving-kindness is for evermore.

---

^a Those who built] In both the Hebrew, and in the old Greek translation, it is 'the builders'. These were not just any builders, but those to whom the construction work was committed. The word was spoken against the Jewish leaders in Matt. 21.

^b Has worked] or 'has acted'. The AV gives another meaning to the verb, 'has made', but it appears to us that the cause of wonder and rejoicing of the psalmist was rather the LORD's intervention in the affairs of men.

^c In this day] Hebrew 'in it'.

^d Hosanna! Save!] The Greek transliteration of the words here, were used by the crowds who met Jesus on 'Palm Sunday' before the Passover. The words mean 'We plead, Save!'. We give the expression made familiar by the Gospel story. The Hebrew uses words of entreaty and pleading in this verse four times. The verse is literally, '[We] plead (Hebrew 'anna' - אָנָּא), LORD, Oh (Hebrew na' - נָא) save! [We] plead (Hebrew 'anna' - אָנָּא), LORD, Oh (Hebrew na' - נָא) give us good success'. See note on Ps. 116:4.

^e Blest] Hebrew *barakh* - בָּרַךְ. See Appendix 2 - Blessing.

^f We bless you all] Hebrew 'we bless you (plural)'. 'We [priests of the house of the Lord] do bless thee, O king David, and the people that is with thee', *Dutch Annotations*.

^g The LORD is GOD] The Hebrew word for God here is *'El* -אֵל. It is combined with 'the LORD' - אֵל יהוה. See Appendix 2 - Names of God.

^h He has shined on us] We have followed the translation of Baron (3).

ⁱ Pilgrim-sacrifice] We have followed the usual interpretation of this verse that makes the reference to 'sacrifice'. The Hebrew is 'bind the *ḥagh* with cords'. *ḥagh* (חַג) is the word for the great pilgrim feasts of Israel. The Jewish authorities Rashi and Ibn Ezra suggest that the word by metonymy means the sacrifice made at these feasts. See Baron (3), de Burgh, etc.

^j Even … horns] We have followed Baron (3) with Delitzsch and many others, concluding that the sacrifice was not bound *to* the horns of the altar, but rather 'the whole space of the court of the priests was full of them [the sacrifices], and the binding of them consequently had to go on *as far as to* the horns of the altar'.

Day 294   Psalm 119:1-8   Aleph. 1st Part

¹ *Blest*^a are those who are blameless in the way!
Those who are walking after^b the LORD's Law.
² *Blest* are those who his testimonies keep!
Those who seek after him with all the heart.

³ Truly, they do not act unrighteously^c,
And they have kept their walk within his ways.
⁴ You have commanded your precepts for us^d
That we might keep them very carefully.

⁵ O that my ways were settled and secure,^e
So I might keep the things that you decree.
⁶ For, if I did^f, I would not be ashamed,
When I look into all that you command.

⁷ I will give thanks to you with upright heart,
And learn the righteous things that you ordain.^g
⁸ And the decrees that you have made, I'll keep;
O do not utterly^h abandon me!

^a Blest] Hebrew *'ašrê* - אַשְׁרֵי. So also in v2. See Appendix 2 - Blessing.
^b After] 'In accordance with'.
^c Act unrighteously] AV 'do no iniquity'.
^d Your precepts for us] These are God's injunctions for man to carry out, his

charge to us. 'For us' is not in the Hebrew but is implicit in the next line. Hebrew *piqqûdhîm* - פִּקֻּדִים. See Appendix 2 - Law - Precepts.

[e] Settled and Secure] One word in Hebrew. AV 'established'.

[f] For, if I did] The avoidance of shame and disgrace depends upon, and follows from, keeping the LORD's decrees, v5.

[g] Things that you ordain] AV 'judgments. Hebrew *mišpaṭ* - מִשְׁפָּט. See Appendix 2 - Law - Judgment.

[h] Utterly] The Hebrew word conveys intensity, and altogether-ness. The same word as used in v4, where we have translated 'very carefully'. De Burgh sees its use in this verse as a response to its use in v4.

Day 295   Psalm 119:9-16   Beth. 2nd Part

[9] How can a young man keep his pathway[a] pure?
By guarding it according to your word.
[10] With all my heart I have sought after you;
From your commandments[b] do not let me stray.

[11] I've treasured up[c] your word[d] within my heart,
To keep myself from sinning against you.[e]
[12] O LORD you only are the blessèd one![f]
Teach your decrees to me, and make me learn.[g]

[13] With my lips I have numbered and declared[h]
All of the ordinances[i] of your mouth.
[14] Your Testimonies' way has made me glad,
As much as riches - wealth of every kind.

[15] Upon your precepts I will meditate;
To all your pathways I will have regard;
[16] And your decrees[j] I will make my delight;
I will make sure I don't forget[k] your word.

---

[a] Pathway] A different word from 'way' in verses 1,3, and 5, where the word (used in Numb. 20:17) may be translated 'road' or 'highway'.

[b] Commandments] Hebrew *mitswâ* - מִצְוָה. See Appendix 2 - Law - Commandment.

[c] Treasured up] AV 'hid'. The word means concealing something with a purpose. Compare Prov. 13:22.

[d] Word] Hebrew *'imrâ* - אִמְרָה - the spoken word, 'what you have said'. Horsley proposes 'oracles'. See Appendix 2 - Word.

[e] To keep myself from sinning against you] Literally, 'for the purpose that I shall not sin against you'. Hiding God's word in our hearts does not automatically prevent us from sinning, but it is part of a discipline that will guard against sin

256

that offends God.

^f O LORD, you only are the blessed one] The sentence (AV 'Blessed art thou, O LORD') occurs nine times in the Psalms, but only here with the emphasis on 'you', we have therefore added 'only' to give emphasis. 'Blessed one' is a passive participle which we take to be a substantive.

^g Teach ... make me learn] Hebrew one word - the causative form of 'to learn'.

^h Numbered and declared] One word in Hebrew, which, in the intensive form here, means 'to recount', 'to number', 'to rehearse', 'to declare'.

ⁱ Ordinances] Hebrew *mišpaṭ* - מִשְׁפַּט. As v7.

^j Decrees] Here the feminine form of *ḥoq* - חֹק. See Appendix 2 - Law - Decree.

^k I will make sure I don't forget] 'I will not forget' is a promise, or statement of intent, rather than just a statement of fact.

Day 296   Psalm 119:17-24   Gimel. 3rd Part

¹⁷ I am your servant. Fully deal^a with me! –
That I may live; so I will keep your word.
¹⁸ Open my eyes and then I will behold
The things of wonder that are in your Law.

¹⁹ I'm just a sojourner^b upon the earth;
Don't hide from me the things that you command.
²⁰ My soul is crushed and broken^c with desire,
Constantly longing for what you ordain. ^d

²¹ You have rebuked the proud – those who are cursed;
Those who are straying from what you command.
²² Take insult and contempt away from me,
Because your testimonies I have kept.

²³ Princes^e have sat and spoken against me;
Your servant meditates on your decrees.
²⁴ Your testimonies – they are my delights;
They are to me as men who give advice.^f

^a Fully deal] AV 'deal bountifully'. See note on 142:7.

^b Sojourner] A special term for a foreigner in Israel, who was in a dependent or vulnerable position (Ps. 39:12; Gen. 23:4; 1 Chr. 29:15). A 'stranger' Gen. 2:22. Hebrew *ger* - גֵּר.

^c Crushed and broken] One word in Hebrew.

^d What you ordain] AV 'judgments'. Hebrew *mišpaṭ* - מִשְׁפַּט. See Appendix 2 - Law - Judgment.

^e Princes] A different word to that which the AV translates 'princes' in Ps. 118:9. It

is used in Gen. 12:15, but it does not necessarily mean 'royalty', rather, a
leader.
[f] To me as men who give advice] 'Counsellors'. Literally, 'men of my counsel' (AV
mg).

Day 297   Psalm 119:25-32   Daleth. 4th Part

[25] My soul is fastened to the dust of earth; [a]
O give me life, according to your word!
[26] I have declared my ways - You answered me;
Teach your decrees to me, and make me learn. [b]

[27] Help me to understand your mapped-out way, [c]
So, on your wonders I will meditate.
[28] My soul's poured out because of heaviness;
Establish me, according to your word.

[29] Remove from me the false unfaithful way, [d]
And graciously impart your Law to me.
[30] The way of faithfulness has been my choice;
Your ordinances [e] I have set for me.

[31] I hold fast to your Testimonies, LORD
O do not leave me hopeless and ashamed! [f]
[32] The way of your commandments I will run;
For you will open and enlarge [g] my heart.

---

[a] Dust of earth] We understand the Psalmist to be speaking of either 'the dust of
death' (see Ps. 22:15,29 - so Calvin) which agrees best with the following line;
or else, more generally of being soiled by worldly, earthly things from which he
desires relief (so Ps. 44:25; Rom. 7:24 - so Bridges).
[b] Teach ... make me learn] See note on v12.
[c] Your mapped-out way] AV 'the way of your precepts'. Hebrew *piqqûdhîm* -
פִּקּוּדִים. The word means the things that God appoints for us. We have here
extended the metaphor of 'way' used by the Psalmist to express this. Compare
'the way of your commandments' v32 and 'the way of your decrees' v33. See
Appendix 2 - Law - Precepts.
[d] The false unfaithful way] The contrast is with the way of faithfulness (v30). See
Perowne.
[e] Ordinances] Hebrew *mišpaṭ* - מִשְׁפָּט. See Appendix 2 - Law - Judgment.
[f] Leave me hopeless and ashamed] One word in Hebrew. See Gesenius *Lexicon*.
[g] Open and enlarge] One word in Hebrew. See de Burgh and Gesenius *Lexicon*.

258

Day 298   Psalm 119:33-40   He. 5th Part

³³ O teach me ª, LORD, the way of your decrees,
And I will keep it to the very end.
³⁴ Give understanding and I'll keep your Law;
I will observe your Law wholeheartedly.ᵇ

³⁵ Cause me to treadᶜ the path of your commands;
For I desire this - It is my delight.ᵈ
³⁶ Unto your Testimonies turn my heart,
And keep it from the selfish love of gain.

³⁷ Divert my eyes from looking at vain things,ᵉ
Quicken and give me lifeᶠ within your way.
³⁸ Your wordᵍ unto your servant please confirm,
For it produces reverence for you.ʰ

³⁹ Make the reproachⁱ I dread to pass from me,
Because your ordinancesʲ are so good
⁴⁰ Behold and see!ᵏ I've for your precepts longed!
Oh, in your righteousness, give life to me.

ª Teach me] 'Point out'. The same word from which *Torah* (*tôrâ* - תּוֹרָה) is derived.
   A different word from 'teach' in v26. See Appendix 2 - Law - Law.
ᵇ Wholeheartedly] Hebrew 'with all my heart'.
ᶜ Cause me to tread] This is the literal meaning. The root of the verb means 'to
   beat' or 'to tread'. AV 'cause me to go'.
ᵈ For I desire this. It is my delight] We have expanded this line to show the fuller
   meaning. The verb does not only mean 'to find delightful', but also 'to desire'.
ᵉ Vain things] Hebrew singular *šaw'* - שָׁוְא. 'Vanity', 'emptiness', 'what is
   worthless'. The verb 'take in vain' is used in the commandment in Exod. 20:7.
   The word is connected with idols as empty things, although another Hebrew
   word for emptiness (*hebhel* - הֶבֶל) is more commonly used in that way. The
   two words are used together in Ps. 31:7.
ᶠ Quicken and give me life] One word in Hebrew – 'to cause to live'.
ᵍ Word] Hebrew *'imrâ* - אִמְרָה. The reference here is to a spoken word (as v11).
   See Appendix 2 - Word.
ʰ For it produces reverence for you] i.e. 'your word is that which stirs men to fear
   God'. Alternatively (as AV) it may refer to the servant 'who is [devoted] to your
   fear'. (See Delitzsch, Perowne).
ⁱ The reproach] Hebrew 'my reproach'. If the reproach that he dreads is breaking
   the LORD's commands, in the second half of the verse he strengthens himself
   against failing, in the confidence that those commands are good.
ʲ Ordinances] AV 'judgments', Hebrew *mišpaṭ* - מִשְׁפָּט. See Appendix 2 - Law -
   Judgment.
ᵏ Behold and see!] Hebrew *hinneh* - הִנֵּה. See Appendix 2 - Behold!

259

Day 299 Psalm 119:41-48 Vau. 6th Part

⁴¹ LORD, let your loving-kindness^a come to me,
And your salvation, just as you have said;^b
⁴² I'll have an answer^c for him who taunts me,
Because I've set my trust upon your word.

⁴³ Do not remove^d your true word from my mouth,
For in your ordinances^e is my hope.^f
⁴⁴ So I will keep your Law continually –
Even forever and for evermore.

⁴⁵ I will walk freely in an open place,^g
Because your precepts I have sought with care.^h
⁴⁶ About your testimonies I would speak,
And before kings I would not be ashamed.ⁱ

⁴⁷ In your commandments which are loved by me
I will make my delight. ⁴⁸ I'll lift my hands
To your commandments, which are loved by me,
And so I'll meditate on your decrees.

---

^a Loving-kindness] Here plural, 'loving-kindnesses'. Hebrew *ḥeṣedh* - חֶסֶד. See Appendix 2 - Loving-kindness.

^b Just as you have said] 'According to your spoken word'. Hebrew *'imrâ* - אִמְרָה. See Appendix 2 - Word.

^c I'll have answer] Literally, 'And I will answer ... a word'. AV 'wherewith to answer'. 'Word' here is Hebrew *dabhar* -דָּבָר - the thing spoken of. See Appendix 2 - Word.

^d Remove] Literally, 'take away utterly'.

^e Ordinances] Hebrew plural. AV 'judgments', Hebrew *mišpaṭ* - מִשְׁפָּט. See Appendix 2 - Law - Judgment.

^f Hope] 'Sure hope'. 'Waiting with confident expectation'.

^g I will walk freely in an open place] Literally, 'I will walk in a broad place'. AV 'at liberty', AV mg. 'at large'. Compare Ps. 118:5.

^h Sought with care] 'Studied', or 'given diligent heed to'.

ⁱ Ashamed] See note on v31.

Day 300 Psalm 119:49-56 Zayin. 7th Part

⁴⁹ The word unto your servant keep in mind^a –
The word that you have made me hope upon.
⁵⁰ In my affliction this is my relief,
Because the word you spoke^b gave life to me. →

⁵¹The arrogant have mocked me, O so much!
But from your Law I have not turned aside.
⁵² Your ancient ordinances^c I recall,
O LORD, I comforted myself in them.

⁵³ Hot indignation then took hold of me,
Over^d the wicked who forsake your Law.
⁵⁴ Psalms were to me the things that you decreed,^e
In this house where I dwell but for a time.^f

⁵⁵ I've kept in mind your name by night, O LORD.
I have observed - Yes, I've observed^g your Law.
⁵⁶ This I have had and this happened to me^h
Because I kept the precepts you appoint.

---

^a Keep in mind] AV 'remember'. The word means more than recalling something that may have been forgotten. So too v55.

^b The word you spoke] Hebrew *'imrâ* - אִמְרָה – 'the spoken word'. Appendix 2-Word.

^c Ancient ordinances] AV 'judgments of old'; 'from everlasting'. 'Ordinances' here is Hebrew *mišpaṭ* - מִשְׁפָּט. See Appendix 2 - Law - Judgment.

^d Over] i.e. 'on account of'.

^e Psalms were to me the things that you decreed] We have translated Hebrew *zemîr* - זְמִיר, from the verb *zamar* - זָמַר as 'Psalms'. See Appendix 2 - *zamar* – זָמַר. Almost all translations reverse the sequence of this line in the Psalm to 'the things that you decree have been my songs'. The Hebrew is literally, 'psalms have been to me your decrees'. Gill uses the usual translation to justify Christians writing songs based on Scripture for congregational singing! Perhaps the text proves the opposite, and it is psalms that are decreed for use in worship.

^f In this ... but for a time] Literally, 'in the house of my sojournings'. The same root as the noun in v19. 'House' may be understood as 'home'. NIV 'wherever I lodge'. Compare 2 Cor. 5:1-10.

^g Observed] We have expanded this line.

^h This I have had and this happened to me] Hebrew literally, 'this was to me'. *Statenvertaling* 'it happened to me'. Bridges refers 'this' to singing psalms and remembering his name (v54,55), which is the fruit of keeping the LORD's commandments.

Day 301   Psalm 119:57-64   Heth. 8th Part

⁵⁷ LORD, you are mine, my portion, and my lot;^a
And I have said that I would keep your words.
⁵⁸ I did entreat your face^b with all my heart;
Be gracious to me, just as you have said^c.   →

⁵⁹ I have considered the ways that I go,
And to your testimonies turned my feet.
⁶⁰ I acted quickly, and did not delay,
So I might keep the things that you command.
⁶¹ The cords of wicked men encircled me;^d
Despite this, I did not forget your Law.
⁶² At midnight I'll get up and give you thanks
For righteous ordinances that you give.^e
⁶³ I am a friend of all those who fear you –
To those who keep the precepts you appoint.
⁶⁴ Your loving-kindness^f, O LORD, fills the earth;
The things that you decree ^g, O teach to me!

---

^a You are mine, my portion, and my lot] Literally, 'My portion, the LORD'. We have expanded the meaning. The word is closely linked to the apportioning of the land of Canaan to the Israelites, which was often by lot. The Psalmist did not just receive a share or portion of the LORD. He, in effect, declares 'My Beloved is mine and I am his' – S of S 2:16.
^b Your face] So the Hebrew. AV and most versions 'favour'.
^c Just as you have said] Literally, 'according to your [spoken] word. Hebrew *'imrâ* - אִמְרָה. See Appendix 2 - Word.
^d The cords of wicked men encircled me] cf. Ps. 18:5. AV 'the bands of the wicked have robbed me'. Two words are in question here. The first is literally, 'cords' and is so translated by the Septuagint and most versions. The AV takes this metaphorically as a 'band' or 'company' (as strings twined together). The second word is literally, 'to repeat' or 'to do again'. It is not used elsewhere in the sense of 'to rob'. If the metaphorical translation is adopted, perhaps 'beset' would be a better word. See Calvin, and de Burgh.
^e Ordinances that you give] Hebrew *mišpaṭ* - מִשְׁפָּט. See Appendix 2 - Law - Judgment.
^f Loving-kindness] Hebrew *ḥeseḏ* - חֶסֶד. See Appendix 2 - Loving-kindness.
^g The things that you decree] Hebrew *ḥoq* - חֹק. See Appendix 2 - Law - Decree.

Day 302   Psalm 119:65-72   Teth. 9th Part

⁶⁵ You have done well unto your servant, LORD;
It's been to me according to your word.
⁶⁶ Teach me good judgement^a; teach me knowledge too,
For I have trusted in what you command.^b
⁶⁷ Before I was afflicted, I transgressed,^c
But now I have kept fast the word you spoke.^d
⁶⁸ For you are good, and you are doing good;
Teach your decrees to me, and make me learn.^e   →

⁶⁹ The arrogant spread falsehood^f about me,
But your precepts I keep with my whole heart.
⁷⁰ Their heart is bloated, and as fat as grease; ^g
But as for me, in your Law I delight.

⁷¹ I was afflicted - it was for my good -
In order that I might learn your decrees.
⁷² The Law of your mouth is good unto me
Better than thousands of silver and gold.^h

---

^a Good judgement] Literally, 'goodness of taste'. Discernment of good and evil; cf.
   Heb. 5:14; Phil. 1:9.
^b What you command] Hebrew plural *mitswâ* - מִצְוָה. See Appendix 2 - Law -
   Commandment.
^c Transgressed] Literally, 'went astray'. Both Bonar and Newton (1) argue for
   expressions that do not imply moral guilt, both here and at v176. They
   consider this Psalm as prophetically spoken by Christ.
^d The word you spoke] Hebrew *'imrâ* - אִמְרָה – 'the spoken word'. See Appendix 2
   - Word.
^e Teach ... make me learn] See note on v12.
^f Spread falsehood] AV 'forge a lie'. The verb means 'to stitch on', 'to smear
   something over', 'to conceal'. We have used the word 'spread' because it
   conveys both 'covering over with something', and because 'spread lies' is the
   English idiom.
^g Grease] Davies *Lexicon* suggests the root of the word is 'smearing', which would
   make a link with the first statement of v69. Compare Ps. 17:10 and Isa. 6] 10.
^h Silver and gold] Hebrew 'gold and silver'.

Day 303   Psalm 119:73-80   Yod. 10th Part

⁷³ Your hands have made me, and have fashioned me.
Give understanding to learn your commands.
⁷⁴ Those who fear you will see me and be glad;
Because in hope I wait upon^a your word.

⁷⁵ I know what you ordain is righteous^b, LORD;
And you in faithfulness afflicted me.
⁷⁶ I plead your steadfast love^c to comfort me;
As, to your servant, you said^d it would be

⁷⁷ Send tender mercies^e to me, and I'll live;
Because your Law is my special delight.^f
⁷⁸ Shamed be the proud! With lies^g they bent me down,^h
But, in your precepts, I will meditate.   →

⁷⁹ Let those who fear you turn again to me,
Even those who your testimonies know. ⁱ
⁸⁰ Let my heart be perfect^j in your decrees,
In order that I may not be ashamed.

---

^a In hope I wait upon] One word in Hebrew 'I wait with confident expectation'.
^b What you ordain is righteous] Hebrew plural. AV 'thy judgments are right'. The Hebrew is literally, 'Righteousness are your judgments'. As elsewhere in Psalm 119, we believe the reference is to what God ordains, rather than right judicial decisions. Hebrew *mišpaṭ* - מִשְׁפָּט. See Appendix 2 - Law - Judgment.
^c Steadfast love] Hebrew *ḥeṣedh* - חֶסֶד. See Appendix 2 - Loving-kindness.
^d Said] Hebrew *'imrâ* - אִמְרָה – 'the spoken word'. See Appendix 2 - Word.
^e Tender mercies] Hebrew 'your tender mercies'.
^f My special delight] Hebrew 'my delights' = my great delight.
^g With lies] with falsehood. It is the only time that the AV translates by 'without a cause'.
^h Bent me down] The root meaning of the word is 'to bend'. AV 'dealt perversely', NASB 'subvert', *Statenvertaling* 'threw me down', Welsh Bible 'made me bent'. See note on Ps. 146:9.
ⁱ Even ... know] We follow the rabbinic correction of the text (*qerê* - הֲרֵי), as AV and Horsley.
^j Perfect] Blameless.

Day 304   Psalm 119:81-88   Kaph. 11th Part

⁸¹ For your salvation, my soul is consumed;
Yet, in sure hope, I've waited^a for your word.
⁸² And, for your word^b, my eyes too are consumed;
For I have said, 'When will you comfort me?'

⁸³ Though I've become a bottle in the smoke;
Yet I do not forget what you decree.^c
⁸⁴ How many are the days your servant has?
When will you judge^d those who so harass me?

⁸⁵ The proud have dug out pits for me to fall^e –
Those who don't act according to your Law.^f
⁸⁶ All your commandments are faithful and true; ^g
They harass me with falsehood. O help me!

⁸⁷ They almost made an end of^h me on earth;
But I your precepts still did not forsake.
⁸⁸ According to your mercyⁱ give me life;
The Testimony of your mouth I'll keep.

^a In sure hope I've waited] One word in Hebrew.
^b For your word] Literally, 'for your spoken-word' or 'for your saying'.
^c What you decree] Hebrew plural, *ḥoq* - חֹק. See Appendix 2 - Law - Decree.
^d Judge] Literally, 'do judgment on'. 'Judgment' here is Hebrew *mišpaṭ* - מִשְׁפָּט.
See Appendix 2 - Law - Judgment.
^e Pits for me to fall] Hebrew simply 'pits', but the metaphor is evidently of pitfalls
set as by hunters to trap.
^f Those who don't act … Law] We take it to be the proud who are not according to
God's Law, rather than the traps ('which …' AV).
^g Faithful and true] One word in Hebrew which has both meanings.
^h Made an end of] The same Hebrew word used in v81 and v82 ('consume').
ⁱ Mercy] Hebrew *ḥeṣedh* - חֶסֶד. See Appendix 2 - Loving-kindness.

Day 305   Psalm 119:89-96 Lamed. 12th Part

⁸⁹ Forever, LORD, your word is firmly set;
Forever in the heavens it is sure.^a
⁹⁰ To generations^b is your faithfulness;
The earth was founded by you and stands firm.

⁹¹ As you've ordained^c, they still to this day stand,
Because all things are servants unto you.
⁹² Unless your Law were my special delight,^d
In my affliction I'd have been destroyed.

⁹³ Your precepts I will never more forget,
For by them you have given life to me.
⁹⁴ Yes, I am yours^e; therefore deliver me,
Because your precepts I have sought with care.^f

⁹⁵ The wicked lie in wait to end my life;^g
Your testimonies I considered well.
⁹⁶ To all perfection I have seen an end;
But your commandment^h is immensely wide.

^a Forever … firmly set … sure] We have extended these lines with repetition of
'forever'. 'Firmly set' and 'is sure' are one verb. For its use as 'sure' see Deut.
13:14 (AV 'certain').
^b To generations] Hebrew literally, 'to generation and generation' i.e. to all
generations.
^c As you've ordained] Hebrew *mišpaṭ* - מִשְׁפָּט. See Appendix 2 - Law - Judgment.
^d My special delight] As v24,77. Plural.

^e Yes, I am yours] Literally, 'I myself am to you', or 'for you'; 'I belong to you'. The 'I' is emphasised.

^f Sought with care] One word in Hebrew.

^g To end my life] One word - 'to kill', 'to destroy', 'to cause to perish'.

^h Commandment] Hebrew singular. God's law is a comprehensive whole, cf. Deut. 11:22. Hebrew *mitswâ* - מִצְוָה. See Appendix 2 - Law - Commandment.

Day 306   Psalm 119:97-104   Mem. 13th Part

⁹⁷ O I do love your Law so very much!
It is my meditation all the day.
⁹⁸ Through your commands I'm wiser than my foes
For it is with me to eternity.^a

⁹⁹ More than my teachers^b, I have understood,
For on your Testimonies I reflect.
¹⁰⁰ I understand more than those who are old,
For I have kept the precepts you appoint.

¹⁰¹ I've kept my feet from every evil path,
In order that I may but keep your word.
¹⁰² I've not departed from what you've ordained,^c
Because you've been a teacher unto me.^d

¹⁰³ How sweet to me^e have been the words you speak^f -
Yes, even more than honey to my mouth.
¹⁰⁴ I, from your precepts, come to understand,
And every path of falsehood I do hate.

^a In this verse there is a singular verb and a plural noun. Literally, this reads, 'Your commandments, it makes me wiser than my enemies, because it is ever with me'. We take it that 'commandments' are here viewed as one comprehensive expression of God's will, as v96, where the singular is used. For comment on agreement of verbs in number, see Ewald *Syntax*, where this verse is referenced. See Soncino also.

^b More than my teachers] Hebrew 'more than all my teachers'.

^c What you've ordained] Hebrew Plural *mišpaṭ* - מִשְׁפָּט. See Appendix 2 - Law - Judgment.

^d Because you've been a teacher unto me] Literally, 'Because you - you have taught me'. 'You' is emphasised in the Hebrew.

^e How sweet to me] Literally, 'how smoothe to my palate'.

^f Words you speak] Hebrew *'imrâ* - אִמְרָה – 'the spoken word'. See Appendix 2 - Word.

Day 307   Psalm 119:105 -112 Nun. 14th Part

[105] Your word is as a lamp unto my foot,
And as a light unto the path I tread.
[106] I swore an oath and surely will fulfil:
To keep the righteous things that you ordain.[a]

[107] I was afflicted, O so very much!
Give life to me according to your word.
[108] My mouth's free offerings[b], O LORD accept; [c]
Cause me to learn the things that you ordain.[d]

[109] My soul is in my[e] hand continually;
Yet, even so, I don't forget your Law.
[110] The wicked ones have laid a trap for me;
But from your precepts I've not gone astray.

[111] Your Testimonies I took for my lot –
For ever! They're the gladness of my heart![f]
[112] I've turned my heart to do what you decree[g] –
For ever! Even to the very end.

---

[a] The righteous things that you ordain] AV 'thy righteous judgments'. Hebrew literally, 'the judgments of your righteousness'. Hebrew *mišpaṭ* - מִשְׁפָּט. See Appendix 2 - Law - Judgment.

[b] Free offerings] 'Freewill' or 'voluntary' offerings. Compare Lev. 7:16; Amos 4] 5; Psalms 54:6 and 110:3, where the word is used. See also Heb. 13:15.

[c] O LORD accept] The psalmist uses a strong word of entreaty (n'a - נָא). AV 'I beseech thee'. See note on Ps. 118:2.

[d] The things that you ordain] AV 'thy judgments' Hebrew *mišpaṭ* - מִשְׁפָּט. See Appendix 2 - Law - Judgment.

[e] My soul is in my hand] A Hebrew idiom, meaning 'my life is in great jeopardy'. See Judg. 12:3; I Sam. 19:5 and 28:21; cf. the English idiom 'to take one's life in one's hands'.

[f] Your Testimonies I took ... heart] AV 'Thy testimonies have I taken as an heritage for ever for they *are* the rejoicing of my heart'.

[g] What you decree. Hebrew *ḥoq* - חֹק. See Appendix 2 - Law - Decree.

Day 308   Psalm 119:113-120 Samech 15th Part

[113] I hate those who are of a double mind,[a]
Because my love is set upon your Law.[b]
[114] You are my hiding place. You are my shield;
And I have hoped and waited for[c] your word.   →

¹¹⁵ Depart from me, you who do wicked things,
Because my God's commandments I will keep.
¹¹⁶ Uphold me, as you said^d, and I will live;
And in my hope^e let me not be ashamed.^f

¹¹⁷ Give strength, support^g me, then I shall be safe;^h
On your decreesⁱ I'll wonder^j constantly.
¹¹⁸ All those who turn from them^k you will reject;^l
For their deceitfulness is but in vain.

¹¹⁹ As dross, you end^m the wicked of the earth;
Therefore your testimonies I do love.
¹²⁰ My flesh shrinks back in trembling fear of you;ⁿ
And your right judgments, they make me afraid.^o

---

^a Those who are of a double mind] A noun from the same root is used in I Kgs.
18:21, cf. Jas. 1:8; 4:8. 'Unstable wavering minds', Newton (13). So too Luther
(*flattergeister*).

^b Because ... Law] Hebrew 'and your Law have I loved'.

^c Hoped and waited for] One word in Hebrew (*yaḥal* - יָחַל), conveying an earnest
watching and expectant hope'. A long patient waiting' Girdlestone.

^d As you said] Hebrew 'according to your [spoken] word'. Hebrew *'imrâ* - אִמְרָה.
See Appendix 2 - Word.

^e Hope] A different word from that used in v114. It may also mean 'hope' or
'wait' and is linked with the idea of examining carefully, as in Neh. 2:13,15.
Compare Matt. 24:32,33.

^f Ashamed] 'Disappointed'.

^g Give strength, support] One word in Hebrew. A different word from 'uphold' in
v116; translated 'strengthen' by the AV at Ps. 41:3; 104:15.

^h Be safe] Or 'be saved' or 'be delivered'.

ⁱ Decrees] Hebrew *ḥoq* - חֹק. See Appendix 2 - Law - Decree.

^j Wonder] The Hebrew word means 'to gaze with devotion', 'to occupy oneself
with'.

^k Them] Hebrew 'your decrees', as v17.

^l Reject] So de Burgh. AV 'trodden down'. Gesenius *Lexicon*, 'despise'.

^m End] 'Cause to cease'. The word is used in connection with keeping the Sabbath
when activity ceases.

ⁿ My flesh shrinks back in trembling fear] AV 'trembles for fear'. Others have used
'flesh creeps'; 'hair stands on end' (the same word as in Job 4:15); 'the hair of
my flesh stands on end' [*Statenvertaling*]. The word translated 'fear' here
derives from a verb meaning 'to tremble' - i.e. great fear and dread.

^o Your right judgments ... afraid] Hebrew 'because of your judgments I have
feared'. We believe the meaning of the Hebrew *mišpaṭ* - מִשְׁפָּט here is in
relation to God destroying the 'dross' of the wicked. We shall not be able to
behold it unless upheld', Newton (13). So too Soncino. Compare 1 John 4:17.

Day 309   Psalm 119:121-128   Ayin 16th Part

¹²¹ I acted justly^a, and with righteousness;
Do not forsake me to those who oppress;^b
¹²² But be the surety for your servant's good;
And do not let the arrogant oppress.

¹²³ For your salvation my eyes are consumed,^c
And for the word of righteousness you speak.^d
¹²⁴ Deal with your servant in^e your steadfast love;^f
Teach me what you decree, and make me learn.^g

¹²⁵ I am your servant. Make me understand;
So that your testimonies I may know.
¹²⁶ This is the season for the LORD to work;
Your Law they've broken and they've made it void.^h

¹²⁷ Therefore I love the things that you command;
I love them more than gold - than finest gold.
¹²⁸ I count your precepts on all things as right;
And every path of falsehood I do hate.

---

^a Acted justly] Literally, 'I have done judgment'.
^b Oppress] Hebrew 'oppress me', here and the following verse.
^c Consumed] See and compare v81,82.
^d The word ... you speak] 'Your saying', Hebrew *'imrâ* - אִמְרָה. See Appendix 2 - Word.
^e In] Hebrew 'according to'.
^f Steadfast love] Hebrew *ḥeṣedh* - חֶסֶד. See Appendix 2 - Loving-kindness.
^g Teach ... make me learn: Hebrew one word - the causative form of 'to learn'.
^h Broken ... made void] One word in Hebrew. AV 'made void', but the meaning of the verb is primarily 'to break'.

Day 310   Psalm 119:129-136   Pe. 17th Part

¹²⁹ Your Testimonies - they are wondrous things;
Therefore, my soul has kept them carefully.
¹³⁰ When your words open^a it makes light to shine;
And so, it makes the simple understand.

¹³¹ With my mouth open wide I gasp and pant;^b
Because I thirst^c and long for your commands.
¹³² Turn to me^d and be gracious unto me;
Just as is right^e for those who love your name

¹³³ My steps keep steady in the word you spoke;^f
Let no iniquity rule over me.
¹³⁴ Redeem me when oppression comes from man;^g
And I will keep the precepts you appoint.

¹³⁵ Upon your servant, make your face to shine;
The things that you decree make me to learn.
¹³⁶ Rivers^h of waters run down from my eyes,
Because of those who have not kept your Law.ⁱ

---

^a Opening of your words] The verb is used of opening a door. The 'unfolding', or 'setting forth' of God's word. Compare Ps. 49:4 where a cognate word is used. See too Luke 24:27,32.

^b Gasp and pant] One word in Hebrew. Compare Jer. 14:6.

^c Thirst] We have added this verb as required by the metaphor of the previous line, and in itself a synonym for 'longing'. Compare Ps. 42:1.

^d Turn to me] Literally, 'turn your face to me' (as Segond). AV 'look upon me'. Compare v135.

^e Just as is right] AV 'as thou usest to do'; AV mg 'according to the custom'. Hebrew literally, 'according to the judgment' (Hebrew mišpaṭ - מִשְׁפָּט). See note at 81:4. We have followed a suggestion of the *Dutch Annotations*. See Appendix 2 - Law - Judgment.

^f The word you spoke] Hebrew 'imrâ - אִמְרָה - the spoken word. See Appendix 2 - Word.

^g Oppression comes from man] This is human (Hebrew 'adham - אָדָם) oppression, violence, injury, extortion. See Appendix 2 - Man.

^h Rivers] Perhaps, better, 'streams' or 'rivulets'. It is a word used for irrigation channels. See Ps. 1:3; Prov. 21:1; Lam. 3:48.

ⁱ Because of those who have not kept your Law] Hebrew 'because they have not kept your Law'.

Day 311   Psalm 119:137-144   Tsadhe 18th Part

¹³⁷ You are the one who is righteous, O LORD;^a
The things that you ordain^b are just and right.^c
¹³⁸ Your testimonies are, by your command,
in righteousness and in great faithfulness.

¹³⁹ My zeal and grief^d is so consuming me,
Because my enemies forgot your words.
¹⁴⁰ The word you speak^e is pure and well-refined,^f
Because of this your servant loves your word.^g

¹⁴¹ I'm only little, and I am despised,
And yet your precepts I do not forget.
¹⁴² Your righteousness is endless righteousness;
It's everlasting^h, and your Law is truth.

¹⁴³ Distress and anguish have took hold on me,
Yet your commandments are still my delights.
¹⁴⁴ Your Testimonies – righteousⁱ evermore -
Give understanding to me, and I'll live.

---

^a You are the one who is righteous, O LORD] The Hebrew emphasises 'You are righteous'.

^b The things that you ordain] Hebrew *mišpaṭ* - מִשְׁפָּט. See Appendix 2 - Law - Judgment.

^c Just and right] One word in Hebrew. The root meaning is 'straight', or 'upright'.

^d Zeal and grief] One word in Hebrew. Calvin and Bridges identify the strong emotion as 'grief'.

^e The word you speak] Hebrew *'imrâ* - אִמְרָה - the spoken word. See Appendix 2 - Word.

^f Pure and ... well-refined] One word in Hebrew. The metaphor is of metals purified in a furnace.

^g Your word] Hebrew 'it'.

^h Endless ... everlasting] One word in Hebrew.

ⁱ Righteous] Hebrew 'righteousness'.

Day 312   Psalm 119:145-152 Qoph. 19th Part

¹⁴⁵ I'm crying out to you with all my heart;
Give answer, LORD, and I'll keep your decrees.
¹⁴⁶ I've called upon you. O deliver me;
And then, your testimonies I will keep.

¹⁴⁷ Ready to meet the dawning I arose;
I cried for help and waited for your word.
¹⁴⁸ Ready to meet each night-watch were my eyes;
To meditate upon the word you spoke.^a   →

271

¹⁴⁹ After ᵇ your mercy ᶜ, listen to my voice;
O LORD, as you've determined ᵈ, give me life.
¹⁵⁰ Those who pursue an evil plan ᵉ draw near;
But they're far off - a long way from your Law.

¹⁵¹ But you yourself ᶠ are near at hand, O LORD;
All the commandments that you give ᵍ are truth.
¹⁵² Your testimonies showed me this of old;
That you have founded them for evermore.

ᵃ The word you spoke] Hebrew 'imrâ - אִמְרָה - the spoken word. See Appendix 2 - Word.
ᵇ After] i.e. 'in accordance with', 'in line with'. Here and the following line.
ᶜ Mercy] Hebrew ḥesedh - חֶסֶד. See Appendix 2 - Loving-kindness.
ᵈ As you've determined] Literally, 'according to your judgments'. Hebrew mišpaṭ - מִשְׁפָּט. 'Determined' is used here in the sense of making a fixed decision as a judge or ruler. We may take this as The Psalmist also seeks life (1) according to God's written word v25,107; (2) according to his mercy v88,159; (3) by his spoken word v154; (4) in his way v37; (5) in his righteousness v40. See v156 and Appendix 2 - Law - Judgment.
ᵉ Evil plan] AV 'mischief'. As Ps. 26:10. See de Burgh.
ᶠ You yourself] the Hebrew emphasises the 'you'. It is God's response to those who pursue an evil plan.
ᵍ Commandments that you give] Hebrew mitṣwâ - מִצְוָה. See Appendix 2 - Law - Commandment.

Day 313   Psalm 119:153-160   Resh. 20th Part

¹⁵³ See my affliction and deliver me,
For I am not forgetful of your Law.
¹⁵⁴ O plead my cause for me ᵃ; redeem me back; ᵇ
And give me life according to your word. ᶜ

¹⁵⁵ Salvation is far off from wicked men, ᵈ
For your decrees they have not sought with care. ᵉ
¹⁵⁶ O LORD, how great your tender mercies are!
According to your judgments ᶠ, give me life.

¹⁵⁷ Many are my pursuers and my foes –
Yet from your Testimonies I've not turned.
¹⁵⁸ I saw transgressors, and I felt disgust; ᵍ
Because they did not keep the word you spoke. ʰ   →

¹⁵⁹ Look – seeⁱ that I have loved your precepts, LORD;
According to your mercy^j, give me life.
¹⁶⁰ The sum and substance^k of your word is truth;
All your right judgment^l is for evermore.

---

^a Plead my cause for me] i.e. 'fight my corner'. Hebrew literally, 'plead my plea'.
   Septuagint κρινον την κρισιν. Welsh Bible 'dadlau fy nadl'.
^b Redeem me back] The word is 'redeem' (ga'al - גָּאַל) in the sense of 'buying
   back' (as in the case of Ruth and Boaz, where he acted as kinsman-redeemer,
   Ruth 2:20ff). See Ps. 19:14.
^c Word] The spoken word, i.e. 'just as you have said'. Hebrew 'imrâ - אִמְרָה - the
   spoken word. See Appendix 2 - Word.
^d Wicked men] Hebrew 'wicked ones', masculine.
^e Sought with care] Gesenius Lexicon 'to apply oneself (to any thing), to study, to
   follow, to practice (any thing)'. Compare Ps. 119:45.
^f According to your judgments] i.e. 'as you have determined'. Hebrew mišpat -
   מִשְׁפָּט. See note on v149 which uses the same expression. 'judgment' is used
   here in the sense of making a fixed decision as a judge or ruler. See Appendix 2
   - Law - Judgment.
^g Felt disgust] AV 'was grieved'. The word is translated 'hate' in Ps. 139:21. It
   indicates strong feelings of revulsion.
^h The word you spoke] Hebrew 'imrâ - אִמְרָה - the spoken word. See Appendix 2 -
   Word.
ⁱ Look - see] One word in Hebrew.
^j Mercy] Hebrew ḥesedh - חֶסֶד. See Appendix 2 - Loving-kindness.
^k Sum and substance] Hebrew one word 'the sum', 'the head'. AV translates the
   word as 'sum' in Ps. 139:17.
^l Your right judgment] Hebrew 'judgment of your righteousness (Hebrew mišpat -
   מִשְׁפָּט)'. Compare the use of the word here with v149 and 156. See Appendix
   2 - Law - Judgment.

Day 314   Psalm 119:161-168   Shin. 21st Part

¹⁶¹ Princes, without a cause, have harassed me;
But, at your word, my heart just stands in awe.^a
¹⁶² I am rejoicing at the word you spoke;^b
Even as one who finds a treasure store.^c

¹⁶³ Falsehood and lying^d I hate and I loathe;
But I have set my love upon your Law.
¹⁶⁴ Within a day I praise you seven times,
For all the righteous things that you ordain.^e   →

273

^{165} Great peace belongs to those who love your Law;
And there shall be no stumbling block^f for them.
^{166} For your salvation I have waited, LORD;
And I have done what your commandments say.

^{167} Your testimonies are kept by my soul;
And I do love them very much indeed.
^{168} Your testimonies and precepts^g I've kept;
For all my ways are manifest to you.

---

^{a} Stands in awe] One word in Hebrew. Not the usual word for 'fear'.

^{b} The word you spoke] Hebrew *'imrâ* - אִמְרָה - the spoken word. See Appendix 2 - Word.

^{c} Treasure store] Hebrew literally, 'much booty', 'great spoils of war'.

^{d} Falsehood and lying] One word in Hebrew.

^{e} The righteous things that you ordain] Literally, 'the judgments (Hebrew *mišpaṭ* - מִשְׁפָּט) of your righteousness', as v160. See Appendix 2 - Law - Judgment.

^{f} Stumbling block] So the Hebrew, equivalent to the word used in 1 John 2:10 in the New Testament. 'Stumbling block' - an expression used for a tree stump (*Oxford Dictionary of English Etymology*).

^{g} Testimonies and precepts] Hebrew 'precepts and testimonies'. See Appendix 2 - Law - Precepts, and Testimony (1).

Day 315   Psalm 119:169-176 Tau. 22nd Part

^{169} Let my loud cry come near before you, LORD;
Make me discern according to your word.
^{170} My prayer for grace^a will come before your face;
According to your word^b, deliver me.

^{171} O let my lips be bursting forth with praise;
For you are teaching your decrees to me.
^{172} My tongue will witness^c to what you have said;^{d}
For all things you command are righteousness.

^{173} O let your hand be ready to help^e me;
Because your precepts are my settled choice.^{f}
^{174} For your salvation I have longed, O LORD;
And your Law also is my great delight.^{g} →

¹⁷⁵ Let my soul live, and it shall give you praise;
Your ordinances^h - let them be my help!
¹⁷⁶ Like a lost sheep, I've strayedⁱ - your servant seek!
For your commandments^j I do not forget.

---

^a My prayer for grace] Or 'my prayer for mercy'. This is the literal meaning. AV
'supplication'. See Gesenius *Lexicon*. It derives from a word meaning 'to be
gracious to', 'to pity'. As in Ps. 6:9 and 55:1.

^b Your word] Hebrew *'imrâ* - אִמְרָה - the spoken word. In verse 169 the word is
dabhar - דָּבָר. See Appendix 2 - Word.

^c Witness] AV 'speak'. Perhaps 'repeat' or even 'echo'. Gesenius *Lexicon*
considers 'sing' as the primary meaning of the verb. Compare Ps. 147:7 and
see the note there.

^d What you have said] Hebrew *'imrâ* - אִמְרָה - the spoken word. See Appendix 2 -
Word.

^e Help] Here and v175. This is the root word used of Eve in Gen. 2:18,20.

^f Are my settled choice] 'To approve after trial, to choose', Davies, *Lexicon*.

^g Great delight] Hebrew 'my delights' = my great delight.

^h Ordinances] Hebrew *mišpaṭ* - מִשְׁפָּט. See Appendix 2 - Law - Judgment.

ⁱ Like a lost sheep, I've strayed] The word translated 'lost' is literally, 'perishing',
'dying', 'being destroyed'. 'Strayed' is used in Isa. 53:6. However, both Bonar
and Newton (1) avoid expressions that imply moral failure here, and at v67.
They consider the whole Psalm to belong to Christ, and interpret these verses
in connection with Heb. 2:10 and 5:8.

^j Commandments] Hebrew *mitswâ* - מִצְוָה. See Appendix 2 - Law -
Commandment.

Day 316   Psalm 120 Song of Ascents (1)

¹ In my distress I cried unto the LORD,
I cried out, and he heard and answered^a me;
² My soul deliver, LORD, from lying lip,
From lying lip, and from deceitful tongue.

³ What shall he give you, O deceitful tongue?
And what more shall he reckon up^b for you? -
⁴ The sharpened arrows of the mighty one,
Even with burning coals of juniper!^c

⁵ Alas for me^d, I am a sojourner;
And, as a stranger, I in Meshech dwell;^e
Among the tents of Kedar I have camped.^f
⁶ My soul has had its dwelling here too long.^g   →

My soul has had its dwelling here too long
Close by him who hates peace; [7]but I am peace!
Yes, I'm a man of peace[h], but when I speak -
I speak of peace; but all they want is war.

---

[a] Heard and answered] One word in Hebrew. Hebrew *'anâ* - עָנָה. See Appendix 2
- Hear and Answer.

[b] Reckon up] literally, 'add'. We take the meaning as a threatening of the LORD's
punishment, 'he' referring to God. See de Burgh and Perowne (note), and
compare 1 Sam. 3:17.

[c] Juniper] We have kept the traditional (AV) translation, following Jerome. Most
modern translations give 'the broom tree'. The metaphor refers to burning
charcoal, which, it is suggested, is especially hot when produced from this tree.

[d] Alas for me] This is an extended form of the word often translated by the AV as
'Woe!' The psalmist is letting out 'a deep heaving sigh', expressing his sadness.

[e] A sojourner ... as a stranger ... I ... dwell] We have expanded the meaning of the
verb (Hebrew *gûr* - גּוּר). It means dwelling as a stranger, as the patriarchs were
in Canaan, (Exod. 6:4), and as Israel was in Egypt (Gen. 15:13). Not being a
part of the resident community.

[f] I have camped] AV 'dwell' (Hebrew *šakhan* - שָׁכַן). Although the word may
simply mean 'dwell', or 'inhabit', it has a strong link with tent dwelling. See
Josh. 18:1 (AV 'set up'), Numb. 24:2.

[g] We have repeated this line as the first line of the following stanza, connecting
the thought between them. We have added 'here'.

[h] But I am peace. Yes, I'm a man of peace] We have expanded the line to convey
the strong and vivid emphasis of the Hebrew. The Hebrew is literally, 'I am
peace' (compare Ps. 109:4 - 'I am prayer').

Day 317   Psalm 121   Song of Ascents (2)

[1] Unto the mountains I'll lift up my eyes,
Asking, 'Where shall the help I need come from?'
[2] My help is with the LORD and comes from[a] him -
The Maker of the heaven and the earth

[3] He'll not allow, nor cause[b] your foot to slip;
The one who keeps you has no slumbering;
[4] Take note of this[c]: he who keeps Israel,
He does not slumber, and he does not sleep.

[5] The LORD's the one who watches over you;
The LORD's your shade[d], and he's at your right hand;
[6] Therefore the sun won't strike you down by day;
Nor will the moon cause harm to you by night.[e] →

⁷ The LORD will keep you from all that is bad;
He'll be a guard and keeper^f of your soul;
⁸ The LORD will keep your going out and in;
From this time onwards and for evermore.

---

^a With ... from] The Hebrew construction is literally, 'my help is from-with the
LORD'. As Welsh Bible *oddiwrth*.
^b Not allow, nor cause] Hebrew 'give'. The verb in Hebrew that is used here has a
range of meanings. Here both the meanings of what the Lord allows and of
what he appoints are clearly present.
^c Take note of this] Hebrew *hinneh* - הַנֵּה. See Appendix 2 - Behold!
^d The LORD's your shade] See Ps. 91:1.
^e Nor will the moon cause harm to you at night] Hebrew 'nor the moon by night'.
^f A guard and keeper] 'He will guard'. The verb, which is used six times in this
Psalm, means 'to guard' and 'to keep', 'to keep watch'.

Day 318   Psalm 122   Song of Ascents (3)

¹ I was made glad by those who said to me,^a
'O come and let us go to the LORD's house';
² Within your gates, Jerusalem, we stand^b -
³ Jerusalem, the city builded up!

The city built and joined in unity.^c
⁴ To it the tribes, yes, the LORD's tribes^d - go up;
A Testimony^e unto Israel;
So that they may give thanks to the LORD's name.

⁵ For there the thrones of judgment are set up -
Even the thrones that are for David's house.
⁶ Pray that Jerusalem may be in peace;^f
Those who love you will prosper peacefully.^g

Pray that Jerusalem may be in peace;
Those who love you will prosper peacefully;
⁷ There will be peace within your city walls;^h
And in your palaces, prosperity.

⁸ For brothers', and for my companions', sake
I will plead thisⁱ: 'May there be peace in you!'
⁹ And for the house – the house of God the LORD -
The LORD our God - I will seek good for you.

277

[a] I was made glad by those who said to me] The cause of the psalmist's joy was not the 'saying' or even the idea of going up to the house of the LORD. His joy was over those who encouraged him to go and worship. This is clear from the Hebrew. See Perowne (note), Motyer (2) and Septuagint.

[b] We stand] Hebrew 'our feet stand'.

[c] Built … joined in unity] cf. Ps. 133:1; 2 Sam. 5:9; Eph. 2:21; 4:16.

[d] The LORD's tribes] Literally, 'the tribes of JAH'. Hebrew YAH - יָהּ. See Appendix 2 - Names of God.

[e] Testimony] Hebrew 'edhûth - עֵדוּת. Modern versions assume that the word here means the law or instruction to go up to Jerusalem for the pilgrim feasts, and translate accordingly 'as was decreed', etc. We have translated the word in the normal way, in which it can stand for the Tabernacle and the Ark. As de Burgh notes, we may take this to be the meaning, in apposition to 'Jerusalem' in v3. See Appendix 2 - Law - Testimony (1).

[f] Pray that Jerusalem may be in peace] Literally, 'ask the peace of Jerusalem'. AV 'pray for …'. The Hebrew word may mean 'request' (AV 'pray for'), and 'enquire after' (cf. Neh. 1:2).

[g] We have repeated this verse at the start of the next stanza.

[h] City walls] The Hebrew word comes from a word meaning 'to surround', hence 'circumvallation'.

[i] I will plead this] Here the psalmist uses a word of entreaty (Hebrew na' - נָא). Literally, 'let me say I implore you'. 'Used in submissive and modest request', Gesenius Lexicon. AV 'now'. See note on Ps. 118:2.

Day 319   Psalm 123. Song of Ascents (4)

¹ It is to you I've lifted up my eyes –
You are the one who in the heavens dwells –
The one who sits in heaven, there enthroned.[a]
² As servants' eyes look to their master's hand,[b]

Like a maid's eyes look to her mistress' hand;
Likewise, our eyes look to the LORD our God,
Until he shall be gracious unto us.
³ Be gracious, LORD, be gracious unto us!

For of contempt we've had more than enough;
⁴ Our soul has had more than enough of this –
The mocking scorn[c] of those who are at ease,
And the contempt heaped on us by the proud.[d]

[a] Dwells … sits … enthroned] We have expanded one line to two to bring out the alternative meanings of the verb. It may be taken as 'seated', 'enthroned', 'dwelling in'.

[b] As servant's eyes … master's hand] The Hebrew calls the reader to take note of

these things. AV 'Behold, as the eyes of servants ...'. Hebrew *hinneh* - הִנֵּה.
    See Appendix 2 - Behold!
^c Mocking scorn] One word in Hebrew.
^d And the contempt heaped on us by the proud] Hebrew 'with the contempt of
    the proud'. We have supplied the English idiom.

Day 320   Psalm 124. Song of Ascents (5)

¹ 'Had it not been the LORD who is for us', ^a
Let Israel thus say with certainty, ^b
² 'Had it not been the LORD who is for us
When up against us men were rising up; ^c

³ 'Surely, they would have swallowed us alive,
Such was their anger burning against us;
⁴ The waters would have overwhelmed us then,
The torrent would have gone over our soul';

⁵ 'Rough waters^d would have covered our soul too'.
⁶ Blest be the LORD who has not given us
Unto their teeth, just as a hunted prey! ^e
⁷ Our soul escaped away, just as a bird –

A bird that's freed out of the trappers' snare;
The snare is broken, so we have escaped.
⁸ On the LORD's name our help and aid depend^f –
The LORD who made the heavens and the earth.

---

^a Who is for us] AV and most translations give 'on our side', but the LORD was not
    merely the deciding factor in a hard-fought battle between two sides. His
    commitment for us ensured our deliverance. We could translate 'the LORD is
    ours'.
^b With certainty] AV 'now'. The Hebrew particle (Hebrew *na'* - נָא) does not
    indicate 'the present time', but emphasises the verb. Compare Scottish
    Metrical Psalter (version 2). The English word 'now' can be used as a word of
    request or entreaty, as can this Hebrew word, which accounts for the AV
    translation. See note on Ps. 118:2.
^c When up against us men were rising up] 'Man' Hebrew singular, but usually
    used in a collective sense. The verbs are plural in the next verse. 'Man' here is
    'adham - אָדָם - Man as a child of Adam. See Appendix 2 - Man. The verb here
    is the Hebrew infinitive with a preposition - 'in the rising up of', as Ps. 126:1;
    Prov. 28:28.
^d Rough waters] AV 'proud waters'. The root meaning of the word is to 'to boil',
    'to seethe', and from that 'to act rebelliously', or 'to act arrogantly'.

279

e Hunted prey] one word in Hebrew.
f On the LORD's name our help and aid depend] Literally, 'our help [is] in the name
    of the LORD'. Compare Ps. 121:2.

Day 321   Psalm 125. Song of Ascents (6)

¹ Those who are putting their trust in the LORD
Are like Mount Zion, which cannot be moved;
For it is set, established[a], evermore
² As mountains are around Jerusalem,

Around about his people is the LORD.[b]
From this time forward, and for evermore.
³ Because of this, the rod[c] of wickedness
Will not rest on the lot of righteous men.[d]

So that the righteous do not stretch their hands
To reach out and to do iniquity.
⁴ O LORD, do good unto those who are good;
And unto those who are upright in heart;

⁵ But as for those who turn themselves aside –
To those who turn unto their crooked ways –
The LORD will, with wrongdoers, lead them off
And upon Israel there will be peace!

a Set, established] Literally, 'seated'. See note on Ps. 122:5.
b As the mountains … Around about his people is the LORD] Compare 2 Kgs. 6:17;
    and Zech. 2:5.
c Rod] The word may mean 'sceptre', and then refer to the dominion (oppression,
    as the Hebrew word 'rest on' can mean) of the wicked over the land of the
    righteous; or (as de Burgh indicates), it may refer to a measuring rod, and then
    indicate that the wicked shall not possess the land allotted to the LORD's
    people.
d Righteous men] 'The righteous ones'.

Day 322   Psalm 126. Song of Ascents (7)

¹ When the LORD turned Zion's captivity,[a]
Then we were like those who are in a dream;
² And then our mouth was full of laughter too;
Our tongue was taken up with shouts of joy.[b]   →

Among the nations they then spoke like this:
'The LORD has done such mighty things for them!'
³ The LORD has done such mighty things for us!
So we rejoice, for we have been made glad.ᶜ

⁴ Turn back again, LORD, our captivity;
Just like the watercourses of the South.ᵈ
⁵ Those who with tearful cryingᵉ sow the seed;
Shall reap the harvest with glad shouts of joy.

⁶ He who goes out, and weeping as he goes;ᶠ
Taking along a measure of the seed;ᵍ
He'll surely comeʰ back, with glad shouts of joy;
Taking along with him his harvest sheaves.

ᵃ Captivity] The word here is different in form from the word used in v4, and may
   be from the same root as 'turned'; i.e. 'turned Zion's returning ones'. De Burgh
   favours the usual reading; but Delitzsch, Gesenius *Lexicon*, Davies *Lexicon*, and
   Theological Workbook link with 'return'.
ᵇ Shouts of joy] As also v5 and v6.
ᶜ So we rejoice, for we have been made glad] One word in Hebrew. Calvin
   'whereof we have been made glad'.
ᵈ The South] Literally, 'the Negev'. The dry and barren land to the South of Israel,
   where, in the wintertime, the wadis fill with rushing torrents after sudden rain.
ᵉ With tearful crying] Hebrew 'with tears
ᶠ Goes out, and weeping as he goes] 'As he goes' - literally, 'going he goes'.
   Perowne, 'may indeed weep every step that he goes'.
ᵍ A measure of seed] The word ('measure') indicates a drawing out of the seed
   (see the verb used in Amos 9:13). Motyer (1) "a 'line' or 'trail' of seed".
   'Basket of seed' - Tregelles (3).
ʰ He'll surely come] Hebrew 'coming he shall come'.

Day 323.   Psalm 127. Song of Ascents for Solomon (8)
¹ Unless the LORD's the builder of the houseᵃ,
Its builders will have toiled on it in vain;
Unless the LORD should keep a city safe,
Its keeper will watch over it in vain.

² For you to get up early is in vain,
To sit up late - eat bread earned by hard work.ᵇ
Surely, he gives to his beloved sleep -
Gives to his loved one even as he sleeps.ᶜ   →

281

³ Behold!ᵈ - sons are a giftᵉ that the LORD gives;
The issueᶠ of the womb is his reward;
⁴ Like arrows in the hand of a strong man;ᵍ
So are the sons you have when you are young.ʰ

⁵ Such *blessings* rest uponⁱ that mighty manʲ -
He who has filled his quiver full of them!
So at the gateᵏ they shall not be ashamed,
When they shall speak there with the enemies.

ᵃ Unless the LORD's the builder of a house] Literally, 'unless the LORD builds a house'.

ᵇ Eat bread earned by hard work] Literally, 'eating the bread of sorrowful labours' or 'pains'. 'Bread' stands for food in general, as the staff of life.

ᶜ Surely he gives ... as he sleeps] In these two lines we have given both meanings suggested by commentators. See Calvin on 'surely' and the interpretation of the verse. The word 'sleep' is a *hapax legomena*, generally understood to mean 'sleep' or 'in sleep' (the NEB calls it 'an unintelligible word'!).

ᵈ Behold!] Hebrew *hinneh* - הִנֵּה. See Appendix 2 - Behold!

ᵉ Sons are a gift] The Hebrew word 'sons' may mean 'children' more generally, and the 'the fruit of the womb' clearly includes daughters. However, 'sons' in v4-6 indicate more a combative male role. 'Gift' is more specifically an 'inheritance' or 'possession'.

ᶠ Issue] Literally, 'fruit'.

ᵍ A strong man] Hebrew *gibbôr* - גִּבּוֹר - Man as a mighty being. See Appendix 2 - Man.

ʰ The sons you have when you are young] Literally, 'sons of youths'. See Prov. 5:18; Isa. 54:6. Compare Gen. 37:3.

ⁱ Such blessings rest upon] Literally, 'O the blessings (or 'happinesses') of' Hebrew *'ašrê* - אַשְׁרֵי. See Appendix 2 - Blessing.

ʲ That mighty man] Hebrew *gibbôr* - גִּבּוֹר - Man as a mighty being. See Appendix 2 - Man. Referring back to v4.

ᵏ At the gate] The area at the gate of a city was where justice was administered and where the (then) adult sons of an older man would be able to defend his cause.

Day 324   Psalm 128. Song of Ascents (9)
¹ How *blest*ᵃ is everyone who fears the LORD!
The person who is walking in his ways;
² The labour of your hands you'll surely eat -
How *blest* you are! It will go well for you!   →

³ Your wife will be just like a fruitful vine
Within the inner chambers of your house;
As olives^b, round your table are your sons.
⁴ So^c shall the man^d be blest^e who fears the LORD.

⁵ The LORD from out of Zion will bless you
And you will see Jerusalem set fair^f -
All of your life's days. ⁶ And also you'll see -
Your children's' children. Peace on Israel!

---

^a Blest] Literally, 'O the blessings (or 'happinesses') of' Hebrew *'ašrê* - אַשְׁרֵי. Here and v2. Compare v4,5. See Appendix 2 - Blessing.

^b Olives] Hebrew 'olive plants'

^c The Hebrew commences the line with *hinneh* - הִנֵּה. 'Behold, thus shall …' See Appendix 2 - Behold!

^d Man] A strong man, a mighty man, a warrior. Hebrew *gibbôr* - גִּבּוֹר - Man as a mighty being. Used of Christ. As in Ps. 127:4,5. See Appendix 2 - Man.

^e Blest] Hebrew *barakh* - בָּרַךְ. Here and v5. Compare v1,2. See Appendix 2 - Blessing.

^f And you will see Jerusalem set fair] Literally, 'and you will look upon the good of Jerusalem'. Of the Hebrew construction here for 'look upon', Gesenius *Lexicon* gives the meaning 'to be pleased with the sight as the eye lingers on objects of pleasure'. The word 'see' may also mean 'live to see' (Ps. 34:13) and 'prove by experience' (Isa. 40:5). The word 'good' has a wide range of meanings, including 'welfare' and 'prosperity' in the widest sense. We understand it of the future time of Jerusalem's promised blessing.

Day 325   Psalm 129. Song of Ascents (10)

¹ 'They have oppressed me much, for a long time,'^a
From my youth up' - May Israel please say^b -
² 'They have oppressed me much from my youth up,
But yet, against me they have not prevailed'.

³ The ploughmen ploughed long furrows on my back.
⁴ The righteous LORD, he cut the wicked's cord;
⁵ They will be shamed, and they will be turned back,
All who are Zion's hate-filled enemies.^c

⁶ They will be as the grass upon the roofs,
Which withers even before it's plucked up; ^d
⁷ It does not fill the hand of him who reaps,
Nor yet the arms^e of him who binds the sheaves.   →

⁸ Nor will the passers-by say unto them,
'The blessing of the LORD be unto you'.
Nor will the passers-by say unto them,^f
'In the LORD's name we give blessing to you'.^g

---

^a Much, for a long time] 'Much' AV margin. Compare Ps. 120:6. The line is repeated in v2.

^b May Israel please say] This is an earnest plea, indicated by the Hebrew word of entreaty (na' - נָא). The AV translates 'now'. See note on Ps. 116:4 and Ps. 118:2.

^c Zion's hate-filled enemies] Hebrew 'those who hate Zion'. The verb 'to hate' is the root of a word translated 'enemy' or 'adversary'.

^d Plucked up] The verb means 'to draw out', as a sword from its sheath, hence it may be translated 'to pluck up'. Alternatively, some translate (as AV) to 'grow, or to 'shoot up' as a plant. Compare Ruth 4:7 where the same verb is used.

^e The arms] Hebrew 'bosom'. The 'lap', or loose fold, at the front of a garment could be used to carry, as here, the ears of corn. Compare Neh. 5:13 and Isa. 49:22, where a closely related word is used.

^f We have repeated this first line of the verse here.

^g We understand this and the previous line as familiar greetings of those who pass by to reapers (compare Ruth 2:4). There is an emphasis on the 'you' in the Hebrew, as though it were underlined, and the verb 'bless' is intensive (piel).

Day 326   Psalm 130. Song of Ascents (11)

¹ Out of the depths, LORD, I've cried unto you;
² My Lord^a, I pray that you will hear^b my voice;
And may your ears listen attentively;
Unto the pleas for mercy my voice speaks.

³ If you, O LORD^c, should mark iniquities,
My Lord, who would be able then to stand?
⁴ But the forgiving pardon^d is with you,
So that, because of this, you may be feared.

⁵ I've waited for the LORD. My soul awaits;
And for his word I've hoped expectantly;
⁶ My soul waits for My Lord - more than the watch -
More than the watchmen who await the dawn!^e

⁷ Hope in the LORD for mercy^f, Israel;
It's with the LORD - redemption plenteous!
⁸ And he himself^g will rescue Israel;
Redeem him^h from all his iniquities.

^b I pray that you will hear] Hebrew simply the imperative - 'hear...'
^c LORD] Hebrew YAH - יָהּ, a shortened form of יהוה, the LORD, JEHOVAH. First used in
   the redemption deliverance of the Exodus (15:2).
^d The forgiving pardon] AV forgiveness'. Hebrew '*the* forgiveness'. The word used
   goes beyond forgiveness to the resulting pardon for sin. See Baron (4).
^e Dawn] The morning. The allusion is most likely to the priestly watchers at the
   Temple who watched for the first indications of morning breaking before
   commencing the daily sacrifice, Baron (4).
^f Mercy] Hebrew *ḥeṣedh* - חֶסֶד. The Hebrew here is '*the* mercy'. See Appendix 2 -
   Loving-kindness.
^g He himself] Not just 'he'. The Hebrew is emphatic as to who will redeem Israel.
^h Rescue ... redeem] One word in Hebrew.

Day 327   Psalm 131. Song of Ascents of David (12)

¹ O LORD, my heart is not raised up in pride,[a]
Nor do my eyes look down as from on high;[b]
I'm not involved in[c] great, important things;
Nor in the things that are too hard[d] for me.

² I've surely calmed and quieted my soul,
Like a weaned child who on his mother rests;
As the weaned child my soul rests upon me;[e]
As the weaned child my soul rests upon me.

³ O Israel, you shall hope in the LORD,
from this time forward, and for evermore;
O Israel, you shall wait on the LORD,
from this time forward, and for evermore.[f]

^a Raised up in pride] Literally, 'lifted up'. When the Hebrew idiom speaks of the
   heart being lifted up, the reference is to pride. See 2 Chr. 26:16ff; Prov. 18:12.
^b Look down as from on high] Hebrew 'are not lofty'. See Ps. 101:5. Motyer (1)
   'the idea here is caught by the expression 'to look down on'.
^c I'm not involved in] Hebrew 'I have not walked in', i.e. in the sense of one's way
   of life.
^d Things ... too hard] Literally, 'beyond one's power', 'wonderful' (AV 'high', AV mg
   "Heb. 'wonderful'"). Adolph Saphir translates the word 'wonderful' (as in Isa.
   9:14) by 'enigma'.
^e Like a weaned child ... my soul rests upon me] The Hebrew is literally, 'As a
   weaned child [is] upon his mother. As the weaned child my soul [is] upon me'.
   We have followed Perowne, who understands the analogy to be to a weaned
   child that lies contentedly upon its mother's bosom rather than being
   distressed or crying for its mother's milk. See too Motyer (1) and Bonar. We

have repeated the second line.

^f We have repeated the last two lines, using this to expand the meaning of the verb (*yahal* - יָחַל), which is 'to wait in expectant hope'. The close of this short Psalm is a confident assertion that Israel will at last be 'weaned' from self-boasting activity, and be still, waiting upon the LORD alone. It ushers in the calm and security of the last three Psalms of Ascents.

Day 328   Psalm 132:1-10. Song of Ascents (13)

¹ For David's sake, O LORD, do call to mind
All his afflictions and his weary toils; ^a
² Of how he swore an oath unto the LORD;
He made a vow to Jacob's Mighty One.

³ 'Into the tent of my house I'll not go;
Upon the couch of my bed^b I'll not go;
⁴ And I will not unto my eyes give sleep;
Nor yet in slumber shall my eyelids close'.

⁵ 'Until I shall find a place for the LORD –
Places to dwell^c for Jacob's Mighty One.
⁶ Behold!^d – We heard of it in Ephrathah;
We found it in the district of Ja'ar.^e

⁷ Into his dwelling places^f we will go;
We'll bow in worship at his footstool there.^g
⁸ Arise, O LORD, into your resting place;
You, and the Ark of your strength and your power.^h

⁹ O let your priests be clothed with righteousness;
Let your beloved onesⁱ shout out for joy;
¹⁰ Let this be for your servant David's sake;
And your anointed's face turn not away.^j

---

^a Afflictions ... weary toils] The word here includes both. See Isa. 53:4 where the word is used (AV 'afflicted'). The root meaning is 'to bestow labour upon something' (Gesenius *Lexicon*).

^b Into the tent ... bed] We have translated these lines literally. 'Tent' and 'house' are here synonyms, as are 'couch' and 'bed'. These 'appositional genitives' evidently serve to emphasise the strong resolve of the vow that was made. Combination of synonyms in this way is also found in Ps. 44. Perowne suggests the translation 'the tent which is my house and the couch which is my bed'. Motyer (2) takes the second phrase to refer to the marriage bed.

286

^c Places to dwell] The Hebrew is plural. The word is more accurately a 'tabernacle' or a 'tent'. The root of the word (*šakhan* - שָׁכַן) is the root of the word Shekinah (*šekhînâ* - שְׁכִינָה), meaning God's Divine presence. In Ps. 46:4 (also in the plural) it refers to the Temple.

^d Behold!] Hebrew *hinneh* - הִנֵּה. See Appendix 2 - Behold!

^e District of Ja'ar] AV 'fields of the wood'. It is now generally accepted that 'the fields (or 'district') of Ja'ar' is a reference to a place - Kiriath Je'arim, where the ark was (1 Chr. 13:5). Ja'ar' means 'the wood', and Kiriath Je'arim 'city of the woods'.

^f Dwelling places] As v5.

^g His footstool there] We have added the word 'there', to indicate a place is referred to. See note on Ps. 99:5.

^h The Ark of your strength and your power] 'Strength' and 'power' are one word in Hebrew. See note on Ps. 78:61. It was at the Ark that his power was displayed. Delitzsch translates 'the Ark of thy Majesty'.

ⁱ Beloved ones] Hebrew *ḥaṣîdhîm* - חֲסִידִים. The Church of England liturgy 'endue thy ministers with righteousness, and make thy chosen people joyful' is taken from this verse, translating *ḥaṣîdhîm* by 'chosen people' - the objects of God's electing mercy. See Appendix 2 - Loving-kindness.

^j Verses 8,9, and 10 also appear in 2 Chr. 6:41,42, which gives the context.

Day 329   Psalm 132:11-18. Song of Ascents (13)

¹¹ The LORD swore unto David what is true;
He won't retract from it, or turn away: ^a
'Of your descendants, who are born to you^b,
For you I'll make them sit upon your throne'.

¹² 'And if your sons will keep my covenant,
And this my testimony that I'll teach; ^c
Their sons shall also sit upon the throne -
They shall sit on your throne for evermore'.

¹³ For Zion has been chosen by the LORD;
He has desired it for his dwelling place: ^d
¹⁴ 'This is my resting place for evermore;
Here I will dwell, for this I have desired'.

¹⁵ 'Zion's^e provision I will greatly bless; ^f
Its needy ones I'll satisfy with bread;
¹⁶ And with deliverance I'll clothe its priests;
And its beloved ones^g will shout for joy'. ^h   →

¹⁷ There will I make a horn for David grow;ⁱ
For my anointed^j I've prepared a lamp;
¹⁸ And I will clothe his enemies with shame;
But his resplendent crown^k shall be on him.

---

^a Retract or turn away from] One word in Hebrew, as v10.
^b Of your descendants who are born to you] Literally, 'of the fruit of your belly' or
'womb'. 'Belly' refers to the inmost part of a person. The Greek translation in
Acts 2:30 means the 'waist' or the 'reproductive organs'.
^c This my testimony that I'll teach] Hebrew 'teach them'. 'Testimony' is Hebrew
'*edhûth* - עֵדוּת. See Appendix 2 - Law - Testimony (1).
^d His dwelling place] The word 'dwelling-place' is derived from the verb 'to sit' in
the previous verse. YLT translates 'a seat to himself'.
^e Zion's] Hebrew 'its' - continuing from v13.
^f Greatly bless] Hebrew 'blessing I will bless'.
^g Its beloved ones] Those who are the object of Zion's love, or maybe (as the word
is usually used) those who are the object of the LORD's love who are 'of Zion'.
Hebrew *ḥaṣîḏhîm* - חֲסִידִים from *ḥeṣedh* - חֶסֶד. See Appendix 2 - Loving-
kindness.
^h Shall shout for joy] Hebrew 'shouting for joy shall shout for joy'. Either 'shall
greatly shout ...' or 'shall surely shout'.
ⁱ There will I make a horn for David grow] 'Grow' - AV 'bud'. The word translated
'branch' or 'shoot' when used of Messiah, is from this verb. Ezek. 29:21; Isa.
4:2; Zech. 3:8, etc. 'Horns' in Scripture signify 'defensive might or victorious
dominion' (Delitzsch).
^j My Anointed] Calvin translates 'my Christ'. Hebrew *mashîaḥ* מָשִׁיחַ = Messiah.
^k Resplendent crown] AV, his crown 'shall flourish'. The Hebrew word strictly
means 'to blossom' or 'to flower'. However, it is also linked to the meaning of
'glisten' or 'shine'. In this connection it gives the name to the golden 'plate' on
the High Priest's crown (Exod. 29:30). Motyer (1) links 'crown' with Nazirite
consecration. There is a wealth of meaning in this verse, part of which is
conveyed by Ps. 72:8-11.

Day 330   Psalm 133. Song of Ascents (14)

¹ Behold!^a How good, and what a pleasant thing!
When brothers dwell and are in unity;^b
² It's like the precious oil^c, upon the head;
Descending on the beard, yes, Aaron's beard

Descending down unto his garments' edge;
³ Like Hermon-dew descends on Zion's hills,
Because the LORD commands the blessing there –
The blessing – even life for evermore.

---

^a Behold!] Hebrew *hinneh* - הִנֵּה. See Appendix 2 - Behold!

^b Brothers dwell and are in unity!] We take this to be an observation of the joyful gathering in Zion, either in the yearly pilgrimages, or of Israel's final gathering and blessing. It is, of course, always 'a good and pleasant thing' whenever it occurs! Ewald *Syntax*, describes the Hebrew expression here as 'mutual relation in such a way that the two sides are represented as belonging to each other'. Motyer (2) likewise shows the central theme of the Psalm to be 'joining together'.

^c Precious oil] Hebrew 'the good oil', but the idiom means 'the best oil', i.e. the holy anointing oil (Exod. 30:22-33).

Day 331   Psalm 134. A Song of Ascents

¹ Take note of this and come[a] and bless the LORD!
All servants of the LORD who stand to serve!
Who stand by night[b] in the house of the LORD;
² Lift up your hands unto the holy place.

Lift up your hands unto the holy place;[c]
So bless the LORD again, and bless the LORD![d]
The LORD from Zion will bless each of you[e] -
The One who made the heavens and the earth.

^a Take note of this and come] Hebrew *hinneh* - הִנֵּה. See Appendix 2 - Behold!
^b Who stand to serve. Who stand by night] Hebrew simply 'stand', but the word is used of the priests and Levites ministering (Deut. 10:8; 1 Chr. 23:30; Heb. 10:11), which service continued day and night (1 Chr. 9:33). Motyer (1) comments that the Passover was, by its very nature, a night festival.
^c We have repeated this line.
^d So bless the LORD again, and bless the LORD] We have expanded this line, which in Hebrew is simply 'and bless the LORD'. It is 'again' after v1.
^e Each of you] The 'you' of previous verses changes to singular here, which we have indicated by our translation.

Day 332   Psalm 135:1-7

¹ O Hallelujah, give praise to the LORD![a]
The LORD's name praise! Praise, servants of the LORD!
² Who stand to serve[b] in the house of the LORD -
Yes, in the courts of the house of our God.

³ Praise! Praise the LORD[c], because the LORD is good;
Sing psalms[d] unto his name for it is sweet;[e]
⁴ For JAH[f] has chosen Jacob for himself:
His treasured property[g] is Israel   →

⁵ I surely know^h the LORD is very great,
And that our Lordⁱ is greater than all gods.
⁶ The LORD has done whatever pleases him
In heaven, earth, in seas, and in all deeps.

⁷ He brings the clouds up from earth's farthest point,^j
And he has made the lightnings for the rain.
He sends the wind out from his treasure stores;
He sends the wind out from his treasure stores.^k

---

^a Hallelujah ... LORD] The first line is simply 'Hallelujah'. We have added the English translation.
^b Who stand to serve] Hebrew is simply 'stand'. But see the note on Ps. 134:1.
^c Praise! Praise the LORD] Hebrew 'Hallelujah' = Praise JAH (Hebrew YAH - יָהּ). See Appendix 2 - Names of God
^d Sing psalms] Hebrew zamar - זָמַר. See Appendix 2 - Sing Psalms.
^e Sweet] AV 'pleasant'. The AV translates the Hebrew word as 'sweet' at 2 Sam. 23:1 and Prov. 23:8. The 'sweetness' or 'pleasantness' may refer either to the LORD's name, or to the singing of psalms to it.
^f JAH] Hebrew YAH - יָהּ a shortened form of יהוה, the LORD, JEHOVAH. See Appendix 2 - Names of God.
^g Treasured property] AV 'peculiar treasure'. From a root meaning 'to acquire' = wealth, property.
^h I surely know] 'I' is emphasised, expressing 'a strong personal conviction' (Perowne).
ⁱ Our Lord] This is not the name 'LORD' or 'Adhonay - אֲדֹנָי. (Appendix 2 - Names of God). The word simply expresses his lordship and power.
^j From earth's farthest point] Hebrew 'from the end of the earth'.
^k He sends ... stores] We have repeated the last line of the section.

Day 333   Psalm 135:8-14

⁸ Egypt's firstborn he struck down, man and beast^a;
⁹ He sent out signs and wonders unto you;
O Egypt, even in your very midst!
On Pharaoh and on all his servants too.

¹⁰ He smote great nations and slew mighty kings:
¹¹ He slew^b Sihon, king of the Amorites;
And then slew Og, the king of the Bashan.
And all of Canaan's kingdoms he smote too.   →

¹² He gave their land up as a heritage –
For Israel, his people's heritage.
¹³ O LORD your name is evermore the same;^c
And your renown^d, LORD, is from age to age.

¹⁴ The LORD will vindicate his people's cause;
And judgment on them he will execute;^e
Yet for his servants' sake he will relent;
And he will have compassion upon them.^f

---

^a Man and beast] Hebrew 'from man to animal'. Although the AV translates 'cattle' in Exod. 12:29, it is the same word as here. It may mean all animals, wild animals, or (most likely, as a plague on the Egyptians) domesticated animals. The word for 'man' here is Hebrew 'adham - אָדָם - Man as a child of Adam. See Appendix 2 - Man.

^b Slew] We have repeated the verb of the previous verse in relation to Sihon and Og. The great nations of Canaan were 'smitten' by the LORD.

^c Your name is evermore the same] Literally, 'your name evermore'. 'Endure' is supplied by most versions, but what is intended is the unchanged continuance of the LORD in all his glorious attributes (his name), not its durability!

^d Renown] AV 'memorial', NKJV 'fame'. See Psalms 30:4 and 102:12. The word is in apposition to 'his name', and we could perhaps translate 'all that his character calls to mind'.

^e Vindicate ... cause ... judgment ... execute] One word in Hebrew - dîn - דִּין. See Appendix 2 - Law - Judgment. The word translated 'judge' by the AV means the decision of a cause; a statement of what is right. The verse is quoted from Deut. 32:35,36. The emphasis may be on vindication (see Deut. 32:43), or (as the verse is quoted in Heb. 10:30) on punishment ('penal judgment', Delitzsch on Deut. 32:34). Bengel comments 'He will judge, in grace and in anger, according as he shall find each individual'.

^f Relent ... have compassion upon them] The word translated 'relent' (AV 'repent') is reflexive ('repent himself' - as being moved by emotion). In contexts with this grammatical construction it refers to the cause of the change of heart - compassion.

Day 334   Psalm 135:15-21

¹⁵ The nations' idols are silver and gold,
The workmanship that human^a hands have made;
¹⁶ They have a mouth, and yet they cannot speak;
They have two eyes, and yet they cannot see.

¹⁷ They have two ears, but they do not give ear^b
And in their mouth there is no breath at all;^c
¹⁸ All^d those who make them will be just like them;
Yes, everyone who puts his trust in them.   →

¹⁹ O bless the LORD, you house of Israel!
O bless the LORD, you who are Aaron's house!
²⁰ O bless the LORD, you who are Levi's house!
And, you who fear the LORD, bless him alone!^e

²¹ From out of Zion the LORD shall be blest;
He who is dwelling in Jerusalem.
Hallelujah, give praise to the LORD!^f
O Hallelujah, give praise to the LORD!

---

^a Human] Hebrew *'adham* - אָדָם - Man as a child of Adam. See Appendix 2 - Man.is used.

^b They do not give ear] So the Hebrew, which strengthens the irony. AV 'they hear not'. We have translated the dual number as 'two eyes', 'two ears'.

^c In their mouth there is no breath at all] A strong negative is used. Delitzsch translates literally, 'there is not a being of breath', i.e. 'not a trace of it'.

^d All] We have added 'all', which corresponds to the following line ('everyone').

^e Alone] The word 'alone' is not in the Hebrew. However, these verses follow after verses about the futility of idol worship, and are in contrast to them. The Hebrew particle *eth* - אֶת is placed before 'the LORD' here to emphasise that he is to be the object of the worship of Israel and Aaron's house, etc, rather than idols.

^f Hallelujah ... LORD] The last line is simply 'Hallelujah'. We have added the English translation and repeated the line.

Day 335   Psalm 136:1-9

¹ O give thanks to the LORD for he is good;
His loving-kindness is for evermore.^a
O give thanks to the LORD for he is good;
Because his loving-kindness has no end.^b

² To him who is the God of gods^c give thanks,
His loving-kindness is for evermore.
³ To him who is Lord of lords^d give thanks;
Because his loving-kindness has no end.

⁴ To him who does great wonders all alone;
His loving-kindness is for evermore.
⁵ To him who made the heavens skilfully;^e
Because his loving-kindness has no end.   →

⁶ To him who on the waters spread the earth;
His loving-kindness is for evermore.
⁷ To him who made in heaven^f the great lights;
Because his loving-kindness has no end.

⁸ Even the sun that it should rule the day;
His loving-kindness is for evermore.
⁹ The moon and stars that they should rule the night;
Because his loving-kindness has no end.

---

^a In the Hebrew the same refrain follows the first line of every verse. We have
alternated two translations; 'His loving-kindness is for evermore' and 'Because
his loving-kindness has no end' The Hebrew is literally, 'because forever his
loving-kindness (ḥeṣedh - חֶסֶד)'. 'Endure' is supplied by most versions, but
what is intended is the unchanged continuance of the LORD's covenant mercy,
not its durability. Compare Ps. 135:13. See Appendix 2 - ḥeṣedh - חֶסֶד.

^b We have repeated the first verse in this stanza to begin the next daily portion
with the deliverance from Egypt. We have had to make a further adjustment
at verses 17 and 18.

^c The God of gods] The Hebrew expression (as 'Lord of lords' which follows)
means the Supreme God, the essence of all that is Divine. Compare 'holy of
holies' = the most holy place. The expressions are a quotation of Deut. 10:17.

^d Lord of lords] Or 'Master of masters'. Compare this expression and 'God of
gods' with Ps. 95:3 and 1 Tim. 6:15. Compare also the titles of the exalted Lord
Jesus in Rev. 17:14 and 19:16.

^e Skilfully] AV 'by wisdom'. Compare Exod. 31:1-5 where the same Hebrew word
(AV 'understanding') is used.

^f In heaven] The Hebrew is simply 'made the great lights'. We have added 'in
heaven', as the verses following indicate this meaning (in accordance with
Gen.1:14).

Day 336   Psalm 136:10-20

¹⁰ To him who struck Egypt in their firstborn;
His loving-kindness is for evermore.
¹¹ And from among them brought out Israel;
Because his loving-kindness has no end.

¹² With a strong hand and with an outstretched arm;
His loving-kindness is for evermore.
¹³ Who into parts divided^a the Red Sea;^b
Because his loving-kindness has no end.   →

¹⁴ And he made Is-ra-el pass through the midst;
His loving-kindness is for evermore.
¹⁵ Pharaoh, his army, shook in^c the Red Sea;
Because his loving-kindness has no end.

¹⁶ He led his people through the wilderness;
His loving-kindness is for evermore.
¹⁷ To him who struck great kings; ¹⁸ slew famous kings; ^d
Because his loving-kindness has no end.

¹⁹ Sihon who was king of the Amorites;
His loving-kindness is for evermore.
²⁰ And Og who was the king of the Bashan;
Because his loving-kindness has no end.

---

^a Into parts divided] Literally, 'parted into parts'. The verb may be translated 'cut' and is used in 1 Kgs. 3:25.
^b The Red Sea] Hebrew 'the Sea of Reeds', or (transliterating) 'the sea of Suph', as also in v25. See note on Ps. 106:7.
^c Shook in] Hebrew 'shook off, i.e. 'he shook them from the land and cast them into the sea', Gesenius *Lexicon*. The verb is also used in Neh. 5:13 (AV 'overthrew'). Calvin 'cast headlong into [the Red Sea]'.
^d To him who struck great kings; slew famous kings] We have given the first line of both v17 and v18. In the Hebrew, each of these lines is followed by the refrain 'his loving-kindness is for evermore'.

Day 337   Psalm 136:21-26

²¹ He gave their land up as a heritage;
His loving-kindness is for evermore.
²² For Israel, his people's heritage;
Because his loving-kindness has no end.

²³ Who in our lowly state remembered us;
His loving-kindness is for evermore.
²⁴ And broke us free from those who were our foes;
Because his loving-kindness has no end.

²⁵ He who gives food^a unto all living things; ^b
His loving-kindness is for evermore.
²⁶ Unto the GOD of heaven, O give thanks;
Because his loving-kindness has no end.

^a Food] Hebrew, 'bread'.
^b All living things] Hebrew, 'all flesh'. As Gen. 6:17,19.

Day 338 Psalm 137

¹ We sat beside rivers of Babylon;
As we remembered Zion, so we wept;
² We hung our harps upon the willows there; ^a
³ For there our captors asked of us a song.^b

For our tormentors urged us^c to be glad;
'Sing some of Zion's songs^d to us' they said; ^e
⁴ Alas, how^f could we sing the LORD's song there?
When we are in a strange and foreign^g land.^h

⁵ If I forget you, O Jerusalem;
Let my right hand forget, ⁶ and let my tongue
Stick to my jaws, if I do not recall;
If my chief joy is not Jerusalem.ⁱ

⁷ Oh, Edom's children do remember, LORD;
Who said in the day of Jerusalem:
'To its foundation, strip it! Strip it bare!'
⁸ Daughter of Babylon who'll be destroyed

Blest^j be the one who will pay back to you;
What you brought on us. ⁹ Yes, and *blest* he'll be –
The one who grasps upon your little ones –
The one who dashes them against the rock.

^a There] Hebrew 'in the midst'. Horsley translates 'willows of the spot', thereby surmising that this was the particular tree of the country.
^b Song] Hebrew 'the words of a song'.
^c Asked of us ... urged us] One verb in Hebrew. AV 'required of us'.
^d Some of Zion's songs] AV 'one of the songs'. Davidson *Syntax* uses the expression in this verse to illustrate the partitive use of the preposition (*min* - מִן), as Gen. 30:4 ('some of the mandrakes'), Exod. 4:9 ('some of the water').
^e They said] The Hebrew does not have 'they said', but it is supplied to indicate that these are the words of their captors.
^f Alas, how ... ?] The form of the Hebrew word for 'how' used here (*êkh* - אֵיךְ) is frequently used in lamentation. See Gesenius *Lexicon*.
^g Strange and foreign] One Hebrew word, which carries both meanings. It may also be linked with hostility and alienation, as Ps. 18:44,45.

[h] Land] Hebrew *'adhamâ* - אֲדָמָה. See 2 Kgs 5:17. See Appendix 2 - Earth.

[i] If my chief joy is not Jerusalem] Literally, 'if I do not exalt Jerusalem as the head of my joy'. The word we have translated 'chief' may mean 'the sum total of' (so Horsley). The word we have translated 'joy' is the same word as translated 'glad' in v3.

[j] Blest] AV 'happy'. Hebrew *'ašrê* - אַשְׁרֵי. This verse and v9. See Appendix 2 - Blessing.

Day 339   Psalm 138:1-5

[1] I will give thanks to you with my whole heart;
Before the gods[a] I'll sing with psalms[b] to you;
[2] Toward your holy Temple[c] I'll bow down;
And I will give my thanks unto your name.

Thanks for your loving-kindness[d] and your truth;
You've made your word great, more than all your name![e]
[3] You answered me in the day when I called;
You gave me courage – put strength in my soul.[f]

[4] All kings of earth will give you thanks, O LORD;
For they have heard the words that your mouth spoke;
[5] And they will sing: of the LORD's ways they'll sing;
Because the glory of the LORD is great.

[a] Before the gods] Various translations or interpretations have been suggested for the use of 'gods' (Hebrew *'elohîm* - אֱלֹהִים). The Septuagint reads 'angels', which are present at the worship of believers (1 Cor. 11:10). Perowne considers these the heathen gods and their worshippers (compare Ps. 95:3). Newton (1) relates this to 'those holding authority from God', to include all the kings of the earth (v4).

[b] Sing with psalms] Hebrew *zamar* - זָמַר. See Appendix 2 - Sing Psalms.

[c] Holy Temple] Literally, 'the Palace (Hebrew *hêkhal* - הֵיכָל) of your holiness'.

[d] Loving-kindness] Hebrew *ḥesedh* - חֶסֶד. See Appendix 2 - Loving-kindness.

[e] You've made ... name] The meaning perhaps is 'the report of what the LORD has done exceeds what we expected from our knowledge of him'. The Hebrew 'word' used here generally indicates the spoken word. *'imrâ* - אִמְרָה. See Appendix 2 - Word.

[f] You gave me courage ... soul] Literally, 'you emboldened me ['made me proud'] with strength in my soul'.

Day 340   Psalm 138:6-8

⁶ The LORD is high, but sees those who are low;
And from afar he knows those who are proud.ᵃ
⁷ If, in the midst of trouble, I should walk,
You will revive me, and preserve my life.ᵇ

Against the anger of my enemies –
Against their anger – you will stretch your hand;
You will deliver me by your right hand;
Yes, you will save me by your own right hand.ᶜ

⁸ The LORD will finish what he does for me;
He brings to pass his purposes for me.ᵈ
Your mercyᵉ is to everlasting, LORD;
Do not forsake the works of your own hands.ᶠ

ᵃ Proud] the word also means lifted up, high. AV 'haughty'. Compare Luke
  1:51,52. It is unrelated to the word in v3 (see note above).
ᵇ Revive … preserve my life] The word can carry both meanings. Compare Ps.
  23:4.
ᶜ We have repeated the last line of v7 with a different wording.
ᵈ The LORD will finish … brings to pass his purposes] We have expanded the line.
  The Hebrew is literally, 'the LORD will finish that which is to me', or 'which
  concerns me'. The same word is used in Ps. 3:3 - the LORD is a shield 'for me'.
  So to in Ps. 57:2. He will fulfil and accomplish his purposes for us. Compare
  Phil. 1:6; Heb. 12:2.
ᵉ Mercy] Loving-kindness, Hebrew ḥeṣedh - חסד. See Appendix 2 - Loving-
  kindness.
ᶠ The works of your own hands] It is probably best to understand this, not as a
  synonym for the psalmist himself, or believers in general, but what he does by
  'his hand', 'his right hand', as in v7 - 'the undertaking he has commenced',
  Bonar.

Day 341   Psalm 139:1-6

¹ LORD, you have searched me, therefore you have known;ᵃ
² You know my sitting down and getting up;
And from afar you understand my thought;
³ My walking and my resting you sift through.ᵇ

You are acquainted well with all my ways,
⁴ For there is not a word upon my tongue,
But, surelyᶜ, LORD, you know about it all;
⁵ Behind, before me, you've surrounded me.   →

297

Your hand you've rested and placed over me.[d]
[6] Such knowledge is too wonderful for me!
It is so lofty, well beyond my reach;
It is so lofty, well beyond my reach.[e]

---

[a] Therefore you have known] 'The form of the verb marks a consequence of the previous action', Perowne. There is no 'me' in the Hebrew after 'known'.

[b] My walking and my resting you sift through] The word we have translated 'sift through' means, more precisely, 'winnow' (AV margin)- 'to submit to minute scrutiny' (see Soncino). AV translates 'compassest', deriving the verb from the word for 'a span' [unit of measurement] - see Koehler, *Lexicon* and BDB *Lexicon*. 'Walking (AV 'path'); and 'resting' (AV 'lying down') [Welsh Bible *'gorweddfa'*, Segond *'couche'*], are infinitives. See Perowne, note.

[c] Surely] Hebrew *hen* - הֵן, drawing attention to the certainty of it. AV 'lo'. See Appendix 2 - Behold!

[d] Surrounded me ... rested and placed over me] Most versions suggest hostile actions by the LORD in v5, by translating 'beset', 'hemmed me in'. 'laid your hand upon me'. 'Surrounded' conveys security (compare S. of S. 8:9). Likewise the word for 'hand' here is rightly 'the palm [or 'hollow'] of the hand', which conveys a more comforting sense, when it is rested or placed over us, as it may be translated.

[e] We have repeated the last line.

Day 342   Psalm 139:7-12

[7] Wherever shall I from your spirit go?
Wherever from your presence[a] shall I flee?
[8] If I should climb to heaven - you are there![b]
If I bed down in Sheol[c] you're there too!

[9] If I rise up as on the wings of dawn;
If I should dwell on sea's most distant shore;
[10] Yet even there your hand would guide me on;
And your right hand would still hold on to me.

[11] If I should say that 'Darkness covers me,
And so, the light around me will be night';[d]
[12] Yet darkness does not darken things from you;[e]
Night shines as day: Darkness and light the same.

---

[a] Your presence] Hebrew 'your face'.

[b] You are there] The Hebrew marks this statement with *hinneh* - הִנֵּה, an urgent interjection to draw attention to something important. See Appendix 2 - Behold!

[c] If I bed down in Sheol] Literally, 'if I spread my bed in Sheol', or 'if I make Sheol

my bed'. Sheol *šeʾôl* - שְׁאוֹל - the place where the dead were. Consistently spoken of as 'down' in Scripture (Numb. 16:29, etc.). See Appendix 2 - Sheol.

^d And so ... night] The contrast (apodosis) of the first line does not come with this second line (as in the AV), but this whole verse contrasts with the following verse. Compare verses 9 and 10 with verses 11 and 12. Verses 10 and 12 each begin with the Hebrew word *gam* - גַּם, which we have translated 'yet'.

^e Yet darkness does not darken things from you] Literally, 'darkness darkens not from you' - see AV margin.

Day 343   Psalm 139:13-18

¹³ You are the one[a] who formed my inner parts;[b]
And you did weave[c] me in my mother's womb;
¹⁴ I will be thankful unto you for this –
That such an awesome wonder I've been made.[d]

The things you've made are awesome, wonderful;
And this my soul knows, O so very well!
¹⁵ My body's frame[e] was not hidden from you;
When I was made within the secret place.

I was complexly made[f] in depths of earth![g]
¹⁶ Your eyes have seen my undeveloped form;[h]
All days were written in your book, as planned;[i]
When there was yet not even one of them.

¹⁷ How precious to me are your thoughts, O GOD!
How vast are they in their entirety![j]
¹⁸ If I should count them, they outnumber sand;
And when I wake, then I am still with you.[k]

---

^a You are the one] We have translated the Hebrew in this way as 'you' is emphatic in the original.

^b Inner parts] Hebrew 'reins' or 'kidneys', which Scripture views as the seat of the feelings and emotions of a person, although it here has its literal meaning. See notes on 7:9 and 16:7.

^c Weave] This is the literal meaning of the Hebrew verb used here.

^d That such an awesome wonder I've been made] There is no word for 'being made' here. The line could be translated 'I am fearfully wonderful'. The root word of 'wonderful' indicates a sign or an enigma. One translator suggests 'signalized by dreadful things' for the meaning here. Segond translates *'je suis une créature si merveilleuse'*. Bishop Lowth, quoted by Horne, sums up the meaning 'with awful joy I view this frame of mine: stupendous monument of power Divine'.

^e My body's frame] Literally, 'my strength' (AV margin). This appears to refer to the skeletal frame; 'complexly made' (v15) seems to refer to the flesh, veins, skin upon it - see Soncino, Horsley, and compare Job 10:11.

^f Complexly made] It is generally agreed that the word means 'variegated'. Gesenius *Lexicon* argues for the meaning 'embroidered'. It is perhaps descriptive of the varied appearance of the organs, veins, sinews, etc. of the human body. It may also be rendered 'knitted together'.

^g In the depths of the earth] This is a metaphor for the womb which, like Sheol, is a hidden, dark place. This does not teach the transmigration of souls, a doctrine of later Judaism. The assumed reference to Sheol has led some (e.g. Bishop Pearson, *Apostles' Creed*; Gill; Alford) to raise the possibility that Eph. 4:9 refers to the Incarnation.

^h Undeveloped form] One word in Hebrew. It means 'something rolled together' as a ball, and hence is taken to mean the human embryo or foetus.

ⁱ All days … as planned] By adding 'my members' (not in the Hebrew), the AV understands this line to mean that every part of his body was pre-defined and fashioned by God ('complexly made', Hebrew *raqam* - רָקַם). Tregelles (1) applies this to Christ's mystical body. We take the meaning as the AV margin ('what days should be fashioned'), which is now favoured by most translations. It is thereby a statement of God's predetermining all of our days, from our birth to our death.

^j In their entirety] AV 'sum'. The Hebrew is plural ('sums') - 'the plural of fullness' - how vast is the sum total of God's thoughts and desires!

^k When I wake … you] As often as he wakes from sleep he is still enthralled with the wonders of God's wisdom and purposes. De Burgh rather applies this to the sleep of death - that we shall never in this life exhaust pondering on these things, even till we enter God's presence.

Day 344   Psalm 139:19-24

¹⁹ Will you not slay the wicked one, O <u>God</u>? ^a
You men of bloodshed^b go away from me!
²⁰ (They speak against you with a scheming plan^c -
Your enemies who raise themselves in vain^d).

²¹ Do I not hate those who hate you, O LORD?
Do I not loathe insurgents^e against you?
²² With utter hatred I have hated them;
And I consider them my enemies.

²³ Examine, search me^f, know my heart, O GOD;
Refine and try me^g, know my anxious thoughts; ^h
²⁴ See if there be a hurtful wayⁱ in me;
And lead me in the everlasting way.

ᵃ God] Hebrew *'Elôah* - אֱלוֹהַ. See Appendix 2 - Names of God
ᵇ Men of bloodshed] Literally, 'men of bloods'. Hebrew for 'man' here is *'enôš* - אֱנוֹשׁ - Frail, mortal man. See Appendix 2 - Man.
ᶜ They speak against you with a scheming plan] We see this verse as a parenthesis. See Perowne (notes) for objections to translating 'speak', and deriving the verb from another root, which accounts for 'rebel' in some versions. Literally, 'with wicked purpose (AV 'wickedly'), from a verb meaning 'to devise', 'to purpose', 'to plot'
ᵈ Raise themselves in vain] AV 'take your name in vain'. There is no 'your name' in Hebrew, and this translation is assumed on the basis of Exod. 20:7.
ᵉ Insurgents] 'Those who rise up'. *Hapax legomenon.*
ᶠ Examine, search me] One word in Hebrew.
ᵍ Refine and try me] One word in Hebrew, used of metal tested in the fire, as Ps. 26:2.
ʰ Anxious thoughts] One word in Hebrew, a different word for 'thoughts' from that used in v3 and v17. NKJV 'anxieties'.
ⁱ A hurtful way] Literally, 'a way that causes grief and pain', as sin and wickedness does.

Day 345   Psalm 140:1-7

¹ Deliver me, LORD, from the evil man;ᵃ
Preserve me from the manᵇ of violence;
² Who in their heart have made up evil plans;
Each day they gather and they stir up wars.

³ Their tongue they sharpen, like a serpent's tongue;
The adder's poison is under their lips. ǂ
⁴ From the hands of the wickedᶜ guard me, LORD;
And keep me from the man of violence.

Those who have schemed to push away my steps;
⁵ The arrogant have hid a trap for me;
With cords they have spread out a net to catchᵈ –
Along the road. They have set snares for me. ǂ

⁶ I said unto the LORD, 'You are my GOD.
O hear my voice – my pleas for help, O LORD.ᵉ
⁷ O LORD My Lordᶠ, you're my salvation's strength;
When battle ragedᵍ you covered upʰ my head'.

ᵃ Man] Hebrew *'adham* - אָדָם - Man as a child of Adam. See Appendix 2 - Man.
ᵇ Man of violence] As also in v4. 'Man' here is Hebrew *'îš* - אִישׁ - Man as an individual, or of higher rank. The Hebrew is 'man of violences', where

'violences' is used to emphasise the extent of his brutality. Both of the words for 'man' in this verse are singular, but the verbs in the next verse are plural, which has led some versions to translate 'evil men' and 'violent men' here. The expression in v11 has 'violence' in the singular.

^c The wicked] Hebrew singular

^d A net to catch] The Hebrew is simply a net, but the word it comes from has the meaning of 'taking', of 'taking possession of something'.

^e O hear my voice ... O LORD] Literally, 'Give ear, O LORD, to the voice of my supplications [entreaties for pity or favour]'.

^f My Lord] Hebrew 'Adhonay - אֲדֹנָי. See Appendix 2 - Names of God.

^g When battle raged] Literally, 'in the day of armour', i.e. when armour was needed.

^h Covered up] Hebrew 'sheltered', 'protected'. From the same verb as the 'booth', Hebrew sukâ - סֻכָּה, of the Feast of Tabernacles.

Day 346   Psalm 140:8-13

⁸ 'Don't give the wicked his desires, O LORD.
Aid not his scheme, lest they be set on high' ‖
⁹ As for the chief^a of those surrounding me –
Their lips make trouble. Lay it upon^b them!

¹⁰ Let hot and burning coals^c fall upon them!
Throw them in chasms deep, no more to rise!
¹¹ A slanderer^d shall not stand in the earth;
The violent man – evil shall hunt down.^e

¹² I know the LORD will judge the poor man's cause;^f
He will give judgment to the ones in need.^g
¹³ Truly, the righteous shall confess your name!^h
And upright ones will dwell before your face.

^a Chief] Hebrew singular. So the Geneva Bible. The Hebrew word generally means 'head'.

^b Lay it upon them] 'Cover them with it'. Not the same word as v7.

^c Hot and burning coals] Hebrew '(hot) coals with fire'. We have followed Calvin in linking 'fire' with 'coals', which eliminates one stich in the AV and makes the next stich 'throw them [or 'he shall throw them'] in deep chasms'. The comparison is then with Sodom in the first line. The following line is then a comparison with Korah, Dathan and Abiram. See Bonar, Tregelles (3), and Jay Green Hebrew-English interlinear.

^d Slanderer] Hebrew 'a man of tongue', compare v3; 101:5. The word used for that 'man' and for 'the violent man' is Hebrew 'îš - אִישׁ -Man as an individual. See Appendix 2 - Man.

^e Hunt ... down] The Hebrew indicates the urgent, speedy, relentless thrusting

down of the violent man.

f Judge the poor man's cause] 'Cause' (Hebrew *dîn* - דִּין) relates primarily to a legal claim or judgment. Hebrew literally, 'do the legal claim of the poor'. The word 'the poor' is singular, and may be translated 'the afflicted' (as the AV). See Appendix 2 - Law - Judgment.

g He will do judgment for the ones in need] 'Judgment' = Hebrew *mišpaṭ* - מִשְׁפָּט. This line uses the same verb, so it is literally, 'do judgment'. See Appendix 2 - Law - Judgment.

h Confess your name] Or 'give thanks to your name'. This form of the verb may carry either meaning, and we understand this as confessing, acknowledging, and affirming all that God is.

Day 347   Psalm 141:1-4

¹ I've called to you, LORD. Quickly come to me!
To my voice listen, when I call on you;
² Let my prayer be ᵃ as incense before you; ᵇ
My lifted hands the evening offering. ᶜ

³ O LORD, please set a watch over my mouth;
And on the door of my lips set a guard;
⁴ O do not let my heart be turned aside;
Let it not turn to any evil thing.

Lest I persist in deeds of wickedness; ᵈ
With the great men ᵉ who work iniquity;
Keep me from feeding on what pleases them.
Keep me from feeding on what pleases them. ᶠ

ᵃ Be] Hebrew 'be established as' - i.e. regularly offered. The word is used of the Temple service in 2 Chr. 29:35.

ᵇ Before you] Hebrew 'before your face'.

ᶜ Offering] Hebrew *minḥâ* – מִנְחָה. In Scripture this usually means the sacrifice of meal and oil, which (like incense) was added to the burnt offering morning and evening. See Perowne.

ᵈ Lest I persist in deeds of wickedness] Literally, 'do deeds of wickedness' or 'occupy myself with occupations of wickedness'. The word form is reflexive, and indicates repeatedly acting, or being busy at. Gesenius *Lexicon* sees the root of the verb in an Arabic word meaning 'to drink', in which case the verse may speak of both drinking and eating.

ᵉ The great men] An unusual plural (*'îšîm* - אִישִׁים) is used for this word for man (*'îš* - אִישׁ). The word is used for men of importance or renown (compare 4:3 and 49:2). See Appendix 2 - Man.

ᶠ We have repeated the last line of the section.

Day 348   Psalm 141:5-10

⁵ The righteous will smite me in faithful love; ᵃ
He will reprove me. It's oil on my head.ᵇ
My head will not refuse, nor disallow; ᶜ
(My prayer is still against their wickedness).ᵈ

⁶ Their judges have been stumbled at the rock; ᵉ
And they shall hear my wordsᶠ, that they are sweet.ᵍ
⁷ Like ploughing, and like breaking up the earth;
At Sheol'sʰ mouth our bones are cast about.ⁱ

⁸ My eyes look unto you, O LORD, My Lord; ʲ
In you I've taken refuge, put my trust; ᵏ
Do not pour out my soul or lay it waste; ˡ
⁹ Preserve me from the trapᵐ they laid for me.

Preserve me from the snares that they have laid –
Laid by the workers of iniquity.
¹⁰ The wicked shall each fall in his own net;
While I myself will pass on safely by.

ᵃ In faithful love] 'In loving-kindness' - Hebrew *ḥeṣedh* - חֶסֶד. PBV 'smite me friendly'. The word stands alone, and could be translated 'it shall be a kindness'; as AV; 'for that is a benefite' Geneva Bible. See Appendix 2 - Loving-kindness.

ᵇ Oil on my head] This 'head-oil' may be taken to be the most precious (chief) anointing oil of Exod. 30:25.

ᶜ Not refuse, or disallow] one word in Hebrew. The verb occurs in Ps. 33:10 ('frustrate'), and Numb. 30:5 ('disallow'). The AV makes 'oil' the subject of the verb rather than 'my head', which then forces a rather strange meaning on it – 'which shall not break my head'.

ᵈ Their wickedness] Hebrew 'their wickednesses'. The reference is to the 'great men who work iniquity' of v4 not to 'the just one'. There is a change of the persons with whom he interacts, from singular ('just one') to plural ('their wickednesses').

ᵉ Their judges ... rock] 'Judges', Hebrew *šôphet* - שׁוֹפֵט. See Appendix 2 - Law - Judgment. The literal translation of the phrase is 'Their judges have been stumbled by the hand of the rock'. this is capable of a Messianic application ('Rock' cf. Isa. 8:13-15; Rom. 9:32,33; 1 Pet. 2:7,8). 'The just one' of v5 may also be applied to Christ. Other interpreters speculatively apply this verse to an unknown event when the judges (of the wicked?) were destroyed by casting them over a precipice!

ᶠ They shall hear ... words: i.e. 'people (not 'the judges') shall hear'. 'Words' - spoken words. *'emer* - אֵמֶר (from *'amar* - אָמַר 'to say'). See Appendix 2 - Word.

ᵍ Sweet] 'Pleasant', 'delightful' (as v4).

ʰ Sheol] Hebrew *šeʾôl* - שְׁאוֹל. See Appendix 2 - Sheol.

ⁱ As ploughing ... cast about] The action is ploughing and furrowing the land,
which leaves broken clods of earth. AV supplies 'wood' (not in the Hebrew) as
being cut and cleaved, in which case the comparison with scattered bones
would then be the debris left afterwards. Compare Ezek. 37:1ff.

ʲ My Lord] Hebrew *ʾAdhonay* - אֲדֹנָי. See Appendix 2 - Names of God.

ᵏ Taken refuge, put my trust] One Hebrew word - *ḥaṣâ* - חָסָה. See Appendix 2 -
Refuge.

ˡ Do not pour out my soul or lay it waste] The Hebrew word conveys both of these
meanings. 'My soul' is an emphatic way of the writer speaking of himself.

ᵐ From the trap] Hebrew 'from the hands of the trap', i.e. from its power and
potency. It is different from the following word and refers more to a spread
out net.

Day 349   Psalm 142

¹ With my voice I'll cry out unto the LORD;
My voice will plead ᵃ for mercy to the LORD;
² I will pour out before him my concern; ᵇ
Before him I will make my trouble known.

³ My spirit was with fainting overwhelmed;
Yet you're the one ᶜ who knows the path I tread; ᵈ
But in the path ᵉ in which I am to walk;
There they have spread a hidden trap for me.

⁴ Look unto the right hand and you will see
There is no-one who has regard for me
The way I could escape is closed to me. ᶠ
There is no-one who seeks for my soul's good!

⁵ I cried to you, O LORD, and I have said:
'You are my refuge ᵍ and my portion too';
A portion in the land of those who live; ʰ
⁶ Attend unto my cry, I'm very low'.

Deliver me from those pursuing me;
They are too strong! ⁷ From prison take my soul!
I'll praise your name ⁱ, the righteous all around; ʲ
Because you will complete your work in me. ᵏ

ᵃ My voice will plead] Hebrew 'with my voice I will plead'.

[b] Concern] anxious concern. The word can mean 'meditation'. AV 'complaint' (in the older meaning of 'complaint' as an expression of grief).

[c] You're the one] The 'you' is emphasised in the Hebrew.

[d] Path I tread] One word in Hebrew. This 'path' is derived from a root that means 'to tread with the feet', a track.

[e] Path] A different word from the 'track' of the previous line. It is from a root that means 'to journey' or 'to wander'. It is used metaphorically of a person's journey through life.

[f] The way I could escape is closed to me] Hebrew 'a way of escape has perished from me'.

[g] Refuge] a different word from the 'place of escape' of the previous verse (both translated 'refuge' by the AV). Here it means a place of safety. Neither of the words is used of 'the cities of refuge' in Numbers 35.

[h] The land of those who live] Compare Psalms 27:13; 52:5; 116:9.

[i] Praise your name] Literally, 'give thanks to your name' or 'confess your name', as in Ps. 140:7.

[j] All around] Hebrew 'all around me'.

[k] Because you will complete ... me] This is, we believe, the correct meaning here. The root meaning of the Hebrew word (גָּמַל - gamal) is 'to complete' or 'to accomplish' [see Koehler Lexicon, BDB, Lexicon, and Motyer (1) and (3)]. A weaned child (whose nursing is complete) is גָּמוּל - gamul (Ps. 131:2). Furthermore (see lexicons) the verb is akin to גָּמַר - gamar, which is used in Ps. 138:8. Cf. Phil. 1:5,6. Davies Hebrew Lexicon considers that there are two root words with this spelling, one meaning ' to reward', 'to requite', and the other 'to complete', but it is better to consider the idea of reward in connection with the meaning 'to ripen' and so bearing fruit (as in Numb. 17:8 and Isa. 18:5).

Day 350　　Psalm 143:1-6

[1] LORD, hear my prayer and to my pleas give ear,
In faithfulness. In righteousness[a] reply;
[2] Don't come unto your servant as a judge;[b]
No living thing is righteous before you.[c]

[3] Because the enemy pursued my soul;
My life he crushed right down unto the ground;
He made me dwell[d] in places that were dark;
Even as those who are forever dead.

[4] Therefore my spirit languishes in me;
My heart within me is filled with dismay.
[5] The days that were of old I call to mind;
I meditate on the things that you've done.　　→

I ponder what your hands have brought about.
⁶ I spread my hands, and I reach out^e to you;
Like a dry land my soul thirsts after you.^f ⊣⊢
Like a dry land my soul thirsts after you.^g

---

^a In faithfulness ... in righteousness] Hebrew 'in your faithfulness ... in your righteousness'. There is no 'and' the Hebrew. We follow de Burgh connecting 'faithfulness' with the hearing, and 'righteousness' with the answer.

^b Don't come ... as a judge] Literally, 'do not come in judgment (Hebrew *mišpaṭ* - מִשְׁפָּט)'. *The Theological Wordbook* states that the meaning here is 'to enter into litigation with'. See Appendix 2 - Law - Judgment.

^c No living thing is righteous before you] The Hebrew verb is not passive (as the AV, 'shall be justified'), but active (see de Burgh). The Septuagint translates as if it was passive, as do Paul's statements in Rom. 3:20 and Gal. 2:16. 'Before you' is literally, 'before your face'.

^d He made me dwell] The verb may be translated 'sit'. Compare Luke 1:79; Isa. 42:7.

^e Spread ... reach out] One word in Hebrew.

^f Like a dry land my soul thirsts after you] The land looks to the LORD for refreshment and for rain, and the stretching out of hands in the previous line indicates the same. The word translated 'dry' is usually used of one who is wearied out with a journey or with work (cf. Gen. 25:29,30; Ps. 63:2) in the context of lack of water or thirst (Isa. 32:2).

^g We have repeated the last line.

Day 351   Psalm 143:7-12

⁷ Give answer quickly, LORD, my spirit fails;
Don't hide your face from me - lest I should be
With those who go descending to the Pit.
⁸ At morning make me hear your steadfast love.^a

At morning^b - for on you I've placed my trust -
Cause me to know the way that I should walk;
For unto you I've lifted up my soul;
⁹ Deliver me, LORD, from my enemies.

Deliver^c, for in you I take refuge;^d
¹⁰ Teach me to do your will; you are my God.
In a plain land^e let your good Spirit lead;
¹¹ For your name's sake, O LORD, give life to me. →

307

In righteousness[f] take my soul from distress;
[12] In steadfast love[g] cut off my enemies;
Destroy all those who cause my soul distress;
For I'm a servant, I belong to you.[h]

---

[a] Steadfast love] Hebrew *ḥesedh* - חֶסֶד. See Appendix 2 - Loving-kindness.

[b] At morning] to keep continuity with the previous line, we have repeated 'at morning' here.

[c] Deliver] To keep continuity with the previous line, we have repeated 'deliver' here.

[d] In you I take refuge] Literally, 'to you I have covered [myself]'. It is argued the verb is reflexive here. See Calvin, and see Perowne's note ('unto you have I hidden myself'). Compare 141:8.

[e] In a plain land] The expression 'plain land' (*Statenvertaling*) or 'level ground' is used in a geographical, literal, sense in Deut. 4:43, where it is used of the (easy) way to a city of refuge. Compare Psalms 26:12 and 27:11.

[f] In righteousness] Hebrew 'in your righteousness'

[g] In steadfast love] Hebrew 'in your steadfast love'. Hebrew *ḥesedh* - חֶסֶד. See Appendix 2 - Loving-kindness.

[h] For I'm a servant, I belong to you] He does not base his request on the merit of his service, but on his calling and his relationship as a servant of the LORD. See Calvin.

Day 352   Psalm 144:1- 8

[1] Blest be the LORD for he is my strong rock;[a]
He is the one who trains my hands for war;
And, for the battle, trains[b] my fingers too –
[2] My Loving-kindness, Fortress of defence.

He's my Deliverer, and my High Tower,
My Shield[c], and in him I take my refuge;[d]
Who makes my people[e] subject under me.
[3] LORD, what is man[f] that you acknowledge him?

LORDM, what is man that you acknowledge him?[g] –
Son of frail man[h] – and you consider him!
[4] And as for man[i], he's only but a breath;[j]
His days are like a shadow passing by.

[5] Bow down[k] your heavens and come down, O LORD;
Just touch the mountains, and they then will smoke;
[6] Flash out your lightnings[l]. Scatter them about;[m]
Send out your arrows. Bring them to defeat;[n]   →

⁷ Your hands send down°; Rescue and snatch me out,
From many waters, from the strangers' hand,^p
⁸ Whose mouth tells false and empty vanity,^q
And their right hand is a right hand of lies.^r

---

^a Strong rock] One word. The word means primarily 'the strength and solidity of stone' (de Burgh). AV mainly translates the word as 'rock', but here as 'strength'.

^b Trains] We have repeated the verb from the previous line.

^c My Loving-kindness, Fortress, and High Tower] The sequence in Hebrew is 'my loving-kindness' (Hebrew, ḥeṣedh - חֶסֶד), 'my Fortress', 'my High Tower', 'my Deliverer', 'my Shield'. He lays personal claim on God by all these figures.

^d In him I take my refuge] AV 'he in whom I trust'. The Hebrew verb is ḥaṣâ - חָסָה 'to flee to a refuge and a place of safety'. See Appendix 2 - Refuge.

^e My people] Although this is the reading of most Hebrew manuscripts and the Septuagint, there are many Hebrew manuscripts that read 'nations'. 'Nations' is also the reading in the Dead Sea Scrolls (11QPs^a), Vulgate (Juxta Hebr.), and the Syriac. Compare v1,6,7, and Ps. 18:47. The difference is a single Hebrew letter.

^f Man] The word for 'man' here is Hebrew 'adham - אָדָם - Man as a child of Adam. See Appendix 2 - Man.

^g We have repeated this line from the previous stanza.

^h The words for 'man' reversed from the order they are given in Ps. 8:4. Here it is 'son of 'enôš - אֱנוֹשׁ - frail, mortal man, with stress on inability and weakness. See Appendix 2 - Man.

ⁱ Man] The word for 'man' in this verse is Hebrew 'adham - אָדָם.

^j Mere breath] One word in Hebrew (hebhel - הֶבֶל). AV 'vanity'.

^k Bow down] See Ps. 18:9.

^l Flash out your lightnings] Hebrew 'lightning your lightnings'.

^m Scatter them about] NIV interprets 'them' as 'the enemies', but it may equally be lightning bolts (as Gesenius Lexicon).

ⁿ Flash lightnings ... send arrows ... defeat] Compare Ps. 18:14.

^o Your hands send down] Literally, 'send your hands from on high'. AV 'hand', following many MSS. and the ancient versions. The Masoretic text has 'hands'.

^p From the strangers' hand] Hebrew 'from the hand of sons of the stranger', as Ps. 18:44,45. 'Stranger' is here used in its original sense of 'a foreigner'.

^q False and empty vanity] One word in Hebrew conveying both meanings.

^r And their right hand ... lies] Hebrew 'lie' (singular). The right hand was raised in taking an oath (see Gen. 14:22; Rev. 10:5,6). The expression indicates being a liar in a most brazen way.

Day 353   Psalm 144:9-15

⁹ I'll sing a brand-new^a song to you, O God!
With ten-stringed lyre^b, I will sing psalms^c to you -
¹⁰ The One who gives deliverance to kings -
His servant David, - from the evil sword.^d   →

¹¹ Rescue and snatch me from the strangers' hand,^e
Whose mouth tells false and empty vanity;^f
And their right hand is a right hand of lies.^g
And their right hand is a right hand of lies^h.

¹² Butⁱ our sons are, in youth^j, as plants full-grown,
Our daughters as carved palace-cornerstones; ^k
¹³ Our stores are full - provide all kinds of things; ^l
Our flocks bear many thousands in our fields.^m

¹⁴ Our cattle bear without mishap or loss;
There is no cry of sorrow in our streets.ⁿ
¹⁵ *Blessèd*^o the people to whom it is so!
Blessèd the people whose God is the LORD!

---

^a Brand-new] The Hebrew word means 'fresh', 'choice', 'polished'.

^b With ten-stringed lyre] Literally, 'with a *nebhel* (נֶבֶל) ten', (AV 'the psaltery [and] an instrument of ten strings'). Compare Psalms 33:2 and 92:3). See Appendix 2 - Harps.

^c Sing psalms] Hebrew *zamar* - זָמַר. See Appendix 2 - Sing Psalms.

^d His servant David, from the evil sword] Hebrew 'who rescues David, his servant, from the evil sword. 'The sword that is engaged in the service of evil', Delitzsch.

^e From the strangers' hand] As v7.

^f False and empty vanity] As v8a.

^g And their right hand ... lies] As v8b.

^h And their right hand ... lies] We have repeated this line.

ⁱ But] See Perowne's note discussing the Hebrew particle - 'whereas' ?

^j In youth] Hebrew 'in their youth'.

^k Corner stones] All versions now seem to prefer 'corner pillars'. Gesenius *Lexicon* suggests *caryatides*, as in heathen temples! See Tregelles' (1) preference for 'corner stones of strength and beauty'.

^l Provide all kinds of things] Literally, 'providing from kind to kind'.

^m Many thousands in our fields] Literally, 'our sheep thousanding, ten thousanding in our out-places'. The word 'out-places' literally means any place outside, and therefore here fields, meadows. Its usual meaning is 'streets' (as in the following verse, and as the AV here), or 'broad open places'

ⁿ Our cattle ... streets] There are differing translations of this verse. The AV applies it to cattle, following the ancient versions. This naturally follows from the reference to 'flocks' (v13). This then indicates cows (as the word is used in Deut. 7:13) being fruitful in bearing, with no abortion, or casting off of their young (see Gill, and *Dutch Annotations*; compare RSV). However, the word frequently means 'princes' or 'chieftains'. The rest of the verse has therefore been taken by modern versions [NIV (inc. text note), HCSB, NRSV] to refer to no 'breaching [of walls]', not 'going into captivity' and no 'cries of distress in the streets'.

Day 354   Psalm 145:1-7

¹ I will exalt you, My God and the King; [a]
I'll bless your name for ever, evermore;
² In each and every day [b] I will bless you;
I'll praise your name for ever, evermore.

³ Great is the LORD and greatly to be praised;
His greatness is beyond all searching out.
⁴ Each generation [c] shall extol your works;
And shall declare your acts of might and power. [d]

⁵ I'll meditate, and I will speak upon [e]
The splendour of your glory's majesty;
And on your wondrous words [f] I'll meditate; [g]
⁶ They'll tell the fearful power of your works. [h]

I will recount your acts of might and power;
⁷ They will speak out, yes, they will pour out words; [i]
Remembering you are so very good; [j]
They'll sing out loud your righteousness with joy.

---

[a] My God and the King] Literally, 'My God the King. The use of 'God' rather than 'LORD', and 'the King' (Hebrew) rather than 'King' emphasises the universality of God's dominion, and 'my' declares David's personal relationship with him.

[b] In each and every day] Hebrew 'every day'. Not only to all eternity (for ever and ever) but without lapse (every day).

[c] Each generation] Hebrew 'generation to generation'.

[d] Acts of might and power] One word in Hebrew. Literally, 'mightinesses'. In parallel to the previous line, the word is referring to acts of God, whether past, present, or prophetically future. So too in v6.

[e] I'll meditate and I will speak upon] One verb in Hebrew. It means going over something in one's mind, either silently, or by giving it expression in words, 'rehearsing' or 'reciting' it.

[f] Words] The Hebrew word (*dabhar* -דָּבָר) may also mean 'deeds' or 'things'. See Appendix 2 - Word.

[g] I'll meditate] We have repeated 'I'll meditate'.

[h] They'll tell] AV and most versions supply 'men' as those who tell. The verse could equally follow on from the previous line, i.e. that it is the 'wondrous words' that will tell. See Calvin.

[i] They will speak out, yes, they will pour out words] Hebrew literally, 'they will

311

pour forth' or 'gush out'. The verb is used of uttering speech in an energetic or uncontrolled way (as Ps. 19:2; cf. Prov. 15:2). De Burgh 'abundantly utter'.
[j] Remembering you are so very good] Hebrew 'the remembrance of the greatness of your goodness'

Day 355   Psalm 145:8-13

[8] The LORD is gracious and is merciful,[a]
Forbearing anger[b], great in steadfast love; [c]
[9] The LORD is good to each and every thing; [d]
His tender mercies over all his works.

[10] Your works shall all give thanks to you, O LORD;
Those you whom you love with kindness[e] will bless you;
[11] The glory of your kingdom they will tell;
And they will speak of all your mighty power.[f]

[12] His acts of might they'll make known to mankind[g] –
The glory of his kingdom's majesty;
[13] Your kingdom is a kingdom without end;[h]
To every generation your domain.[i]

[a] Merciful] AV 'full of compassion', in Exod. 34:6 AV translates 'merciful'.
[b] Forbearing anger] As in Prov. 25:15.
[c] Steadfast love] Hebrew ḥeṣedh - חֶסֶד. See Appendix 2 - Loving-kindness.
[d] To each and every thing] Literally, 'to the all'. The following line ('over all his works') indicates the meaning is not restricted to mankind.
[e] Those whom you love with kindness] One word in Hebrew. AV 'saints'. Hebrew ḥaṣîdhîm - חֲסִידִים from ḥeṣedh - חֶסֶד. See Appendix 2 - Loving-kindness.
[f] Your mighty power] One word in Hebrew. The singular of the word used in v4 and v11 'acts of might and power').
[g] Mankind] Hebrew 'sons of men (Hebrew 'adham - אָדָם)'. Man viewed in a general sense. Here is the contrast between those who have come under the influence of grace (those 'whom you kindly love', v10), and those who only partake of Adam's character and nature. See Appendix 2 - Man.
[h] A kingdom without end] Literally, 'a kingdom of all eternities'
[i] To every generation your domain] Compare Dan. 7:13,14,18.

Day 356   Psalm 145:14-21

[14] The LORD upholds all those about to fall;
He raises up all those who are bowed down.
[15] The eyes of all things wait in hope[a] on you;
You give their food in its appointed time.   →

¹⁶ Your hand you open and, as pleases you,
You fill the need of every living thing.^b
¹⁷ In all his ways the LORD is right and just; ^c
And he is merciful^d in all his works.

¹⁸ The LORD is near to all who call on him –
Unto all those who call on him in truth.
¹⁹ For those who fear him, he meets their desire;
He saves them when he hears their cry for help.

²⁰ All those who love the LORD he guards and keeps,^e
But all the wicked ones he will destroy;
²¹ The praises of the LORD my mouth will speak;
All flesh will ever^f bless his holy name.

---

^a Wait in hope] One word in Hebrew - 'to anxiously await'.

^b Your hand ... living thing] We have here followed the Geneva Bible, Calvin, the Statenvertaling, and the Welsh Bible. We understand the 'desire' or 'good pleasure' to be that of the LORD, not of the creature. The Hebrew word (ratsôn - רָצוֹן) usually applies to God's good pleasure. However, in the working of his grace, believers then find their own desires conform to those of God himself – see verse 19.

^c Right and just] One word in Hebrew tsadîq - צַדִּיק, or 'the righteous one'.

^d Merciful] Hebrew ḥasîdh - חָסִיד - Here the meaning is that the LORD is the one who shows loving-kindness and covenant love (Hebrew ḥesedh - חֶסֶד) rather than receives it. Compare 18:25 and Jer. 3:12. See Newton (11), p352. See Appendix 2 - Loving-kindness.

^e Guards and keeps] One word in Hebrew.

^f Ever] Hebrew 'for ever and ever'.

Day 357   Psalm 146

¹ Hallelujah^a. O praise the LORD my soul!
While I yet live, I'll give praise to the LORD.
² While I have being, I'll sing psalms^b to God.
While I have being, I'll sing psalms to God.^c

³ Don't trust in princes^d, nor a son of man: ^e
For there is no salvation^f found in him.
⁴ His breath departs; he goes back to his earth; ^g
In that same day his thoughts and plans^h die too. →

⁵ *Blest*ⁱ is the one whose help is Jacob's GOD,
Whose hope is resting on the LORD his God;
⁶ He who has made the heavens and the earth,
And the sea too, and all that they contain.

He is the one who keeps truth evermore;
⁷ Judgment he gives^j to those who are oppressed;
To those who suffer hunger He gives food;^k
The LORD is freeing those who are bound up.

⁸ The LORD is giving sight unto the blind;^l
The LORD is raising those who are bowed down;
The LORD has loving care^m to righteous men;ⁿ
⁹ The LORD protects the strangers in the land.^o

The orphan, and the widow, he sustains;
He makes the wicked's way to twist and turn;^p
¹⁰ Zion, Your God, the LORD, forever reigns!
Your God all generations!^q Praise the LORD!^r

---

^a Hallelujah] = Praise the LORD.
^b Sing psalms] Hebrew *zamar* - זָמַר. See Appendix 2 - Sing Psalms.
^c We have repeated the last line of this stanza.
^d Princes] See 118:9. This is the traditional translation via the Vulgate (Wycliffe onwards), but see note on Ps. 118:9.
^e A son of man] Man as a child of Adam. Hebrew *'adham* – אָדָם. See Appendix 2 - Man.
^f Salvation] AV 'help'. The AV margin is 'salvation' and the AV mostly translates the word by 'salvation'. 'Help' in verse 5 is a different word.
^g Earth] 'Ground'. Hebrew *'adhamâ* - אֲדָמָה. Note the link with Hebrew *'adham* - אָדָם of the previous verse. See Appendix 2 - Earth.
^h Thoughts and plans] One word in Hebrew that has both meanings.
ⁱ Blest] The word (Hebrew *'ašrê* - אַשְׁרֵי) is plural - 'O the blessednesses of ...'. See Appendix 2 - Blessing.
^j Judgment he gives] Literally, 'he does judgment', as Ps. 119:121. Hebrew *mišpaṭ* - מִשְׁפָּט. See Appendix 2 - Law - Judgment.
^k Food] Hebrew 'bread'.
^l The LORD is giving sight unto the blind] Hebrew 'the LORD opens the blind'. There is no word for 'eyes' here.
^m Has loving care] Hebrew 'loves'. God's love is not just a warm sentiment, but is always expressed in his care and his intervention (e.g. John 3:16).
ⁿ To righteous men] 'To righteous ones'.
^o Strangers in the land] Hebrew 'strangers', or 'sojourners' (Hebrew *ger* - גֵּר) were entitled to protection by the children of Israel. We have added 'in the land' to give that context. See Deut. 10:18,19.

^p To twist and turn] One word in Hebrew. To be tortuous and crooked. Horsley
'to turn aside [from right]'. AV 'to turn upside down'.
^q All generations] Hebrew 'to generation and generation', i.e. to all generations.
^r Praise the LORD] Hebrew 'Hallelujah'.

Day 358   Psalm 147:1-6

¹ O Hallelujah, give praise to the LORD!^a
For it is good to sing psalms^b to our God;
For it is pleasant: praise - a comely thing.
² The LORD is building up Jerusalem!

And Israel's outcasts he will gather up;
³ The broken-hearted heals, and binds their wounds;^c
⁴ Yet he appoints^d the number of the stars!
And every one of them he calls by name.^e

⁵ Great is our Lord, and of abundant power;
His understanding is just measureless;
⁶ The poor, afflicted ones^f the LORD sustains;
But brings the wicked down unto the ground.

^a Hallelujah ... LORD] The first line is simply 'Hallelujah'. We have added the English
translation.
^b Sing psalms] Hebrew *zamar* - זָמַר. See Appendix 2 - Sing Psalms.
^c Their wounds] Literally, 'their sorrows', or 'their griefs', [so the Welsh Bible -
doluriau].
^d Yet he appoints] 'Yet' is not in the Hebrew, but the contrast is clear. 'He
appoints', or 'reckons up', 'counts'.
^e And every one of them he calls by name] Literally, 'to all of them he calls
names'.
^f Poor, afflicted ones] The Hebrew word may be translated both 'poor' and
'afflicted'.

Day 359   Psalm 147:7-11

⁷ Respond^a unto the LORD by giving thanks;
Sing psalms^b unto our God upon the harp.
⁸ He covers up the heavens with the clouds;
And he appoints the rain upon the earth.   →

Upon the mountains he makes grass to grow;
⁹ And for the cattle he provides their food; ᶜ
And he does likewise for the ravens' young;
Even for ravens' young when they do cry.

¹⁰ The horse's strength does not give him delight;
He takes no pleasure in the legs of man: ᵈ
¹¹ The LORD takes pleasure in those who fear him –
Those who in hope wait for his steadfast love.ᵉ

ᵃ Respond] 'Respond' or 'answer' is the primary meaning of the verb. In Ezra 3:11
the AV translates 'they sang together by course', i.e. responsively. See de
Burgh. Compare Welsh Bible - *cyd-genwch* [sing together]. See note on
Ps.119:172.
ᵇ Sing psalms] Hebrew *zamar* - זָמַר. See Appendix 2 - Sing Psalms.
ᶜ Food] Hebrew 'bread'.
ᵈ The horse's strength ... legs of man] It is generally agreed that the imagery
relates to warfare. Compare Eccles. 9:11; Job 39:19-25 and Ps. 20:7 in relation
to a horse; and 2 Sam. 2:18 (Asahel) in relation to speed in running. See also
Amos 2:14,15. The word translated 'leg' is the leg from the knee to the foot -
see Delitzsch.
ᵉ Steadfast love] Hebrew *ḥeṣedh* - חֶסֶד. See Appendix 2 - Loving-kindness.

Day 360   Psalm 147:12-20

¹² Jerusalem, commend the LORDᵃ with praise!
And Zion bring your praise untoᵇ your God!
¹³ For he's made strong the bars upon your gates;
He's blest your childrenᶜ who are in your midst.

¹⁴ He is the one who makes your border peace;
He satisfies you with the finest wheat.ᵈ
¹⁵ He sends out his commandᵉ upon the earth;
And then his word runs very speedily.

¹⁶ He is the giver of the wool-like snow;
The frozen dewᶠ like ashᵍ he scatters round;
¹⁷ He casts about the fragments of his hail;
And who is able to withstand his cold? ʰ

¹⁸ He sends his word, and he makes them to melt;
He makes his wind to blow; the waters flow.
¹⁹ It is to Jacob he declares his wordⁱ –
Decrees and judgmentsʲ unto Israel.   →

²⁰ He has not dealt with any nation^k thus;
As for his judgments, they're to them unknown.
O Hallelujah, give praise to the LORD!^l
O Hallelujah, give praise to the LORD!^m

---

^a Commend the LORD with praise!] One word in Hebrew - *šabhaḥ* - שְׁבַח . Not the
usual word for praise in the next line. Compare the Hebrew of Eccles. 8:15
('commend'). See Gesenius *Lexicon*.

^b Bring your praise unto] Hebrew simply 'praise' - the more usual verb (Hebrew
halal הָלַל). The words for 'praise' in this verse are both used in 117:1.

^c Children] Hebrew 'sons'.

^d Finest wheat] Literally, 'the fat of wheat', as in Deut. 32:14. So too in the
promise of Ps. 81:16 fulfilled in the circumstances described here.

^e His command] His spoken word, his fiat of command. Hebrew *'imrâ* - אִמְרָה.
See Appendix 2 - Word.

^f Frozen dew] 'Hoar frost'.

^g Ash] Hebrew 'ashes'.

^h Withstand his cold] Literally, 'stand before the face of his cold'.

ⁱ Word] The text as it is written (*kethîbh* - כְּתִיב) is singular - 'word'. 'Words'
(plural) is the rabbinic correction of the text (*qerê* - קְרִי).

^j Decrees and judgments] Hebrew 'his decrees and his judgments'. See Appendix
2 - Law - Decree, and Judgment.

^k Nation] The word used here is the word usually applied to the Gentiles in
contrast to Israel (*gôy* - גּוֹי).

^l Hallelujah] The first line is simply 'Hallelujah'. We have added the English
translation.

^m We have repeated the last line.

Day 361   Psalm 148:1-6

¹ O Hallelujah, give praise to the LORD!^a
And from the heavens praise the LORD alone!^b
Praise^c in the heights! ²All you his angels, Praise!
Praise all his host! ³Praise him both sun and moon!

Praise him all stars - praise all you stars of light!^d
⁴ Heavens of heavens, give your praise to him!
You waters, that are over heaven too!^e
⁵ O let them praise - give praise to the LORD's name!^f

For he created them at his command;
⁶ He has established them for evermore;
And he has given to them a decree;
Which none can break. It will not pass away.^g   →

[a] Hallelujah … LORD] The first line is simply 'Hallelujah'. We have added the English translation.

[b] Praise the LORD alone] Here and v7 in this Psalm. This is not 'hallelujah'. The construction of the Hebrew emphasises the LORD as the object of praise. We have added 'alone' to make this emphasis. See Ps. 117:1.

[c] Praise] Hebrew 'praise him', and so through v2,3.

[d] We have repeated half this line. The Hebrew of this line is simply 'praise him all you stars of light'.

[e] You waters that are over heaven too] As Gen. 1:7.

[f] O let them praise - give praise to the LORD's name] We have split the sentence.

[g] Which none can break. It will not pass away] We have here given both possible translations. The AV, following the Septuagint, the Vulgate, and the Syriac understands the verb to mean that the decree will not pass away. However, the verb is never elsewhere used of the passing away of a law, and its usual meaning is the transgression of a law. Hence it may also be translated that they (all the heavenly creation that the LORD has made and established) are constrained by his natural law(s), which they cannot pass over or transgress.

Day 362   Psalm 148:7-14

[7] From earth give praise unto the LORD alone![a]
You great sea creatures[b], praise[c]; and all you deeps.
[8] Both fire and hail; together, snow, and smoke,
With stormy wind, fulfilling his command.[d]

[9] Give praise to him, you mountains, and all hills;
Trees that bear fruit, and all the cedar trees;
[10] Wild beasts, and all domestic cattle, Praise!
The things that creep, and birds upon the wing.

[11] Praise, kings of earth, and all the peoples too,
Princes, and all you judges[e] of the earth!
[12] Praise him young men! Praise him young women[f] too!
Praise him you old men, with the children, Praise!

[13] O let them praise - give praise to the LORD'S name,[g]
For his name only is the name most high;
His splendour[h] is above that of the earth,
His splendour is above the heavens too.

[14] And for his people he's raised up a horn.[i]
He is the praise of all those whom he loves;[j]
A people near him - sons of Israel.
O Hallelujah, give praise to the LORD![k]

318

[a] Give praise unto the LORD alone] As in v1. This is not a simple 'hallelujah'. See note on Ps. 117:1.

[b] Great sea creatures] AV 'dragons'. As Gen. 1:21 (AV 'whales').

[c] Praise] we have added the verb throughout v7-12. The Hebrew simply lists things from which praise is due.

[d] Fulfilling his command] We take 'fulfilling his command' in this verse as referring to five agencies used by the LORD, principally in judgment. The word 'smoke' is from a verb mainly used of the smoke of incense or sacrifice. It is used Gen.19:28 and Ps. 119:83. Others translate the verse as referring to atmospheric phenomena.

[e] Judges] Hebrew *šôphet*. See Appendix 2 - Law - Judgment.

[f] Young women] The Hebrew normally means a virgin, but see Joel 1:8.

[g] As v5.

[h] Splendour] A different word from that used in Ps. 113:4. The word is used in Ps. 8:1 (AV 'glory').

[i] And for his people he's raised up a horn] See Luke 1:69 and Ps. 75:4. The lifting up of the head, or horn, is a picture of strength, relief, and deliverance.

[j] Those whom he loves] Those on whom he sets his love. Hebrew *ḥaṣîdhîm* - חֲסִידִים. As in v1

[k] Hallelujah ... LORD] This line is simply 'Hallelujah'. We have added the English translation.

Day 363   Psalm 149:1-4

[1] Praise the LORD![a] Sing a new song[b] to the LORD –
Praise[c] in the company[d] of those he loves.[e]
[2] Rejoice in him who made you, Israel!
Let Zion's children be glad in their king –

[3] With dancing, praise his name, with tambourine;
With harp, sing psalms[f] to him. [4] The LORD is pleased –
Pleased with his people; and he beautifies –
Gives beauty with salvation to the meek.

[a] Praise the LORD] Hebrew 'Hallelujah'.

[b] New song] A fresh, choice, polished, song.

[c] Praise] Hebrew 'his praise'

[d] The company] Or 'the assembly'. The Septuagint translates the word by *ekklesia* (ἐκκλησια), which is used for 'Church' in the New Testament. The word is also used in Ps. 22:22 (quoted in Heb. 2:12) and translated the same way by the Septuagint.

[e] Those he loves] Hebrew *ḥaṣîdhîm* - חֲסִידִים, from *ḥeṣedh* - חֶסֶד. See Appendix 2 - Loving-kindness.

[f] Sing psalms] Hebrew *zamar* - זָמַר. See Appendix 2 Sing Psalms.

Day 364   Psalm 149:5-9

⁵ Those the LORD loves^a in glory shall rejoice.^b
And they shall sing for joy^c upon their beds,
⁶ With GOD's exalted praises in their mouth,^d
And in their hand a sword, a two-edged sword.^e

⁷ Vengeance upon the nations to requite,
And punishments upon the peoples too;
⁸ To bind their kings as prisoners in chains,^f
With iron fetters bind their honoured ones.

⁹ To execute the judgment upon them,
Even the judgment that's been written down.^g
This honour is for all of those he loves.^h
O Hallelujah, give praise to the LORD!ⁱ

---

^a Those the LORD loves] Hebrew *ḥaṣîdhîm* - חֲסִידָיו. The Hebrew does not have
'the LORD', but it follows from v1. See Appendix 2 - Loving-kindness.

^b In glory shall rejoice] 'Rejoice' here is a strong word, meaning 'exult in triumph'.
T&J Latin translates by *gestio*, the Collins Latin Dictionary definition of which is
'jump for joy'. *Statenvertaling* 'leap up'. 'In glory': Gill suggests (1) the glory
that has been placed upon them (2) the glory of the LORD now manifest (3) the
manner of their rejoicing - 'gloriously'.

^c Sing for joy] The verb may also be rendered 'shout (for joy)' as *Statenvertaling*.

^d With GOD's exalted praises in their mouth] AV 'High praises'. The word 'praise' is
not present in the Hebrew, which is literally, 'exaltations', 'heights'. Mouth =
Hebrew 'throat'.

^e A sword, a two-edged sword] Hebrew, 'a sword of mouths'. Septuagint 'two
edged'. Ehud made 'a sword of two mouths' - Judg. 3:16: cf. Rev. 1:16; 2:12.

^f Bind ... as prisoners] One word in Hebrew. This is the fuller meaning of the verb.
See Gen. 40:3,5. We have repeated the verb in the next line ('bind').

^g The judgment that's been written down] This is more than just a judicial role.
Mišpaṭ - מִשְׁפָּט [see Appendix 2, Judgment] encompasses executive, legislative
and judicial functions. Newton (1) describes verses 6-9 as 'the office of the
saints at the resurrection' (compare 1 Cor. 6:2,3; Matt. 19:28). We may take
'written' literally, or as 'confirmed and settled'.

^h Those he loves] Hebrew *ḥasîdh* - חָסִיד from *ḥeṣedh* - חֶסֶד. See Appendix 2 -
Loving-kindness.

ⁱ Hallelujah ... LORD] This line is simply 'Hallelujah'. We have added the English
translation.

Day 365   Psalm 150

[1] O Hallelujah, give praise to the LORD![a]
Give praise to GOD within his holy place![b]
Praise him within his firmament[c] of power!
[2] Give praise unto him for his acts of power!

Give praise to him as he is very great![d]
[3] Give praise to him with sound of the shofar![e]
Give praise to him with lyre[f], and with the harp!
[4] Give praise to him with tambourine and dance!

Give praise to him with strings[g], and with the flute![h]
[5] Give praise to him with cymbals sounding loud![i]
Give praise to him with cymbals sounding high![j]
[6] All breath shall praise the LORD[k]. Hallelujah!

---

[a] Hallelujah ... LORD] The first line is as Ps. 149:9.

[b] His holy place] his Sanctuary.

[c] Firmament] AV 'firmament' follows the Vulgate. The heavens are not characterised by 'firmness', but the term in English use means 'the vault of heaven' 'the heavens' (SOED). The Hebrew could be translated 'the spread-out heavens'. See Gen. 1:6-8; Ps. 19:1; 68:34.

[d] As he is very great] 'According to', and 'fitting to' his abundant, surpassing, greatness.

[e] Shofar] The ram's horn blown at the year of Jubilee (Lev. 25:9), the New Year (*Rosh HaShannah*, Lev. 23:24), and on other occasions in Israel.

[f] Lyre] AV 'psaltery'. See Appendix 2 - Harps.

[g] Strings] This is the literal translation. This may indicate all kinds of stringed instruments. The second half of the verse may then indicate all kinds of wind instruments.

[h] Flute] singular. AV 'organs'. 'Flute', is now most generally accepted as the instrument to which the word refers, possibly a shepherd's flute (Gen. 4:21), so Perowne. 'Organs' were much later instruments.

[i] Cymbals sounding loud] Literally, 'cymbals of hearing' - i.e. that can be [easily] heard.

[j] Cymbals sounding high] The Greek word used in 1 Cor. 13:1 is related to the word used in the Septuagint here. It indicates a shrill sound, or the shout of an alarm.

[k] All breath shall praise the LORD] This is the literal Hebrew. The word 'LORD' is, however, the abbreviated form JAH (*YAH* - יָהּ). 'Praise' is future tense, ending the Psalms on a prophetic note. The Hebrew word for 'breath' here is mostly used in Scripture of the breath of man (see Gen. 2:7. Perowne therefore paraphrases 'above all, the voice of man'). However, the translation here may be given as 'the totality of breath', 'the whole of breath', or possibly (Ewald *Syntax*) 'every kind of breath', i.e. every breathing thing.

APPENDICES

APPENDIX 1

Transliteration

This transliteration attempts to represent each of the letters of the Hebrew alphabet as they are used in the Scriptures. Beyond identifying the use of 'letters used as vowels' it does not attempt to fully represent the vocalisation of vowels. The pronunciation is intended as a rough guide.

Note that when a dot *(dagheš lene)* occurs in the body of the consonants ב, ג, ד, כ, פ, ת (bh, gh, dh, kh, ph, th) the sound of the letter is hardened.

א	'	Unpronounced. Lets a word begin with a vowel sound
ב	bh	An 'aspirate b' sounds like a 'v'. A soft 'b'
בּ	b	'b' as in 'bottle'
ג	gh	An 'aspirate g'. An 'r' at the back of the throat
גּ	g	'g' as in 'goat'
ד	dh	An aspirate d'. As the 'th' in 'the'.
דּ	d	'd' as in 'dog'
ה	h	'h' as in 'hello'
ו	w	'w' as in 'wet'
ז	z	'z' as in zoo
ח	ḥ	'ch' as in Scottish 'loch'
ט	ṭ	Difficult to distinguish from ת. A dull 't'
י	y	'y' as in 'you'
כ	kh	An aspirate 'k'. A little lighter than the 'ch' in 'loch'
כּ	k	'k' as in key
ך	kh	Simply the form כ takes at the end of a word

לְ	l	'l' as in 'lamb'
מ	m	'm' as in 'mother'
ם	m	Simply the form מ takes at the end of a word
נ	n	'n' as in 'no'
ן	n	Simply the form נ takes at the end of a word
ס	ṣ	A dull 's' sound. Hard to distinguish from שׂ
ע	ʿ	Unpronounced. Originally a gulping sound?
פ	ph	An 'aspirate 'p'. 'f' as in 'funny'
פּ	p	'p' as in 'pig'
ף	ph	Simply the form פ takes at the end of a word
צ	ts	'ts' as in 'rats'. A hissing 's'
ץ	ts	Simply the form צ takes at the end of a word
ק	q	A hard 'k' sound at the back of the throat
ר	r	'r' as in 'ruby'
שׂ	ś	's' as in 'silent'. Dot on the left
שׁ	š	'sh' as in 'show' Dot on the right
ת	th	'th' as in 'thin'
תּ	t	A hard 't' as in 'top'

VOWELS		
הָ	â	A long 'a' as in 'Amy'
ֵ	ê	A long 'e' as 'ey' in 'obey
ִ	î	A long 'I' as in 'machine'
וֹ	ô	A long 'o' as in 'phone'
וּ	û	A long 'u' as in 'lute'

324

APPENDIX 2

Notes on the translation of some Hebrew words

This Appendix explains the translations adopted for the following words. We have given the numbers used in Strong's Concordance for each word commented on in this appendix.

BEHOLD hen - הֵן [2005] and hinneh - הִנֵּה [2009]

Hebrew uses hen - הֵן and its longer form hinneh - הִנֵּה to draw attention to something important. These words are 'markers'; interjections used to emphasise or to call attention to something. These words are sometimes used as a 'particle of incitement' (Gesenius Lexicon), as in Ps. 134:1 AV 'Come, praise the LORD'.

The English 'Behold!' and 'Lo!' are frequently used by the AV to translate these words. They provide a close, concise, equivalent for translating, but have fallen out of use in current English. The Hebrew words can sometimes be replaced by 'surely', 'yes' (yea), or 'verily' but their force as an urgent interjection is then largely lost. Some modern versions (notably NIV), omit, or significantly reduce, the force of these words.

A footnote has been given where the words are used, and their translation has been given according to the context.

BLESSING barakh - בָּרַךְ [1288, 1293]

and 'ašrê - אַשְׁרֵי [835]

Two different Hebrew words are connected with 'blessing'.

barakh - בָּרַךְ. This is the main word used in connection with blessing. The root meaning of the word barakh is probably 'to bend the knee'. It is used in asking for, or giving a blessing. In the Psalms it mostly expresses a desire for God's glory. It is in this sense closely associated with praise and adoration, e.g. Ps. 34:1. It is also used of seeking blessing upon another person in God's name, e.g. Ps. 129:8. Perhaps most importantly, it is used of God declaring a blessing, e.g. Psalms 29:11; 118:26. When God blesses, it means that he bestows and shows his favour.

'ašrê - אַשְׁרֵי. Gesenius Lexicon suggests the root meaning of this word is 'to go straight on', and hence to be successful and prosper. It is never used of man 'blessing' God. The word is plural and occurs 25 times in the Psalms. It could be translated 'O the blessednesses of'. To be 'blessed' in the sense of this word, man generally has to do something - trust in the LORD, not walk in the counsel of the ungodly, etc. It is a consequence of trusting and obeying God.

The AV translates 'ašrê by 'happy' at Psalms 127:5; 128:2; 137:8,9; 144:15; 146:5. Modern versions (and De Burgh) prefer this translation of the word. Nevertheless, we think 'happy' says too little, and 'blessed' too much.

To summarise: barakh, when used of God's action, means his bestowal of his favour and benefits. 'ašrê describes the state of a person, usually as a result of a person's spiritual condition.

We have (as the AV), with little variation, translated both words by 'blessed', but we have always used italics for the 'ašrê blessing to make a distinction, and have added a footnote.

To assist those using this psalm-book in singing we have written 'blest' (one syllable) and 'blesséd' (two syllables).

EARTH

Four words are used for the 'earth' or 'world' in the Psalms:

'erets - אֶרֶץ [776]; tebhel - תֵּבֵל [8398]; 'adhamâ - אֲדָמָה [127]; ḥeledh - חֶלֶד [2465]

'erets - אֶרֶץ is the usual Hebrew word used for the earth, in distinction from the heavens. It is used 188 times in the Psalms. There is frequently difficulty in translation, as it can also mean 'the land'. Careful consideration must be given to the context in which it is used. The same difficulty occurs with the Greek word gē - γῆ in the New Testament. Consider the use of these Hebrew and Greek words in Zech. 12:1-12, and as quoted in Rev. 1:7.

tebhel - תֵּבֵל generally refers to the inhabited and fertile world although it can be the equivalent to 'erets - אֶרֶץ (see Ps. 18:15), or 'the earth' in distinction from 'the sea' (Ps. 98:7). It is uniformly rendered 'the world' by the AV, apart from Prov. 8:31 where 'the habitable part (of the earth)' is used. The Greek Septuagint almost always renders it by oikoumenē - οἰκουμένη in the Psalms. The Greek word likewise means 'the inhabited earth', and came to be used of the Roman Empire (Luke 2:1), as it was earlier used of the empire of Xerxes. The word 'ecumenical' has its origin from this word. A footnote has been provided at each of the fifteen times where tebhel is used in the Psalms.

'adhamâ - אֲדָמָה is also translated 'earth' (83:10; 104:30; 146:4) or 'land(s)' (137:4; 49:11) in the Psalms in the AV. It is translated 'ground' in 104:35. It generally

327

relates to the ground or soil to which man ('adham - אָדָם) returns, (cf. 1 Cor. 15:47). It sometimes refers to owned land. A footnote has been provided where this word occurs.

heledh - חֶלֶד is translated 'world' twice in the Psalms (Ps. 17:14; and 49:1). Motyer (1) defines the meaning when it is used in this way as 'the world of time and space, the world as transitory, lasting only as time lasts'. It primarily relates to time, and is used in that sense in Ps. 39:5 (AV 'age' - the duration of my life); and 89:47 (AV 'time'). Compare the use of the Greek word aiōn - αἰών in Heb. 1:2; 11:3. See also Girdlestone.

HARPS

Kinnôr - כִּנּוֹר [AV 'harp' 3658] and Nebhel - נֵבֶל [AV 'psaltery' 5035]

Two stringed instruments are named in Scripture. The exact nature of these instruments is unknown. Any modern terms used will not accurately describe them.

Kinnôr - כִּנּוֹר. The traditional translation of 'harp' for kinnôr has been adopted. It is today common to regard the kinnôr as being more like a lyre (ESV, RSV, NIV).

Nebhel - נֵבֶל. The nebhel - נֵבֶל (AV 'psaltery') is currently thought to have been like a small harp, and is translated 'harp' in the ESV, NIV and NASB. It is associated with (perhaps identified with) a ten stringed instrument: see Psalms 33:2; 92:3; and 144:9.

The traditional translation of 'psaltery' for nebhel derives from the Greek Septuagint, which also translated the unrelated word mizmôr - מִזְמוֹר by 'psalm'. This translation makes a false link not present in Hebrew between sung-praise (psalm) and an instrument (psaltery). We have translated ne<u>bh</u>el by 'lyre'. It would, perhaps, have been better if the obsolete word 'nable' had been used, which is found in Wycliffe's translation. Calvin, and the Reformation Latin translation of Tremellius and Junius, use nablum or nablium, and the Welsh Bible translation (transliteration) is 'nabl'.

HEAR AND ANSWER

'anâ - עָנָה [6030]

The AV translates 'anâ - עָנָה as 'to hear' twenty times in the Psalms. It is not the main word used for hearing. Most translations now, along with Calvin, Delitzsch and others in the past, consistently translate 'anâ - עָנָה by 'to answer'. The explanation for the 'to hear' translation lies in the special use of the word 'hear' in a liturgical or 'Scriptural' sense where it means 'listen to with favour: grant a prayer' (SOED). We feel it is better to avoid this special use of 'hear' as it will not be recognised by most readers.

The word seeks a response. In almost every case where it is used the Psalmist is not just asking God to hear; he is asking for God to act (see Psalms 22:2; 34:4; 108:6).

We have translated this frequent word in the Psalms by 'answer' wherever possible, particularly where the Psalmist cries out to God.

LAW WORDS

This section considers the following words:

mi<u>ts</u>wâ - מִצְוָה   [4687] [commandment]
ḥoq - חֹק   [2706] [decree]
mišpaṭ - מִשְׁפָּט   [4941] [judgment/ordinance]
dîn - דִּין   [1779] [judgment]

tôrâ - תּוֹרָה [8451] [law]

piqqûd̲hîm - פִּקּוּדִים [6490] [precepts]

'edh̲ûth̲ - עֵדוּת [5715] [testimony]

'edh̲â - עֵדָה [5713] [testimony]

Various words relating to God's laws and requirements are used in the Psalms, and particularly in Psalm 119. In that Psalm one of them occurs in practically every verse as the object of the psalmist's delight. This translation attempts to distinguish and consistently translate these words. Where we have not been able to do so because of the constraints of verse, a footnote has been added to identify the Hebrew word.

Accurate and consistent translation is important. The Holy Spirit has not given different words for the sake of variety, even if we cannot in our present state of knowledge always grasp the distinctions that the Scriptures make. Nevertheless, at various points in the Old Testament, the terms are used together, and apparently interchangeably. See, for example: Deut. 6:20; 8:11; 30:16; 1 Kgs. 2:3; 2 Kgs. 23:3 (=2 Chr. 34:31); Jer. 44:23; 1 Chr. 29:19; Neh. 9:34.

Commandment. mit̲swâ - מִצְוָה. From Hebrew t̲savâ - צָוָה meaning 'to set up', or 'to confirm'. These are definite commands imposed by authority, whether by God or man. There is little debate about the meaning of this word. It occurs 26 times in the Psalms, 22 times in Ps. 119. The AV always translates by 'commandment' in the Psalms.

We have translated mit̲swâ – מִצְוָה by 'commandment' or 'command'

Decree. ḥoq - חֹק. The word means an 'enactment' or 'decree' and derives from a word meaning 'to cut in' or

330

'to engrave', and hence something that was written down, or solemnly declared as a law. It is used 29 times in the Psalms, 19 times in Psalm 119. The AV translates the word by 'statute' 24 times in the Psalms. However, 'statute' in English has come to mean 'an enactment by a legislative body expressed in a formal document' rather than a decree made by a person. The AV uses 'decree' for ḥoq - חֹק in Psalm 2, where verses 7-9 illustrate the nature of a decree. The feminine form, ḥuqqâ - חֻקָּה, is used in Psalms 18:22; 89:31 and 119:16 where the AV again translates by 'statute'.

We have translated ḥoq - חֹק by 'decree'.

Judgment. - mišpaṭ - מִשְׁפָּט and dîn - דִּין

Two different Hebrew words are translated 'judgment' and 'judge' in the Authorised Version. We believe it is important to distinguish them in the translation, or at least by footnotes in this expanded edition. In this translation mišpaṭ - מִשְׁפָּט has generally been translated by 'judgment'. In Psalm 119, as noted below, it has mainly been translated by 'ordinance' or 'what God ordains'. dîn - דִּין is translated more narrowly as 'a vindication' or 'a judgement on a cause'. In Psalms 7:8; 9:8; 72:2, the verbs connected with judgement šaphat - שָׁפַט and dîn - דִּין are used together. In Psalm 76:8,9 the nouns mišpaṭ - מִשְׁפָּט and dîn - דִּין are used together.

mišpaṭ - מִשְׁפָּט comes from the verb šaphat - שָׁפַט, which is usually translated 'to judge'. It includes ordering and governing. The Hebrew word for 'the judges' who ruled Israel after Joshua is a participle of this verb (šophetîm - שֹׁפְטִים) = 'the judging ones'. The Biblical 'judge' had executive, legislative, and judicial power.

Whenever mišpaṭ - מִשְׁפָּט is used in the Psalms it is important to keep in mind God's ordering of all things and his active government; his past giving of his laws to be kept; his current acting to vindicate the cause of the needy and oppressed; and his future government in righteousness. Judgment (mišpaṭ - מִשְׁפָּט) and righteousness are often combined (see Psalms 9:4; 33:5; 37:6; 72: 2; 75:3; 89:14; 94:15; 97:2; 99:4; 119:7,62,75,164). It also follows that mišpaṭ - מִשְׁפָּט, when used in the Psalms, is frequently a Messianic word. Messiah sits as a king on the 'throne of judgment' (Psalms 72:1; 97:2; 89:14; 99:4; 122:5). The use of the word in Psalms 9:4,7,16 expresses this clearly; he has the royal prerogative to rule and judge, and he executes judgment. When the Hebrew expression 'do judgment' is used in 9:17; 119:84; 146:7; 149:9 (see also 105:5; 140:12) the idea of implementing judgment and vindication is the main idea.

In Psalm 119 the emphasis is upon God as the lawgiver and the use of the word is somewhat different. The word mišpaṭ - מִשְׁפָּט in that Psalm generally refers to God's laws (see verses 102,106,108,120 - see also Ps. 147:19,20). In Psalm 119 the word 'ordinance' has been used to translate mišpaṭ - מִשְׁפָּט. The English word 'ordinance' has a similar root meaning - 'to order', 'to set up' or 'to arrange'. An 'ordinance' is an 'order', or law, given by God's authority. It also has a religious association which conveys both a duty and a privilege. It is a more extensive word than 'judgment' - it is 'what God ordains'. Compare the Afrikaans (1953) translation in Psalm 119 (verordeninge). See, however, the footnotes at Ps. 119:132,149.

332

dîn - דִּין as a verb is a judicial word that usually relates to a decisive act (passing judgment and settling a case). It is used eight times in the Psalms, and seven times is translated 'to judge' by the AV. When viewing the injustice of this world which seems to go unpunished the Jews look to the final outcome They use dîn - דִּין and the derived word dayyan - דַּיָּן (a judge) in the saying 'there is a Judgment and there is a Judge' to comfort them in all their trials. dîn - דִּין as a noun occurs three times in the Psalms, (Psalms 9:4, 76:8, 140:12), and is translated 'cause' and 'judgment' by the AV. Neither the verb nor the noun are used in Psalm 119.

Law. tôrâ - תּוֹרָה. This word is from a verb meaning 'to point out', 'to direct', or 'to teach'. B.W. Newton (1) refers to it as 'God's Directory'. The word is used in connection with 'The Book of the Law' in Deut. 28:61. It is commonly used as a name for the first five books of the Bible – the Torah. However tôrâ - תּוֹרָה in the Psalms is a general word for all that God has given to direct his people in his ways for their good. It may be understood of Scripture as a whole.

tôrâ - תּוֹרָה has been indicated by the translation 'Law' (capital letter).

Precepts. piqqûdhîm - פְּקוּדִים. The word is only used in the Psalms and is only used in the plural (piqqûdhîm - פְּקוּדִים). The root meaning is 'to take oversight or to take charge'. It is the charge which God has given, or that which he appoints. A related word is used in Ps. 109:8 (AV 'office') and quoted in Acts 1:20 in connection with Judas.

piqqûdhîm - פְּקוּדִים has been translated by 'precepts', or 'precepts he appoints'.

333

Testimony (1). ʿedhûth - עֵדוּת. This word is mostly used in the plural. It is derived from a verb meaning 'to bear witness'. It generally refers to a command of God, testifying to his character and attributes, and to Israel's relationship and responsibilities to him. The word is especially used of the tables of the law (Exod. 25:21,22; and 31:18). See the note on Ps. 122:4.

ʿedhûth - עֵדוּת has been indicated by 'Testimony' (capital letter).

Testimony (2). ʿedhâ - עֵדָה. Most translations do not distinguish this feminine form of ʿedhûth - עֵדוּת. The distinction is small. When used in the plural ʿedhâ - עֵדָה always refers to God's solemn statements of covenant obligations (Deut. 6:20).

ʿedhâ - עֵדָה has been indicated by footnotes.

LOVING-KINDNESS

Ḥeṣedh - חֶסֶד [2617] - loving-kindness

Ḥaṣîdh - חָסִיד [2623] generally the one who is the object of God's loving-kindness

We have placed these two words together. Ḥaṣîdh - חָסִיד Is derived from ḥeṣedh - חֶסֶד and we have sought to preserve the link in meaning in our translation.

Ḥeṣedh - חֶסֶד. The AV renderings of this word in the Psalms are kindness, pity, mercy, favour, goodness, loving-kindness. Modern translations add to these 'unfailing love' 'steadfast love', or simply 'love'.

Girdlestone[a] notes that the word shows God's dealings with man, and how we ought to deal with one another. We may describe it as 'covenant love'. It is used in Exod.

---

[a] Robert B. Girdlestone: *Synonyms of the Old Testament.*

20:6, 'showing mercy unto thousands of them that love me and keep my commandments'. How we ought to deal with one another is best shown by the Good Samaritan, 'who showed the mercy' (Lk.10:37). The word used by Luke (eleos - ἔλεος) is the word that the Septuagint uses 135 times to translate ḥeṣedh in the Old Testament.

The Shorter Oxford English Dictionary defines loving-kindness as follows: 'Kindness arising from a deep personal love, as (in Christian use) the active love of God for his creatures; affectionate tenderness and consideration'.

It has been unavoidable but to translate ḥeṣedh - חֶסֶד in different ways, but a footnote has been added wherever it is used.

Ḥaṣîdh - חָסִיד. This word comes from the same root as t ḥeṣedh - חֶסֶד. The AV renderings of the word in the Psalms are 'saints' (15 of 32 times), 'him that is godly', 'godly man', 'Holy One' (16:10), 'the merciful' (18:25). The Authorised Version margin translates the word at Ps. 86:2 by 'one whom thou favourest'. The Dutch Statenvertaling translates consistently throughout by gunst genoten - one who enjoys favour.

The Greek Septuagint, with few exceptions, uses the Greek word hosios (ὅσιος) to translate ḥaṣîdh - חָסִיד. This translation is given in Acts 2:27 (AV 'Holy One'). Hosios (ὅσιος) in Classical and Koine Greek meant pious, devout, religious. The Septuagint thus gives the word an active sense - one who acts rightly to God and to man. Bengel notes on Acts 2:27 "the Hebrew has, 'Thy Gracious One'"[a]

---

[a] John Albert Bengel, *Gnomon of the New Testament,* (Fausset)

The Hebrew word, unlike the word for 'saint' in the New Testament (hagios - ἅγιος), does not mean 'holy', or refer to personal 'holiness'. Nevertheless, the AV frequently translates both the regular word for 'holy' (qadhôš - קָדוֹשׁ) and ḥaṣîdh - חָסִיד by 'saints', even though the Hebrew words are quite different. In the Psalms this is done in Psalms 16:3; 34:9; 89:5,7; 106:16.

ḥaṣîdh - חָסִיד is used in the active sense (one who shows loving-kindness - e.g. Jer. 3:12) in relation to God (Jer. 3:12). However, when used of man, we contend that the passive sense predominates - one who has experienced the loving-kindness (ḥeṣedh - חֶסֶד) of God, and who is in covenant relation to him (see Ps. 50:5). In the plural it is almost always accompanied by a possessive pronoun 'my', 'your' (singular), 'his' ḥaṣîdhîm - חֲסִידִים (the exceptions are in Ps. 149:1 and 2).

The Dutch Annotations, commenting on Ps. 4:3, define the term [AV 'him that is godly'] as 'myself, to whom God sheweth undeserved kindness, favour and bounty; the enjoying and experience whereof, also maketh me disposed and heartily inclined to shew favour and kindness to others'.

The term was appropriated by the followers of Judas Maccabaeus (1 Macc. 2:42; 2 Macc. 14:6). The Pharisees probably had their origin from them. It was used of a medieval Jewish pietistic movement (ḥaside ashkenaz), and is used of modern day, ultra-orthodox, Jews. Unfortunately, this only serves to confuse the Biblical meaning of the word.

ḥaṣîdh - חָסִיד has not been translated by 'saint' or 'holy one', but rather in line with the Hebrew as a recipient of the LORD's mercy (ḥeṣedh - חֶסֶד). We have expressed this in various ways as suited to the versification.

336

MAN

Five different Hebrew words are used for 'man' in the Psalms. It has sometimes been possible to distinguish them in the translation. However, footnotes have not been provided every time the more common words are used.

Often it is hard to distinguish differences in meaning. However, there are differences, though these should not be forced in every context. The following five Hebrew words are used for 'man' in the Psalms.

'adham - אָדָם [120] Man as a child of Adam, human. Often used collectively for mankind or the human race.

'îš - אִישׁ [376] Man as an individual; a person of higher rank (see Dan. 9:21); A husband, a male (Gen. 2:23, where 'îš - אִישׁ is 'man', and 'îššâ - אִשָּׁה is 'woman' (or 'wife'); a manly man (1 Kgs. 2:2).

'enôš - אֱנוֹשׁ [582] Frail, mortal man, with stress on inability and weakness. In Ps. 8:4 it is applied to Christ in the weakness of his humanity (see Heb. 2:6).

gibbôr - גִּבּוֹר [1368] Man as a mighty being; strong; a warrior. Adolph Saphir considers it to be 'a title of Messiah. He is mighty to save'[a], and 'el gibbôr - אֵל גִּבּוֹר. The mighty God.
gebher - גֶּבֶר [1397] a word from the same root - is also used of man as one who is strong, with an emphasis on maleness (Deut. 22:5). It is used of a warrior or soldier Psalms 120:4; 127:4.

methîm - מְתִים [4962] Always used in the plural, 'men'. It emphasises man's mortality, if (as suggested) the

---

[a] Adolph Saphir, *Expository Lectures on the Epistle to the Hebrews*, on I:8 (and therefore on Psalm 45).

word is to be associated with the Hebrew word for death. It is only found four times in the Psalms.

NAMES OF GOD

We have distinguished the Hebrew names of God used in Psalms, and have provided footnotes when the less frequent words are used. The following names are given in the Psalms.[a]

LORD - יהוה [3068]

'Adhonay - אֲדֹנָי [136]

'El - אֵל [410]

'Elohîm – אֱלֹהִים [430]

'Elyôn - עֶלְיוֹן - the Most High [5945]

JAH - YAH – יָה [3050]

Marôm - מָרוֹם - Highest of All,

The High One [4791]

Šadday – שַׁדַּי [7706]

LORD - יהוה. We have followed the traditional convention of writing 'Lord' in capital letters to represent the unpronounced name of God. We have avoided the use of 'Jehovah', 'Yahweh', 'The Eternal', etc. In one sense this is the only true 'name' of God – his proper name. Calling on "the name of יהוה" is frequently used in Scripture. It, of course, does not mean 'lord'.

My Lord –'Adhonay - אֲדֹנָי. The general word Adhôn - אָדוֹן - is translated 'lord' in the Old Testament in reference to God and men. This special form of the word - 'Adhonay - אֲדֹנָי - is only used of God. It is the word that

---

[a] See R.B. Girdlestone, *Synonyms of the Old Testament* for a fuller consideration of the names of God.

Judaism substitutes for the name of God, which it refuses to utter (יהוה). However, the form of the word has led to much discussion and debate. It appears to be a plural form. Many explain this as 'the plural of majesty'. Gesenius Lexicon states that the name is used chiefly (in the Pentateuch always) 'wherever God is submissively and reverently addressed'.

Many Hebraists also consider its ending is the suffix of the first person singular = 'My Lord'. This was the view taken by Ewald, and Gesenius in his Thesaurus. Tregelles also takes this view in his comment in Gesenius Lexicon.

It may be that its form, as a name of God, has become standardised, and the possessive sense is not always prominent (cf. the French word monsieur), but very often, we believe, the psalmist is declaring God's lordship over him personally, and the translation 'My Lord' is wholly appropriate. This suggestion has been followed where possible, or a footnote has been provided.

It is often distinctively applied to Christ, as Ps. 110:1.

GOD 'El - אֵל. This is a singular word, which may be applied to a false god (as in Psalms 44:20; 77:13; 81:9), sometimes in irony. Where 'El - אֵל is used of the true God, it emphasises God's power and might. The word is never used in the plural ('elîm – אֵלִים) of the true God. 'El - אֵל is sometimes used in connection with things, to emphasise their greatness and excellence (e.g. Ps. 36:6 'the mountains of God', 80:10 'the cedars of God' - see the AV translations). The word is first used in connection with Melchizedec, who was 'the priest of the Most High GOD' (Gen. 14:18-22). Koehler

Lexicon gives a full summary of the use of this word in Scripture.

The use of this word for 'God' has been highlighted by capitalising the first letter putting the rest of the word in small capital letters (GOD) and, occasionally by 'Mighty GOD' with a footnote. Where a false God is referred to, we have just used small capitals - GOD.

God Elôah - אֱלוֹהַ. This word is most frequently used in the book of Job. It is only found four times in the Psalms, where it is only used of the true God. In the Psalms it is used of God as the safe refuge of his people and as a terror to the wicked and his enemies. Its first use is in connection with worship Deut. 32:15-17.

Most consider it to be the singular form of the usual (plural) word for God - 'Elôhîm - אֱלֹהִים.

This word for God in the text has been indicated by simply underlying it (God) with a footnote. The word is used in Psalms 18:31; 50:22; 114:7; and 139:19.

God - 'Elohîm - אֱלֹהִים. This is generally regarded as the plural form of 'Elôah - אֱלוֹהַ. It is however used as a singular noun (with a verb). When it is used in this way it always refers to the one true and supreme God. Girdlestone therefore suggests the meaning is 'Godhead'. It is the usual Hebrew word translated as 'God' in the Bible. We have therefore not routinely noted the Hebrew. It can be used of false gods (e.g. Judg. 2:3).

The Most High - 'Elyôn - עֶלְיוֹן. The AV generally translates this as 'the Most High.. This name is first used as a name for God in Gen. 14:18 (Melchizedek). It means the Highest, the Supreme Being. It is sometimes used in combination with other words for

God: 'El 'Elyôn - אֵל עֶלְיוֹן; LORD 'Elyôn יהוה עֶלְיוֹן; and 'Elôhîm 'Elyôn - אֱלֹהִים עֶלְיוֹן.

A footnote has been added where this word is used. We have generally translated 'the Most High'.

JAH - YAH - יָהּ. This is generally understood to be a shortened form of LORD - יהוה. It is frequently used in the Psalms, especially in the phrase Hallelu-jah - הַלְלוּ־יָהּ

The name is first found in Exod. 15:2, and its use in the Psalms frequently coincides with narratives concerning the Exodus or the Passover. Motyer (1), calls it 'a diminutive of endearment' from the name יהוה (LORD).

We have usually 'translated' the name as 'LORD' with a footnote, but on some occasions have transliterated, as does the AV at Ps. 68:4.

Highest of All, The High One - Marôm - מָרוֹם -.
The older versions (Calvin, Geneva Bible, Tremellius and Junius, Statenvertaling with The Dutch Annotations, AV, and Welsh Bible) generally translate this word as a title of God at Psalms 56:2 and 92:8. It is used similarly at Mic. 6:6. It is accepted as a title of God by Rashi, Kimchi, and the Targum. Marôm means 'height' or 'what is high'. The verb from which it is derived is used in relation to God at Psalms 99:2; 113:4; and 138:6. Modern versions and most modern commentators do not accept it as a stand-alone title of God, but treat it as an adjective with various shades of meaning. See de Burgh and Perowne for an explanation of this latter view of the word.

We have distinguished this word from 'Elyôn - עֶלְיוֹן by using the translation 'God Most High', as the Welsh Bible.

The Almighty - Šadday — שַׁדַּי (traditionally transliterated Shaddai). This is a title of God that the AV, following the Septuagint, translates as 'The Almighty'. We have followed that translation. It was

341

the under this name that God manifested himself to Abraham (Gen. 17:1). Although it occurs 44 times in the Old Testament, it only occurs twice in the Psalms (Psalms 68:14 and 91:1). In Gen. 17:1 the Geneva Bible translates El Shaddai as 'God All-sufficient'.

REFUGE

ḥaṣâ – חָסָה [2620] and baṭaḥ - בָּטַח, [982]

The AV translates two Hebrew words by 'to trust' in the Psalms. They are rarely distinguished. The usual word is baṭaḥ - בָּטַח, [982] – literally, 'to lean upon'. It is used 44 times and is translated by 'trust' 41 times.

The word ḥaṣâ – חָסָה is used 23 times in the Psalms. The AV always translates it by 'trust' apart from Ps. 57:1[a]. It is often found in contexts where 'flee for refuge or safety' would be more suitable, for example in Ps. 11:1. The word for 'refuge' which is derived from it (maḥṣeh – מַחְסֶה) is almost always translated 'refuge' by the AV.

A footnote has been added wherever ḥaṣâ – חָסָה is used. We have translated the word in connection with finding refuge, often of making the LORD our refuge.

SHEOL

še'ôl – שְׁאוֹל [7585]

This is the Hebrew word for the place of the dead, the prison-house of the disembodied soul after death. The AV translation 'the grave' wrongly implies a place of unconsciousness or burial. The other AV translations 'Hell' and 'the Pit' are equally wrong.

---

[a] See Newton (14) for further comment on the three Hebrew words that are used for trusting.

The Hebrew word is equivalent to Hades (ᾅδης) in the Septuagint and the Greek New Testament. It is not the place of final torment (Gehenna – γέεννα, or the Lake of Fire) or of eternal blessedness (Heaven), still less of fictional Purgatory. It is the place where all the dead were before the resurrection of Christ.

There is not space in this book on worship to enter into a fuller explanation of Sheol's meaning. The word has simply been transliterated, thus avoiding common misconceptions, and directing the reader (and singer) to further study of this important subject.

SHIELDS

Two words for 'shield' are found in the Psalms. The AV translates the two words indiscriminately as 'shield', 'buckler', 'defence'.

Maghen – מָגֵן [4043] is the commonest word. It was a 'buckler' or 'target' – a small, round shield, used by light infantry and for attack. The word is used seventeen times. Maghen – מָגֵן has been translated as 'shield', which is the most easily understood English word. The sole exception is Ps. 35:2, where it occurs with tsinnâ – צִנָּה. It is there translated by 'buckler', the more precise meaning.

Tsinnâ – צִנָּה is used three times. It refers to the large body-shield. The equivalent Greek word is related to the word for 'door'. Tsinnâ – צִנָּה has been translated as 'great shield'.[a]

---

[a] Yigael Yadin, *The Art of Warfare in Biblical Lands,* p14. 'Also in use in ancient times was the very large shield. This was carried by a special shield bearer who was constantly at the side of the fighter he was protecting',

The word Ṣoherâ – סֹחֵרָה is translated is translated 'buckler' by the AV in Ps. 91:4. Strictly it means 'what goes around', hence, armour or a protecting wall. We have translated 'armour round about'.[a]

SING PSALMS

Zamar – זָמַר [2167]

This word is usually translated in the AV by 'sing', or 'sing praises'. Twice it is translated 'sing psalms' (1 Chr. 16:9; Ps.105:2). This verb is the origin of the word for Psalm (mizmôr – מִזְמוֹר). It is used 44 times in the Old Testament and each time this refers to singing. With one exception, the Septuagint translates the word by psallo (ψαλλω), which is the word used in Jas. 5:13 – 'Is any be merry? Let him <u>sing psalms</u>'. Calvin's commentary, the Dutch Reformation translation commissioned by the Synod of Dort (Statenvertaling), and the Reformation Latin translation of Tremellius and Junius consistently translate the Hebrew verb as 'sing psalms'[b].

Most commentators and translators now consider the word relates to 'melody' or even playing instruments. Whatever the linguistic arguments, these interpretations coincide with the abandonment of the Psalms as the vehicle for Christian praise and the adoption of instruments in worship. As there are other words for singing, and for praising, this word has been translated as 'sing psalms' wherever possible.

There are three other, related, words used in the psalms.

---

[a] See Davies *Lexicon*, Koehler *Lexicon* etc. Compare Septuagint, and Wycliff 'he shall compass thee as a shield'. NASB 'bulwark', NIV 'rampart'

[b] So too B.W. Newton.

344

Zimrâ – זִמְרָה [2172]. This is used in Psalms 81:2 (AV 'Psalm'), Psalm 98:5 (AV 'Psalm'); Isa. 51:3 (AV 'melody'), Amos 5:23 (AV 'melody'), and rendered by us 'psalm' and 'psalmody'. Bishop Horsley considers the word to be a (unknown) musical instrument and simply transliterates 'zimrah'.

Zemîr – זָמִיר [2158]. This is used in Ps. 95:2 (AV 'with psalms') and 119:54 (AV 'songs'). In 2 Sam. 23:1, where the AV says that David was 'the sweet psalmist of Israel', the literal translation is that 'David was pleasant in the psalms of Israel' (RV margin).

Zimra<u>th</u> – זִמְרָת [2176]. This is generally taken as equivalent to zimrâ – זִמְרָה. However, Koehler Lexicon, links it with a root meaning 'strength' (compare Hebrew of Gen. 43:11). Translated 'Psalm' by the Dutch Statenvertaling. This word occurs three times in the Scriptures in the AV expression 'the LORD is my strength and song' – i.e. the object of my song. Exod. 15:2; Ps. 118:14; Isa. 12:2.

WORD

da<u>bh</u>ar –דָּבָר [1697] and 'imrâ – אִמְרָה [565]

Two main words are used in Hebrew for 'word' – da<u>bh</u>ar –דָּבָר and 'imrâ – אִמְרָה. They are usually both translated as 'word' in English, without distinction. It is often difficult to distinguish their meaning.

The most common 'word' comes from 'to speak' – da<u>bh</u>ar – דָּבַר [1696]. It emphasises the thing or substance that is spoken about.

The other main 'word' comes from 'to say' 'amar – אָמַר [559]. It is much less frequently used. It is more about

345

the act of speaking – the mode in which the 'word' is given – the 'saying'.

The difference can be seen in Ps. 105:19. 'Until the time that his word (dabhar –דָּבָר) came, the word ('imrâ - אִמְרָה) of the LORD tried him' - i.e. until the substance and fulfilment of the word of the LORD came, the mere words he recalled from his dreams were a test and a trial to Joseph.

A footnote has been added every time 'imrâ - אִמְרָה is used. It occurs frequently in Psalm 119, where a number of modern versions (RSV, NEB, ESV, NIV) translate the word 'promise'.

A note has been added where other rarer words derived from 'amar - אָמַר are used ('emer - אֵמֶר, and 'omer - אֹמֶר). These two words are, of course, also closely associated with 'saying'. However, in many cases the context makes the meaning clear - that the spoken word is intended.

APPENDIX 3

Psalm Titles, Selah (סֶלָה),
and Higgaion (הִגָּיוֹן)

The Psalm titles and the words 'Selah' and 'Higgaion' (Higgayôn) are present in the oldest manuscripts of the Psalms. We therefore accept them as fully canonical. They also appear in the very early translations of the Greek Septuagint and Aramaic Peshitta, with some variations.

Although the titles, 'Selah', and 'Higgaion' are all sung in synagogue worship, and although the titles frequently become verses in their own right in Jewish editions and translations, it is clear that these have a supplementary purpose. They are not, strictly speaking, a part of the words of praise, and therefore do not form part of this version of the Psalms for singing. However, consideration of them may help us to 'sing with understanding'.

The titles relate to authorship, historical context, and the character of a Psalm (e.g. maskil, a Psalm of instruction). We find the work of J.W. Thirtle[a] on the Psalms convincing. The Psalms were first written as a continuous manuscript without punctuation. There may been confusion in what precedes and what follows after the cessation of Temple worship. Thirtle applied the pattern of the beginning and end of Habakkuk 3 as the rule for determining what precedes and follows. This appears to resolve certain problems caused by putting the 'title' material at the beginning of successive Psalms.

It has been usual to exclude Ps. 72:20 from versions of the Psalms for singing[b]. It has been included in this translation as providing closure on this Psalm of future glory – that the desires of David's heart are accomplished when the things declared in this Psalm are fulfilled.

---

[a] J.W. Thirtle, *The Titles of the Psalms*
[b] The Sandemanian psalter included it. John Metcalf, *(The Psalms of the Old Testament in Metre)*, also included it, somewhat apologetically.

Higgaion occurs untranslated once in the Authorised Version (Ps. 9:16), and we have likewise included it for singing there. It also occurs in relation to instruments in Ps. 92:3, where the AV translates 'with solemn sound', and Motyer (1) with soft 'meditative music'. It comes from a word that the AV translates 'to meditate' in Ps. 1:2 and elsewhere. In Ps. 19:14 it is translated 'meditation'.

Selah also occurs in the body of the text of the Psalms. We consider it as primarily referring to the subject matter, and not to musical instructions. We follow Rabbi Kimchi, Bishop Horne, de Burgh, and many others in this. It is the traditional view.

It is primarily a call to pause and note what is said carefully, as 'NB' is used. Robert Hawker comments on Ps. 62:8 'My soul, the Holy Ghost hath marked this verse with Selah; therefore, pray observe it'. It is a mark of emphasis, showing something important[a]. C.H. Spurgeon writes, 'Wherever we see 'Selah', we should look upon it as a note of observation. Let us read the passage which precedes and succeeds it with greater earnestness, for surely there is always something excellent where we are required to rest and pause and meditate, or when we are required to lift up our hearts in grateful song'[b]. It may have a role in signalling a change of subject.

Attention has been drawn to the presence of Selah by the use of the symbol ‖ where it occurs in the Hebrew text.

---

[a] See T&J Latin where the presence of *Selah* influences the translation.
[b] C.H. Spurgeon, *Treasury of David*, on Ps. 3:2. See also the interesting book of sermons by Archibald G. Brown, *'Selah', or Think of That*.

APPENDIX 4

Resources used in preparing this Psalter

A large number of Bible versions have been consulted in preparing this psalter, as we sought a helpful and accurate turn of phrase that would fit the metre. However, we have primarily sought help from Reformation and post-Reformation versions. These have included the translation which accompanies Calvin's commentary (1557); the Geneva Bible (1560); the Latin translation of Tremellius and Junius (1575); the Welsh Bible (1620); the *Statenvertaling* Dutch Bible commissioned by the Synod of Dort (1637); and, of course, the Authorised Version (1611). The Segond French translation (revised 1910) has also been helpful, as has Young's Literal Translation (revised 1907).

The Dutch Annotations (1657), the English translation of the *Statenvertaling* and its marginal notes by Theodore Haak, Westminster Assembly, has been invaluable.

We have used a several key commentaries to clarify the meaning of the Hebrew. As well as Calvin's commentary we have particularly used the commentaries Dr Gill, J.J. Stewart Perowne, Keil and Delitzsch, and Alec Motyer.

The exegetical comments of a select group of expositors have been carefully considered. These have included: Bishop Samuel Horsley, William De Burgh, Andrew A. Bonar, Benjamin Wills Newton[a], Adolph Saphir, and David Baron.

The Hebrew lexicons of Gesenius, Davies *(Student's Hebrew Lexicon)*, Brown-Driver-Briggs, Koehler-Baumgartner, and the *Theological Wordbook of the Old Testament* have been used to clarify the meaning and usage of Hebrew words. Girdlestone's *Synonyms of the Old Testament* has been helpful throughout. *The Interlineary Hebrew and English Psalter* Some of its

---

[a] We will shortly be publishing the definitive catalogue of the works and remains of B.W. Newton and have therefore been able to use a number of his minor works, giving his comments on the Psalms.

translations of difficult words have been adopted (e.g. on Ps. 68:13).

Constant reference has been made (particularly in the latter part of this work) to Gesenius *Hebrew Grammar* and the Hebrew Syntaxes of A.B. Davidson, and of Heinrich Ewald.

Versions and Publications referred to in the footnotes

Bibles and Versions

PBV	Prayer Book Version (1539, 'sealed' in 1662).
Geneva	Geneva Bible, 1599 edition.
Calvin	The translation accompanying Calvin's Commentary on the Psalms, translated from the Latin and French by James Anderson.
AV	Authorised (King James') Version 1611.
RV	Revised Version 1884 (Interlinear Bible 1907)
YLT	Young's Literal Translation (1898 edition).
JPS	Jewish Publication Society of America Tanakh 1917
RSV	Revised Standard Version 1947.
NEB	New English Bible 1970.
NIV	New International Version 1984 edition.
NASB	New American Standard Bible 1995 edition.
Welsh Bible	William Salesbury's Psalms 1567, revised by William Morgan 1588, and finally revised by John Davies and Richard Parry, 1620.
Segond	French Bible (Louis Segond), 1910.
Statenvertaling	Dutch Bible (1637) Commissioned by the Synod of Dort. We have used Theodore Haak's Translation to English (1657), reportedly commissioned by the Westminster Assembly.
T&J Latin	Immanuel Tremellius and Franciscus Junius Latin Bible (1575).
BHS	Biblia Hebraica Stuttgartensia (1990) (Rudolf Kittel).
Septuagint	Henry Barclay Swete (1909).

Publications

Alford	Dean Henry Alford (1810-1871, Dean of Canterbury), *The Greek Testament … and a Critical and Exegetical Commentary.*
Baron (1)	David Baron (1855–1926, founder of the Hebrew Christian Testimony to Israel), *The Shepherd of Israel and His Scattered Flock* (Ps. 80).
Baron (2)	David Baron, *Israel in the Plan of God.*
Baron (3)	David Baron, *The Conclusion of the Hallel.*
Baron (4)	David Baron, *Types, Psalms, and Prophecies.*
BDB *Lexicon*	Brown, Driver, Briggs, *Hebrew and English Lexicon of the Old Testament.*
Bengel	John Albert Bengel (1687-1752, Lutheran scholar and liguist)), *Gnomon of the New Testament* (unedited).
Bonar	Andrew A. Bonar (1810-1892, Free Church of Scotland minister), *Christ and His Church in the Book of Psalms.*
Bridges	Charles Bridges, *Exposition of Psalm 119.*
Calvin	John Calvin, Bible commentary and accompanying version (1563) Calvin Society edition, Baker Book House.
Davidson *Syntax*	A.B. Davidson, *Hebrew Syntax.*
Davies *Lexicon*	Benjamin Davies, *Student's Hebrew Lexicon* (founded on Gesenius and Fürst).
De Burgh	William de Burgh, *A Commentary on the Book of Psalms.*
Delitzsch	C.F. Keil and F Delitzsch [the Psalms by Delitzsch] Commentary *on the Old Testament.*
Dickson	David Dickson, *A Brief Explication of the Psalms.*
Dutch Annotations	*The Dutch Annotations upon the Whole Bible* (1657) translated by Theodore Haak with a translation of the Dutch

	Statenvertaling,
Ewald *Syntax*	Heinrich Ewald, *Syntax of the Hebrew Language of the Old Testament* (translated by James Kennedy).
Gesenius *Grammar*	William Gesenius, *Gesenius Hebrew Grammar.* Translated from Roediger's edition by Benjamin Davies.
Gesenius *Lexicon*	William Gesenius *Hebrew and Chaldee Lexicon to the Old Testament Scriptures* (1846) (Bagster's complete edition translated by Samuel Prideaux Tregelles).
Gill	Dr John Gill (1697-1771, Calvinistic baptist pastor whose Church was a forerunner of the Metropolitan Tabernacle, London), *Exposition of the Old Testament.*
Girdlestone	Robert Baker Girdlestone (1836-1923, first principal of Wycliffe Hall, Oxford), *Synonyms of the Old Testament their bearing on Christian Doctrine.*
Horne	Bishop George Horne, *A Commentary on the Book of Psalms.*
Horsley	Bishop Samuel Horsley, *The Book of Psalms; translated from the Hebrew: with notes explanatory and critical.*
Kirkpatrick	A.F Kirkpatrick, *The Book of Psalms* (The Cambridge Bible).
Koehler *Lexicon*	Ludwig Koehler and Walter Baumgartner, *The Hebrew and Aramaic Lexicon of the Old Testament,* 2001.
Motyer (1)	Alec Motyer, *Psalms by the Day. A working translation with analysis and explanatory notes.*
Motyer (2)	Alec Motyer, *Journey. Psalms for Pilgrim People* (Psalms 120-134).
Muraoka	T. Muraoka, *Hebrew/Aramaic Index to the Septuagint.*

Newton (1)	Benjamin Wills Newton, *Dark Sayings upon the Harp. Studies in Some of the Psalms* (posthumous; from notes of Newton's lectures).
Newton (2)	Benjamin Wills Newton, *Notes on Psalm 1* (*Occasional Papers 2*).
Newton (3)	Benjamin Wills Newton, *Thoughts on Parts of the Prophecy of Isaiah.*
Newton (4)	Benjamin Wills Newton. From MSS notes of A.C. Fry held by C.W.H. Griffiths.
Newton (5)	Benjamin Wills Newton, *David King of Israel.*
Newton (6)	Benjamin Wills Newton, *Ancient Truths.*
Newton (7)	Benjamin Wills Newton, *Notes on Psalm 84* (*Occasional Papers 4*).
Newton (8)	Benjamin Wills Newton, *Babylon and Egypt.*
Newton (9)	Benjamin Wills Newton, The Millennium and Israel's Future.
Newton (10)	Benjamin Wills Newton, *Notes on Psalm 68* (*Occasional Papers 4*).
Newton (11)	Benjamin Wills Newton, *Thoughts on the Apocalypse.*
Newton (12)	Benjamin Wills Newton, *Narratives from the Old Testament.*
Newton (13)	Benjamin Wills Newton, *Psalm 119. Christ's Daily Life-work for us. Patmos 39.* (posthumous; from notes of Newton's lectures).
Newton (14)	Benjamin Wills Newton, *Notes on Psalm 2* (*Occasional Papers 2*).
Perowne	J.J. Stewart Perowne 1823-1904, Bishop of Worcester), *The Book of Psalms; a new translation with introductions and notes explanatory and critical* (unedited, 2 volumes).

SOED	Shorter Oxford English Dictionary
Soncino	A. Cohen, *The Psalms. Hebrew text, English Translation, and Commentary* (Soncino Press).
Theological Wordbook	R. Laird Harris (Ed.), *Theological Wordbook of the Old Testament* (Moody Press).
Tregelles (1)	Samuel Prideaux Tregelles (1813–1875, Hebrew and Greek scholar), Critical notes on Gesenius's interpretations, in Tregelles's translation of *Gesenius Hebrew Lexicon.*
Tregelles (2)	Samuel Prideaux Tregelles, The Man of Sin.
Tregelles (3)	Samuel Prideaux Tregelles[a], *The Interlineary Hebrew and English Psalter.*
Tregelles (4)	Samuel Prideaux Tregelles, *Remarks on the Prophetic Visions in the Book of Daniel.*

---

[a] *The Interlineary Hebrew and English Psalter,* 1845: 'Whilst we have no definite information, it is likely that this is at least partly the work of Samuel Prideaux Tregelles ...' , Letter from Bagsters (publisher) 1966. Quoted in *Catalogue of English Bible Translations*, W.J. Chamberlin, 1991.

APPENDIX 5

How to sing this book

In some ways, Psalm-singing will never be 'easy'. As praise and worship of our most holy God, it requires effort. As an expression of love to the Lord, it should be done with all our heart, all our soul and all our mind. Singing may be 'easy' in a large gathering, singing a well-known song, to loud accompaniment, in congenial surroundings. Such a description would fit a beach party where alcohol has been flowing freely, but personal and family worship is something different.

Psalm-singing requires singing with understanding, often singing unfamiliar words (at least unfamiliar at first). James 5:13 indicates that our singing of Psalms should be when we are by ourselves, as well as when we are in Church. In family terms there may be challenges in terms of the age of our children, learning disability, or dyslexia.

The task could be made easier for the singer in various ways. The number of Psalms sung could be reduced to a limited number of favourites; but personal choice exercised in relation to God's Word is a very dangerous thing. It can be easier to sing with accompaniment, but one should always remember that the essence of Christian worship is 'the fruit of our lips' (Hebrews 13:15), not skill at a keyboard. The one providing accompaniment is often impeded or prevented from singing God's praise by their role. Well-formed rhyming verse is no doubt easier to sing, but as we have noted elsewhere rhyming verse severely limits the available vocabulary to accurately translate and express words given by the Holy Spirit.

Psalm singing should give sufficient time for the singer to think on the words, and gain blessing from them. Unless this psalter is used many times, the wording will remain unfamiliar. It has to be sung slowly enough for the singer to profit from it.

By using only one metre, it is hoped that the added complication of new words + new music will be avoided, so that the singer's focus will be on the words. This was the principle adopted by Edmwnd Prys for his Welsh language Psalter (1621) and by the Scottish Metrical Psalter (1650). All the Psalms in this book are set to the 10.10.10.10. metre. This means that they can all be sung to the tune 'Eventide' (the usual tune for the hymn 'Abide with me') or, perhaps even more simply, to the two line tune 'Pax Tecum' (the usual tune to the hymn 'Peace, perfect peace in this dark world of sin').

We suggest the following tunes, several of which we have simplified. They are available as pdfs and as playable audio files on the Pearl Publications website. The character of the passage should determine the tune type chosen

A. Prayerful, Restful and Didactic
- Eventide.
- St Agnes (aka Langram, or Hoyland).
- Pax Tecum.

B. Cheerful and Rejoicing
- Waldo.
- Ffigysbren.
- Speranza.

C. Confident and Strong
- Toulon (Old 124th shortened, aka Navarre).
- Huntingdon.
- Bont-newydd.

D. Sorrowful and Plaintive
- Georgetown.
- Ellers.
- Griddfaniad.

The tunes follow in alphabetical order

Bont-newydd (C)

John Roberts [Ieuan Gwyllt] (1822-1877)

Ellers (D)

(aka Benediction)

Edward J. Hopkins (1818-1901)

Eventide (A)

Dr W.H. Monk (1883-1929)

Ffigysbren (B)

Welsh hymn tune 1840

Georgetown (D)

From *Hymns of Consecration and Faith*, 1902

Griddfaniad (D)

Morris Davies (1796-1876)

Huntingdon (C)

S. Wellens

Pax Tecum (A)

George T. Caldbeck (1852-1918)
and Charles Vincent (1852-1934)

Speranza (B)

C. Leflaive (1864-1938)

St Agnes (A)

aka Langram, or Hoyland)

James Langram (1835–1909)

Toulon (C)

(aka Navarre)
Adapted from the Genevan Psalm 124 tune
Claude Goudimel (1510-1572)

Waldo (B)

Anonymous 1855

Chosen – Called - Kept

In 1619 all the Reformed Churches of Europe met to discuss the great subject of 'How God saves'. That gathering was the Synod of Dort. Its decisions were unanimous. Chosen-Called-Kept is a new and very accessible translation of its conclusions. Its imaginative typesetting is designed to encourage regular and prayerful reflection on these great truths. It is not an edited version or a paraphrase. It is particularly useful for the catechising of children and young people.

First published in September 2022.

Chosen – Called – Kept. The Conclusions of the Synod of Dort translated and arranged for prayerful reflection and study
Paperback   ISBN 978-1-901397-01-7
Hardback   ISBN 978-1-901397-02-4

Pearl Publications books are available online on Amazon (and Takealot in South Africa), and from bookshops via wholesale distributors. Ebooks are available from a range of outlets. Enquiries are invited for direct bulk sales to Churches and Colleges.

Pearl Publications is operating on a not for profit basis and would welcome proposals, including conventional book printing and distribution proposals, that would enable the sale prices of its books to be reduced.

Printed in Great Britain
by Amazon

22447833R00218